GREAT REVOLUTIONS COMPARED

GREAT REVOLUTIONS COMPARED
The Outline of a Theory

Jaroslav Krejčí

Professor Emeritus, Lancaster University

Assisted by

Anna Krejčová Ph.D.

NEW YORK   LONDON   TORONTO   SYDNEY   TOKYO   SINGAPORE

First published 1994 by
Harvester Wheatsheaf
Campus 400, Maylands Avenue
Hemel Hempstead
Hertfordshire, HP2 7EZ
A division of
Simon & Schuster International Group

Typeset in 10/12 Times
by PPS Limited, London Road, Amesbury, Wilts.

Printed and bound in Great Britain by
T.J. Press (Padstow) Ltd

British Library Cataloguing in Publication Data

A catalogue record for this book is available from
the British Library

ISBN 0–7450–1408–9

1 2 3 4 5   98 97 96 95 94

Contents

Preface

The present study has its origin in an article published as long ago as 1968 in two issues of the *Czech Sociological Review*, under the title 'A sociological model of the revolutionary process'.

The main work, undertaken eleven years later in the School of European Studies at Lancaster University, was sponsored by the Social Science Research Council in London. The generous four-year grant enabled me to call upon the full-time cooperation of my wife, Dr Anna Krejčová, previously the Principal Lecturer at Preston Polytechnic, now the University of Central Lancashire. My colleague Professor A.H. Woolrych provided me with invaluable comments on the chapter on the English revolution, and my colleague Dr Graham Bertram helped me most efficiently with the editorial work.

The first edition of the book was published by Harvester Press in the Wheatsheaf Books series in 1983.

Within ten years of its publication, many things happened which called for a new edition; meanwhile the book went out of print. At the welcome request of the publishing house, Simon & Schuster, which took over the original publisher, I have prepared a new, updated and extended text which has been altered in places. I gratefully acknowledge the assistance of the Nuffield Foundation in London which contributed towards my research expenses for four consecutive years.

The updating mainly concerns the revolutions in Russia, Turkey and China. The discussion of the about-turn in Russia is expanded with comments on the emancipation of its former satellites. By way of extension, two more twentieth-century revolutions, in Iran and in Mexico, have been added to the six case studies analysed in the first edition (Hussite Bohemia, England, France, and the previously mentioned revolutions in Russia, Turkey and China).

Further substantial additions have been made, often combined with alterations, in the general section of the book, both in its introductory and concluding parts. A new typology of revolution is suggested and reference is made to a wider range of comments by other authors. In order to illustrate the perennial nature of the phenomenon 'revolution', there is a brief account of some revolutions in the Middle Ages and antiquity. The new edition also contains a full and updated bibliography.

Apart from the unstinting, essential cooperation of my wife, I am indebted to my colleagues Alan Airth, Peter Gedge and Melanie Hardman, for their invaluable editorial work, and Thelma Goodman, Mike Hutchinson and John Illingworth for their prompt and efficient librarian help. Kay Roberts deserves a particular mention for her precise and thoughtful typing.

Part I

General considerations

INTRODUCTION

In the last fifty years or so the study of revolution has almost become a specialised area of social science. The phenomenon has been tackled from the sociological, political, economic and psychological points of view, and in a few instances, even historians have discarded their dislike of conceptual approaches and generalisation and joined in the search for a theoretical explanation of revolution as a social phenomenon.

Various angles of observation, different foci and different methods of investigation have produced a wide range of theories seeking to explain a phenomenon that, despite all these efforts, still awaits a satisfactory conceptual framework.

In this book no attempt is being made to review the work already undertaken in this field. There are many good and critical studies on what others had to say. Suffice it to mention just two works: first, the comprehensive, well-structured and clearly written book, *The Phenomenon of Revolution* by Mark N. Hagopian, published in 1974;[1] and second, to bring us up to date, albeit with a narrower focus, Michael S. Kimmel's *Revolution: A sociological interpretation*, published in 1990.[2]

The fact that this study does not explicitly review findings and theories of other authors does not mean, however, that they are ignored. On the contrary, their findings and ideas are not only often referred to but also abundantly quoted wherever I find them illuminating or useful. I am particularly indebted to historians who provided me with material for the analysis of individual revolutions and gave me insight into the range of social atmosphere with respect to historical time and geographical space. Furthermore, I have to extend my gratitude to the social scientists who, between them, covered so much ground that, possibly, very little more work is needed to convert their findings into a coherent theory.

I do not share the narcissistic view held by some scholars that as in the natural sciences so too in the social sciences theories should be 'parsimonious and elegant'. Since one of the characteristics of social change is its complexity, a theory, in my opinion, should not eschew this particular feature of the subject matter. However interesting individual sociological, socio-psychological, economic or political theories may be (I am using Stan Taylor's frame of reference),[3] a good understanding of the phenomenon of revolution requires a comprehensive approach.

Right at the start, I should perhaps also point out my intention of avoiding those biases which are brought to the study of revolution by the background of a specific discipline. Writings of the outstanding and widely quoted American scholars Hannah Arendt[4] and Theda Skocpol[5] provide good examples of this tendency. As a philosopher, Arendt succumbed to the temptation of introducing a political value judgement into her considerations. In Arendt's view 'freedom', understood as the ability to participate in political decisions, is opposed to 'liberation', understood as the endeavour to rid oneself of poverty and oppression. Only revolutions that aim at and achieve 'freedom' are pure, successful revolutions, while those that fight for 'liberation', for resolving the social question, ensue in a 'grand tragedy'. Unfortunately for Arendt, people do not always choose to take lessons from a philosopher. As Arendt put it: 'The sad truth of the matter is that the French Revolution, which ended in disaster, has made world history, while the American Revolution, so triumphantly successful, has remained an event of little more than local significance'.[6]

Judging from Theda Skocpol's popularity, the academe seems to prefer a radical sociological approach, free from any psychological consideration. In a determined opposition to prevalent theories, in particular to those that accept that societal orders are based on consensus, Skocpol establishes as the first major principle of adequate understanding of social revolutions (i.e. those revolutions that Arendt describes as tragedies) 'a non-voluntaristic, structural perspective of their causes and processes'.[7] In this respect Skocpol is adamant. Even Marxists, who of all schools of thought are closest to her, are castigated because in emphasising class consciousness or hegemony they allow the voluntaristic theories to creep into their reasoning.[8] However, careful reading of Skocpol's otherwise sensible writings (I shall refer to her findings in the appropriate context) reveals that her arguments are not that much obscured by her declared principle as she asserted it. As Kimmel says in his comment on Skocpol: 'Consciousness and conscious social action play an ambiguous role in her analysis: they are there, but she does her best to ignore them'.[9] By the way, authoritarian governments are more sensible, when they are inclined, as a matter of precaution, to bar those ideas that may influence the consciousness of their subjects in an undesirable way.

As any social phenomenon is, by its very nature, also a historical phenomenon, its study has to pay particular attention to its historical dimension. Conceptualisation has to be matched with the overview of its occurrence both in historical time and in geographical space: we shall call this part of our study 'topography'. Not only the incidence but also the relevance of revolutions for the development of the society must be evaluated. Each individual specimen of the revolution species deserves its topographical classification and an assessment of its individual causes and course (development). Possible similarities or regularities can then provide the basis of theoretical conclusions. The heuristic or methodological framework will then consist of six sections:

1. Concept and types (taxonomy or typology) of revolution.
2. Occurrence (topography) of revolutions.
3. Causation (etiology) of revolutions.
4. Course or development (morphology) of revolutions.
5. Outcome (consequences) of revolutions.
6. Conclusion, a theoretical outline.

The typology is intended to be comprehensive, the topography illustrative. The etiology is the summary of other authors' findings corroborated by the case studies. The morphology is wholly based on the case studies; these are supposed to represent the most significant specimens of the species 'revolution'. The outcome of revolutions is discussed in the context of individual case studies and in the conclusions.

As in the first edition of this book, the main test cases are three 'Western', 'historical' revolutions (the Czech Hussite, the English and the French), and three 'Eastern', 'modern' revolutions (in Russia, Turkey and China). In addition, observations are made on revolutions in Iran and in Mexico, and on the collapse of the Soviet empire.

With respect to the time span under observation, we should talk about revolutionary processes rather than about revolutions. These processes are followed from their first violent preludes or turmoils, but their development is already foreshadowed by the origins of the issues which were later at the heart of revolution. The end of this process is marked by the completion of changes that are deemed to be irreversible.

Until now there has been no general agreement on what should be considered the end of a revolutionary process. Although its very beginning may also sometimes be a matter for discussion, the start of the revolution itself is usually marked by a manifest outbreak of violence. On the other hand, as L.P. Edwards says, 'a revolution dies out in a curiously insignificant and inconsequential way'. Edwards sees the end of revolution in a 'process of accommodation' culminating in 'an arrangement ... whereby the different factions in the revolutionary society have their reciprocal relations defined, and their spheres of action worked out ... The main principles which the revolution has established cease to be matters of controversy'.[10] This seems to be an appropriate demarcation of the end of a revolution.

In this study, we want to follow each revolutionary process through to such an end. In doing so, we shall find that the winding up of a revolutionary process need not be characterised by insignificant or inconspicuous events; only the dramatic flavour that marks the start of revolution will of necessity be missing.

What is more difficult to assess is whether the change produced by the revolution was of long duration. I prefer this as a defining characteristic to the more apodictic term 'irreversible'. As will be shown in the final part of the book, some revolutionary changes were, in the long run, reversible. Realism demands that we be satisfied with the condition that changes brought about by revolution lasted centuries rather than decades. This may still seem too vague or arbitrary, but I hope to show the utility of this approach as our discussion progresses.

Since we understand revolution not as a single event but as a process, it follows that all its characteristic elements need not materialise at once or in a particular phase of that process. This holds also for the use of violence, which may break out at frequent or less frequent intervals.

In individual cases, it may sometimes be difficult to decide whether or not a substantial change occurred in the socio-economic structure or, to put it another way, whether the ceaselessly occurring gradual changes attained such a magnitude that they may be considered as substantial. An illustration of this may be found in the case of the English Puritan revolution. In L. Stone's words, 'It was a political revolution with potential, but abortive, social consequences'.[11] The so-called commercial revolution was an earlier phenomenon; the so-called agricultural and industrial revolutions came later. What, in my opinion, justifies the view that the English Puritan revolution should be considered in this context, is its legacy, revealed in subsequent developments. Although the revolutionary forces were – after a twenty-year struggle – defeated, their moderate factions recaptured most of the ground after a further twenty-eight years. At least some of the achievements of the revolution became permanent. Constitutional parliamentary monarchy, a wider scope for religious tolerance and the free play of market forces became the main long-term features of the British societal system.

CONCEPT AND TYPES OF REVOLUTION

If all possible meanings of the term 'revolution' were to be encompassed within a short definition, then perhaps three words would suffice: 'sweeping dramatic change'. This definition is broader than that of the *Oxford English Dictionary*, which reads: 'a complete overthrow of the established government in any country or state by those who were previously subject to it, a forcible substitution of a new ruler or form of government'. The latter understanding of the concept may be described as the revolution in technical terms. Concepts such as 'industrial, cultural, scientific or neolithic' (etc.) revolutions are revolutions in the figurative sense.

In the real world, the change of the form of government usually has wider implications; they are often the main reason for its overthrow and the main issue in the process of substitution. It is not only the sphere of government or political regime that is at stake, but the whole complex of power relationships with their impact on wealth, social status and social stratification. David Robertson, in the *Penguin Dictionary of Politics*, takes this into account when he says: 'A revolution, properly so-called, is a violent and total change in a political system which not only vastly alters the distribution of power ... but results in major changes in the whole social structure'.[12] This is revolution in the sociological sense.

Force is being used on both sides and not necessarily only within the country involved. The complete overthrow of a government and a change of the political regime, however, may occur several times. Revolution then appears to be not a single event but a protracted period of turbulent, dramatic events, which, as previously stated, may be better styled as a 'revolutionary process'.

This is what makes any discourse on the phenomenon of revolution a complex undertaking. As Krishan Kumar pointed out, it is no wonder that John Stuart Mill found that the term 'revolution', as a name for any sort of principles or opinions, was not English. The English would speak of particular events, like 'the French Revolution', or 'the English Revolution'. The general usage, which derived from France, was to be deplored. 'It proceeds from an infirmity of the French mind, which has been one main cause of the miscarriages of the French nation in its pursuit of liberty and progress; that of being led away by phrases, and treating abstractions as if they were realities which have a will and exert active power.'[13]

Here the famous Englishman, revealing the long-standing Anglo-French rivalry, made a point which, if transferred from the ethnic to the professional sphere, could refer to traditional historians. Yet the difficulty with using general terms cannot always be brushed aside by merely substituting the specimen for the species.

Some scholars, mainly from Princeton University, came up with the idea that it would be better to drop the term 'revolution' altogether and replace it with the term 'internal war'. This would then be defined as 'any attempt to alter state policy, rulers or institutions by the use of violence when violent competition is not the norm and well-defined institutional patterns exist'.[14] This definition is only slightly different from that of the *Oxford English Dictionary* mentioned earlier.

The tendency to avoid the term 'revolution' also stems from those who understand revolution mainly in terms of social change. If it is a sudden and thorough change, they prefer to talk of social transformation. This is the case with some sociologists in Eastern Europe who, being at a loss as to how to handle their 'velvet revolutions' theoretically (in fact, negotiated transfers of power conditioned by turmoil), look to the consequences rather than to the technique of the crucial acts that make the breakthrough for change. The gap between those, on the one hand, who look primarily at individual acts of illegitimate violence and those, on the other hand, who want to see the process of transformation in its wholeness, is so vast that it would be better to use the different names for the different foci of observation: respectively, revolution and social transformation.

Homonyms, however, are widely used, and English is particularly rich in them. A proper meaning of the term has to be looked for within its context. It is primarily historians who, quite in line with their ontological position, take advantage of such a linguistic opportunity. Social scientists have to be more careful; ambiguous terms present a challenge to their analytical skill, and if they do not want to drop such a term altogether, they have to work out a sensible typology. Abolition of entrenched concepts in scholarly language is not an easy undertaking; perhaps it is not even advisable. Quite a few significant historical events in which both the violent change of government and social transformation took place, already bear the indelible common term 'revolution', and any attempt to change this would be a preposterous act of pedantry which, in any respect, would hardly be shared by most scholars in the field.

Nevertheless, a little pedantry may be useful. It is logic, in particular, which should not be thrown overboard. This is precisely what happened with Chalmers Johnson's famous typology of revolution based on a combination of two methods: (a) the selection of outstanding cases which are then considered as paradigms characterising a particular type; and (b) the use of generic concepts. Applying such a methodological hybrid, Johnson arrived at a sixfold typology: Jacquerie, millenarian rebellion, anarchistic rebellion, Jacobin-communist revolution, conspiratorial *coup d'état* and militarised mass insurrection. As only one type is labelled revolution, one may wonder why the epithet 'Jacobin-communist'? Does it mean that there may be yet another type of revolution of a non-Jacobin, non-communist nature? All the other categories are (a) rebellions (in principle unsuccessful), or (b) *coups d'état* (why only conspiratorial?), or (c) militarised mass insurrections which may, according to circumstances, issue either in a war of liberation or in a revolution of more-or-less Jacobin-communist type. The lack of a system and of terminological consistency is surprising. Some categories overlap, others leave uncovered ground between them.[15] Johnson's elaborate typology also fails to encompass all uses of the general terms (revolution, rebellion, insurrection, etc.) to which he refers.

Looking for a comprehensive and systematic typology we must first decide whether we want to use the term 'revolution' only for single acts or for the whole process. If we decide for single acts, the focus would be on a violent overthrow of government. During one revolutionary process there may be a series of such overthrows. Individual overthrows would be adequately described by the conventional epithet of historiography, such as the February Revolution

(Paris, 1848) and the Great October Revolution (Russia, 1917); the categorisation would then be most concerned with the border between genuine revolution and a mere *coup d'état*.

If we opt for using the term 'revolution' as a process, then the focus will be on social change or transformation of society. Individual specimens could then be identified either by the name of the country or by the names of those sections of the population that were the driving force behind the revolutionary action (puritans, bourgeois, proletarians, etc.). The categorisation of revolutionary processes may also take into consideration the main features in the outcome of revolution. This means which, and/or to what extent, individual social aspects were affected; or whether the transformation concerned mainly the political regime, or whether also the socio-economic parameters (such as the change of property control, of social stratification, of social status, of hierarchy, etc.) were also profoundly affected; or whether the main achievement was the greater efficiency (modernisation) of the economy and state bureaucratic organisation.

In this book I shall be using a typology which (a) considers revolution primarily as an accelerated, and in some phases violent, process of a significant social change; and (b) looks for the criterion of differentiation relating to the origin of that process.

As far as the origin of such a process is concerned, there are, as Table I.1 demonstrates, three basic alternatives:

1. Action initiated from below (originating with the subjects).
2. Action initiated from above (originating with the rulers).
3. Action initiated from the side (from abroad).

Only revolution from below can be considered as a revolution in the proper sense of the word.[16] Action from above and from the side can be styled as revolutions only in a broader meaning. The main reason for the extended use of the term is the significant and dramatic changes that occur in the wake of a violent act.

In the case of 'revolution' from above, violence may or may not be legitimate. Whether the use of force was legitimate or not may be difficult to answer unequivocably. As both the Russian and the Japanese emperors were sovereign, they were in that capacity entitled to act according to their will. However, in both countries there was also a long-standing tradition which regulated the relationship between emperor and the foci of lesser authority. *Streltsy* in Russia and the shogun in Japan both have customary rights and could consider their resistance to the emperor's orders as legitimate. What eventually decided the conflicting claims was force.

'Revolution' from the side is a revolution which is 'exported' from the country of its origin and, via military conquest or infiltration, 'imported' to another country. In the 1790s, the French revolution was 'exported' to the neighbouring countries in this way. However, its export beyond the Rhine and to Italy only had a temporary success. Communists, in their 'exports' of revolution, were

Table I.1 Types of revolution (the main examples)

| | Revolution from below (revolution in a strict sense) | | | Revolution in a broader sense | | |
	Vertical		Horizontal	Revolution from above	Revolution from abroad	Hybrid revolution (from below and above)
	Endogenous (internal impulses)	Exogenous (responses on external impulses)	Secessionist war			
	Bohemia (1419)	Russia (1905)	Netherlands (1566)	Russia (Peter I – 1689)	Netherlands, Italy (from France 1795)	Italy (1922)
	England (1642)	Turkey (1908)	North America (1773)	Japan (ōsei fukko – 1867)	East-Central Europe (from Russia – 1944)	Germany (1933)
	France (1789)	China (1911)	Latin America (1810)	Russia (Gorbachev – 1985)	Tibet (from China – 1951)	Libya (1969)
	Mexico (1910)	Iran (1906)	Algeria (1954)			
	Cuba (1953)	Ethiopia (1974)				

Note: The data in brackets indicate the first explosion or the beginning of action.

successful only in much later stages of the revolutionary process in Russia, i.e. as a result of the Second World War. This issue will be discussed in more detail in the corresponding case studies (Chapters 3 and 4). The outcome of contemporary attempts to 'export' the Iranian Revolution which, in socio-economic terms, is of a particularly specific nature, remains to be seen.

Most difficult to categorise are those revolutions that started both from below and from above. Italian fascists took the state by organised action from below but with the connivance of some sectors of the military and political establishment of the day. Hitler became chancellor (prime minister) legally but in circumstances approaching civil war; he then extended his power illegally while using considerable violence against his opponents. Franco rose to power by a military insurrection supported by a part of the official establishment against the legitimate government. All these and similar instances may be described as 'hybrid revolutions'. Not only the way in which the societal power was taken over, but also the ensuing transformation of the society, can be seen as 'hybrid' – a mix of innovative and conservative measures.

Turning to the core type of revolution (revolution from below), we may find several further aspects of type differentiation. Revolution may be directed against the government which is at the same time located in the country and enjoys a full sovereignty there. Large-scale military activities may then be considered as internal or civil wars. These terms may be regarded as synonyms. But 'civil war' implies that the belligerents have a more equal social status and power position, as in wars between groups of citizens in Graeco-Roman antiquity or in modern times. Also the war between the king and Parliament in seventeenth-century England is conventionally described as civil war.

But the issue may be between people in one country and a government seated in another country, which is in the dominant position over the country where dissent is being voiced. If the ensuing struggle develops into a war, it is then usually called a 'secessionist war' or a 'war of liberation'. If the term 'revolution' is to be further used for these two different types of confrontation, revolution against sovereign authorities in the home country may be called 'vertical revolution' and revolution against the sovereign authorities seated in another country 'horizontal revolution'.

As far as societal transformation is concerned, it is more likely to be an effect of a 'vertical' rather than a 'horizontal' revolution. Yet the fact of political secession itself, while creating conditions for a different legal order and social relationship, always has wider implications: this, too, may be described as social transformation, albeit of a less sweeping and dramatic nature than is usually the case with 'vertical' revolutions. Quite a few modern secessionist wars even established political regimes that made societal transformation their *raison d'être* (for example, North Vietnam, Algeria, Angola etc.). Here, however, an important caveat is to be made: the nature of ensuing social change is not a matter of the type of revolution, but of the general socio-historical context, as will be shown throughout this book, in particular in the test cases.

In this context we have to mention yet another, more subtle, differentiation applicable to the typology of revolution. Despite Theda Skocpol's emphatic denial, each revolution is a complexity of conflicting purposeful activities. They may be irrational, confused and counter-productive; but not only the leaders, but also the rank-and-file actors in revolution, always have some aims in mind which, in their opinion, make their efforts meaningful; in most cases there is a specific goal to be accomplished.

Although there is always a gap between the intentions of revolutionaries on the one hand, and the outcome of their confrontation with the countervailing forces on the other, there is nevertheless a certain line of development, an image of orientation or a sense of socio-historical direction which links the beginning and the end of the revolutionary process.

The image of orientation ensues from the source of inspiration which may come either from the domestic or from the foreign cultural, or, to use a more general term, civilisational tradition. As in the first edition of this book, I am using this difference as a further nuance in my typology. I describe those vertical revolutions that were inspired by the tradition of the countries where they took place as endogenous; whereas vertical revolutions where the inspiration came from the challenge of foreign values, habits and institutions are described as exogenous. In this edition, however, I would like to confront this particular distinction with another theoretical approach.

The difference between the domestic and the foreign elements in a revolution can follow two conceptual lines of investigation. One is the line of global, supranational socio-cultural entities usually called civilisations. Here it is the general mental orientation towards a particular world-view and set of values embodied in the codes of behaviour, symbols and institutions which constitute and demarcate individual civilisations.

The other line is that of supranational entities defined in economic or political terms. For Theda Skocpol the global category is 'the international states system as a transnational structure of military competition ... Throughout modern world history, it represents an analytically autonomous level of transnational reality – interdependent in its structure and dynamics with world capitalism, but not reducible to it'.[17]

For Immanuel Wallerstein the term of reference is the Modern World System constituted by the tissue of the capitalist economy and by its foreign trade and movement of capital and their political implications.[18] Whereas Skocpol's position does not point to any general line of typological differentiation between individual revolutions, Wallerstein's concept brings to the fore of the theory of revolution the distinction between the core and the periphery related to his world system.

As the Modern World System does not incorporate all countries to the same depth or with the same intensity, the contrast between the more developed core and the periphery becomes a key factor in modern political history and also in the occurrence of revolutions. Although at first sight this perception seems to make more sense with respect to horizontal revolutions (wars of liberation), as regards the typology of revolution, it is more useful when applied to vertical revolutions.

In horizontal revolutions it could operate both ways. The uprising of the Netherlands provinces against the Spanish Crown can be viewed either as a war of liberation within the core of the capitalist world, or as a revolution of the nascent core country against a country that put an ideological brake on its economic development. But when the African colonies revolted against their European masters it was beyond any doubt a revolution of the periphery against the core. But the key issue, the secession, was the same. There is no reason for further differentiation within the type of horizontal revolutions. If we pass over the strong cultural (ethnic and religious) aspects, the Dutch revolted because they wanted to modernise faster, and the Africans, etc., because they wanted to modernise in their own way.

As will be shown in our test cases of vertical revolution, the reference to the contrast between a revolution within the core on the one hand, and that between the periphery and the core on the other, may be helpful. In circumstances of increasing economic and political linkage a peripheral country usually looks to the core as an example. Catching up requires not only learning appropriate skills and attitudes, but also harmonising with the domestic cultural tradition. This usually constitutes a serious complication or even a stumbling block in the process of 'modernisation'. In contrast, revolution within a core country has to create the image of what should be achieved from its own resources. There is a case for bold innovation; the source of inspiration can hardly be other than the domestic tradition. Images from an idealised past, sometimes a very remote one, mix with images of the future visualised within the conceptual framework of the present.

The first six case studies will illustrate this point. In the Russian, Chinese and Turkish revolutions, it was the daunting challenge and example of the modern (capitalist, democratic, technologically advanced) West that spurred the quest for the abolition of shameful backwardness. The main issue was to what extent to adopt the Western model and to what extent national cultural identity should be preserved. On the other hand, in the Czech and in the English example it was idealised, pristine Christianity that inspired the attempts at reform. In the English Revolution, however, there was also a more articulated interest in political innovation and economic awareness. The French revolutionaries were inspired by the earlier pagan Roman tradition rather than by the Christian tradition; their aroused imagination, sustained by the changing spirit of the time, led them to more significant innovations than was the case with previous revolutions in Europe.

It is evident that, unlike the three European revolutions, the later, more Eastern revolutions cannot be properly understood without reference to the foreign impact on their countries. Although the three European revolutions also occurred in a constellation of domestic and foreign circumstances, the foreign element, whether this was the image of prosperous England in the case of France, or the example of the city state of Venice in the case of Bohemia, did not impinge on the common culture (civilisation). There was no question of recasting the whole society according to the foreign example.

We must not forget that in the three Eastern revolutions it was not only the economic or political catching up but the wide-ranging cultural reorientation that was supposed to modernise the country. Capitalism, nation-state and pluralistic democracy became the dominant features of the modern West because its spiritual orientation was inspired by values other than those of medieval, Latin Christianity. It was a lengthy and dramatic process which, through a dialectical rhythm of renaissance, reformation, counter-reformation, enlightenment and romanticism, transformed the religion-orientated Latin Christian civilisation into a mundane civilisation where a peculiar combination of spontaneity and discipline created conditions for unprecedented efficiency in most walks of life.

Max Weber rightly realised that any change in political and economic organisation presupposes a change in mental orientation, i.e. either a new interpretation of the established principles or turning to another kind of reasoning.[19] Wallerstein pushed the Weberian balance back to the Marxian reductionist stance. Thus, for instance, in his understanding, 'the French Revolution was . . . the moment when the ideological interpretation finally caught up with the economic base. It was the consequence of the transition, not its cause or the moment of its occurrence'.[20]

Here we come across an issue which is not a matter of substance, or a matter of empirical evidence. The concept that the economy is the base and ideas are the superstructure depends on the angle of observation. Looking at the major changes or shifts within contemporary societies, we are struck by the crucial role of the twin processes of industrialisation and urbanisation and their psychological and structural effects. Peasant groups or whole nations, when caught up in these processes, experience a disintegration, or even total loss of their traditional values. They adapt themselves gradually, and often painfully, to the lifestyle dictated by industrial work and urban life. In this case 'being', exemplified by the position in the production process and the living environment, may be rightly considered the independent variable, whereas the consciousness (exemplified by the symbolic systems of culture) of the people affected by the change may be classified with all due allowances for the intergenerational time-lag as the dependent variable.

However, when the observer takes a higher vantage point and looks at the issue from a historical perspective, another type of dependence emerges as the obvious one. Industrialisation is unimaginable without a series of inventions and innovations which in their turn were due to a substantial change in many people's mentality and value orientation, i.e. in their ability to develop their thoughts along previously untrodden paths. Without an analysis of the changes in human images of reality and in human valuation, we can hardly understand the historical breakthroughs by which new discoveries, techniques and skills brought individual societies and, eventually, a substantial part of humankind as a whole to a higher level of cognition and consequently to a more effective command over their environment.

Yet as Max Weber has amply demonstrated, not only the study of breakthroughs (the analysis of diachronic processes) but also the comparative examination of contemporaneous social formations (in a synchronic analysis) can profit from focusing first on people's views and values.

In connection with the typology of revolution, a few words have to be said about some labels for similar but less weighty events. These labels are *coup d'état*, rebellion, revolt, uprising and insurrection. The *coup d'état* has already been mentioned. Literally, as Hagopian pointed out, it is not a problematic term; it means a sudden attack on the government. But within a broader context it may look different. Usually, *coups d'état* are restricted in their objectives and happen to be rather mild affairs.[21] Occasionally, however, a *coup d'état* may initiate a period of turbulent events or a watershed in a revolutionary process. As will be shown in the case of the French Revolution, a series of *coups d'état* marked the turning points in the course of that revolution.

Rebellion, revolt, uprising and insurrection usually describe violent actions with particular, more or less limited aims; they are undertaken by a particular group of people (social, ethnic, religious or political) and are more likely to be unsuccessful in their objectives. These terms can be used also for failed attempts at revolution. However, there are historians who use these terms for processes which sociologists prefer to describe as revolutions.

There is a whiff of illegitimacy about the term 'rebellion', often coupled with a lack of sophistication. Monarchs used this term when describing the armed uprisings of their vassals, as did aristocratic landlords when describing the uprisings or protest movements of their peasants. Most often the aim of such a rebellion was the restoration of the previous position of one social group – of an earlier relationship between rulers and ruled, which was supposed to be more advantageous for those who started to rebel. In a rebellion there would be little new ideology, but there could be a quite significantly different interpretation of the common social philosophy concerning the relationship between rulers and ruled in the society. One has only to remember the different understandings of the Bible exemplified by the verse 'When Adam ploughed and Eve span, who then was the gentleman?'

Finally, we have to mention a word with still more specific meaning – 'mutiny'. This is applicable to uprisings of the rank-and-file soldiers against their officers, or of a crew on a ship against their captain, etc. During a revolutionary process, mutinies, too, may occasionally occur but they are unlikely to become turning points in its course.

People using the term 'revolution' may sometimes have in mind the violent form and sometimes the scope and intensity of the change. If it is the violent form, it is more likely that they will not see so clearly the difference between revolution on the one hand and revolt, rebellion etc. on the other. These people are also more likely to consider revolution as a short-term event rather than as a long-term process. The stress on the scope and intensity of the change, however, makes it easier to understand revolution as a process and to see individual violent acts in their broader perspectives. An accelerated, fundamental change in particular aspects of society, which occurred without any use of collective violence may also be described as revolution; this is the case with 'industrial revolution'. But everybody is quite clear that the term 'revolution' is used here as a metaphor.

The subsequent section will shed some additional light on the demarcation between revolution as a process and revolution as an instantaneous event.

TOPOGRAPHY OF REVOLUTION

Counting and weighting revolutionary events

Those who understand revolution merely as a change of government brought about by force or by menace of force may see no reason for making a distinction between revolution and other, supposedly less weighty, acts of collective violence such as rebellion, revolt, uprising, etc.

Historians need not bother too much about conceptual nuances. Since they like to see all historical events as unique phenomena, it is for them of no particular importance to stick to rules concerning the use of generic concepts. Thus, for instance, M. Mollat and P. Wolff, in their overview of what they call *The Popular Revolutions of the Late Middle Ages,*[22] gloss over the main violent mass movements in Western Europe from the Jacquerie of 1358 to the 1391 pogrom in the Iberian Peninsula and only lightly touch on the Hussite wars in fifteenth-century Bohemia. Similarly, but in a more systematic way, the German medievalist F. Seibt, in his *Revolution in Europa*, discusses seven cases starting with 'Rienzo's Roman Revolution' in 1347 and ending with the 1618 defenestration in Prague.[23]

On the other hand, social scientists either try to maintain conceptual rigour or make a broad sweep. In either approach, they may be attracted by the charms of quantification which turns out to be a Sisyphean task.

Conceptual rigour is defended by Peter Calvert, a political scientist, who describes his subject matter as 'revolutionary events' and accepts the definition of revolution offered by the *Oxford English Dictionary*. According to this definition (referred to earlier), the essential mark of the term is the 'complete overthrow of the established government' by its 'previous subjects', i.e. the revolt, uprising, etc. has to be successful in order to fit the term 'revolution'.[24]

Using this definition as a demarcation, Calvert identified 446 revolutionary events world-wide during the time span from 1901 to 1969. This means more than six such events per year on the global scale. Most of these events were of short duration. Of the cases listed between 1961 and 1969 only a quarter lasted longer than one month. More than a third were one-day events. In terms of conventional typology, they were mainly *coups d'état* or mere assassinations of the head of state. Only a few of them initiated or were the turning points in what, in our terminology, could be described as a revolutionary process, such as the events in Mexico in 1911 and subsequently each year from 1913 to 1916.

Studying individual revolutionary events as isolated specimens of a species may sometimes be useful from a military or technical point of view (this is what Calvert attempts to assess and even quantify) but it can hardly help us to understand the phenomenon of revolution as a particular case of social change. The geographical location of revolutionary events studied by Calvert (most of which took place in Latin America, Africa and the Middle East) indicate that in a study of the incidence of revolution, the particular socio-historical and cultural context has to be taken into account.

The sociologist Pitirim Sorokin, writing before Calvert, was among those who preferred the broad-sweep approach. In particular, he attempted to assess the incidence and magnitude of revolutionary events. In his third volume of *Social and Cultural Dynamics*, a volume entitled *Fluctuation of Social Relationships, War and Revolution*, Sorokin, in cooperation with N.S. Timasheff and S. Oldenburg, provided a list of 1,622 'internal disturbances' (occasionally also referred to as revolutions) which occurred in ancient Greece and Rome, in Byzantium and in the main countries of medieval and modern Europe.[25]

According to the author's assessment, most of these disturbances were violent. Only about 5 per cent occurred without violence and 23 per cent with a little violence (p. 477). Within the researched time span (which differs with respect to individual countries), Sorokin discovered that the frequency of notable social disturbances in the social bodies under consideration was, on average, about one in six years. Furthermore, he stated that the indicators of the magnitude (duration and masses involved) 'show no continuous trend' and that 'there is hardly any definite periodicity in the ups and downs of internal disturbances' (pp. 482–3). However, some periods were more turbulent than others.

The common denominator of Sorokin's list is the mere occurrence of disturbance, irrespective of whether any social and/or political change resulted from it. It might be assumed that individual disturbances, especially those that cropped up in rapid sequence in particular areas, point to a process of social transformation – a process of transition from one pattern of social and political relationship to another one. However, having compared the most turbulent periods with the account of the general development, Sorokin concludes: 'Disturbances occurred not only in the periods of the decay and decline of society, but in its periods of blossoming and healthy growth' (p. 495). (This might be a boost to the conflict theorists. However, with respect to what has been said about the average incidence of disturbances, there is still enough scope for the functionalists to defend their ground.) In spite of the lack of a trend in the course of the disturbances, the indicators of their frequency and magnitude lead Sorokin to observe 'three main peaks; in the eighth, in the thirteenth and fourteenth centuries; and in the nineteenth and twentieth centuries. After each peak the wave of disturbances subsides and remains low till the next peak' (p. 496).

Although this observation provides Sorokin with an additional argument for his general idea of a 'tripartite trendlessly fluctuating cyclic movement or super-rhythm', it is difficult to accept the plausibility of Sorokin's reasoning. Suffice it here to quote one of his propositions:

> During the thirteenth and fourteenth centuries the European culture and society moved from the ideational to the sensate form, from the feudal to the modern system of social relationship (from predominantly familistic to coercive-constructural; from theocracy to the secular *régime*, from ideational freedom to sensate, from the feudal *régime* to the national monarchies and so on). (pp. 496–7)

This is obviously a cavalier judgement; the process of change which Sorokin allocates to the thirteenth and fourteenth centuries was much more protracted. After the sensate spirit of the renaissance came the ideational backlash, first in the form of reformation and then as counter-reformation; in both, theocracy or, rather, hierocracy reappeared with full vigour. Only the enlightenment of the eighteenth century, of which the French Revolution was an integral, albeit not fully consistent part, made that breakthrough which Sorokin predated by 400 years.

There is yet another problem with Sorokin's topography of revolution. Individual disturbances are reviewed in isolation, irrespective of whether they were linked together by chains of cause and effect. Historical processes are dissected into incoherent events. Thus the most important part of sociological analysis is left out.

Another attempt to count wars, including those that can also be considered as revolutions, was undertaken by Evan Luard. In his *War in International Society*,[26] he is looking primarily for the social function of war (if any) and for changing patterns of warfare. Luard's list of wars is impressive: it starts at 1400 AD and, as time goes on, the geographical focus is extended from Europe to the whole of the world. The civil wars in Europe are counted until 1790, then there is a special category of wars of national independence and wars of decolonisation, which corresponds with our category of horizontal revolutions. They are listed irrespective of whether they were successful or not. Unfortunately, with regard to the most recent period (1917–83), Luard abandons the classification by the nature of war and gives the breakdown only by geographical areas.

The era of large-scale wars of liberation (or decolonisation) came only after the Second World War. Indonesia, Vietnam, Algeria, Angola and Mozambique are the best-known examples. There were also similar transformative revolutions in countries that were more-or-less independent, such as Cuba and Ethiopia, but where the involvement of foreign powers may be considered a horizontal element in otherwise vertical revolutions.

Recently, a review and recount of revolutions in Europe during the last 500 years (1492–1992) was undertaken by Charles Tilly.[27] Compared with the authors mentioned earlier, Tilly pays more attention to conceptual considerations and to the historical background of individual types of revolution which he identifies in the course of the epoch.

Tilly's working definition of revolution reads as follows:

a forcible transfer of power over a state in the course of which at least two distinct blocs of contenders make incompatible claims to control the state, and some significant portion of the population subject to the state's jurisdiction acquiesces in the claim of each bloc (p. 8, and more explicitly on pp. 49–50 and 241–2)

The reasons for raising incompatible claims may vary, but in the course of the 500 years under study, some types of underlying issues may be typical for particular periods or sets of circumstances. In Tilly's words, '*Dramatis personae* of political conflict, collective action and revolutions changed fundamentally between 1492 and 1992' (p. 28). This range may be exemplified by the predominance of dynastic wars and barons' rebellions in the earlier periods and social revolutions and wars of liberation in modern times. The focus is not on 'revolutionary events', as is the case with Calvert, but on 'revolutionary situations' and 'revolutionary outcomes'. The revolutionary situation is defined by the emergence of 'multiple sovereignty' ('dual power' or 'second-pivot situation' in our vocabulary). The revolutionary outcome is understood as a substantial transfer of power. It is clear that the latter may occur also without a revolutionary situation such as, for instance, by conquest. Contrarily, a split in the polity (revolutionary situation) need not result in a transfer of power (i.e. there is no revolutionary outcome). Thus: 'Only in the minority of instances where the new power holders emerge from multiple sovereignty can we properly speak of full-fledged revolution' (p. 15).

Unfortunately, the table that summarises Tilly's count of revolutionary situations by region and period between 1492 and 1992 – 709 cases altogether in six main areas of Europe (p. 243) – is not matched by a corresponding table of revolutionary outcomes; thus the suggested theoretical tool for the identification of full-fledged revolutions has not been used. In spite of some illuminating comments on individual cases, and especially on the general trend of development, Tilly's counting of revolutions does not go far beyond the works of Sorokin, Calvert and Luard.

To what extent is revolution a modern phenomenon?
A look into bygone ages

There is a widely shared view that revolution, understood in the terms outlined in the section above on 'Concept and types of revolution' (pages 6–16), is a modern phenomenon. This may be true as far as a particular type of revolution is concerned: revolution, whether vertical or horizontal, that brought about a significant restructuring of society, or in other words, revolution as a result of which the social barriers were either attenuated or realigned.

Before the French vertical and American horizontal revolutions at the close of the eighteenth century, we would scarcely find any similarly structured processes of societal transformation. The 'social climate' was not prepared for a drama of that kind. Yet dramatic, large-scale and profound changes of another sort did occur many times and their social impact can hardly be considered less significant than that of modern revolutions.

Most changes of that kind happened as a result of foreign conquest. Not only the European conquests in other continents, which mark the dawn of 'modern times', but many other expansions in which force was amply used, such as Graeco-Macedonian expansion to the Middle East, the Roman conquests beyond the Alps, and the conquests of Arabs and other Muslims in Asia, Africa and Europe – all produced significant changes in the conquered societies. The European conquest of the Americas, when millions of people were put under the strain of uprooting and a new, exhausting form of exploitation, can be considered a particularly drastic example of this kind.

The difference between such conquests and revolutions from abroad is subtle but obvious. Most conquerors of the aforementioned kind implanted their establishment on the subject population, which was then variously treated. Sometimes they were evicted (in particular if they were nomads or hunting people); sometimes they were enslaved or made bondsmen (such as most settled Amerindians). However, most often their social structure and hierarchy of status was not fundamentally altered but gradually absorbed the structure of the newly imposed social arrangements. Significant sections of the old élites often opted for a wholehearted collaboration within the new order.

Conquests motivated or justified by revolutionary ideologies (such as was the case in the French and Russian revolutions) also resulted in some form of exploitation, but the main aim was the restructuring of the society in the conquered country – the change of its political regime and economic system; changes sympathetic to those who felt somehow disadvantaged by the domestic regime. Leadership of the conquering countries and some sections of the population in the invaded countries were inspired by common ideals.

What the French revolutionaries did in the early stage of their revolution, their Russian counterparts also tried to do, but with little success; their main thrust came more than twenty years later and, with intervals, was carried out for a further forty years. Then, however, as will be shown in more detail in

Chapter 4, the nations to which the Russian revolution was exported, rose up and rejected the import. This happened in a way that may be symbolically described as a war of national liberation or horizontal revolution.

It is true that one type of revolution, namely the large-scale transformative revolution, is a phenomenon of the modern age, or to give it a proper name, of the age of Europeism. Modernity, like fashion, is always with us; it moves with time itself, and implies a certain rejection of the past. The epoch of Europeism which began with the transoceanic expansion of European states and nations, is, like the epoch of Hellenism 2,000 years earlier, a transient phenomenon. The twenty-first century may see its demise. At the close of the twentieth century there are enough pointers to the waning of European superiority on the global scale.

Our modernity, i.e. the epoch of Europeism, is often described as the age of capitalism, of the nation-state, of political mobilisation of the masses, or by other structural characteristics. All this may be correct, but it does not refer to the heart of the matter. The underlying common denominator of Europeism is the awakened consciousness of each individual's right to self-determination; hence the elusive vision of equality, not only before God, but also before law and, in principle, also among individuals.

In another context, I have described the transition from the European culture before the eighteenth century and that which gradually emerged hereafter to as a societal transformation exemplified by a fourfold shift: from fideism to empiricism, from religious to ethnic loyalties, from inequality and obedience to equality and self-assertion, and from muscles to machines.[28] With such a mutation, the propensity to rebel was particularly enhanced. No wonder that the main breakthrough occurred in the process of two great revolutions (the American and the French); the last quarter of the eighteenth century can be metaphorically described as a historical watershed.

The consequences of the aforementioned shifts provided the West European nations with unprecedented technical, military and economic superiority over other parts of the world; European ideas exerted a corrosive influence on the domestic cultures in those countries that were exposed to European pressures. Rejection or adoption of the European ways of thought and work became the Hamletian question of the day. With it the proclivity to revolt acquired a new impetus and justification. Likewise in Europe the sense of relative deprivation acquired a new, multifaceted dimension.

We have to bear in mind, however, that relative deprivation, in whatever form it may be sensed, does not provide a sufficient explanation for why people rebel.[29] Unless the people concerned are at such a low level of rationality that they are driven to action only by spontaneous strong feelings, in order to revolt they need to feel that their cause is justified. Barrington Moore, who certainly cannot be suspected of 'idealist' leanings, observed this on several occasions in his writings, in particular in his book *Social Origins of Dictatorship and Democracy*, published in 1966,[30] and then again twenty-two years later in a more explicit way, in a book with the telling title *Injustice: The social bases of obedience and revolt.*[31]

Taking the decision to rebel requires motivation to this effect. Where there is a strong feeling of injustice, which adversely affects human beings who take that decision, the motivation is quite obvious. There need not be, however, an explicit feeling or conviction about the particular injustice. Propensity to rebel or, on the other hand, acceptance of hardship and discrimination as a matter of course, may spring from within the particular culture in which individuals set their mind on action.

As Max Weber has amply demonstrated, suffering or discrimination, perceived as a justified way of life, may be a serious inhibition to revolt. If people believe in reincarnation and if their prospects for the next life depend on their observance of the code of behaviour valid for the present life, then they will humbly bear their distress which is bound to bring some comfort in the future. According to the karmic law of the Hindus, to borrow Max Weber's words:

> the world is viewed as a completely connected and self-contained cosmos of ethical retribution. Guilt and merit within this world are unfailingly compensated by fate in the successive lives of the soul, which may be reincarnated innumerable times ... Each individual forges his own destiny exclusively, and in the strictest sense of the word.[32]

As long as the basic values of Indian culture (whether Hindu or Buddhist) were fully accepted by Indian peoples, a social revolt or revolution was an unlikely event. Wars, whether dynastic, tribal or occasionally even religious, did occur, but all these were more like interstate wars than revolutions. Such wars were waged by people for whom fighting was a legitimate vocation. Only with the arrival of Islam in India, and with the development of syncretic religions such as Sikhism, was there scope for disturbances similar to vertical revolutions according to our typology.

In China, as opposed to India, vertical revolution was accepted almost as an element of political culture. The imperial power styled as the August Perfection or Noble Pinnacle was supposed to provide the link between humanity and what was around and above it.

The emperor was seen as the Mandatee of Heaven and in that capacity he was deemed to be responsible for the orderly course of society and of its natural environment, such as the weather. Any serious disturbance, whether caused by nature or by people, was a sign that the Heavens were about to withdraw their Mandate from the emperor of the day. If the disturbance ensued in a revolt and the government succeeded in suppressing it, the Mandate was upheld, but if the revolt turned out to be a successful revolution, its leader got the chance to become emperor in his own right and to found a new dynasty. Usually such a change of ruler was accompanied by measures that re-established order, improved the efficiency of imperial administration, and possibly brought about some improvement in the economy.

The best examples of dynastic changes that can be interpreted in terms of revolution are the rise and fall of the Qin dynasty and the subsequent ascent of the Han dynasty – events that happened in the fourth and third centuries BC.[33] The Qin story can be described as revolution from above (the stage of building up a tough 'modern' state) and from abroad (conquest of, and imposition of the new type of state on, the other Chinese states). The Han story can be described as endogenous vertical revolution.

The revolution from above in the state of Qin occurred between 361 and 339 BC, when Qin was transformed from a peripheral backwater, riven with anarchy and brigandage, into an efficient machine for work and war. First, law and order were established by drastic measures. These included the division of the population into groups of five or ten families jointly responsible for one another. The fiefs and the communal holdings were abolished and land became private property, from which taxes in kind proportionate to the size of the field were levied. The draining of the marshes and the construction of canals substantially increased the cultivated area, and refugees from other kingdoms, attracted by the good prospects for entrepreneurs, further improved the economic potential. Efficiency in all walks of life was enhanced by the substitution of merit for privileges of birth. Instead of the old aristocracy, a new system of honours was introduced to reward military achievements. Later, honorary posts could also be bought for money.

In their incessant fighting with the neighbouring barbarians, the Qin soldiers acquired both the practical skills and the endurance which, combined with the extensive use of iron weapons and cavalry, became their main assets in the struggle with other kingdoms which were less successful in terms of technical and organisational innovation.

The final round of internecine warfare began in 246 BC and was completed in 221 BC, when the last rival of the Qin, the state Qi (in what is now the province of Shantung) was defeated. The victorious king assumed the imperial title, Qin Shi Huangti; under the ideological guidance of the Legalists, who, unlike the Confucians, believed in the efficiency of punitive measures rather than education, the political and socio-economic system of the state was extended to cover the whole empire. As has been said already, this can be understood as revolution from abroad.

The unifying measures included a single currency, common measures of length and capacity, a new simplified standard writing, standardisation of the gauge of cart-wheels and large-scale construction of roads and canals. Protective walls around individual kingdoms were pulled down and the new Great Wall against the northern barbarians was built. The possession of arms was made illegal and the highest-ranking aristocracy of the conquered states had to settle without arms in the imperial capital.

Finally, in 213 BC, ideological pluralism was abolished. All writings, with the exception of those written by the Legalists and writings of a technical nature on subjects such as agriculture, construction, military matters, medicine and divination, were ordered to be burned. Further copying of the banned books became a capital offence and their possession was punished with forced labour. The revolutionary transformation of China was to be complete. Tradition was not to hamper the will to direct life towards greater economic and military efficiency. Yet, and this was to become typical of ideological purges in China, the emperor retained a college of seventy representatives of the various schools, perhaps in case there might be something valuable in them. Superstition was not to disappear from the cultural climate. Divination continued to be an important element of political decision-making, which also kept alive an interest in the Taoist practices.

Unfortunately, the unification of China did not mark the end of warring. The push to the south had to be continued and the struggle with the barbarians of the Northern Steppes was to be carried on more vigorously.

Thus the new regime asked for too much at once. It estranged too many people whose influence still mattered. The growing tax burden and the growing claims on military service and various kinds of corvée were also disturbing. Last but not least, the second emperor who took the helm lacked the ability necessary for such a task. Within a year uprisings broke out. The revolting forces soon became divided into two blocks: one led by a nobleman, the other by a minor official of lowly birth, Liu Bang. In 203 BC Liu Bang won and founded a new dynasty which was to become one of the most glorious in Chinese history, the dynasty of Han.

There are many astonishing things about this revolution, which ousted the son of the emperor unifier but preserved the unity of the empire. It was a vertical, not a horizontal, revolution. The Mandate of Heaven was apparently withdrawn from Qin for reasons other than the enforced unification; it was bestowed for almost four centuries upon the Han because they knew better how to preserve the necessary harmony. Such would be the traditional Chinese explanation. In our view, Liu Bang and his descendants were able to strike a more sensible balance between the innovations sponsored by the Legalists and the tradition for which the Confucians stood. Liu Bang, however, was not concerned with theories, but had the common sense to ensure a firm power base for his victory; he bequeathed to his descendants a solid establishment.

Tax reductions, the emancipation of slaves and a less severe penal code were without doubt popular measures. The land tax was fixed at one-fifteenth of the yield, while everyone between 15 and 56 was liable to the poll tax. Private ownership and saleability of land were preserved. A particular innovation was the right of villagers to elect their own magistrates from persons over 50. From these the authorities then chose the district officials (one district containing about a hundred villages). It is difficult to say whether this measure marked a return to the ancient custom of communal autonomy which some authors of a Marxist inclination believe held sway in the prehistorical era, or whether it was a brand new innovation. Given the fact that the prehistorical era was about 1,500 years earlier, the innovation has to be considered an epochal event anyway.

Enterprising people had many opportunities to enrich themselves. The royal coinage was abolished and minting became a matter of private banking. Free trade of all sorts was supported by the government's care for the infrastructure, for roads and for river transport, which together facilitated the transfer of goods from areas with a surplus to areas suffering from inadequate supply. Thus, at the turn of the third and second centuries BC, China moved close to what may be described as a kind of proto-capitalism.

Yet this was only one element, though a substantial one, of her complex structure. The difficulty lay in how to placate the aristocracy, made jealous by the promotions to government office from the middle classes. Liu Bang attempted to strike a balance between what may be called the capitalist and the feudal elements. To appease the nobles, the highest imperial offices were reserved for them; in addition some kinds of conspicuous consumption could be indulged in exclusively by that class. Furthermore, aristocratic titles involving land but not tenure of office were renewed, and the emperor himself did not hesitate to bestow fiefs upon his supporters and family members, although he often withdrew them again. Government officials and army officers were rewarded with personal benefices.

A compromise was also sought in cultural matters. The edict of 213 BC, prohibiting books of all schools not favoured by the Qin dynasty, became obsolete and was formally revoked under Liu Bang's successor in 191 BC. Actually the ban had been enforced for only two years, during which time about 450 scholars were sentenced to death and many more to forced labour. This was surely not enough to destroy the 'Hundred Schools'. In Maspero's view, the studies of traditional literature were more affected by the simplification of the script, which was at the same time facilitated by the invention of the brush as a writing tool.[34]

The story of the two-tier transformation of China not only provides an additional example to our typology of revolution, but also foreshadows our morphological model: a radical innovative move is followed by reversal and the whole process is eventually consolidated approximately at the mid-point of the amplitude between the new and the old.

Another area where the social climate was conducive to vertical revolutionary action long before the European challenge is Iran. Following the path indicated by Max Weber, we may first ask ourselves what the view of Iranian religion was on this point. Zoroastrian religion, although shrouded in mystery, ritual and superstition, had a realistic glimpse of the nature of the polarity between Good and Evil. Each had its hypostatic supranatural representative. They fought each other and the followers of Zarathushtra were supposed to fight on the side of the Wise Lord of the Truth (Ohrmazd) against the Evil Spirit, Lord of Darkness (Ahriman). Although, at the end of time, the victory of the Wise Lord was guaranteed, it was still far off and there was scope for action.

The Zoroastrian religion was not an ascetic one. One of its virtues was prosperity, both in a spiritual and in a material sense; all the followers of

Ohrmazd were entitled to enjoy this virtue. As Zaehner put it, 'Zarathushtra is the Prophet of life and of life ever more abounding'.[35]

This was the theory. In practice, as ever, some could enjoy it more than others. It was up to somebody from the upper estates (the priesthood or the nobility) to invite those in need to take action; and such an invitation had to fall on fertile ground. The situation was to become revolutionary. Widespread relative deprivation, remedial action considered justified, weak government, high tension between royalty and the aristocracy, menace from abroad, and a determined religious leader: all this was present in the 490s in Sassanid Iran.

The issue was threefold and simple: redistribution of granaries, harems and landed property. Womenfolk, land and goods were too heavily concentrated in the hands of the upper aristocracy. Although the historical records are not clear about how all this came about, the main gist of the story cannot be doubted. Some redistribution was effected. For twenty-five years Mazdak, the leader of the whole action, managed to play the role of one pivot in a precarious tripartite balance: the king in the middle, the high aristocracy and clergy on the right, and the Mazdakites on the left. Eventually, when the heir apparent to the throne made a common cause with the nobility and clergy, Mazdak's revolution was doomed. He was put to death with many of his followers in 528 or 529 AD.

The new king, Khusraw (531–579 AD), embarked on reforms which were to ensure that something similar to the Mazdakite rebellion could not happen again. Common sense dictated the strengthening of royal power and the spreading of the Zoroastrian virtue of prosperity a little more evenly. Thus, on the one hand, the powers of the most powerful magnates and of the high priest were trimmed and a considerable section of unruly nobility was made into a more obedient court aristocracy; on the other hand, the treatment of the peasant became more considerate, with respect to both his working and his tax-paying capacity. In the middle, the role of the gentry and yeomanry was strengthened. Estate barriers, however, were made more impregnable. According to the Arabic historian at Taalibi, Khusraw even forbade the education of children from the lowest estate, on the grounds that, if educated, they could demand better jobs and thus affront the nobles.[36] Khusraw apparently had a good grasp of who might rebel and why. The deprivation of the lowest strata of society was eased and the power of the highly placed was curbed, but both were to be kept in their place. On the other hand, what was then the middle class was to get more opportunity for self-advancement.[37]

With the arrival of Islam, the propensity to rebel received a new ideological impetus. As Muhammad was not only a prophet, but also a political leader and statesman, Islam does not recognise a clear borderline between religion and politics. Various interpretations of the Koran and Islamic tradition are just as likely to lead to political schisms as to religious ones. In such a social climate, violent confrontations of various kinds occurred, and some of them can be described and interpreted in terms of revolution, either horizontal or vertical.

The uprising of various groups of zealots against the Umayyad dynasty of caliphs in the mid-eighth century AD can be regarded as the most significant vertical revolution within Islamic society. With the seat in multicultural Damascus, the Umayyads became increasingly lax in religious matters; on the other hand, they continued to observe the privileges granted to Arab Muslims and this was resented by the growing numbers of non-Arab converts to Islam. It was the Persian (Iranian) converts in particular who, being comparatively more sophisticated and having embraced Islam wholeheartedly, could not swallow the privileged position of the Arabs, and became staunch supporters of those Arab factions that showed more sympathy for the desire for greater equality among the believers.

The revolution was successful. The caliphate went over to a new dynasty – the Abbasids. Privileges granted to the Arabs were abolished, the seat of the caliphs was transferred nearer to the Arab-Iranian ethnic border, to a newly founded city, better known under its local Persian name, Baghdad (i.e. the Gift of God), than its newly coined Arabic name, Dar as-Salam (i.e. Abode of Peace). As a result, the Islamic Arab polity, which had been imposed upon the conquered territories of the Middle East and North Africa, began to develop as a multi-ethnic Islamic civilisation. As the involvement of the Iranians in the breakthrough was essential, so was their participation in the further development of Islamic polity. The caliphate was transformed into a bureaucratic institution to which the Persian imperial tradition made a significant contribution.[38]

Strengthening of the state via revolution is not a novelty of modern European history. An Islamic historian/political scientist might have made a similar observation on the Abbasid revolution, as did de Tocqueville on the French revolution more than a thousand years later.

European antiquity, with its particular concern for human self-assertion in society, is especially rich in events that could be described in terms of revolution. The transformation of the traditional, fully tribal societies, based on blood relationship and ruled by a monarchic type of government, into the modern, semi-tribal polities based on local citizenship and ruled by some kind of representative government, did not occur peacefully nor overnight. As is well known, there were many revolts and uprisings and much in-fighting between factions – in short, violent events – which marked the course of that transformation. It was a prolonged process which, in individual parts of Greece, took a different course and developed various forms of representation. It can hardly be conceived of as one great revolution; it is better to speak about a ramified and variegated revolutionary process. The structure that eventually emerged could be viable only in the short term, and eventually had to give way to the monarchic principle on a higher level, and with a wider geographical scope, of integration.

In the first phase of this process, which lasted from c. 600 to 338 BC (the defeat of the alliance of the Greek cities by Philip of Macedon at Chaironea), Sorokin listed fifty-eight 'internal disturbances in inter-group relationships', i.e.

revolts or revolutions predominantly of the vertical type. From the establishment of the Macedonian hegemony to the time when Rome took over this role (the sacking of Corinth in 146 BC) there were twenty-six further internal disturbances recorded on the territory inhabited by ancient Greeks.[39] This meant a significantly higher frequency in the latter period, i.e. when the quest for a representative government was already superseded by attempts at establishing the monarchy on a larger scale. In the latter period, however, not all internal disturbances are likely to have been recorded. The main issue of these disturbances throughout the whole epoch was the extent of political franchise; but redistribution of land and abolition of debts were also frequent causes of disturbance. In short, there was wide scope for vertical revolutions.

W.G. Forrest, in his account of the emergence of the Greek democracy, identifies (for the sake of exemplification) three transformative processes which he describes as revolutions: in chronological order, they occurred in Corinth, Sparta and Athens. The Corinthian revolution is credited with the invention of political theory, and that of Sparta with providing the paradigm, whereas Athens was the city-state where the quest for democracy was brought to fruition in the most effective and broadly based way.[40]

During these transformative processes, the desire for participation in power was spreading down the scale of social stratification; in Athens it reached the bottom tier of the free population. It is remarkable that the breakthrough in this process was usually achieved by way of compromise; the preceding violent confrontation was often aimed at strengthening the negotiating position without the wish to destroy the other side altogether. Violent confrontation, which made political and social change so often a revolutionary event, was a matter of political culture; this has to be taken into account when we want to compare it with our own epoch.

The Roman historical epoch, encompassing almost the whole millenium (from 509 BC to 476 AD) reveals, according to Sorokin's calculations, only a slightly higher frequency of internal disturbances than was the case with the Greek epoch. We have to bear in mind, however, that Roman history took place over gradually extending territories which eventually spread beyond what the Greeks could consider their historical ground.

In contrast to Greek history, the internal disturbances of the Roman epoch were more of a horizontal than of a vertical nature. Revolts of subjected peoples constituted a substantial part of them. In addition, the civil wars between various factions of the upper class were increasingly frequent. Their peak period was in the last century BC, when the republic began to break down and the process of transformation into a monarchy set in. Ronald Syme described the events that happened between 60 BC and 14 AD which effected the social transformation as the Roman revolution.[41] But was it really a revolution? Perhaps in figurative terms, as a revolution from above. But the term 'civil war' is certainly more appropriate. Historians, as we said earlier, feel free to use generic terms according to their evaluation of the change.

The great transformative processes in Roman history did not occur by way of revolution. The main means were internal political strife for full civic rights and political representation, civil wars between the pretenders for the top leadership, and, as far as the spread of Roman power and societal arrangements abroad were concerned, external wars. Perhaps only the insurrections of Italian cities in 90–89 BC, claiming civic rights in the Rome-dominated association of city-states, can be described as a revolution of the vertical type. In political terms this insurrection, known as Italic or Marsic war, was successful; its positive result concerned a substantial part of the population in what was then the orbit of Roman hegemony. With respect to the main issue of this confrontation – granting equal rights within society – there is a parallel with the Abbasid take-over of the caliphate in Islamic society.

The renaissance of the cities that took place in Western Europe in the eleventh and twelfth centuries brought to the fore similar problems of social and political stratification to those that have been highlighted within the cities of Greek and Roman antiquity. The political strife was violent more often than not, or at least the threat of violence was present. There was again ample scope for 'revolutionary events', to borrow Calvert's term. However, only a few of them would justify the label 'revolution' in its proper sense as it is understood in this book.

In Italian cities there was first a replay of the strife between the plebeians and patricians which in the thirteenth century led in many cities to the establishment of special people's offices, such as the *Capitano del Popolo* and the special people's councils. The interplay of these institutions with the magistrates (*podesta* and council) of the commune was usually not adequately regulated and, as in ancient Greece (and to a lesser degree in ancient Rome), the use of violence became an almost legitimate feature of political life.[42]

The social divide between the well-to-do (*popolo grosso*) and those less endowed with material means (*popolo minuto*) led to another kind of tension which also often culminated in 'revolutionary' events. But they had little impact on the main transformative changes; they were incidental happenings rather than acts effecting social change. It was during the fourteenth century particularly that this type of conflict became frequent and virulent.

The struggle went on not only on the vertical line, within the cities, but also on the horizontal line, with the cities bidding for hegemony or trying to liberate themselves from domination. Another area of potential conflict was the encroachment by aristocratic landlords aiming to carve out their sovereign domains from the wider political framework of what was nominally a kingdom or empire.

Apart from northern Italy, this type of three-cornered contest took place in many parts of Europe, especially in the Low Countries and in northern France. Cities in Flanders and other places where foreign trade preponderated over local industry became, in particular, a setting for revolutionary disturbances. Within the cities, the *poorterie* (high bourgeoisie), the mass of small craftspeople and the cloth workers were the main parties of the confrontation which was often extremely bitter and violent. The outside authorities (the king, the count, the bishop, or whoever) occasionally interfered, but in essence it was a vertical three-cornered contest, a struggle for the greater share in the proceeds of these groups' work.

Henri Pirenne, the unrivalled authority on this topic, says 'The struggle took on more and more the appearance of a class war between rich and poor, but it was in appearance only'. His comment deserves to be quoted in full:

> There was no common understanding among the mass of workers in revolt. The fullers, whose wages the weavers claimed to fix, or, rather, to reduce, treated the latter as enemies and, in order to escape from their exploitation, supported the cause of the 'good people'. As to the small-scale crafts, all detested the 'odious weavers' who interfered with their work and injured their business, and whose communistic aspirations dismayed them as much as they dismayed the ruler and the nobility. But perpetually in a state of revolt as they were, the exasperation of these people only increased, when they perceived that, in spite of all their efforts and even when they were in authority, their situation did not improve. Incapable of understanding that the nature of the great commerce and of capitalistic industry inevitably condemned them to the insecurity of a wage-earning class and to all the misery of crises and stoppages, they believed themselves to be the victims of the 'rich' for whom they laboured. It was not until the ruin of the cloth industry forced them to emigrate to seek a living elsewhere that the struggle which they had waged indomitably up to that moment came to an end.[43]

This assessment is also revealing on another point. The issue was never clearly resolved and eventually petered out altogether. Confrontation on similar issues elsewhere, sometimes on a much larger scale (such as the concentrated attempt of the cities in southwest Germany to extricate themselves from the supremacy of the regional aristocratic authorities) had a similar result.

Only where the issue was broadened and lost its exclusively class- or estate-based nature, and where other issues joined in and wider strata of the population became involved, could a revolt with little prospect of success have turned, temporarily at least, into a successful vertical revolution. Such a combination of issues and cooperation of estates was possible where a strong ideological amalgam was available. At the time under discussion, this would be religious.

A telling example of such a case is the Hussite revolution in Bohemia in the first half of the fifteenth century. It succeeded on the following counts: (a) the Czechs established their own, albeit diluted, version of Catholic orthodoxy; (b) their urban estate (the burghers) significantly improved their political and economic position; and (c) the use and prestige of the Czech language was promoted within and also without the lands of the Bohemian Crown. No wonder, then, that the Hussite revolution was dubbed 'proto-protestant, proto-bourgeois and proto-national'. The story is told in more detail as the first case study in this book.

ETIOLOGY (CAUSES) OF REVOLUTION (VERTICAL TYPE)

Etiology of revolution is the best-elaborated part of the theory of revolution, in particular as far as vertical revolution is concerned. The comparatively rich supply of observations and suggestions on this topic can be arranged under three headings.

1. The general social climate: the prevalent hierarchy of values, the view (acceptance or rejection) of inequality, admissibility of violence, etc.
2. Preconditions: the increasing number of disturbing issues, the solution of which appears to be beyond the regulatory capability of the political regime or of the spontaneous social relationships (civil society).
3. Precipitants: the activation of those people who prefer to resolve a complicated situation by a short-cut.

The disposition of particular social climates towards vertical revolutionary action has already been touched upon in the preceding section. There are no general conclusions that could be deduced from a comparative study of various world-views and of their impact on social structure and institutions. The pioneering work of Max Weber indicates the path to be taken.

In the previous section, a reference was made to the key factor of irritation, conventionally described as relative deprivation. Here we are considering the state of mind of people within a broader context of irritating factors, factors conducive to conflict. As long as the conflict situations are manageable within the given institutions and social relationships, these can still be considered normal or functional. As soon as the conflicts exceed the legal or customary framework for conflict resolution, the situation becomes dysfunctional. If there is a wider range of such situations, we may speak about a multiple dysfunction.

'Functional relationship' and 'conflict' are concepts applicable to phenomena of real life, which often cannot be disentangled one from another. There is no reason for making the bases of contradictory theoretical reasoning from them. We may say that there is a kind of sensible dialectic in the practical use of these two concepts.

Seeking to identify individual factors in a multiple dysfunction, we come across particular contrasts or disproportions in social relationships. In describing them we refer back to the work of the first scholars in this field. The best-known contrasts which are supposed to underlie the 'multiple dysfunction' should be mentioned first: the 'Weberian disproportion' and the 'Marxian contradiction'.

First, the Weberian disproportion is usually described as the discrepancy between a group's position on the one hand within the class hierarchy manifested mainly by wealth, and on the other within the status hierarchy manifested mainly by prestige and lifestyle. The role of the disproportion as a precondition of revolution has been elaborated more by Max Weber's followers than by Weber himself. Thus, for example, Benoit-Smullyan located a revolutionary impetus in the blocking of the natural tendency to adapt to each other the different positions within the two hierarchies.[44] This disproportion has been stressed mainly with respect to the French revolution, where the wealth of the rising bourgeoisie was not matched by an adequate rise in their social status.[45]

In this context, we have to understand 'status' in the Weberian sense, namely as a lifestyle and prestige which together provide a separate element of social stratification. In Talcott Parsons' translation, the term 'social status' in Weber's understanding applies to

> a typically effective claim to positive or negative privilege with respect to social prestige so far as it rests on one or more of the following bases: (a) mode of living, (b) a formal process of education ... or (c) the prestige of birth, or of an occupation.[46]

Thus, in Weber's terms, social status is an element of a triad, the others being, broadly speaking, wealth and power.

In some more recent sociological writings, however, the term 'status' is used as a common denominator for the overall position in the stratification hierarchy. Thus, for instance, in Lenski's view, social status means, on the strength of American evidence, a relative position in four hierarchies: those of income, occupation, education and ethnicity.[47] Within these hierarchies, social status may either tend towards congruence (consistency or crystallisation) or towards decomposition (inconsistency).

To avoid a possible misunderstanding, we shall alternatively define the Weberian disproportion as a disproportion between wealth, power and prestige within social status. Each element may be considered separately, thus providing a wider scope for possible contrasts.

The apparent paradox which was noticed by Brinton, namely that 'revolutions seem more likely when social classes are fairly close together than when they are far apart',[48] may also be better understood in terms of the Weberian disproportion.

Second, Marx saw the main precondition for revolutionary change in the contradiction between the productive forces on the one hand and the mode of production on the other; or to put it more explicitly, between the state of technology (technical possibilities) and the socio-economic system (the utilisation of those possibilities by a particular socio-economic formation). R.C. Tucker sums up the Marxian contradiction as follows:

> the source of revolutionary energy in a class is the frustration of man in his capacity of producer, his inabilities to develop new powers of production to the full within the confines of an existing mode of production or socio-economic order ... the effect of the revolution is to eliminate a set of social relations of production that has become ... a 'fetter' upon the evolving productive powers of the species, and thus to 'emancipate' these powers.[49]

This basic contradiction between the productive forces and the mode of production is, in the Marxian view, brought to a head by a contradiction between the social classes with antagonistic interests: one for the preservation of the existing mode of production, the other striving to change it. The intensified class struggle is supposed to be the prime mover of revolution.

As is well known, Marx's theory of revolution, which extends far beyond the above-mentioned key contradiction, provided inspiration both for thought and for action, quite in accordance with Marx's claim that 'a correct theory is the consciousness of a practice that aims at changing the world'.[50] Yet in both these fields of inspiration, thought and action, there are many difficulties to be overcome, many deviations and aberrations to be undergone, if a plausible explanation of events or an appealing programme is to be put forward. The faithful followers of Marx, however, always sought to justify their own interpretation by reference to one or other of Marx's statements.

In Johnson's model, the Marxian contradiction corresponds to the dissynchronisation between the changes in environment and values.[51] Johnson further subdivided both categories into endogenous and exogenous. Although in the context of Johnson's abstract reasoning this may be, as Stone observed,[52] of little consequence, when applied to the socio-historical context of individual revolutions it may prove, as will be shown later in this book, to be very relevant indeed.

Both the Weberian disproportion and the Marxian contradiction can be considered the so-called objective factors, i.e. phenomena observable from outside without reference to any awareness and/or conceptualisation of them on the part of the people concerned. They are, however, unlikely to play any significant role without such an awareness or conceptualisation.

As many students of revolution have realised, no class interest can by itself exploit any propitious circumstances to revolt unless there is a conviction on the part of the people concerned that their plight is not only unbearable, but also unjust in terms of a value system which, in one way or another, differs from that accepted by the people in power.

This cognition is, in fact, the gist of what may be called the Aristotelian contradiction, because Aristotle was the first known scholar who saw in people's contradictory concepts of justice, manifested in different evaluations of inequality, the main causes for revolutions and/or class wars.

Barrington Moore, although starting from different theoretical premises, rediscovered this Aristotelian truth in his comparative empirical studies:

> Massive poverty and exploitation in and by themselves are not enough to provide a revolutionary situation. There must also be felt injustice built into the social structure, that is, either new demands on the victims or some reason for the victims to feel that old demands are no longer justifiable.[53]

The Aristotelian contradiction, however, may be understood more broadly, as a *pars pro toto*: the concept of justice reflected in evaluation of inequality is a key concept of social philosophy which in its turn may be related to a particular world view. Thus the clash between contradictory concepts of justice may imply the contradiction between normative and/or cognitive systems, between different paradigms for understanding our position within a society and often also within the universe.

Such a broader view of the Aristotelian contradiction was taken by many students of revolution, such as de Tocqueville and other classics in the field (Brinton, Edwards and Pettee). Recently, P. Schrecker made of this contradiction a general principle, a key issue of revolution, whether in the technical or the metaphorical sense of the term.[54] Also T. Kuhn,[55] although having only the scientific sphere in mind, contributes to the understanding of any sort of revolution when he explains the essence of a scientific revolution as the replacement of one paradigm by another, i.e. the change of the conceptual scheme at the highest level which governs all experimentation and theory at a lower level.

A combination of 'objective' and 'subjective' factors occurs in what may be described as the contradiction between achievements and expectations. The scholarly discovery of this contradiction may be traced back to de Tocqueville's *Ancien Régime and the French Revolution* (pt 3, ch. 4). Like the Marxian, the Tocquevillian contradiction also provided inspiration for further elaboration and ramification, in particular the theory of relative deprivation.

Occasionally there has been a tendency to focus de Tocqueville's proposition on the economic field. J.C. Davies[56] and M. Olson[57] are the most renowned representatives of this approach. However, the precision achieved by this reduction was counterbalanced by a considerable decrease in the applicability of that theory. Adequate economic data are hard to come by, especially with respect to past revolutions and revolutions in underdeveloped countries; furthermore, as Stone rightly stresses, the psychological responses to changes in wealth and power are more precisely related to political changes, which in themselves are more significant than the material changes.[58] Again, Barrington Moore may be quoted: 'It is nearly always possible to find an economic aspect in any social movement. But such a discovery cannot justify the claim that economically-based protest constitutes the most important part of the explanations'.[59]

The theory of relative deprivation, as represented by the so-called J-curve suggested by Davies and further elaborated into three alternatives (decremental, aspirational and progressive deprivation) by Ted Gurr,[60] appears to be a suitable theoretical device for explanatory purposes. It has so far, however, proved susceptible to empirical confirmation in the political rather than in the economic sense. Davies actually based his theory on only three empirical instances: the Russian revolution of 1917, the Egyptian revolution of 1952, and the Dor rebellion in 1842 in the American state of Rhode Island. These are three very different types of social disturbance: only the first can be considered a full-scale revolution.

Perhaps Kramnick's reformulation may be considered the best redefinition of the Tocquevillian disproportion: 'a sudden widening of the gap between expectation and gratification when it is perceived, correctly or incorrectly, that the governing *régime* is either responsible for, or incapable of, dealing with this intolerable situation'.[61]

In our view, however, the Tocquevillian contradiction might be applied, with equal justification, to the field of moral authority and its impact on social cohesion. As is well known, if a society is to hold together and abide by its own rules either through conviction or imitation rather than coercion, its ruling élite has, *inter alia*, to enjoy a certain degree of moral authority. A decline in this authority produces a gap between the subjects' expectations and the reality of what is considered to be the moral standard of the ruling élite (a case of Gurr's decremental deprivation).

Finally, there is a particular disproportion which also may become a precondition of revolution: this is the lack of vertical social mobility. This idea was put forward by Vilfredo Pareto. In his opinion, a healthy development of any society requires a certain amount of openness, a reasonable scope for social mobility, or, as Pareto prefers to say, for 'circulation of the *élite*'. The gist of Pareto's argument runs as follows:

> It is not only the accumulation of inferior elements in a social stratum that is harmful to society, but also the accumulation in the lower strata of *élite* elements which are prevented from rising. When simultaneously the upper strata are full of decadent elements and the lower strata are full of *élite* elements, the social equilibrium becomes highly unstable and a violent revolution is imminent.[62]

Although Pareto's further elaboration of this argument may be taken with reservations,[63] the basic idea appears to be a matter of common sense. The impressionistic view, based on widely shared life experience, indicates that in-breeding is not the only cause of degeneration; another factor is the closely knit upper classes who close ranks against newcomers from other strata, and stagnate in their capability to react creatively to the changing impacts of their social environment. Thus an inadequate circulation of the élite may be an additional cause of weakened resistance to revolution.

All the aforementioned preconditions do not, in themselves, make the situation ripe for revolution. The 'combustible material', so to speak, has to be further 'prepared' before 'ignition' takes place. A sufficient number of people have to be deeply disturbed by the development. Their perception of the causes of their trouble may vary; individuals or groups may even take opposing views, but they are united by their discontent with, or hatred of, the government.

In order to become dangerous, the discontent must be given a direction. This is usually done in two ways: one of them was described by Crane Brinton as 'desertion of the intellectuals'.[64] Lynford Edwards put it more explicitly: 'the transfer of the allegiance of the intellectuals'.[65] Indeed, intellectuals do not merely desert the government camp but switch sides; this is the crux of the matter. As we shall see in our test cases, there were always educated people who, in normal circumstances, would have climbed up the echelons of social status, or sometimes already did enjoy such a status, but who, in a situation beset by the irritating contrasts or disproportions mentioned earlier, chose another path. These people often became leaders of the movement that precipitated the course of events turning the call for reform into a revolution.

The other precipitant is the creation of a focus of influence, or alternative power, from which the opponents of the regime may launch their campaign for change. This alternative source of power may be an ancient institution, which has not performed its function for some time, but which becomes re-activated as a rallying point for the opposition. The best-known example of this type of development is the re-emergence of the General Estates in France. Or a new focus of influence and/or power could be a brand new institution. The Soviets in the Russian revolution are a classic example. Lenin called the situation in which they operated 'dual power'. The *samizdat* author, F. Znakov, termed this alternative focus 'the second pivot'.[66]

Using the second pivot to their advantage, the deserting intellectuals played a crucial role in each successful revolution. They helped to articulate the mental ferment which, in its turn, became a hotbed of purposeful action. G. Pettee compared such a situation with 'cramps'.[67]

A particular impetus in this sort of situation may be a lost foreign war. In Russia, the defeats suffered by the Imperial Army were the main precipitants of revolution in both 1905 and 1917. Similarly, the defeat of the Ottoman army in the First World War, and the subsequent encroachments of the victors upon the Turkish territories, unleashed violent resistance to the sultan's government as it yielded to foreign pressure.

A military disaster may considerably aggravate the economic situation and thus precipitate revolution. Sometimes a lost foreign war may even be a remote precondition, which enters the range of precipitants as one cause of the protracted financial crisis. Again, this can be seen in the case of the French Revolution.

A particular precipitant of revolution may also be the inconsistency of government policy. If a government ignores the time-honoured Roman advice, *principiis obsta, sero medicina paratur* (take preventive action; it is late to take medicine), it does so at its peril. The critical moment comes when the government tries, in de Tocqueville's words, 'to mend its fences'. Belated attempts to put things right make matters still worse. By relaxing censorship and thus allowing more publicity for the alternative influence or alternative power centre, the government risks weakening its position even further. When the government realises that all concessions were in vain and goes into reverse gear, then the situation can easily become explosive. New repressive measures, in particular manifest ones, may become the precipitants that trigger the outbreak of revolution. What this means and what the future course of events is likely to be, will be shown in the subsequent section on the morphology of revolution.

To sum up the considerations in this section: there is no single cause of revolution. Theories that explain revolution in terms of one cause or one issue being at stake are misleading. It is the structure of causation rather than one particular cause or one particular aspect of development which helps us to understand the phenomenon of revolution.

As has been said earlier, the failure to uphold the moral standard is one of the preconditions that may lead to disturbances and, eventually, to revolution. If those who should be the custodians of the moral standards legitimised by tradition or by principles declared in the constitution (or another normative document) do not fulfil their function, the door is open to criticism and dissent. Thus a crucial element of multiple dysfunction starts to unsettle the social climate.

Moving on from the preconditions to the precipitants and then the first stages of revolution, the contrast in moral standards may be observed from yet another vantage point, that is with respect to the different attitudes of the revolutionaries on the one hand, and the representatives of the *status quo* on the other. For this observation, we are indebted to Pareto, whose theory of élite circulation was mentioned earlier.

For the purpose of this study, Pareto's view on this point may be slightly adapted and reformulated as follows. Efficient rule by any power élite requires a sufficient number of able, energetic and resolute people – in Pareto's simile, lions. As long as there are enough such lions within the élite, and as long as potential lions born among the lower strata are allowed, via upward mobility, access to the élite (thus compensating for the natural decay at the top, and allowing the circulation of élites), revolution is unlikely. If, however, either the energetic, resolute people in the élite are replaced by those who appreciate soft methods or ruse rather than strength (foxes in the simile), and furthermore the access of new lions to the élite is restricted or even made wholly impossible, the potential lions in the lower echelons of the social pyramid become frustrated and will look for another opportunity for their self-assertion, including revolt. Whether this is a rebellion, a *coup d'état* or a revolution depends on circumstances. If they strive merely for the promotion of their own persons, they may instigate a *coup d'état*. If they put themselves at the head of a spontaneous popular movement aiming for improvements in government practice rather than for a systemic change, their action may issue in a rebellion. If the lions from the bottom embrace a new social philosophy, a new paradigm, they may become a revolutionary counter-élite and eventually instigate a revolution.

Finally, there is yet another important contrast which operates mainly when the revolutionary process is already in full swing, namely the contrast between the fighting spirit of the rank-and-file revolutionaries and that of their opponents. Although, despite the increasing relevance of high technology, many revolutions of the modern age reveal the continuous presence of this contrast, its importance has been understood more by the active revolutionaries than by the theoreticians of revolution.

For a classical formulation of that contradiction, we have perhaps to go back to late-fourteenth-century Muslim scholarship, which, in the work of Ibn Khaldun, built quite a few cornerstones of sociology as a science. Although Ibn Khaldun was concerned primarily with the relationship between nomadic and sedentary societies (the salient issue of his, Islamic, civilisation),[68] his contrast between societies with different levels of *esprit de corps* (*assabiya*) is not necessarily applicable to horizontal conflicts only. Ibn Khaldun's thesis that religion can achieve a more efficient social cohesion, dedication and striking power than the tribal *assabiya* fits well into our context. A strong ideological conviction nurtures a high fighting spirit which contrasts favourably with the effete mood on the other side. This can be demonstrated by the example of the different types of warriors of God, the 'new model armies', *levées en masse*, etc., through which the revolution attained its most striking successes.

With the Khaldunian case, our survey of preconditions and precipitants has come full circle: from the objective circumstances, via the strength of conviction and resulting dedication to the just cause, to the creation of new objective circumstances by the force of arms.

MORPHOLOGY (COURSE) OF REVOLUTION (VERTICAL TYPE)

The course of revolution and the phasing of revolutionary processes was given less attention in the specialist literature than the causes and outcomes of revolutions. The protagonists in the field are Lynford Edwards, Crane Brinton and George Pettee (quoted earlier). Edwards and Brinton were the first to come up with a model, based on the example of the French revolution. According to the model, the course of revolution runs roughly as follows: first, the moderates take over power; they are then pushed out by the radicals who, having unleashed terror, bring destruction upon themselves; and a tedious return to normality, to a new, non-revolutionary 'equilibrium', then sets in.

This model was rightly criticised as too schematic. Hagopian suggested a more sophisticated alternative in conceiving the course of revolution and its rhythm in terms of two countervailing tendencies: hypertrophic and entropic.

> Hypertrophy refers to the increasingly radical thrust of revolutions once they became manifest. Revolutionary entropy counteracts hypertrophy by dissipating the moral and physical energies required to sustain a frenetic pace of political and social change ... The fate of every revolution is determined by the relative strength of hypertrophic and entropic forces. If there is any 'dialectic' of revolution, surely it is in the contest between the two sets of factors.[69]

Furthermore, Hagopian exemplified his dialectics of revolution by pointing to some hypertrophic and entropic events or tendencies in the French, Russian and Chinese revolutions. However, the general, rather commonplace, theory was not particularly advanced by this attempt. The Edwards–Brinton model remains a better starting point for a further refinement of the morphology of revolution, a refinement which is, among other things, suggested in this book.

The proposed refinement is a model derived from the case studies which will be examined in the course of this book. The model is based on the following general observations.

In every revolution that gets beyond its initial stage (i.e. is not suppressed right at the beginning), the revolutionaries do not proceed in unity, but are divided as far as their programmes and interests are concerned. This is more complex than a simple division into moderates and radicals and, possibly, conservatives. Instead, four basic categories can be identified, conveniently labelled right, centre, left and extreme left. When the opponents of revolution (the counter-revolutionaries) are included in the total, there are five positions. The scale from right to left indicates the increasing amount of required change, or, in other words, the radical nature of the stance.

The further development of a revolution depends on changes in the relative strength of these positions: this results in conspicuous shifts in the balance of power between individual positions. The shifts in the balance of power reveal some similarities which, however, may vary according to the type of revolution.

These similarities do not appear to be accidental; they reflect the socio-psychological pattern of behaviours which may be considered typical for revolutionary situations and processes. The terms 'hypertrophy' and 'entropy' may be used as labels for the contrasting tendencies.

The revolutionary process can be regarded as concluded only when the main issues which caused the revolution have lost their acuteness and other issues have become matters of primary concern, or, to borrow Edwards' terms, when the main principles which the revolution has established cease to be matters of controversy.[70] This assumption extends the temporal dimension of the model to more than half a century, thus implying a longer duration of what is usually seen as one revolution.

The course of the revolutions under study in this book points to a common rhythm which can be described in terms of the following sequence of phases.

At the *onset*, before the outbreak of revolution, there is a prolonged period of innovative, reformist moves within part of the society's cultural élites, which try to respond to the challenges resulting from the disproportions or contradictions reviewed in the preceding section. As a corollary to these moves, which may be described as the 'alienation or defection of intellectuals', there takes place a progressive political activation of large groups of the population.

These developments culminate in a sort of *institutionalisation* of what are still reformist rather than revolutionary forces. This assumes the form of taking over old, or creating new, institutions which possibly become the power base of the opposition. This means the emergence of dual power (the second pivot) within the society; but in view of the fact that a kind of dual power may have existed in the society since long before the revolution, I prefer the term 'institutional-isation', i.e. of reform or revolutionary movements.

The government tries to temporise but eventually finds this development dangerous and attempts to clamp down on it. This phase can be described as the *compression* of what is still a reformist rather than a revolutionary movement.

As this attempt either comes too late or is not carried through resolutely enough (either because of a lack of resources or a lack of fighting spirit, or both), but has immediate effects that are highly irritating, the compression is answered by a violent outburst; this, an *explosion*, is the starting point of the revolution proper.

A successful explosion sets the whole political fabric in motion, and at this time substantial differences emerge among the revolutionaries concerning the required changes to the *status quo*. Different political groupings start to compete for power, revealing a wide range of political demands and ideological positions. In view of the fact that the seat of power tends to oscillate between these positions, this phase can be described as a phase of *oscillation*.

The contest intensifies, while the political activation and commitment to particular political programmes attains its apogee, until the oscillating seat of power is intercepted by that revolutionary group which succeeds in mobilising the most efficient military support. This turning point can be described as *interception*.

As the victorious group has to hold its power not only against the counter-revolutionaries (who in that phase often rely on foreign help rather than on domestic forces), but also against the other revolutionary groups (which in that phase may appear more formidable), it is bound to tighten its grip and introduce a kind of revolutionary dictatorship. Such a *tightening* results in a gradual decay, or even perversion, of revolutionary ideals. Terror is its extreme form.

In its effort to gain absolute command, the revolutionary dictatorship tries to destroy those political groups that have more radical requirements and programmes than its own. By the use of force the enemies to the left of the revolutionary dictatorship are driven from the political arena for good. If their programmes reappear and are eventually implemented, it happens much later (a century or more), under completely changed circumstances.

A contingent foreign intervention is a challenge that tends to be answered by terror against the potential supporters of the intervention, and eventually, by a counter-attack, which often issues in an *expansion* of the revolutionary rule into some neighbouring countries.

Such an expansion, however, overstrains the already strained forces and resources of the revolutionary establishment. Large sectors of the population become disappointed with the insufficient or distorted realisation of the revolutionary programmes, or simply get tired and exhausted from the inter-necine warfare. The increasing economic and psychic exhaustion brings all the opponents of the revolutionary dictatorship closer together. As the forces of the far left are virtually destroyed, the only remaining opposition forces that matter are those on the right. Thus the revolutionary right strikes a compromise with the counter-revolutionaries; this deal issues in a kind of *reversal* of the revolutionary process.

Such a reversal may either produce an explicit restoration of the pre-revolutionary regime, or result in a more discreet, disguised restoration of some of its elements, under the slogans and rhetoric of revolutionary tradition.

At that point the revolutionary process takes a different course. Where there was a formal restoration, there is a prolonged period of uneasy compromise between the revolutionary right and supporters of the *ancien régime* (*restoration compromise*). However, gradually the latter attempt to tilt the balance more and more to their side. Such moves may be described as *restoration pressure*. This pressure upsets the existing alliances. The revolutionary right refrains from giving further support to the counter-revolutionaries and eventually makes an alliance with the other remaining groups which, in one way or another, supported the revolution. When the restoration pressure attains a point where it becomes obvious that a compromise is no longer tenable, the united 'latter-day revolutionaries' organise a violent overthrow of the restoration regime – a kind of 'glorious revolution' or, in general terms, a *consolidation overthrow*. With this event there begins the final phase of consolidation, which shifts the seat of power approximately to the position of what had been the revolutionary centre.

Where there was no formal restoration, the consolidation takes the form of a rather prolonged process during which policies of a more restorative type alternate with others which are more revolutionary, often executed by the same leadership. This phase may even be marked by intense strife with conspicuous reversals of the revolutionary trend. On the whole, however, the amplitude of these policy shifts tends to decrease.

Thus, as we have shown, the process of a vertical revolution may be described as a sequence of ten to twelve phases, depending on whether there is a formal restoration or not.

To sum up, where there is a formal restoration, the phases are as follows: onset, institutionalisation, compression (these three are pre-revolutionary stages), explosion, oscillation, interception, tightening, expansion, reversal, restoration compromise, restoration pressure and consolidation overthrow. Where there is no formal restoration, restorative measures, though less conspicuous, are carried out by the revolutionary authorities themselves until some sort of consolidation is established.

As far as the pre-revolutionary period is concerned, the model covers the occurrence of precipitants and triggers, but does not go back far enough to describe the full development of the preconditions. It must also be added that some phases may be repetitive. This seems to reflect a complex situation when a particular policy does not succeed at a stroke and has to be repeated until the revolutionary process can take its 'regular' course.

The model of the morphological pattern of revolution may be visualised with the help of a two-dimensional graph, one dimension being time and the other the right–left spectrum of political positions. The shifts of the seat of power between them are indicated by a curve, the course of which illustrates the phases of the revolutionary process described above. The graph serves illustrative, not sociometric, purposes; it is not based on any quantitative measurement but on qualitative assessment. The shifts in the seat of power are derived from historians' accounts of individual revolutionary processes.

All graphs, together with explanatory chronological tables, can be found in Chapter 7 following the discussion of the six revolutions which provide the test cases for our theoretical considerations.

I am aware of the fact that historians, as a rule, do not like this type of model. On the other hand, the quantitatively orientated social scientists may deprecate the lack of precise measurability of its parameters. Each may be right as far as the methodology of their respective disciplines is concerned. Yet here we are working in a field in which we need to find our own way. To stick to mere verbal analysis would make comparisons less distinct; an attempt to base conclusions mainly on statistical data would reduce the analysis to a few, more-or-less economic or demographic, indicators,[71] or would narrow the concept of revolution merely to its political aspects.[72] I am aware of the risk of the middle road – yet I do believe that this risk is worth taking.

In following the middle road, I have to steer between the devil and the deep blue sea, to avoid cumbersome detail on the one hand and too much abstraction on the other. I do not believe in the viability of exclusively idiographic or nomothetic methods in social science. Especially where long-term phenomena and processes are studied, an idiographic approach is to a certain extent inevitable. And without a nomothetic venture, historiography is a vast sea on which, having no stars or compass to look at, we can only float aimlessly.

For historians, I would like to make clear that in this type of work there is no place for studying primary sources. I have to rely on the findings of historians, and am grateful for the immense work they have done. If I have to be selective, it is because the historians' work is so immense that I would need more than one life span to read all that has been written on the eight revolutions discussed in this book. I have to limit my focus to what may be called the strategic material.

To sociologists and other social scientists, I would like to say that I cannot afford to follow all their subtle and elaborate abstract reasoning, because in doing so I might lose touch with the historians' findings and their caveats. Where I have to choose, I prefer the bumpy road of factual analysis to the elegance and conceptual rigour of a theory.

Finally, a note on the epistemological nature of this model. It reflects the understanding of revolution as a series of conflicting purposeful actions interconnected by specific issues that, for people in a particular territory, became of paramount importance.

Conflicting purposeful activities, however, are not a specific feature of revolutions, revolts, rebellions, etc. These activities are present in any human society, being a part of human nature itself. It is the scope and intensity of such activities that are the main difference between what may be described as a revolutionary (or similar) situation on the one hand, and more-or-less peaceful evolution on the other. Conflict theories may thus be applicable to any situation, irrespective of whether it may be classified as revolutionary or not.

The reluctance to recognise purposeful action as an explanatory element in the theory of revolution seems to be mainly due to the fact that, as a rule, such actions do not achieve the intended aim. The outcome is always different from what had been envisaged, to a lesser or greater extent, when the particular action was initiated. It is similar to the theory of vectors in physics, where each vector has a magnitude and a direction and the result of their movements reflects the relative strength of these properties.

Any society at any time, but particularly in turbulent periods such as revolution, can be compared to a field of vectors; individuals and groupings with common interests can be considered as social vectors. Their magnitude is determined by the number of their supporters, armaments and economic resources. The direction is given by their aims and by the amount of energy with which they are pursued. Comparable to the addition of vectors in physics, the addition of social vectors produces results that need not correspond to the direction of any individual vector; in social terms, the result of a revolution differs from the wishes of its participants.

Notes

1. M.N. Hagopian, *The Phenomenon of Revolution* (Harper & Row, New York, 1974).
2. M.S. Kimmel, *Revolution: A sociological interpretation* (Polity Press, Cambridge, 1990).
3. S. Taylor, *Social Science and Revolutions* (Macmillan, London, 1984).
4. Hannah Arendt, *On Revolution* (Faber & Faber, London, 1963).
5. Theda Skocpol, *States and Social Revolutions* (Cambridge University Press, London, 1979).
6. Arendt, p. 49.
7. Skocpol, *States*, p. 14.
8. *Ibid.*, p. 16.
9. Kimmel, p. 180.
10. L.P. Edwards, *The Natural History of Revolution* (reprint Russell & Russell, New York, 1965), pp. 186 and 194.
11. L. Stone, *The Causes of the English Revolution 1529–1642* (Routledge & Kegan Paul, London, 1972), p. 57.
12. D. Robertson, *Penguin Dictionary of Politics* (Penguin, London, 1985), p. 290.
13. K. Kumar (ed.), *Revolution: The theory and practice of a European idea* (Weidenfeld & Nicolson, London, 1971), p. 26.
14. Stone, *Causes*, p. 4.
15. Chalmers Johnson, *Revolution and the Social System* (Hoover Institution Studies, Stanford University Press, CA, 1964).
16. 'From below' does not necessarily mean 'from the bottom' but rather from a lower echelon of the power hierarchy, such as the House of Commons in the English

revolution and the *tiers état* in the French. From here the revolutionary activity spreads to lower strata, possibly touching for a while the bottom of the stratification pyramid.

17. Skocpol, *States*, p. 22.
18. I. Wallerstein, *The Capitalist World System*, vol. I (Cambridge University Press, New York, 1979), and *The Modern World System*, vol. II (Academic Press, New York, 1980) and vol. III (Academic Press, San Diego, CA, 1989).
19. Max Weber's view on this point is scattered throughout his many writings. For consultation, the best is *The Sociology of Religion* (Social Science Paperbacks in assoc. with Methuen, London, 1966).
20. I. Wallerstein, *The Modern World System*, vol. III (Academic Press, San Diego, CA), p. 52.
21. Hagopian, pp. 3–9.
22. M. Mollat and P. Wolff, *The Popular Revolutions of the Late Middle Ages* (Allen & Unwin, London, 1973).
23. F. Seibt, *Revolution in Europa: Ursprung und Wege innerer Gewalt* (Süddeutscher Verlag, Munich, 1984).
24. P. Calvert, *A Study of Revolution* (Clarendon Press, Oxford, 1970).
25. P. A. Sorokin, *Social and Cultural Dynamics*, vol. III, *Fluctuation of Social Relationships, War and Revolution* (Allen & Unwin, London, 1937).
26. E. Luard, *War in International Society* (I.B. Tauris, London, 1986).
27. C. Tilly, *European Revolutions, 1492–1992* (Blackwell, Oxford, 1993).
28. J. Krejčí, *The Human Predicament: Its changing image* (Macmillan, London, 1993), pp. 106–24.
29. T.R. Gurr, *Why Men Rebel* (Princeton University Press, NJ, 1971).
30. B. Moore, Jr, *Social Origins of Dictatorship and Democracy* (Penguin, Harmondsworth, 1966).
31. B. Moore, Jr, *Injustice: The social bases of obedience and revolt* (Macmillan, London, 1978).
32. M. Weber, *Sociology of Religion*, p. 145.
33. My account is based mainly on Henri Maspero, *China in Antiquity* (University of Massachusetts Press, Dawson, 1978) and Jean Gernet, *A History of Chinese Civilization* (Cambridge University Press, London, 1982).
34. H. Maspero and J. Escarra, *Les Institutions de la Chine* (Presses Universitaire de France, Paris, 1952), p. 56.
35. R.C. Zaehner, *The Dawn and Twilight of Zoroastrianism* (Weidenfeld & Nicolson, London, 1961), p. 40.
36. O. Klíma, *Mazdak: Geschichte einer sozialen Bewegung im Sassanidischen Persien* (ČSAV, Prague, 1957), p. 250.
37. For more details on the Mazdakite revolution see Jaroslav Krejčí, *The Civilizations of Asia and the Middle East* (Macmillan, London, and in the US *Before the European Challenge, the Great Civilizations of Asia and the Middle East*, State Univ. of New York, Albany, 1990), pp. 89–96.
38. Of the many sources on this topic, suffice it here to mention the most comprehensive one: P.K. Hitti, *History of the Arabs*, 10th edn (Macmillan, London, 1973).
39. Sorokin, *Social and Cultural Dynamics*, vol. III, pp. 578–80.
40. W.G. Forrest, *The Emergence of Greek Democracy* (World University Library, Weidenfeld & Nicolson, London, 1966), pp. 98ff.
41. R. Syme, *The Roman Revolution* (Oxford University Press, London, 1960).
42. D. Waley, *The Italian City-Republics* (World University Library, Weidenfeld & Nicolson, London, 1969).

43. H. Pirenne, *Economic and Social History of Medieval Europe* (Kegan Paul, London, 1947), pp. 206–7.
44. E. Benoit-Smullyan, 'Status, status types and status interrelations', *American Sociological Review*, vol. IX, 1944, pp. 151–61.
45. E.G. Barber, *The Bourgeoisie in Eighteenth-Century France* (Princeton University Press, NJ, 1955).
46. M. Weber, *The Theory of Social and Economic Organisation*, ed. Talcott Parsons (Free Press, New York, 1969), p. 428.
47. G.E. Lenski, 'Status crystallization: A non-vertical dimension of social status', *American Sociological Review*, vol. XIX, 1954, pp. 405–15.
48. C. Brinton, *The Anatomy of Revolution* (Jonathan Cape, London, 1953), p. 278.
49. R.C. Tucker, *The Marxian Revolutionary Idea* (Allen & Unwin, London, 1969), p. 18.
50. Quoted from H. Marcuse, *Reason and Revolution* (Routledge & Kegan Paul, London, 1969), p. 321.
51. C. Johnson, *Revolutionary Change* (University of London Press, 1968), pp. 63ff.
52. Stone, *Causes*, pp. 96 and 112.
53. B. Moore, Jr, *Social Origins*, p. 220.
54. P. Schrecker, 'Revolution as a problem in the philosophy of history', *Nomos*, vol. VIII, *Revolutions*, 1966, pp. 34–53.
55. T. Kuhn, *The Structure of Scientific Revolution* (Chicago University Press, 1970).
56. J.C. Davies, 'Towards a theory of revolution', *American Sociological Review*, vol. XXVII, no. 1, 1962, pp. 5–19.
57. M. Olson, Jr, 'Rapid growth as a destabilising force', *Journal of Economic History*, vol. XXIII, 1963, pp. 529–52.
58. Stone, *Causes*, p. 17.
59. Moore, *Injustice*, p. 88, n. 5.
60. Gurr, *Why Men Rebel*, pp. 47–55.
61. I. Kramnick, 'Reflections on Revolution: Definition and explanation in recent scholarship', *History and Theory*, vol. XI, 1972, p. 44.
62. V. Pareto, *Manuale di economica politica* (Edizioni Bizzarri, Rome, 1965), p. 249.
63. For a neat critical assessment of Pareto's argument see Hagopian, pp. 52 and ff.
64. Brinton, p. 45.
65. Edwards, p. 38.
66. A. Shtromas, 'How the end of the Soviet system may come', in A. Shtromas and M. Kaplan (eds), *The Soviet Union and the Challenge of the Future*, vol. I (Paragon House, New York, 1988), pp. 205–8.
67. G. S. Pettee, *The Process of Revolution*, reprint (H. Fertig, New York, 1971), p. 3, original edition Harper & Row, New York, 1938.
68. Ibn Khaldun, *The Muqaddimah: An introduction to history*, vol. I (Routledge & Kegan Paul, London, 1958).
69. Hagopian, pp. 233 and ff.
70. Edwards, p. 194.
71. For instance, R. Tanter and M. Midlarsky ('A theory of revolution', *The Journal of Conflict Resolution*, vol. XI, no. 3, 1967, pp. 264–81) in their attempt to quantify frustrated aspirations have to be satisfied with the per capita GNP, primary school enrolment ratio and Gini's coefficient of income or land inequality.
72. This is the case with Calvert, Luard and Tilly quoted earlier.

Part II

The main case studies

1

□

Bohemia (1403–58)

Of the six revolutions discussed in this book, the Hussite is possibly the least known both to the general reader and to the student of revolution. Therefore I consider it expedient to discuss this particular revolution and its socio-historical context in more detail than will be the case with the other revolutions. Fortunately, during the last forty years or so, the specialist literature in the English language has been enriched by a series of thorough descriptive and analytical studies of the subject to which I can refer for more detail.[1]

General preconditions

From the ascent of the Luxemburg dynasty to the Bohemian throne in 1310, Bohemia and Moravia became more intensively involved in European affairs, and their political, economic and also cultural weight within the European context increased. In 1346, the Electors chose Charles IV, son of John of Luxemburg, as the Roman king. In 1355 he was crowned emperor in Rome and held all his realms firmly until his death in 1378.

Charles IV made Bohemia the bulwark of his power. In 1344 the bishopric of Prague was elevated to the status of archbishopric. In 1348 the University of Prague was founded as the first university north of the Alps and east of the Rhine. In the same year, Charles founded the New Town of Prague which more than doubled the size of that capital city. Under his reign there was a long period of comparative peace and prosperity, but his endeavour to strengthen the royal power against that of the higher nobility was only partly successful.

Throughout the fourteenth century there was a continuous growth of the market economy. The so-called emphytheutic tenure of land (brought into the country with the German settlers in the twelfth and thirteenth centuries), which gave the tenant full possession (surface ownership) of the land for a fixed rent in cash, continued to spread further, where no new settlements were created. On the whole, this development is supposed to have benefited the farmers. (However, there is evidence of instances where the transformation of the traditional law into the new emphyteutic one was connected with the extraction of a lump sum, a payment which, under the conditions of a new settlement, would not be imaginable.) Further, there was a considerable flow of people from the countryside to the towns, which increased the population there, in spite of higher mortality than natality in urban areas. In contrast to the European West, which was much more affected by the great epidemics (such as the Black Death of 1348–50), such shifts pulled the wages of the urban workforce down.

In the towns there was an increasing tension between the commercial patriciate and the artisanate. Charles's policy favoured free trade and the craftsmen's guilds were allowed to function only for social and religious purposes. The excess of imports over exports was balanced by bullion from the prosperous silver mines, but in the internal market the gradual worsening of the mint created inflationary pressure. Its effects on prices and also on different groups of the population seem to have been very uneven.

In general it can be supposed that until about the end of the fourteenth century, per capita real income was increasing, but so were income differentials. This produced new kinds of tension. The land-owning patriciate of the capital city and the silver-mining town of Kutná Hora wanted to be considered equal with the nobility. The prosperous craftsmen resented their inferior status *vis-à-vis* the commercial patriciate, while prosperous peasants, whether freehold or tenant, tried to enjoy privileges belonging to the country squires. On the whole there was ample scope for what has been described in our etiological comment as the Weberian disproportion.

By about the end of the fourteenth century, the general upward trend of the economy seems to have been brought to a halt. It may be assumed that this produced a widespread mood of relative deprivation.

The fourteenth century also saw a great advance in the Roman Catholic Church's bid for power. The transfer of the Holy See from Rome to Avignon by no means diminished the papacy's claim, exemplified by its policy from the time of the struggle for investiture. That part of the Hildebrandian reform (in contrast to the part that dealt with the fight against simony and the incontinence of the clergy) continued to be enforced with increasing vigour, even in outlying provinces of the Catholic world, and this whole policy was supported by the increasing participation of the Church in what may be described in metaphorical terms as the commercial revolution. The papal *Curia* became a world financial and banking centre, keen to extend its network into every corner of the Christian community.

When, in 1378, the attempt to bring the Holy See back to Rome resulted in a papal schism, the superstructure of the papal administration became even more onerous. The two *Curiae* competed for allegiance and income and intensified the practice of selling offices, some vacant, but some long before they were to be vacated. Thus simoniac and other unholy practices increasingly undermined the moral authority of the Church. The disappointment of true believers can be classified as a decremental deprivation of a spiritual type. In other words there was a frustration resulting from the failure to maintain values.

The contradiction between religious expectations and ecclesiastical achievements became of paramount importance because the Church was dispensing the sacraments which led everybody safely, from the cradle to the grave, towards a salvation in which, we can reasonably assume, there was universal belief.

Specific preconditions and the reform programme

The disproportions and contradictions mentioned so far, however, were issues throughout Europe, and the above-mentioned socio-economic tensions were not peculiar to the Czech Lands either. Why, then, only in Bohemia and Moravia did the quest for reform become so urgent that, when confronted with attempts at repression, it broke out into revolution?

The majority of the population in the two countries were of the Czech tongue; the rest spoke German. The German speakers inhabited mainly some frontier areas, and also some royal boroughs where they had settled during the great Germanic migration to the east in the twelfth and thirteenth centuries. Where these boroughs were founded within the Czech hinterland, the migration from the countryside changed their ethnic composition, yet in many royal boroughs the Germans continued to hold the wealth and the power. Social tensions were combined with, and eventually superseded by, ethnic tensions in which both sides welcomed a religious justification for, or rather consecration of, their cause.

A similar development took place within the seat of intellectual activity, the University of Prague. As it was founded for a larger area than the Czech Lands, the 'Bohemian nation' had only one vote in the quadripartite administration, the other three belonging to the so-called Bavarian, Saxon and Polish nations (the latter included mainly German-speaking Silesians). Towards the end of the fourteenth century ethnic differentiation at the university became exacerbated by the so-called dispute about universalia. German masters – with a few notable exceptions[2] – joined the nominalist camp led by the University of Paris, while most Czech masters opted for the realist school, whose main protagonists were in the University of Oxford.

This philosophical issue, however, also had a theological meaning and practical religious consequences. For the nominalists, reason and faith were different matters; not so for the realists. For the nominalists the Church was compounded of its visible representatives, such as the pope, bishops, monks, parsons, etc. The realists saw in the Church an entity of all those, past and present, who were predestined for salvation, i.e. including the predestined laity, and excluding the foreknown clergymen. For the nominalists the misbehaviour of individual representatives did not invalidate the institution. For the realists the spread of unholy practices cast a shadow on the institutions themselves. Therefore, the realists looked instead to the Bible as the infallible source of religious authority.

Thus it may be inferred that wherever the realists dominated higher education, there was scope for a reform movement which went beyond mere moralisation and became concerned with institutional alternatives. This paved the way for the defection of intellectuals, the rise of the counter-élite and thus the crystallisation of a full-scale contradiction of the Aristotelian type.

An important element of this contradiction was a doctrine enunciated by FitzRalph, Archbishop of Armagh in Ireland, and further elaborated by Wyclif, namely that nobody in the state of mortal sin has a true lordship over other creatures according to God.[3] This doctrine, of course, affected not only secular, but also spiritual, dominion. Here the theoretical issue touched the hard core of everyday life: sacraments administered by evil priests put the salvation of laymen into jeopardy. Such a state of affairs could not be tolerated but, as the Church representatives were not in a position to help, the reform had to be carried out by the wielders of secular power.

In taking this position, the realist masters extended a helping hand to the popular preachers who knocked in vain on the door of the ecclesiastical establishment. But, significantly, this particular link between the realist academics and popular preachers materialised only in Bohemia. In the other bastion of realism, England, the reform remained a more-or-less intellectual and theoretical undertaking. The Lollards, although gaining some support among the middle classes, never became a mass, let alone a revolutionary, movement. If they wanted to take part in such a thing, they had to go to Bohemia, like Peter Payne in 1413; there he became one of the leading theologians – and diplomats – of what later became the Hussite or Utraquist establishment.

In contrast to the English, the Czechs possessed all the ingredients necessary for turning the word into flesh. Popular preachers of the Czech tongue who started their campaign in the late 1360s were joined by theologians, who, in their persons, united all three driving forces of the Czech reform: indignation over the Church's betrayal of its Christian mission, practical suggestions as to who should see to improvements, and finally the belief that reform was the sacred duty of the whole nation, which by virtue of this stance became a sort of Chosen People.

The linkage of these three elements of the Czech reform was epitomised in its main spokesman, John Hus. Nothing can better illustrate the sensible combination of theoretical position with practical concern than the interpretation by Hus and his associates (such as Jacobellus de Misa) of the doctrine of dominion. For them the sacraments were valid to the recipient, even if administered by an evil priest, but the administration of the sacraments was to the evil priest's damnation.[4] Thus no feeling of insecurity could ensue: the believer had to be helped, not scared. Furthermore, religion had to be made more understandable for the believer. Therefore, vernacular was to be used more extensively, and eventually the rediscovered source of supreme authority in the Church, the Holy Writ, was to be translated. The simplification and standardisation of Czech orthography undertaken by John Hus effectively helped to further this purpose. An extraordinary spread of literacy in fifteenth-century Bohemia and Moravia was testified to by foreign observers.

The extent of the Czech nation as a chosen, even sacrosanct, community was demarcated by another reform theologian, Jerome of Prague, as follows:

> from the king to the knight, from the knight to the squire, from the squire to the peasant; from the archbishop to the canon, from the canon to the lowliest priest; from the mayor of the town to the councillor and the burgher, from the burgher to the lowliest worker.[5]

Thus in the religious context, the unity of the nation was conceived in much broader terms than in the political context. Unfortunately, in practical terms, this extended concept found its echo only among the armies of the left, the so-called field communities or military brotherhoods, who nevertheless continued to respect fully all differentials of hereditary status.

The programme of Czech reform hammered out in the years 1416–20 was condensed into four articles, the so-called Four Articles of Prague, which in the final version of October 1420 read as follows (the text is substantially abbreviated):

1. That the Word of God shall be freely and without hindrance proclaimed and preached by Christian priests in the kingdom of Bohemia.
2. That the Holy Sacrament of the body and blood of Christ under the two kinds of bread and wine shall be freely administered to all true Christians who are not excluded from communion by mortal sin.
3. That since many priests and monks hold many earthly possessions against Christ's command and to the disadvantage of their spiritual office and also of the temporal lords, such priests shall be deprived of this illegal power and shall live exemplary lives according to the Holy Scripture, in following the way of Christ and the apostles.
4. That all mortal sins, and especially those that are public, as also other disorders contrary to the divine law, shall be prohibited and punished by those whose office it is so that the evil and false repute of this country may be removed and the well-being of the kingdom and of the Bohemian nation may be promoted.[6]

The onset and institutionalisation

By the time the Four Articles of Prague took this form, the revolution was already in full swing. Let us now turn to it and examine the sequence of events.

The key element of the onset was the growing frustration due to the lack of 'maintenance values'. Its manifest reflections can be seen in the following events. In 1363 King Charles, concerned with the decaying morals of the clergy (Tocquevillian and Paretian disproportion), invited the Augustinian monk, Conrad Waldhauser from Vienna, to help to bring about a religious revival in Prague. In 1369 his place was taken by a Czech lay mystic and ascetic, Jan Milič of Kroměříž, who had earlier exchanged a promising career in the royal chancellory for pastoral work. (He died in 1374 in Avignon, where he had cleared himself of the charge of heresy.) Soon afterwards, Matthew of Janov, graduate of Paris University and Canon of Prague, declared the Holy Writ to be the only source of faith and religious knowledge. A country squire, Thomas of Štítný, who devoted his life to moral reform, wrote a telling indictment in Czech of how the higher estates behaved badly and exploited the common folk, mainly peasants. Puritanism became the main unifying factor of the reformers.

Meanwhile, on the political front, the successor to Charles, King Wenceslas IV, attempted to carry his father's policy further, aiming to strengthen royal power at the expense of the higher aristocracy, an issue characteristic of most European countries of that epoch. The lower nobility and royal boroughs were the king's natural allies in that struggle. Yet at the beginning of the fifteenth century, the king's endeavour was, after a prolonged struggle, stopped by a coalition of the lords with his half-brother, Sigismund, and other members of the royal family. The lords reaffirmed their position in the country's administration and the king had to be content with sovereignty in his own royal domain. This happened at a time when the economic upsurge also suffered a breakdown.

The struggle to strengthen royal power in his own country led the king to neglect the empire's affairs, and eventually resulted in his deposition as emperor and the election of another. Only when the so-called conciliar party in the Church hierarchy summoned a council to Pisa with the intention of healing the schism, did King Wenceslas regain his interest in international matters; he favoured the Pisan Council against the stance of the archbishop of Prague, who supported the acting pope in Rome. As this was a question of ecclesiastical law, it was brought to the university, where the German majority decided against the king. This provided a welcome opportunity for the Czech realist minority to persuade the king to change the statutes of the university: in January 1409, by the Decree of Kutná Hora, the king granted three votes to the Bohemian nation against one to be held by the three foreign nations (considered from then on as one Teutonic nation). This act proved to be an important precondition of the revolution. The Czech reformers acquired an influential institution for their cause. The *Curia*'s condemnation of seventeen writings by Wyclif as heretical was contested by the university, where John Hus became the main link with the popular movement.

As long as the archbishop of Prague continued in his allegiance to the Roman pope, while the king acknowledged the pope elected in Pisa, the archbishop's measures against the Wyclifites were ineffective. Only when he switched sides and acknowledged the pope elect in Pisa could he take effective measures against John Hus. Preconditions of revolution turned to precipitants. In February 1411, Hus was anathematised by the Pisan pope. To make things still worse, John Hus decided to condemn as immoral and sacrilegious the sale of indulgences, the proceeds of which were to finance the war of the Pisan pope against the supporters of the Roman pope; as the king was to participate in the proceeds of these sales, the tension between him and Hus increased.

The situation became increasingly acute. The Pisan pope reaffirmed the anathema against Hus, who then left Prague and spent two years under the protection of his friends from the lower nobility. The reform party hardened its stance. A university master, Jacobellus de Misa (Jakoubek of Stříbro), more radical than Hus in those days, declared the pope to be anti-Christ and, towards the end of 1414, started to serve, in defiance of the explicit disapproval of the *Curia*, the Holy Communion in both kinds (*sub utraque specie*; hence the reformers were also called Utraquists). Communion of both kinds became a symbol of the equality of laymen with the clergy before God.

Compression and explosion

Meanwhile a new Council was summoned to Constance with the aim of abolishing the threefold schism, reforming the Church and dealing with the heretical teachings. John Hus, who always demanded a public hearing, accepted Sigismund's warrant of safe conduct and went to Constance. There, however, he was arrested and, in the teeth of protests both from the Czechs present in Constance and from others who sent letters from Bohemia, was condemned for holding the Wyclifite heresies and burned at the stake (July 1415). Thus the reform movement got its martyr, soon to be venerated by his followers as a saint. From then on, the movement which had earlier been largely known as Wyclifite, was styled either Hussite, after its saint, or Utraquists or Calixtins, after its symbol.[7]

Shocked by this disregard for, and contempt of, Czech feelings, 58 barons and 391 members of the lower nobility concluded a covenant and sent a letter to the Council protesting against Hus's condemnation. By way of response, the Council indicted all who signed the protest and burned at the stake yet another reformer, Jerome of Prague. The University of Prague promptly declared Hus and Jerome innocent of heresy, but in 1416 the Council retaliated by suspending the activity of the university.[8] In August 1417, while a large chiliastic movement was spreading through the country, the Hussite priesthood elaborated the first draft of the Four Articles of Prague.

As the king did not want to oppose the Council's decision, he put pressure on the royal boroughs and, albeit less effectively, on the nobility. According to our model, a period of compression set in (1417–19). Yet the pressure only spurred the reformers on, and triggered the revolution.

In response to royal pressure, the Hussite nobility started to disregard the ecclesiastical prescription controlling the filling of offices and took care to provide their churches with Utraquist priests.[9] In Prague all but four of the churches were returned to the Romanists on the king's orders. The king also appointed new city councillors, all Romanists, and forbade all processions. On 22 July 1419, however, a procession led by a Hussite radical, John Želivský, violently turned a Romanist church mass into a Utraquist one, and then went to the town hall to demand the freeing of the Hussite prisoners. When their request was not granted, they stormed the town hall and threw the councillors out of the windows – the so-called first defenestration of Prague, which heralded the explosion of the revolution. When the king received news of the event he suffered a series of strokes and died. As he was childless, his half-brother, Sigismund, was the legitimate heir.

In the country, however, the Hussite movement held power over several institutions without whose consent Sigismund could not take possession of his heritage. At first it seemed that the Hussite nobility, the university and the councillors of the city of Prague would yield to Sigismund's double game of appeasing and menacing tactics, but as soon as he had shown his true intentions, namely to suppress the Hussites by force (the pope declared a crusade at his instigation), the mood changed and the opposition stiffened. Those Romanists who still remained in Prague had to leave the city and their property was confiscated. They were mainly Germans, of whom only a few became Utraquists. Meanwhile, the radical Hussites, hard-pressed in their towns and assembly places, founded a new town of their own in southern Bohemia named after the biblical mountain, Tabor. Another Hussite faction established its camp on the mountain called Horeb in eastern Bohemia. The royal borough Hradec Králové became their main urban centre.

The revolutionary spectrum and its social context

The spread and institutionalisation of Hussitism was accompanied by its fission. Soon the full spectrum of political groupings typical of any revolution at that stage unfolded. We shall review them first from the point of view of their social background.

The most moderate Hussites, the right wing of the Prague party (the revolutionary right in our model), were represented by a portion of the higher nobility and some university masters. The revolutionary centre, the mainstream of the Prague party, was represented by several noble families, most university masters and some gentry, but their main stronghold was in the Old Town of Prague (after it became converted into the Czech city) and in some other royal boroughs which acknowledged Prague's leadership.

The revolutionary left had two centres: one in Tabor, the other in Horeb; their followers were mainly peasants, burghers and gentry. In its original form,

Tabor was a settlement of those who were largely imbued with the adventist spirit; a kind of consumer communism was practised, but this was soon abandoned, apparently when the prophecies of the Day of Wrath passed unfulfilled and a more realistic approach had to be adopted. In religious matters, however, Tabor continued to be more radical, although it ceased to be a haven for overtly heretical teachings.[10] The Horebites took up a position between that of Tabor and that of Prague. The New Town of Prague, too, inclined to the left.

The extreme left was, in principle, recruited from the same social classes as the main left, but it seems that the peasants were more strongly represented than in the other groups.

The main differences between individual factions were religious; the key issue was the Eucharist and religious rites. The Hussite right was satisfied with serving the Holy Communion in both kinds and in all other matters conformed to the Roman Church. The centre was more resolute in trying to implement the Four Articles of Prague in practice; what was most conspicuous was that they wanted a simplification of the rites, and also stood for dispensing the Eucharist to children.

The Taborite left abandoned the solemn rites altogether and denied quite a few orthodox beliefs, such as the belief in purgatory, and the belief in the efficacy of consecrations, of auricular confession, of the intercession of saints, etc. With regard to the Eucharist they did not stick firmly to the orthodox doctrine of transubstantiation, but were more inclined to follow Wyclif's doctrine of remanence. They saw themselves as the Primitive Church reincarnate, as an autonomous section of the Church Militant.[11] They were not inhibited by the desire to preserve unity with the universal Catholic Church, and elected their own bishop (Nicholas of Pelhřimov) in a non-canonical way. The Horebites followed a similar practice but in a less conspicuous fashion.

Only the extreme left did not hesitate to outrage the Romanists and the Hussites alike by their open heresies, the most apparent of which was the denial of any presence of Christ's blood and body in the Eucharist. This heresy, characteristic of the so-called Pikharts, who were to be found all over Europe, went so far that even the main left could not accept it. The leading Pikhart theologian, Martin Húska, was eventually burned at the stake, after attempts by the chief Horebite priest, Ambrose, to convert him had failed. As the Holy Communion in both kinds became the main common symbol of all the Hussites, they were highly sensitive to any dilution of its sacramental value.

The extreme left was the least coherent group. Nevertheless, we can consider as its hard core a community known as Adamites, who, imbued with the heresy of 'free spirit' (endemic throughout the whole of Western Europe), seceded from Tabor and established themselves in a nearby fortress, where they practised their licentious lifestyle and from where they undertook raids upon the surrounding countryside until they were annihilated by the Taborite forces. In contrast to the Adamites, there was a gentle, pacifist extreme left, represented by the independent thinker, Peter Chelčický, who, as we shall show later, left a permanent impact on the Czech reformation.

Religious differences made individual factions easily distinguishable from one another. Although individuals might fluctuate and the political positions of individual factions might change, the doctrinal demarcation remained quite distinct throughout the whole revolutionary process.

The question may arise as to how far these differences in religious programmes reflected other, from the point of view of our epoch, more tangible differences. As the main programmes were conceived in religious terms, it is difficult to deduce from these statements their precise political meaning. To ascertain this, we have to observe the actual behaviour of the different factions.

On the whole, those factions that deviated from Catholic doctrine in matters of rites only (right and centre), stuck to the idea of unity with the universal Church, and were not particularly interested in political or socio-economic changes. Moral regeneration would, in their view, heal all wounds. However, alongside the acceptance of the general social framework, there was a strong endeavour on the part of certain individuals to improve their legal and/or economic position within the estate structure of the society. The Third Article of Prague provided a welcome religious justification for the confiscation of the Church's property (which before the revolution was about one-third of the land in Bohemia), a lure which not even the Romanists could resist.

This Article might be considered an opportunity for rallying the higher nobility, which might make the most practical use of it, behind such a programme. In fact, however, only about one-third of the barons joined the Hussite camp; here they sided mainly with its right or centre factions which, in principle, favoured a compromise with the Church and the king. From the latter's decisive victory a full-scale restoration of ecclesiastical property must have been expected. Perhaps, however, the barons were pragmatist enough to understand that the longer the disruption lasted, the less the restoration of property rights would be feasible. This might have been an additional reason (the other being the fear of having one's property devastated) that the domestic Romanist party was not too keen on the suppression of the Hussite movement by foreign conquest.

As the strength of the Taborites and Horebites resided mainly in the royal boroughs, they were naturally interested in the promotion of their status in the country's diet and government. Within Prague, the left, led by John Želivský, favoured the so-called Great Community, i.e. the general assembly of burghers (as a rule, but not necessarily at that time, owners of houses in Prague), while the centre relied rather on the *seniores* (Senior Community), a body of burghers enjoying social, economic and political prestige in the city. Both these communities acquired importance at the expense of the traditional administration represented by the city councillors. Naturally the Great Community, as an unwieldy body with irregular attendance, could not exert much direct power, but it had considerable influence, especially in cases of emergency. Otherwise the main initiative seems to have been with the Senior Community, although executive power remained with the councillors.[12] Furthermore, the prestige of the leading boroughs, such as Prague, Tabor and Hradec Králové, was enhanced by their virtual sovereignty in religious matters. The priesthood of each party seated there decided, sometimes with the participation of laity, what should be believed, or rather how religion should be practised, within its sphere of power.

In national policy, the left was against any compromise with Sigismund, but in principle did not object to a king from another dynasty, provided he adhered to the Four Articles of Prague. As it turned out, another Sigismund, Sigismund Korybut, a prince related to the Jagiellon dynasty of Poland-Lithuania, became a serious candidate for the Bohemian throne.

Thus all three secular estates – barons, knights and royal boroughs – had a stake in what was going on in the revolution. To what extent the peasants, who were the most numerous socio-economic group, were affected, is difficult to assess. A few sources, not always clearly worded, indicate that in the high days of revolution, villages became recognised as communities participating in some matters concerning the country's administration,[13] but the practical impact of this position is difficult to evaluate. Those who settled in the towns or who joined the Taborite or Horebite armies found some prospects of individual advancement. It is, however, impossible to draw a reliable picture of the general economic situation of the Czech peasantry. It seems that the disorders in the country resulting from the war were more to their disadvantage than to their advantage: fighting armies and the mutual devastation of property were the biggest nuisance for them, while the lightening of the tax burden resulting from the neglect of tax collections for central government may have been outweighed by the exaction of extraordinary contributions by the warring parties. (There are many complaints to this effect in the documents of that epoch, complaints directed against both sides in the conflict.) As far as the peasants' attitudes are concerned, it may be reasonably assumed that at the beginning many of them expected from the reform an improvement of their lot. In so far as their religious needs were catered for by the Utraquist clergy, they may have felt satisfied by having obtained in the communion from the chalice an equal religious status with the clergy, and lower ecclesiastical dues (the contribution to the *Curia* was abolished) may also have been appreciated. Unfortunately, there is not enough evidence on how the peasant majority of the Czech nation coped with what, in contrast to the experience of the three higher secular estates, may have been an ordeal rather than an opportunity for advancement.

We must also bear in mind the imperfect position of what we would nowadays call the state. Before the revolution, secular power was divided, as elsewhere in the West, between the king (Margrave in Moravia) and the political nation represented by three estates, of which the upper and lower nobility had a majority in the diet and in the courts of the kingdom. The nobility owned most of their lands as freehold, not as a fief.[14] Each lord was master in his domain, and if he was strong enough he could defy an external power. At a time of civil war each baron, and even each squire and – when the royal power was vacant – each royal borough, could choose their political allegiance according to their own will. The conquest of a fortified castle or walled city was a difficult matter, and most warfare was waged at the expense of the peasantry. It is no wonder that the country was regionally divided between individual parties, often in perplexing enclaves without continuous borders. However, most of eastern and central Bohemia was Hussite, whereas in the west the Romanist domains prevailed. The south and the north were almost equally divided between the two camps. In Moravia the Hussites were in a minority.

In considering the concept of the seat of power according to our model, we have to make a qualification in view of the imperfect organisation of the state. Throughout the revolutionary process until its consolidation phase, each of the main factions, with the exception of the extreme left, preserved some geographical area for itself; what changed was the size and importance of that area. Consequently, in Figure 7.1 (page 193) the changes in the seat of power reflect these regional shifts rather than any changes in the composition of what might be considered the central authority.

Oscillation

In terms of our morphological model, the five years from 1419 to 1424 can be considered a period of oscillation. The course of events can be summarised as follows. Negotiations with Sigismund failed, partly because he could not agree with the Four Articles of Prague, but partly also because he was unwilling to allow a public disputation on them as the Hussites required; military means proved ineffective. The crusade declared by a papal bull and organised by Sigismund failed. The united armies of the Prague and Taborite parties, under the leadership of an extremely able military commander from the lower gentry, John Žižka, proved a match for the invading army (a battle took place on Vitkov, a hill east of the Prague walls) and Sigismund eventually preferred diplomacy to war. Although both sides considered themselves God's warriors, only the Hussites proved to be truly imbued with that spirit; what we have called the Khaldunian contrast developed in their favour.

The only success of Sigismund's diplomacy was in getting the leading representative of the Hussite right, Čeněk of Vartenberk, to make it possible for Sigismund to be crowned King of Bohemia in Prague castle. Yet this was not recognised by the other Hussites, who meanwhile started to negotiate for another king from (linguistically related) Poland. Because of the international implications, these negotiations were a delicate and protracted matter.

By 1421 the non-baronial Hussites were organised into three associations or, as they styled themselves, communities, each under the leadership of the most powerful city – Prague, Tabor and Hradec Králové. In April 1421, the Archbishop of Prague, Conrad of Vechta (of German origin), joined the Prague party (the centre), thus providing the Hussites with the possibility of an orderly canonical consecration of their priests (important for the centre, who wanted to preserve the Apostolic succession).

At the same time, John Žižka, at the head of his Taborites, liquidated the militant community of the Adamites, who, more than any other group, deviated from the Catholic orthodoxy and from the basic norms of contemporary society. There thus took place something that was to be repeated in most future revolutions: in the early phase of the revolutionary process, the extreme left was liquidated by the neighbouring group on the left.

The year 1421 also witnessed an attempt to rule Bohemia as a republic of estates. A diet, summoned to the royal borough of Čáslav, and attended not only by all the Hussite factions but also by most Romanists,[15] elected a committee of twenty governors. Its composition characterised the shift in the relative power and prestige of individual estates. Eight representatives were from royal boroughs, seven from the gentry, and only five from the baronial ranks. To make the reversal of importance still more explicit, the burgomaster and councillors of the Old and New Town of Prague were placed first on the roll.

At the beginning of autumn 1421, the second crusade against the Hussites collapsed ignominiously near the West Bohemian royal borough of Žatec. In January 1422, a more formidable attack by Sigismund's Hungarian army (Sigismund had acquired the Hungarian crown in 1387) was defeated in several battles in central and southeastern Bohemia.

The Hussite armies possessed not only a superior fighting spirit, but were also helped by a new military technique; the main innovation was fortified wagons armed with artillery usable mainly for defence, but in favourable circumstances also for attack. Many other weapons, including farmers' implements such as nailed flails, were also introduced into the Hussite armoury. The use of new weapons required new tactics and strategy, in which Žižka proved to be without match.

Being sufficiently strong to repulse foreign attacks, the Hussites had enough scope to indulge in their in-fighting. During the period of oscillation (1419–24), the regime in Prague changed several times, from the centre to the left and back again. The king designate, Sigismund Korybut, nephew of the king of Poland, Wladyslaw II, and of the archduke of Lithuania, Witold, came to Prague, where he tried to work for compromise, but favouring the nobility over the boroughs, he failed. Confronted with the disapproval of his candidature by his uncles, Korybut left the country in March 1423. Before this happened, however, his diplomacy contributed to the indecisive outcome of the third crusade led by Frederick, the Elector of Brandenburg.

Meanwhile, sometime during 1422, Žižka swapped parties, crossing from Tabor to Horeb, whose clergy was less keen on innovations (the Taborites saw in them a return to the Primitive Church) and less assertive. In contrast to Tabor (or the Old Tabor as it became widely styled), which was in fact a hierocracy, the Horebite brotherhood (the New, Lesser Tabor) was deemed to be a theocracy – God's law was supposed to be revealed to everybody reading or listening to His word.

At the time, Žižka was said to have been the creator of his military order, a sort of covenant signed by individual representatives of the army. It was a significant document providing an interesting insight into the social structure and hierarchical ranks of the Horebite military brotherhood.[16]

Soon after the shift within the left, there was a regrouping on the right. In autumn 1423, there was a rapprochement between the Romanists and the Hussite right. At the diet on St Giles' Day in Prague a new twelve-member government was elected, composed half of Hussites and half of Romanists, with the higher nobility in the majority. Yet this move could not but exacerbate the relationship between the left and the centre, which had already turned sour because of the competing claims to the city of Hradec Králové. Confrontation became unavoidable.

Interception, tightening and expansion

In June 1424, at Malešov (close to Prague), in what was one of the bloodiest battles in the Hussite wars, the united Horebite and Taborite brotherhoods under Žižka defeated the army of the new compromise government of Bohemia. In the following months most royal boroughs associated with Prague went over, or were forced to go over, to the Taborite and Horebite associations. There was even the danger that Žižka would launch an attack on Prague. Yet the leading theologian of the centre, John Rokycana (who had succeeded the deceased Jacobellus), persuaded Žižka to refrain from this intention, and a peace between Prague and the brotherhoods (September 1424) was sealed by the agreement to undertake a common expedition to Moravia, where the comparatively weak Hussite camp was to be strengthened.

In October 1424, Žižka died. In 1426 a priest, Prokop the Shaven – a man of military and diplomatic skill – became the supreme commander of the combined Taborite and Horebite brotherhoods. In the same year, a synod of Taborite clergy succeeded in resolving some internal differences and in codifying their religious doctrine. In June 1426, a Saxon intervention was defeated, and so too, in August 1427, was the fourth crusade.

Meanwhile, one more internal hurdle which obstructed the tightening of the Hussite rule had to be overcome. By mid-1424, Korybut was again in Prague at the invitation of the Prague party, but he now supported the right (minority) wing of that party (led by John of Příbram), which wanted to use his help to bring about reconciliation with the king and the *Curia*. When it was discovered that Korybut was conducting secret negotiations to this effect (April 1427), a *coup* against him led by the newly emerging leader of the main body of the Prague party, Rokycana, put an abrupt end to any attempts at a rapprochement with the Romanists. Korybut was taken prisoner and, in autumn 1428, banned from Prague for good.

The period between September 1424 and April 1427 can be considered as the period of interception of the oscillating seat of power within the Hussite camp in Bohemia. The left, led by Prokop, became the stronger partner in the coalition and Prague fell under the control of the radical (Rokycana) wing of the centre. From 1427 until 1433 the Hussite rule in Bohemia was both at its most intensive and at its most extensive (the phase of tightening in our model).

As these things happened, there was also a growing feeling that the war had reached a stalemate. Foreign intervention proved ineffective, but so too did the attempts of the Hussites to establish the unity of the country on the basis of the Four Articles of Prague. People were starting to tire of the continuous warfare, and to long for peace, but this could not be achieved without the consent of the main powers in Europe, the papal *Curia* and the royal/imperial court.

In that situation, the Hussite leaders decided that only if they took the war abroad would they induce the powers to negotiate on the basis of equality. Thus, from spring 1427 to May 1433, the united Hussite armies undertook a series of raids into neighbouring countries. Significantly, the military forces of the empire were not in a position to offer adequate resistance. Many cities preferred to pay ransom rather than be sacked. This six-year period can, in terms of our model, be described as the period of expansion. It coincided with the phase of tightening of revolutionary rule which started with the Rokycana coup in Prague in 1427, and finished with the events in Prague towards the end of 1433 to which we shall refer shortly.

During that period, Hussite propaganda also intensified. Pamphlets defending the Utraquist position and calling for a critical approach to the practices of the Roman Church were distributed all over Europe.

The successful Hussite raids into German and Hungarian domains eventually convinced the pope that he had to accede to the request of the Council party in the Catholic hierarchy and summon a new Council, this time to Basle, where among other issues the Hussite problem had to be solved.

Most Hussites were genuinely interested in reconciliation with the Roman Church. As their deviations from the acknowledged religious standard were of a ritual rather than a dogmatic nature, they considered themselves good, even better, Catholics than the others. As their maximal requirement, they wanted the Church to accept their view, which they claimed to be based on the Scriptures and the practice of the Early (Primitive) Church only, whereas the Roman Church was blamed for having introduced many 'adnovations'. These, however, were considered by the *Curia* to be superior and more dignified than the practice of the Primitive Church. Oddly, but significantly, the revolutionaries wanted to return to the past, while the counter-revolutionaries did not want to give up their 'modernity' – rather, they insisted on its continuation throughout the whole Catholic Church.

By way of a compromise, the Hussites would content themselves with an agreement according to which Hussite practice would be recognised as legitimate and as generally applicable throughout the kingdom of Bohemia. They did not want to create a schismatic Church, but an acknowledged national branch of the universal Catholic Church.

Negotiations started in April 1429, but the Hussites' request to obtain a public hearing from the Council was the main obstacle to agreement. Meanwhile, the last attempt was made to curb the military power of the Hussites. The fifth crusade (1431), in which perhaps the largest number of crusaders, recruited from all over Europe, took part, virtually dissolved at the very border when approached by the Hussite army. The Khaldunian contrast was demonstrated in a manifest way.

Only then did the pope and the emperor get ready to accept the Hussite demand for a public hearing. This was to take place at the Council of Basle, which started its dealings in 1431. In the preliminary talks between the Hussites and the envoys of the Council in Cheb (Eger) in May 1432, it was agreed that both sides should accept the Bible and the practice of the Early Church as the criteria for discussion. Thus, where a reformer – John Hus – failed, the revolutionaries succeeded. They not only obtained a public hearing, but commanded respect. In view of the Hussite military strength, there was no attempt to hinder the safe conduct of the Czech delegation, some 300-strong, which arrived in Basle during the first months of 1433. The leaders of the Hussite delegation were the commander-in-chief, Prokop the Shaven, and one baron. Among the four main speakers, each defending one Article of Prague, was Peter Payne, the Oxonian Lollard.

During the negotiations, or rather disputations, in Basle, a delegation of the Council visited Prague; they realised that there were essential differences within the Hussite camp, and entered into closer contact with the Hussite right. This faction was becoming increasingly concerned by the continuation of the war, which badly affected both the economy and cultural intercourse with other countries.

Another worrying factor was the worsening of discipline in the armies of the military brotherhoods, where mercenaries began to appear increasingly side by side with the dedicated warriors of God. This was a dangerous development for the military superiority of the left, the parties of Tabor and Horeb, or, as the latter called themselves after Žižka's death, the Orphans. It bore witness to a disturbing perversion of the revolutionary ideal, which in its turn provided the background for a rearrangement of alliances.

As the negotiations in Basle approached the decisive stage, the Hussite left wanted to tilt the balance of power in their favour by the conquest of the most important Romanist borough in Bohemia – Plzeň. In order to force the city to surrender through starvation, strong armies were concentrated around it, yet the great numbers of beleaguering soldiers were difficult to feed, especially as it was a year of bad harvests. Under such circumstances foraging became strongly resented by the peasant population of the area: the foraging contingents had to spread into wide areas and were often met with armed resistance. In order to avoid clashes with the Czech peasants, they went foraging in neighbouring Bavaria, where on one such occasion a strong contingent was almost completely annihilated. This was a heavy blow to discipline in the army, where some dangerous signs of insubordination cropped up. There were also some defections, the most serious being that of a Taborite captain who secretly helped to supply the beleaguered city of Plzeň.

Meanwhile in Prague, the left was overtaken by yet another disaster. The assembly of the Hussite centre and right, held towards the end of 1433 in Prague, elected, instead of the twelve members of government who had been acting till then, one baron (of the Hussite right) as administrator of the kingdom. He, in agreement with the Romanist faction and the Hussite councillors of the Old Town of Prague, declared a general peace in the country and asked the New Town of Prague to join in. As the New Towners refrained, they were overwhelmed by force.

As a result of this event, the siege of Plzeň was lifted and Prokop prepared for the decisive confrontation with the unified forces of the Prague party and the domestic Romanists. The centre-right coalition was numerically stronger. In military technique there was no significant difference – all the Hussite innovations were used on both sides – and neither does there seem to have been too much difference in spirit. Apparently there was little scope for the Khaldunian contrast. In the Battle of Lipany, on 30 May 1434, the united Taborite and Orphans' armies were utterly defeated.

Restoration: compromise and pressure

Although this was not the end of them, the Taborite and Orphans' parties were deprived of their military arm, and could not check the fateful reversal of the revolutionary process. As the military power of the radicals was eliminated, it was possible for the Hussite right and centre to make a deal with the Council on the basis of a compromise interpretation of the Four Articles of Prague. The form agreed in Basle – the so-called Compacts of Basle – was a diluted form of their original version. The Articles about freedom of preaching and the punishment of mortal sins were accepted in a general way, but with a more precise definition of those who should have the right to preach (i.e. only ordained persons) and of the authorities that should be entitled to proceed against sinners. The Article against the worldly dominion of the Church was worded in the Compacts in a way that made it impossible to use it as a justification for further confiscations of Church property. Oddly enough, the most difficult agreement was the one concerning the communion from the chalice to the laity. As Heymann points out, this type of communion never became an issue between the Roman and Greek Orthodox Churches, but here, within the Czech context, it had a deep political connotation. It was a symbol of equality between the laity and clergy and also a symbol of Czech specificity which the universalistic spirit of Latin Christian Europe was not ready to accept. Nevertheless, the representatives of the Council (but, unfortunately for the Hussite case, without the approval of the pope) agreed 'that the chalice be given to those men and women who were used to it and expressly demanded it as long as otherwise they lived in the favour and the ritual of Christ and the Sacred Church'.[17]

In that form, the Compacts of Basle were finally signed in a common diet of the Bohemian and Moravian estates, which took place in July 1436, in the Moravian city of Jihlava. This act made manifest the formal reconciliation of the Hussites with their Romanist counterparts, as far as they were represented by the Council of Basle, and with Sigismund of Luxemburg as the legitimate king of Bohemia. This was a typical restoration compromise in terms of our model, a compromise whose fragility, however, was revealed sooner than in other revolutions.

In 1435 the Hussites, i.e. the Prague party, who acted then on behalf of the whole movement, elected their own archbishop, John Rokycana, and, after the signature of the Compacts, wanted him to be appointed according to canonic law by the pope. Yet, as has been said already, the pope did not approve the Compacts, so he did not appoint the Utraquist candidate; even among the representatives of the Council there were many who had serious reservations concerning the validity of the Compacts. In their view, the peculiarities of the Bohemian Church should be tolerated only as long as was absolutely necessary, i.e. as long as there were people able to defend them by force of arms. Thus the upholding of the compromise became a delicate power game.

As soon as Sigismund installed himself in Prague, the restoration pressure set in. (An outward symbol of the end of official puritanism in the city was the return of prostitutes, whose whole community had been banned with the explosion of the revolution.) In Prague, only the Hussite right, led by the university master, John of Příbram, was tolerated as the legitimate partner of the Romanists. The leader of the Hussite centre, their archbishop elect, John Rokycana, had to find refuge with his east Bohemian supporters (1437). Paradoxically, meanwhile, Tabor, in a separate deal, acknowledged Sigismund as king of Bohemia and received from him the charter of a royal borough.

The restoration pressure continued after the death in December 1437 of Sigismund, who had not had long to enjoy the throne that had taken so much to recapture. From then on, there was for many years virtually no royal power in the country. In principle, there were two serious candidates for the Bohemian throne, one from the Austrian Habsburgs (Albrecht) and the other from the Polish Jagiellon dynasty (Kazimír). But the premature death of the former (1439), and the irresolute action of the latter left the matter unresolved.

The country was still divided into four religious parties, each of which held its own power zone. The Romanists held most of western and a good deal of southern Bohemia, the Hussite right shared power with the Romanists in Prague, while eastern Bohemia was solidly under the captains of the Hussite centre. After the Battle of Lipany the Orphans joined the Prague party (i.e. the centre), as did most of the royal boroughs in other parts of Bohemia, and the Hussite left was reduced to the city of Tabor and a few allied boroughs in south Bohemia. The Utraquist clergy of the centre, led by their archbishop elect, attempted in vain to establish complete unity between all the Hussite factions. For Rokycana it was easier to strike a compromise with the Hussite right, led by Příbram (1442), than with the Hussite left, whose leader, Bishop Nicholas of Pelhřimov, was, from the point of view of the Compacts of Basle, schismatic. The discussion with the left culminated in the condemnation of the Taborite doctrine by the Utraquist clergy of the reunited Prague party (1447).

Within the Romanist party in Bohemia and Moravia, the priesthood was less tolerant towards the Utraquists than was the laity. The clergy supported the pope against the aspirations of the Council and, following his stance, did not recognise the Compacts. (In 1448 a papal legate even attempted to deprive the Czechs of the original copy of that document.) On the other hand, the Romanist nobles were more inclined to observe the compromise. The nobles on both sides of the divide were not interested in the re-establishment of a strong royal power: they preferred the precarious, indecisive balance of power when order in the kingdom was upheld by regional truces, the so-called *Landfrieden*, agreed by the local barons, knights and royal boroughs.

Consolidation

The consolidation had to come from the Hussite centre, which was apparently the strongest faction numerically, and dominated the east Bohemian *Landfrieden*. From 1444, George of Poděbrady became their leader; he possessed a considerable talent for combining diplomacy and force. Having about a third of Bohemia solidly behind him, he could embark on a well-prepared campaign for the unification and pacification of the country. In 1448 he took by force – with minimal casualties – the city of Prague. In 1449 the Romanist nobility united in a counter-league (the League Strakonice), but they did not dare to take up arms. In 1452, most of them attended a diet which elected George governor of the kingdom for two years. Soon after that, Tabor surrendered to George's military expedition, which put an end to its political and religious sovereignty. The Taborite bishop, Nicholas, and his close associate Koranda, ended their lives as George's prisoners. Thus the whole country acknowledged his command and the consolidation process could be started.

In 1453, Ladislas the Posthumous, the thirteen-year-old son of Albrecht the Habsburg, was crowned as the Bohemian king, but in 1457, amid preparations for his wedding with a French princess, he died. This time, however, the Bohemian estates did not look abroad for a suitable candidate. There had been too many disappointments with candidates from abroad; they preferred the comparative stability achieved by George of Poděbrady. In March 1458, they elected him king of Bohemia. The Moravian estates accepted the election later in the same year; only the royal borough of Jihlava had to be brought to submission by force of arms. Oddly enough, it was the 'little people' of that city, mainly of German tongue and of strong anti-Hussite feeling, who opposed the 'heretic' king.[18]

As far as the Czech situation was concerned, the revolution was over, and issues other than religious ones came to dominate political divisions. If the religious issues nevertheless remained on the cards, it was because of the papal *Curia* which was not willing to recognise even so moderate a deviation from the uniform ritual standard as communion from the chalice for everybody. It may be worth noting that it took 500 years before the Roman *Curia* could stomach this practice of the Primitive Church – its legitimacy was recognised by the Second Vatican Council (1962–4).

The end of the revolution, however, was not the end of Czech reform. Although the political establishment stuck to the Compacts of Basle, which provided too tight a framework for the specificities of Utraquism, the reformation did not stop. In 1457, in an east Bohemian village, a small community picked up Chelčický's tradition and constituted itself as the Unity of Brethren (*Unitas Fratrum*). After having passed its period of childhood devoted to Primitive Christian revival, it developed into a most articulate, autocephalous denomination of the Czech Reformation.

In 1462, Pope Pius II declared the Compacts nullified, and in 1466 anathematised George of Poděbrady. What followed was a fight not against a revolution, but against a 'schismatic' king who, despite all the wounds inflicted on him, could not be curbed. Nevertheless, to forestall further heretisation and the wars that would ensue, George refrained from founding a dynasty; he recommended, wisely from the religious point of view but less so with respect to political developments, the candidature of the Polish dynasty. Thus in 1471 the throne went to Vladislav, who, though being a faithful Romanist, duly acknowledged the dual religious character of the country as had been agreed in the Compacts of Basle.

Religious tension in the country eased and in 1485 the diet of Kutná Hora sealed the religious peace on the basis of the Compacts and of the existing divisions of parishes and churches between the two parties. Only the newly created Unity of Brethren was not included in that compromise. The Hussite establishment stuck to the Compacts. Within their framework, however, the freedom to communicate according to Romanist or Utraquist rite was granted both to the upper estates and to the peasantry. This was a virtual denial of the principle *Cuius regio eius religio*, which during the Hussite wars had become the common practice; thus the final full-stop after the Hussite revolution resulted in a religious tolerance unprecedented in Latin Christian Europe. The Unity of Brethren, which was not officially recognised, survived under the protection of some Utraquist barons. Religious divisions ceased to be the primary bone of contention in Czech society. For the next generation other issues, of a purely economic or political nature, came to the forefront of public life and when, in the 1520s, religion again re-entered the arena of strife, it was in the context of European Reformation and under considerably changed social and political circumstances.

Notes

1. There are several outstanding works in English on the key issues, personalities and social background of the Hussite reform and revolution. H. Kaminský in *A History of the Hussite Revolution* (Berkeley and Los Angeles University Press, 1967) provides an excellent, detailed and extremely well-documented analysis of the initial period of revolution, with particular reference to the broad ideological spectrum into which the reformers and/or revolutionaries became divided. A detailed narrative of the course of events, supported by a penetrating analysis of how and why things happened, can be read in two monographs by F.G. Heymann, *John Žižka and the Hussite Revolution* (Princeton University Press, NJ, 1955) and *George of Bohemia: King of heretics* (Princeton University Press, NJ, 1965). The former book discusses the early period and the latter the final epoch and epilogue of the revolutionary process. An alternative account of the later period is provided by O. Odložilík, *The Hussite King: Bohemia in European affairs 1440–1471* (Rutgers University Press, NJ, 1965). Hus's teaching is analysed with much understanding by M. Spinka in *John Hus at the Council of Constance* (Columbia University Press, New York, 1965), *John Hus and the Czech Reform* (Archon Books, Hamden, 1966) and *John Hus: A biography* (Princeton University Press, NJ, 1968). *Essays in Czech History* (Athlone Press, London, 1969), a posthumous edition of articles by R.R. Betts, contains valuable information on the intellectual origins of the Hussite reform, its relationship to Wyclif, and the philosophical controversies of the epoch. The revolutionary implications of Wyclif's ideas are analysed in H. Kaminský, 'Wyclifism as ideology of revolution', in *Church History*, vol. 32 (1963), pp. 57–74. A crucial event, the negotiations between the Hussites and the Roman Church, is discussed by E.F. Jacob in 'The Bohemians at the Council of Basle 1433', in *Prague Essays*, ed. R. Seton-Watson (Clarendon Press, Oxford, 1949). On the social background, with particular reference to urban problems, the reader may learn from Heymann's articles 'The role of the towns in Bohemia of the later Middle Ages', in *Journal of World History*, pt. 5 (Paris, 1954), p. 326, and 'City rebellions in 15th-century Bohemia and their ideological and sociological background', in *The Slavonic and East European Review* (London, June 1962) pp. 324–40. A sociological analysis of the nobility's position is supplied in a monograph by J.M. Klassen, 'The nobility and the making of the Hussite Revolution', in *East European Quarterly* (Boulder, New York, 1978).

   For information on the position of the peasantry, however, we have rather to look into the Czech sources. The standard book of reference is *Dějiny selského stavu* (*History of the Peasant Estate*) by K. Krofta (Laichter, Prague, 1949). Another highly important Czech book for which there is no equivalent in the English literature is by Rudolf Urbánek, *Lipany a konec polních vojsk* (*Lipany and the End of the Field Armies*), Melantrich, Prague, 1934. An account and evaluation of the main foreign interventions against the Hussite reform is given in F.G. Heymann, 'The crusades against the Hussites', in *A History of the Crusades*, ed. K.M. Setto, vol. III, *The Fourteenth and Fifteenth Centuries* (H.W. Hazard, Madison, WI, 1975). Useful information on the pre-revolutionary process can be found in R.E. Weltsch, *Archbishop John of Jenstein 1348–1400* (Mouton, The Hague–Paris, 1968). Ideas of the reformed denomination which survived the Hussite period are analysed in P. Brock, *The Political and Social Doctrines of the Unity of the Czech Brethren in the Fifteenth and Early Sixteenth Centuries* (Mouton, The Hague, 1957). A general account of the Hussite period by K. Krofta is available in the *Cambridge Medieval History*, vol. VIII. A brief evaluation of the period can be found in my article, 'The meaning of Hussitism', in *Journal of Religious History*, vol. VIII, June 1974, pp. 3–20.

The Czech literature on the topic is vast and it would be out of place to review it in this context. Virtually all of it is referred to in the above-mentioned books published in English. A long list can also be compiled of books in other languages, especially in German and French. From this rich source of information I would like to quote only four which, in my opinion, are most relevant to what is being discussed in this book: F. Seibt. *Hussitica: Zur Struktur einer Revolution* (Böhlau Verlag, Köln-Graz, 1965) and 'Die Hussitenzeit als Kulturepoche', *Historische Zeitschrift*, Bd. 195, 1962, pp. 21–62; R. Kalivoda, *Revolution und Ideologie des Hussitismus* (Böhlau Verlag, Köln–Wien, 1976) and K. Hrubý, 'Senior Communitas: Eine revolutionäre Institution der Prager Hussitischen Bürgerschaft in Bohemia', *Jahrbuch des Collegium Carolinum*, Band 13 (R. Oldenburg Verlag, München–Wien, 1972). The last two contributions are the adapted versions of the Czech originals. Kalivoda's book is a Marxist reappraisal of the ideological roots of the Hussite Revolution which, for the first time in Marxist historiography, characterises this revolution as an early bourgeois one. Hrubý's analysis is in line with Seibt's sociological approach. A comprehensive review of books and articles published on the topic in different European languages up to 1976 is supplied in a bibliographical study guide, *The Hussite Movement and the Reformation in Bohemia, Moravia and Slovakia 1350–1650*, ed. J.K. Zeman (Michigan Slavic Publications, University of Michigan Press, 1977).

2. The most original and influential German-speaking reformer was Nicholas of Dresden, whose radicality in several respects surpassed that of the Czech reformers.

3. Betts, p. 79.

4. On Hus, see Betts, p. 84, and on Jacobellus de Misa (Jakoubek of Stříbro) see Kaminský, *A History*, p. 201.

5. Quoted from Klassen, p. 67.

6. Quoted from Odložilík, pp. 4–5.

7. The name 'Hussite' was originally a pejorative nickname used by their enemies. It became used by the followers of Hus only much later (towards the mid-century) but even then the terms 'Utraquist' or 'Calixtin' were more common. For detail, see for instance Seibt, *Hussitica*, pp. 10–13.

8. The interdict which the *Curia* imposed on Prague was only intermittently enforced by the Archbishop of Prague, Conrad, and when this happened it affected virtually only the Romanists, who then had to stop their services and the dispensing of sacraments (with the exception of baptism), while the Utraquists carried on, and on top of that took possession of the vacant Romanist churches (Kaminský, *A History*, pp. 159–61 and 223).

9. The Hussite lords actually returned to the ancient practice common before the Hildebrandian reform, which might be considered as a class-conscious attempt to regain lost rights. But the loyalties of the nobility were divided; of the lords, the majority remained faithful to the Roman Church, and there is no clear-cut evidence that only the Hussites, because of their patronate rights, were in a position to appoint the parsons; it would therefore be preposterous to consider this action of the Hussite nobility as a matter of class rather than of religious consciousness. Klassen, pp. 99ff.

10. Although scholarly opinion is divided on the issue, it seems most probable that Taborite religious radicalism was due to two influences: the teaching of radical

masters from Prague University, such as Nicholas of Dresden and the young (in contrast to the mature) Jacobellus de Misa (Jakoubek of Stříbro) on the one hand, and contacts with Waldensian communities in South Bohemia on the other. (For a detailed evaluation of this issue, see Kaminský, *A History of the Hussite Revolution*, pp. 141–220.)

11. *Ibid.*, p. 145.
12. This is an intricate problem lacking clear reference in primary sources. For a systematic attempt to sort out both primary and secondary sources, see especially Seibt, *Hussitica*, pp. 133–45, and Hrubý, pp. 9–43.
13. Seibt, *Hussitica*, pp. 149–60.
14. Klassen, pp. 47–8.
15. The exception was the so-called *Landfrieden* (regional covenant) with its seat in Plzeň – a royal borough in West Bohemia, a centre of staunch Czech-speaking Romanists in the kingdom.
16. This brotherhood, or Žižka's army, was divided vertically into military units following the hierarchical command of superiors, and horizontally into groups of common social status whose elected representatives or elders had some say in religious, political and other non-military matters. The lowest horizontal group was that of the peasants, who were not included among the groups signing the covenant. They were, however, entitled to have their elected elders take part in the distribution of booty. The clergy was supposed not to interfere in either of the two dimensions of the organisation. For further detail see Heymann, *John Žižka and the Hussite Revolution*, pp. 381–2.
17. Quoted from Heymann, *George of Bohemia*, pp. 8–9.
18. A similar situation developed later in the city of Wrocław (Breslau) in Silesia, where again the lower strata showed the most opposition to the recognition of George of Poděbrady as the sovereign. This issue is dealt with by Heymann, 'City rebellions'.

2

□

England (1628–89)

Nature of the revolution: can we call it 'Puritan'?

The English revolution of the seventeenth century is in many respects reminiscent of the Hussite revolution 200 years earlier. Although political considerations played a more important and largely independent role, religion was a strong factor in shaping the tissue of contradictions. Although the first, introductory phase of reformation was over, the tendency to leave it only half completed persisted. The Anglican Church, as it emerged from the Henrician and Elizabethan eras, did not want to go as far as the Lutheran or Calvinist Churches. There was a parallel with the Utraquist Church in Bohemia, which had also not wanted to follow its more radical wing – the Taborites and later the Unity of Brethren. Only in the severance of all links with Rome was the Anglican Church in line with the Reformation on the Continent. Thus there was a growing feeling that the religious Reformation in England had somehow been left unfinished.

The English revolution broke out when the European continent was fully engaged in its Thirty Years War, which was at first wholly, and at the end partly, being waged for the sake of a re-demarcation of Catholic and Protestant domains in Europe. Then, after the conclusion of the Peace of Westphalia, it was the war between France and Spain, lasting until 1659, that prevented those powers that would have been most likely to intervene from taking part in British events. When foreign wars eventually began to be fought, they were neither wars of intervention nor of revolutionary expansion, but wars of protection and the furthering of English commercial interests. Thus, enjoying its insular position, England was not thrown into European war but could afford to solve its problems through an internal war without risk of foreign interference.

That the religious overtones in the English revolution were somewhat weaker than in the Hussite revolution (but on the other hand much stronger than those brought to a head in the French revolution) has to do with socio-historical developments in Western Europe as a whole, a point that will be discussed in Part IV of this book. On the other hand, the ethnic element that also entered the field of controversy was real only in the Czech case. References to the bad Normans and good Saxons in the English revolution, and to the bad Francs and good Gauls in the French revolution, were myths invented for propaganda purposes.

In view of the complexity of the causes and issues fought for, the description of the English revolution as 'Puritan' may seem one-sided or even misleading. Christopher Hill's opinion that 'The Puritan revolution was a nineteenth-century invention' is, in view of the findings of more recent scholarship, no longer viable.[1] Hill's view may be plausible if we want, with one appropriate epithet, to characterise the whole breadth and depth of what others prefer to call the great rebellion or, simply, the civil war. Yet as we shall see in the case of other revolutions in this study, one characterising epithet is never satisfactory on its own. It may indicate only one particular feature in the causation and development of a revolution, without claiming to cover the whole complexity of that chain of events. If we want to be absolutely accurate, we should drop such an epithet altogether and talk simply of the English revolution of the seventeenth century, the French revolution of the end of the eighteenth century, etc. Yet this procedure would not do justice to the sensible endeavour to characterise each revolution by an apposite, simple label which would pinpoint the most salient, specific feature of that revolution.

We have to bear in mind that several revolutions may be described by one and the same term, such as, for instance, the term 'bourgeois revolution'. In the traditional Marxist view, both the French and English revolutions, and in the modern Marxist view (see note 1 to Part II, Chapter 1) also the Czech Hussite Revolution, fall into this category. In this context we are using individual epithets as denotations of specific differences; for that purpose the term 'Puritan' seems to be the most appropriate in the case of the English revolution. Puritanism is a label of attitude or mood rather than of political party or programme. Therefore it covers a wider area than one specific political grouping. Although not all the actors on the anti-Stuart side can be described as Puritans, the spread of Puritan attitudes and feelings is one of the characteristic features of that period of English history.

In my view, there is no reason to reject this term on the grounds put forward by Hill that such a term 'assumes an element of conscious will among an identifiable group of those who made the revolution', while 'a sociological interpretation preferred by our contemporary historians need not make any assumption about purpose'.[2] As I understand it, an interpretation of social action that does not take into account its purpose, is no interpretation at all. Hill's own writings amply refute his argument.

There is, however, yet another qualification in Hill's rejection of the Puritan concept, namely his emphasis on the role of secular, scientific reasoning in the intellectual origins of the English revolution. This was by no means a negligible element in the social climate of seventeenth-century England, but one that in itself could hardly contribute as much to the fatal decision to revolt as did the Puritan ideas of calling and self-righteousness which motivated dedicated men to resolute actions. In the seventeenth century the vigour of religious feelings among large sections of the population was still formidable. There was not only a proliferation of sects (most of them with strong puritanical leanings and a belief in government by the virtuous), but also a revival of millenarianism which, with the Fifth Monarchy Men, sought for itself a political role.

Furthermore, scientists' views in those days were not divorced from religious beliefs, as some may imagine. This point is illustrated by the fact that Comenius, a Czech refugee from Moravia, participated in the scientific activity of the group around Samuel Hartlib (Hill called them all the Comenians), endeavouring to spread knowledge and universal education on the basis of discovery and experimentation. As bishop of the Unity of Brethren (founded in the consolidation phase of the Hussite revolution and banned by the forcible reconversion of the Czech Lands to Catholicism after 1620) and at the same time a renowned pansophist and educationalist, Comenius symbolised the symbiosis of very intense religious beliefs with nascent science. All these people shared the conviction that scientific enquiry was the right way to learn to understand God's Creation, for it was to God that they were responsible for their own works.

Causes and onset

Reviewing the causes and the course of the English revolution presents a more difficult situation than in the case of the Hussite revolution. There we were confronted with many gaps in historical evidence. Here in the English case, we are rather embarrassed by the riches of information. There the diverging interpretations concerned mainly the tenor, the socio-historical meaning of that revolution; here we have to struggle through different interpretations of what seem to be the same facts or the same observations.

This study is not the appropriate place for a critical appraisal of views and sources on this matter (it would also be a foolish undertaking on the part of somebody without adequate specialisation in the field). Thus, I may be excused for merely selecting from the almost endless reading list what seems to be most relevant for my task, i.e. for testing the main disproportions or contradictions, for applying my morphological model, and last but not least, for evaluating the English revolution in a wider socio-historical and geographical context. Unlike my treatment of the revolution in fifteenth-century Bohemia, I shall not attempt in the English case to reproduce any narrative. I shall simply review the course of events in so far as they are relevant to the morphological model.

As far as the etiology of the English revolution is concerned, I am most indebted to the synthetic analysis by Lawrence Stone, representative *par excellence* of the historian and sociologist in one person. In Stone's analysis, we can trace all the disproportions or contradictions listed in the section on etiology of revolution (pages 31–8).

Let us start with the Marxian contradiction which, in different forms and from different angles, has been considered by many modern historians, British and foreign alike. For many of them the crucial questions are: who made the revolution, which class carried it and which opposed it; or if it was not the classes whose forces clashed in that revolution, but merely political factions of one and the same class or independent of class, how can the English Revolution be interpreted in terms of a contradiction between productive forces and mode of production?

Although it may be accepted that the state machinery of early Stuarts did not correspond with the development of the productive forces in England in those days, it is more difficult to pass judgement on whether the social organisation as a whole, the mode of production, was in some contradiction to these forces. If we look only into the period demarcated by the years of the revolutionary process (by my reckoning 1628–89), we can hardly maintain that there was a conspicuous change in the socio-economic system; but this does not in itself mean that there was no particular contradiction of the above-mentioned type. We can only say that this contradiction was not solved (Marx's favourite term, *aufgehoben*, would fit here) by that revolution.

The contradiction between the productive forces and the mode of production underlying the English Puritan revolution was an issue for much longer than the time span of the seventeenth century, and its essence was much broader than one expressed merely in terms of technology and social organisation. Tawney described this contradiction appositely as follows:

> Politically, one can see different views of the basis of wealth in conflict, that which measures it by the number of tenants 'able to do service' contending with that which tests it by the maximum pecuniary returns to be got from an estate, and which treats the number of tenants as quite a subordinate consideration. The former is the ideal of philosophical conservatives, is supported, for military and social reasons, by the Government, and survives long in the North; the latter is that of the new landed proprietors, and wins in the South.[3]

Thus understood, the contradiction reveals not only the Marxian but also the Aristotelian criteria: economic versus social justice, efficiency versus assured status. This contradiction stirred English public life for about 400 years (the evidence collected by Tawney stretches from the early fifteenth century until the end of the first third of the nineteenth century).[4] And it was not so much the economic pressure itself as the political support of the government that helped the economic concept of justice to its final victory, making English agriculture highly effective and at the same time reducing the number of its operators (farmers) on the national scale to the minimum.

If there was any conspicuous acceleration, or perhaps a leap forward in that policy, it happened after the revolution when, together with the absolutist aspirations of the Crown, there fell away the last, however thin and ineffective, shield of social justice for the peasantry and rural labourers. The identity of interest and policy between the great landlords and the government which, in Tawney's words,[5] characterised the period between 1688 and 1832, was the most conspicuous result of the revolution in the socio-economic field. 'If economic causes made a new system of farming profitable, it is nonetheless true that legal causes decided by whom the profits should be enjoyed.'[6] It seems that this was in socio-economic terms what the revolution was about. It accelerated the trend towards commercialisation and secured its fruits for the landowning class which – imbued with the entrepreneurial spirit – emerged from the structured shifts during the process of revolution.

Only in that sense, perhaps, can the English Puritan Revolution be described as a bourgeois revolution, and this with more justification than the Czech Hussite revolution. Although in the short run the participation of the bourgeoisie as a conscious class (estate of royal boroughs) was more impressive in the Hussite than in the English revolution, in the long run, it was the English revolution that more effectively paved the way for the ascent of what may be called bourgeoisie. The Hussite Revolution brought only a temporary advance for that social group.

Demographic estimates show that between 1540 and 1640 the English landed classes trebled in number, while the total population scarcely doubled.[7] With respect to the distribution of wealth and income this fact may be interpreted variously, according to our assumptions concerning the increase of economically utilised land and the increase of per capita GNP. Scattered evidence on the increase of rents and on the decline of real wages, however, points to increasing rather than decreasing income differentials. Also the increase of vagrancy and pauperism, which in many contemporary sources is attributed to enclosures, points to a widening gap between rich and poor, although the situation of course varied considerably from county to county.

Common economic interests do not seem, however, to have demarcated the main political groupings; these, rather, cut across the economic divide. Neither were the fronts of political confrontation uniformly determined by the shifts in economic or social status. Although these circumstances played their part, the main factor that seems to have influenced the taking of sides at the beginning of the revolution was the ideological, i.e. basically religious-cum-political, orientation. As Tawney said, 'the bourgeoisie were on both sides', and the same can be said of the aristocracy.

The main ideological justification for the defiance of royal power came from the Calvinist political doctrine, with its clearly circumscribed theory of resistance:

Revolt is never justified except when led by people who are themselves magistrates – i.e. responsible citizens, men of property with a stake in the country, whether they be princes of the blood in France, the States-General in the Netherlands or Parliament in England. 'Private men' should never take the law into their own hands, but should tarry for the magistrate.[8]

The English revolution had neither its Hus nor its Rousseau; Hill's quest for their substitutes in thinkers such as Bacon, Coke and Raleigh has proved questionable.[9] However, what happened could not have occurred without a mental ferment in which the inquisitive spirit combined with the Puritan sense of destiny and emphasis on self-help, thus preparing people for events to come. Most of them acted within the Calvinist limits, ruling out revolt by people without political status, by the 'many-headed monster' of a popular uprising. Thus revolution obtained not only justification (or rather consecration) but also a framework within which it could be better steered towards success and avoid the kind of excesses that people saw, for instance, in the peasants' revolts.

Within these limits, Puritanism became, as Stone put it, 'a generalised conviction of the need for independent judgement based on conscience and Bible reading ... a driving enthusiasm for moral improvement in every aspect of life'.[10] It provided the basis for mental ferment and also for the shift of loyalties necessary to turn already existing institutions into revolutionary organisations.

Institutions that could be used as bases of revolutionary power were those whose leaders were devoted to the common law and to the principle that the monarch has to rule in a balanced harmony with the aristocratic and timocratic representatives of the country. Since the king attempted to tilt this balance in his favour, as other European monarchs tried to do at that time, by depriving both Parliament and the traditional judiciary of their prerogatives, and to this purpose tried to exploit the cooperation of the Church of England, the dissatisfaction with its half-hearted reformation could not but be accentuated.

As in the case of the Hussite revolution, there was a frustration resulting from the lack of 'maintenance values'. The moral decay affected both the secular and the ecclesiastical élite. This widened the gap between the generally required standard on the one hand and the real behaviour of these élites on the other, a typical case of decremental deprivation in the moral sphere. The change in the quality of élites can also be described in terms of the Paretian simile, in which lions, having lost their self-confidence,[11] turned into foxes, and new lions emerged from the lower social strata and eventually became the counter-élite.[12]

Moreover, as there was more social mobility (although historians cannot agree on its proportions and on the prevailing directions of the main moves),[13] there was a growing opportunity for jealousy and resentment which, in their turn, strengthened the feeling of relative deprivation.

This can be classified as a multiple Weberian disproportion. As Stone put it:

wide discrepancies ... developed between the three sectors of wealth, status and power ... One economically rising group, the merchants, felt themselves denied

social prestige ... successful lawyers and the greater squires felt themselves excluded
from power by the Court ... Of the declining groups the wage earners [were]
squeezed between rising prices and lagging wages ... The clergy lamented their
loss of income and status relative to those of the laity ... Overeducated and
under-endowed, the younger sons of the gentry were condemned by the laws of
primogeniture to slide down the social scale ... The universities were turning out
an educated clergy and laity in excess of suitable job opportunities.[14]

Such people are not only most prone to embrace a new revolutionary ideology,
they are also the best qualified to articulate and spread it, thus eventually
becoming the recruiting ground for the revolutionary élite.

There is, however, little evidence for any pattern of development which could
be visualised as a J-curve in the economic sphere; nor has Stone's view that
this curve is applicable to the changing distribution of political power (in Stone's
view, the greater gentry and great Puritan peers suffered a setback in their
aspirations)[15] found adequate corroboration in the findings of other historians.

Compression, institutionalisation and explosion

The year 1628 can be taken as a convenient date from which to follow the
process of the English revolution in the light of our morphological model. In
that year the House of Commons declined to discuss the fiscal requirements of
the king, unless he agreed to the Petition of Right, limiting royal discretion in
several, clearly circumscribed matters. As the king formally yielded to this
demand, but in fact carried on collecting the customs which were not agreed
by the House, opposition in the House became strong. In 1629, the king dissolved
Parliament, imprisoned nine of its leaders and proclaimed his intention of
reigning without them. Thus, without any delay, the phase referred to in our
model as compression set in.

As Stone has shown, this compression – or, in the language of contemporaries,
'Thorough' – was quite complex. A vigorous religious reaction initiated by
Archbishop Laud gathered momentum, the aim being to recover the power and
prestige of the bishops, and to revive the ecclesiastical ritual to the point of a
return to sacramentalism, while Calvinist predestinarian determinism was to
be replaced by its moderate Arminian version. The king continued to increase
his fiscal claims; the increased taxation was coupled with the corruption caused
largely by a new wave of selling of offices and titles to the highest bidder and
also by a new wave of manipulating industrial and commercial monopolies to
the benefit of court favourites. Eventually there was an attempt to supervise
the local powers of gentry when functioning as Justices of the Peace. In the
economic field, guild organisations were imposed on numerous crafts and trades,
monopolies were strictly enforced and fines were imposed for violations of the
anti-enclosure laws; this could only anger those who broke the law without

bringing any help to the peasants affected. In short, as Stone puts it, 'the objective of "Thorough" was a deferential, strictly hierarchical, socially stable, paternalist absolutism based on a close union of Church and Crown'.[16]

In the late 1630s, a series of events acted as triggers; they can be summarised as follows. In 1639 the decision to use armed force to quell the Scottish unrest and opposition against attempts to impose on the Scottish clergy the uniformity of the Anglican Church provoked an outright uprising in Scotland – the first, rather peripheral, explosion in the context of the English revolution. The English troops were unwilling to fight and were defeated, which led the king to lose control over the armed forces; the cost of the war, coinciding with the 'Short Parliament's' refusal to raise an additional sum, followed by a partial taxpayers' strike and a refusal by the City of London to provide financial help, forced the king to summon Parliament again in November 1640 (the 'Long Parliament').

At the start Parliament wrung considerable concessions from the king: the destruction and neutralisation of the personnel and machinery of personal government; the condemnation of the measures and policies of arbitrary rule; triennial summoning of Parliament etc.[17] The most valuable achievement was the abolition of the courts of Star Chamber and High Commission and of all non-parliamentary taxation. (In this context, it is difficult not to apply the simile of the Paretian fox to the king's behaviour in sacrificing his main counsellors, lions as it were, Strafford and Laud.)

But the situation was too complex to be resolved by the constitutional settlement in London. In late October 1641, a Catholic uprising broke out in Ulster and this led to a new polarisation between what can be described as royalists and parliamentarians. The need to raise an army against the rebels was obvious, but could the king be trusted with one? Parliament wanted control over the armed forces and also the right to choose royal ministers and councillors. In addition, the threat of a more radical reformation of the national Church than the conservative Anglicans could stomach deepened the polarisation between the Royalists and the Parliamentarians. Remonstrances were followed by counter-remonstrances, and eventually, in August 1642, the 'paper war' gave way to a 'hot war' between the armed forces of the king and of Parliament. The beginning of the civil war can be seen as the second (the main) explosion in terms of our model.

Oscillation and the revolutionary spectrum

The first three years of the war between the king and Parliament were inconclusive. In the winter of 1644–5, the parliamentary forces suffered a considerable setback. The cause was sought for not only in the 'errors of man, but in the judgement of God'.[18] This spurred the Puritan propaganda on to new efforts, but also led to the introduction of organisational measures: the self-denying ordinance (eliminating all MPs from civil and military service) and a reorganisation of the army. The New Model Army which resulted from this reorganisation turned the tables in favour of the anti-Royalist forces.

The New Model Army, first under Fairfax and then under Cromwell, can be roughly compared to the warriors of God of the military brotherhoods in the Hussite revolution. Starting with Cromwell's victory at Naseby (June 1645), their fortunes in war reveal what we have described as the Khaldunian contrast in the revolutionary process. Unlike the case of the Hussite revolution, however, where the warriors of God emerged at the very beginning of the armed struggle, the Puritan warriors of God came onto the stage of revolution much later and their high morals did not penetrate the whole New Model Army. Woolrych characterises the position in these words:

> Strong as the corporate spirit of the New Model was soon to become, it did not stem from the original convictions of the mass of its rank and file, most of whom were reluctant conscripts and not a few ex-royalists. Only the hard core of the cavalry, the men of the Eastern Association, were devoted from trooper to general to an ideology – and not to any single creed or sect, but to a belief in the common purpose of all God's saints and a conviction that they were fighting the Lord's battles.[19]

The intervention of the New Model Army shifted the balance of forces between sections of the power élite; this in turn led to what may be called the opening of a second front in the contest. To borrow Schenk's dictum, 'the Parliamentarian revolt became a revolution by spreading';[20] in it the lower strata, for a while at least, found their forum and articulated their wishes. Thus, towards the late 1640s, the full spectrum of ideological and political positions characteristic of great revolutions unfolded.

When trying to describe the main positions within the political spectrum we encounter considerable difficulties, more serious than in the other revolutions discussed in this book. The political groupings were not clearly demarcated and their membership and often also their policies were subject to considerable fluctuations. Nor do their religious denominations, although more susceptible to a clear-cut demarcation, provide a reliable clue. As J.H. Hexter discovered, and D. Underdown further elaborated,[21] there was a poor correlation between religious Presbyterians and Independents on the one hand, and the political groupings described by the same labels on the other. Thus any attempt to differentiate some clearly identifiable groups within the political-cum-ideological spectrum can only be approximate. In our scheme, individual positions represent only the hard core of groupings, or rather their ideal types, within an otherwise continuous spectrum. Bearing this qualification in mind, we may proceed to draw up the political spectrum as follows.

On the counter-revolutionary right, there were the Royalists who, however, did not necessarily support the king's absolutist claims. Many of them rallied behind his cause more because of their dislike of the other political groupings than because of sympathy with the king's policy. More often the Royalists were described as Cavaliers, a term which fits their style of life better than their political orientation. Nevertheless, there might have been the germ of an ideology in this concept.

On the right of the revolutionary groupings were the good Anglican Parliamentarians, whose opposition to the Crown and Archbishop Laud was aroused by the excessive pressure and rigour of their policies (the 'Thorough'), rather than by a basic disagreement with the Church and State constitutions as such. In view of their religious views and in contrast to the main body of the centre, they may be described as Episcopalians. The number of their active adherents seems to have fluctuated considerably during the revolutionary process, falling most in the high days of revolution during the late 1640s.

The revolutionary centre was represented by men who were described as Presbyterians, either religious or political. Their crystallisation as a political party in Parliament was helped by two pressure groups – the government of the City of London, and the Scottish commissioner residing in England.[22] Supported mainly by the propertied bourgeoisie of London, they were not anti-Royalist, but wanted to give Parliament more independent power and to stop the drift of the revolution further to the left. In religion they ranged from moderate Anglicans to right-wing Puritans; they wanted the Anglican Church transformed along their own lines.

The revolutionary, and by implication also the Puritan, left were described as the Independents; in politics they ranged from those who wanted a strong Parliament and firm restraint on the power of the monarch to incipient republicans. In religious matters they included Presbyterians and Congregationalists as well as sectarians.[23] The main ally of the political Independents was the New Model Army, which became a political force in its own right in spring 1647.

Within the army's pan-Protestant framework there was sufficient scope for differentiation according to the various political and socio-economic interpretations of Puritan Christianity. A succession of very bad harvests in the later 1640s, resulting in price increases, brought economic grievances to the forefront of current issues. Rank-and-file soldiers felt that they had to take care of their political and economic interests more vigorously.

In the spring of 1647, the soldiers of each regiment elected their own representatives, called Agitators. The supreme command conceded the establishment of the General Council of the army consisting, in addition to the staff officers, of two soldiers and two officers from each regiment. In mid-1647, some elements in the army united with some radical Puritans outside the army, such as Lilburne, etc., and worked out a common manifesto, the 'Agreement of the People', which became the programme of the extreme left, known under the nickname of Levellers.

Although there were many shades of opinion among the Levellers, their main common aim was equality before the law. This, however, did not imply equality of social status or property. Only a few envisaged equality in that sense, and only the Diggers ('True Levellers') attempted to put a working commune into practice. Otherwise, the Levellers' programme demanded that supreme authority be vested in a representative body, which should be elected on the basis of a much wider franchise (all men of age except those totally unfree, such as domestic servants, apprentices and wandering beggars).[24] It also called for a considerable devolution of state power to local communities; legal and economic reforms in order to protect and benefit small men in town and country; and, last but not least, a complete freedom of religious worship and organisation.

Cromwell, however, was a practical politician and did not want to alienate people whom the Independents would need in the event of new parliamentary elections. Therefore, the army leaders stuck to the principle that they shared with most Parliamentarians, namely that only those who had 'a permanent fixed interest in this kingdom' (i.e. landed or industrial property) had the right to vote.[25] Thus, the Aristotelian-cum-Marxian contradiction *par excellence* ran through the very heart of the Independents' party. However, the Levellers' appearance as a significant factor within the revolution was a comparatively short one (1647–9).

Another extreme within the political-cum-religious spectrum was represented by the Fifth Monarchy Men, whose lack of realism, however, did not allow them to go beyond the claim that it was the saints who had to rule, and that in order to do so, they had to overturn all 'carnal' or worldly governments.

Interception, tightening and expansion

The seat of power oscillated only for a short time between the five groupings in the political spectrum. In November 1647, the Army Council was disbanded and, in January 1648, the leading Levellers were imprisoned. In August, the second civil war ended with a decisive defeat of the Royalist forces. In December the army entered London for the second time and purged Parliament of most of its Presbyterian members (Pride's Purge). In January 1649, Charles I was sentenced to death and executed. Between February and May the opposition of the Levellers in the army was suppressed and so, later, was the movement of the Diggers, who campaigned for social and economic equality. In March the House of Lords was abolished and in May 1649, England was proclaimed a commonwealth, i.e. a republic.

Thus the oscillating seat of the executive power was intercepted at the position of the revolutionary left. As the power basis of the Independents' government was rather narrow, the interception was followed by a considerable tightening of their rule. Yet, and this is significant, it did not go as far as in other revolutions. The judiciary preserved its traditional leanings towards independence; an outstanding example was the case of the leading Leveller, Lilburne, whom the jury twice found not guilty, despite strong political pressure in the opposite direction. On the whole, the number of political executions does not seem to have exceeded the pre-revolutionary norm. In comparison with the other revolutions under study, revolutionary terror was not practised in the core, in England, but on the periphery, in Ireland.

Also the expansion which soon followed was, in contrast to the Hussite and French revolutions, of a muted nature. It focused on what may be called dependent territories (Ireland and Scotland) rather than abroad. In Ireland, which was in fact an English colony, it took the form of a national and pan-Protestant venture: namely, the enforcement of English rule and Protestant domination against the insurrection of the Catholic Irish people. Scotland, which was united with England only through the personal union of the monarch, estranged itself, mainly from the Independents, by recognising Charles II as its king. Cromwell's campaign was aimed at bringing Scotland into line with the revolutionary establishment in England.

Only when these two campaigns within the British Isles were completed (May 1652) did England enter into conflict with foreign countries (June 1652). The war against the United Netherlands, which until then had been considered as the best friend of English Presbyterians and Independents, and as a kind of paradigm for them, shows how much commercial interests could upset ideological alliances. Only after this war had been won did a token of real expansion, still however on economic lines, take place. The war resulting from Spain's denial of free access for English ships to her colonies and her refusal to stop the persecution of English sailors by the Inquisition, ended with the English conquest of Jamaica and Dunkirk.

Cromwell's intercession on behalf of the persecuted Waldensians in the Duchy of Savoy aroused false hopes among the oppressed Protestants in other European countries. The issue as to whether overseas wars were to promote religion or commerce was resolved in favour of the latter alternative. The treaty with the strongest Protestant powers of Sweden and Denmark, countries that did not compete commercially with England to any great extent, was a merely cosmetic manifestation of Protestant unity.

Thus, in contrast to the Hussite revolution, where expansion was designed to bring the Church and Europe to negotiations, and in contrast to the French revolution where, at least in the original stage, the expansion was aimed at exporting the revolution, the expansion of the English Puritan revolution remained focused on limited aims: the securing within the British Isles of the religious, political and economic interests of the dominant party, and the promotion overseas of the economic interests of England as a whole. Instead of fighting the Catholic oppressors of the Protestants in European countries, as many zealots demanded, Puritan England fought – as *quid pro quo* – the Irish Catholics in their homeland, and subjected them not so much to a policy of mass conversion as to harsh economic exploitation and political discrimination. Economic nationalism unashamedly entered the stage, although some millenarian zealots among the Fifth Monarchists attempted to give it an appearance of a crusade against the kingdom of Antichrist.[26]

A successful expansion within the above-mentioned limits could not, however, solve the internal problems. During the ten-year period of interception (1649–59), England was ruled by the Independents with, until 1658, Oliver Cromwell at the helm. As neither the English constitutional tradition nor the country's political culture was favourable to autocratic rule, the problem was by what kind of more representative institution the country should be governed. The Rump Parliament, as it survived after Pride's Purge, enjoyed little prestige. A new Parliament composed of Cromwell's nominees – good Puritans but mainly of mediocre quality – proved ineffective. According to the new constitutional arrangement of 1653, which turned the 'Commonwealth' into the 'Protectorate', the national government was to be shared by the Lord Protector (Cromwell) and the House of Commons (elected on the basis of newly demarcated constituencies).

Yet in his relations with Parliament, the Lord Protector soon appeared to be in a cul-de-sac similar to that in which Charles I had found himself. The only significant differences were that Cromwell was in command of an efficient army and that his enemies were bitterly divided. On the right, the Presbyterian opposition was pushed towards an understanding with the supporters of the monarchy; on the left there was a considerable body of Independents favouring not only more equality or social justice but also less concentration of power in one person. There was a growing feeling that the revolutionary ideal had been perverted.

In this situation a new political grouping emerged at the national level, described by Woolrych as traditionalist Cromwellians. They stood for 'a mixed government and a balanced polity, against either personal autocracy or unlimited sovereignty claimed for Parliament by the Republicans',[27] and they opposed sectarian enthusiasm and military dominance over civil government. Although Cromwell tried to keep a balance between these people and his more radical, republican, followers, he was nevertheless pushed towards the position of his traditionalists. Although he rejected the offer of the Crown, the return to a bicameral Parliament and some disciplinary measures in the army heralded a shift towards a more central position within the revolutionary spectrum. In 1658, however, Cromwell's death prevented a further development in that direction.

Reversal and restoration compromise

Under Cromwell's son and heir, Richard, the pendulum shifted again to the left. In the spring of 1659 a *putsch* conducted by army officers enforced the dissolution of the new Parliament and the return of the old Rump Parliament from the time of the Commonwealth. After that, realising that he was only a 'cipher',[28] Richard Cromwell resigned. But the old quarrel between the army and the Rump soon flared up again. The Rump was again dispelled in October and again restored in December. London was sinking into anarchy.

In the general tangle of cross-currents some Presbyterians moved closer to the Royalists; the dissensions between the army leaders made it extremely difficult for the revived Commonwealth to follow a coherent policy. Meanwhile the army commander in Scotland, the Presbyterian General Monck, cautiously moved into the forefront of events. During his march on London, the opposition of dissenting army units collapsed. The purged members returned to the Rump Parliament and Monck was able to execute his grand design of reconciling the Presbyterians with the Court. On his advice Charles II made the Declaration of Breda which – like the Compacts of Basle – paved the way for a restoration compromise. No military defeat of the warriors of God was necessary, no parallel to the Battle of Lipany had to occur.

Why did the reversal proceed so smoothly? It seems that the power base of the Cromwellian establishment was all too narrow. For the propertied classes it had moved too far to the left, while for the common folk, it did not mean all that much. Both ends of the social stratification spectrum became estranged from it. The nobility and gentry, the bulk of the electorate, realised, as R.A. Beddard put it, 'that, in challenging the ancient structure of royal and episcopal authority, they have unwittingly struck at the foundations of their own power'.[29]

The Presbyterians found themselves not only excluded from the Protectorate's government, but also menaced in their ecclesiastical aspirations by the corroding spirit of the Nonconformist denominations. They hoped that a restored royal power, by way of recompense for their support, could help them to compromise with, and restructure, the Church of England. The Levellers and Diggers looked on Cromwell's policy as an act of betrayal and, having realised that any political, let alone military, action to promote their cause was doomed to failure, turned largely to the cultivation of the inner religious life; some of them became Quakers. The others, the masses – mostly uneducated people – had, in the words of J.R. Jones, been

> only briefly influenced by the revolutionary ideas of 1647–9. They had never had a chance to participate in political or electoral processes under any of the Interregnum régimes, so that apart from those purged in the corporations or disabled from acting as office-holders there, few men lost any political rights by the Restoration. For most humble people, all governments were a burden on their backs; the less they weighed the better. After 1660, there was far less actual government – no large army that required heavy direct or indirect taxation and yet continued to engage in requisitioning and free quarter. There were no special or extraordinary courts, no major-generals. People seldom thought that government intervention in their daily lives was intended for their benefit, or to increase the prosperity of the nation. Experience had taught them that under each successive régime the purpose was to confer special advantages on the favoured associates of those who controlled political power.[30]

Under these circumstances, the restoration compromise had a good chance of success as long as the king was willing to keep to its basic points. He did quite well in trying to help Presbyterians to find a *modus vivendi* with the Church of England and in promoting religious tolerance towards both Nonconformists and Catholics. Yet he failed because, for the reasons mentioned above, a decisive majority of the political nation, nobility and gentry, embraced Anglican Episcopalianism as their worldly salvation. Presbyterians were pushed towards the Nonconformists, together with whom they became hated and persecuted by the rising Anglican orthodoxy.[31] From the mid-1670s both had to look for protection to one of the two political groupings into which the English political nation became divided after the Restoration;[32] the Whig party was the only force that stood for some bits and pieces of the revolutionary heritage, while the Tories provided a suitable framework for the amalgamation of the counter-revolutionaries and the revolutionary right. As long as the king did not attempt to curtail their parliamentary power and their Episcopal Church, the compromise was secure; and it could have lasted much longer than the twenty years or so that it did. This was at any rate the longest period of uninterrupted restoration compromise in any of the revolutions under study here. The Habeas Corpus Amendment Act of 1679 can be considered one of the achievements of this period.

Restoration pressure and the consolidation overthrow

Yet the Stuarts moved into a new period of crisis. Not only was Protestant consciousness irritated by repeated attempts to extend indulgences for Catholics and to conclude alliances with Catholic powers, but the king's brother, James, heir apparent to the throne, converted to Catholicism. In such an atmosphere the Whigs, campaigning for the exclusion of James II, won two parliamentary elections. In 1681, Charles II responded by dissolving Parliament and, supported by the loyalty of the Tory party, started to rule in a more authoritarian way.

Only after James II took over from his deceased brother in 1685, and the restoration pressure gathered momentum, did the Tories decide in favour of their religion and parliamentary rights against their loyalty to the king. The sequence of events is well known – the extension of the army, the appointment of Catholic officers, and eventually the granting of equal rights for the Catholics, i.e. the virtual abolition of the Test Act, by which in 1673 the Tory Parliament had guaranteed the dominant position of Anglicans in the state service, based on the Uniformity Act of 1662. The response to this challenge was quick and resolute. The Tories abandoned the king, who of his own volition ceased to be theirs, and, jointly with the Whigs, called William of Orange, husband of James's elder daughter, to the English throne. The 'Glorious Revolution' of 1688, a consolidation overthrow *par excellence*, occurred without bloodshed. In 1689 the Bill of Rights and the Act of Toleration for the Nonconformist Protestants concluded, in a manifestative way, the sixty-year-long revolutionary process in seventeenth-century England. The course of this revolution in terms of our morphological model is shown in Figure 7.2 (page 195).

It remains to be evaluated what the consolidation brought about – what justifies the judgement that, after having run through its full cycle, the revolution was, at least in part, successful. We can perhaps summarise the main revolutionary achievements as follows.

The attempts at autocracy, whether by a monarch or a dictator, were utterly defeated. This achievement became a lasting one. In place of the absolute personal political power which had to go for good, however, another absolute power was enthroned, namely that of individual rights in general and of private property in particular. Whether we see in the latter an echo of the reception of the Roman law which from the sixteenth to the eighteenth centuries was taking place on the Continent, or whether we see in it the culmination of a domestic trend, a 'reinforcement of English institutions' as David Ogg might say,[33] we cannot fail to realise that all the crucial turning points (1649, 1660, 1688) in a way helped to strengthen the unlimited concept of private property.

This development paved the way for an unprecedented upsurge of economic efficiency. Its main advantages came to those who could exploit their solidified right of possession by their entrepreneurial skills. The aristocracy did well in the ensuing competition with the upstart newcomers. If we have to decide which class profited most from the Puritan revolution, we may say that it was the squirearchy which turned bourgeois and the bourgeois whose social status matched that of the squires. In socio-economic terms, the English Puritan revolution may be described as a revolution of gentlefolk.

But we must not forget religion, which in different ways provided the motivation and justification for different revolutionary or restorative actions. On the whole it may be said that the revolution performed a most valuable service for the Church of England. In its first round, it gave it a taste of discrimination or even oppression, treatment which any Church wanting to be worthy of the name badly needs for its legitimation. Then, in the second round, under the Restoration, the Church of England could not be prevented from taking its revenge on those who wanted to push it further than it wanted to go. The Glorious Revolution saved it from remaining too oppressive for too long; it had to accept some modification of its dominant position in allowing the true heirs of the revolution, the Puritans of Calvinist and Nonconformist hue, to recover some legal ground.

Although, despite the Toleration Act, the Nonconformists remained for some time under the shadow of one dominant established Church, almost like non-Islamic 'millets' in the Ottoman Empire, and although the Catholic minority survived under even more stringent limitations on its rights and practices, nevertheless in contrast to France at the time and to the Habsburg Empire, England's post-revolutionary religious pluralism was by no means a negligible socio-cultural achievement.

With the symbolic acts, such as the Bill of Rights and the Act of Toleration, however, developments in England had not yet reached that point that can be considered the final stage in the whole revolutionary process. The main principles that the revolution had established had not yet ceased to be matters of controversy. According to L. Stone's analysis, it took three more decades for the process of accommodation to be completed.[34] The danger of yet another restoration disappeared only when the succession in the Hanoverian line legalised by the Act of 1701 materialised (1714), and the Jacobite armed bid for power was defeated (1715). During the subsequent five years or so the tension between individual factions in the political nation (about a quarter of a million if the parliamentary vote can be taken as a yardstick) slackened to such an extent that they could be reasonably well contained within the generally accepted procedure of conflict regulation.

If we want to conclude this summary by pointing to some thinkers whose ideas contributed to, or reflected, the course and outcome of the English revolution, we may perhaps mention two theoreticians of the main opposing forces which clashed in the revolution: Locke versus Hobbes. Understood in these terms, the place of the English Puritan revolution in European history appears all the more significant.

Notes

1. C. Hill, *Puritanism and Revolution* (Secker & Warburg, London, 1965), p. 5.
2. C. Hill, *Change and Continuity in Seventeenth-Century England* (Weidenfeld & Nicolson, London, 1975), p. 279.
3. R.H. Tawney, *The Agrarian Problem in the Sixteenth Century* (Longman, London, 1912), p. 2.
4. *Ibid.*, pp. 12–14.
5. *Ibid.*, p. 14.
6. *Ibid.*, pp. 406–7.
7. L. Stone, *The Causes of the English Revolution, 1529–1642* (Routledge & Kegan Paul, London, 1972), p. 72.
8. C. Hill, *Intellectual Origins of the English Revolution* (Panther, London, 1972), p. 284.
9. *Ibid.*, p. 289.
10. Stone, *Causes*, p. 99.
11. *Ibid.*, p. 84.
12. The Paretian mutation can also be corroborated in terms of military skill. According to the evidence supplied by H. Miller (*The Early Tudor Peerage, 1485–1647*, MA thesis, 1950, p. 181) and L. Stone ('The crisis of the aristocracy', in *Social Change and Revolution in England, 1540–1640*, Longman, London, 1977), every able-bodied adult peer had seen service in the wars of the 1540s, but in 1576 only one peer in four had any military experience.
13. Cf. discussion on the English gentry reviewed, for instance, in L. Stone (ed.), *Social Change and Revolution in England, 1540–1640* (Longman, London, 1977) and R.C. Richardson, *The Debate on the English Revolution* (Methuen, London, 1977).
14. Stone, *Causes*, pp. 96 and 112.
15. *Ibid.*, p. 125.

16. *Ibid.*, p. 126.
17. R. Ashton, *The English Civil War: Conservatism and revolution 1603–1649* (Weidenfeld & Nicolson, London, 1978), p. 135.
18. M.A. Kishlansky, *The Rise of the New Model Army* (Cambridge University Press, London, 1979), p. 274.
19. A.H. Woolrych, *Battles of the English Civil War* (Batsford, London, 1961), p. 98.
20. W. Schenk, *The Concern for Social Justice in the Puritan Revolution* (Longman, London, 1948), p. 10.
21. J.H. Hexter, *Reappraisals in History* (Longman, London, 1961), pp. 163–84, and D. Underdown, *Pride's Purge: Politics in the Puritan Revolution* (Clarendon Press, Oxford, 1971), p. 2.
22. Kishlansky, pp. 278–80.
23. Ashton, p. 240.
24. Here I am following the interpretation by K. Thomas, 'The Levellers and the franchise', in G.E. Aylmer (ed.), *The Interregnum: The quest for settlement 1646–60* (Macmillan, London, 1972), pp. 57–78.
25. A.S.P. Woodhouse (ed.), *Puritanism and Liberty* (Dent, London, 1974), p. 53. Later, however, there was a tendency to compromise with the army leaders on this matter (*ibid.*, p. 357).
26. Even the Dutch War was seen in this light. Woolrych's summary of sermons of those days (1653) states that war 'was the doing of Providence, and it had a cosmic purpose: Holland was to be the landing-place for a march of conquest that was to end in Rome itself, when all the lesser seats of Antichrist had been destroyed'. A.H. Woolrych, *Commonwealth to Protectorate* (Clarendon Press, Oxford, 1982), pp. 286–7.
27. A.H. Woolrych, 'Last quests for a settlement 1657–1660', in G.E. Aylmer (ed.), *The Interregnum: The quest for settlement 1646–1660* (Macmillan, London, 1972), p. 187.
28. I. Roots, *The Great Rebellion 1642–1660* (Batsford, London, 1966), p. 241.
29. R.A. Beddard, 'The Restoration Church', in J.R. Jones (ed.), *The Restored Monarchy 1660–88* (Macmillan, London, 1979), p. 156.
30. J.R. Jones, 'Main trends in Restoration England', in J.R. Jones (ed.), *The Restored Monarchy 1660–88* (Macmillan, London, 1979), pp. 23–4.
31. Like so many other instances of religious persecution, this one, aimed at Puritans in general, also had its high and low points and its avenues of escape. For the ups and downs of the religious policy of the restoration, see for instance G.R. Cragg, *Puritanism in the Period of the Great Persecution, 1660–1688* (Cambridge University Press, London, 1957) and J.R. Western, *Monarchy and Revolution: The English State in the 1680s* (Blandford, London, 1972), pp. 156–238.
32. Oddly enough, as M.P. Schoenfeld has shown, it was from the House of Lords and not the House of Commons that the Nonconformists could obtain some protection against the vengeance of the super-orthodox Tories (M.P. Schoenfeld, *The Restored House of Lords*, Mouton, The Hague–Paris, 1967, p. 224).
33. D. Ogg, *England in the Reigns of James II and William III* (Clarendon Press, Oxford, 1955).
34. L. Stone, 'The results of the English revolutions of the 17th century', in J.G.A. Pocock (ed.), *Three British Revolutions: 1641, 1688, 1776* (Princeton University Press, NJ, 1980), pp. 75–89.

3

□

France (1776–1884)

Introductory remarks on the nature of the revolution

The French revolution which exploded in 1789 set in motion a process of social change which took almost a century to complete. Its consequences affected a much wider geographical area than did the two revolutions discussed so far. Furthermore, its occurrence provided empirical material and inspiration for the first theoretical ventures on the phenomenon of revolution, ventures which in their turn supplied the would-be revolutionaries of later days with a model from whose successes and failures they might be able to learn.

Like the epithet 'Puritan', as applied to the English revolution, the epithet 'bourgeois', by which the great French revolution has as a rule been characterised, became subject to scholarly criticism. This, however, was due mainly to the fact that the discussion centred on the issue of who made the revolution rather than who won it. Looking at the revolution from the latter angle and taking into account the whole time span during which the issues of that revolution remained alive, we find the label 'bourgeois' substantiated. This term, even if all possible qualifications are taken into account, pinpoints the salient feature of the complex social change which in the long run resulted from the revolution; namely, the substitution of wealth for birth (or ennoblement) as the main yardstick of social stratification.

Why, however, are we ready in this case to accept a socio-economic label as a characterising epithet, whereas in the case of the Czech and English revolutions we preferred an ideological-cum-political label? The reason is that there is no single term general enough to characterise this aspect of the French revolution. Nor is the terminology of the epoch of any help. In the first stages the supporters of revolution called themselves patriots and addressed each other as citizens.

Neither of these terms is typical enough to distinguish the French revolution from others. Furthermore, they do not apply throughout the whole length of the revolutionary process. Any other term, such as republican, liberal, or even Jacobin, would characterise only a part, one particular segment of the revolutionary spectrum. Oddly enough, the ideological content of the French revolution appears more diversified than that of the other two revolutions. Its common denominator can best be found with the help of socio-economic criteria.

In the long run the French revolution changed many things. It abolished the patrimonial concept of the monarchial state and attached all the attributes of power to the juridical construct of a nation-wide collectivity (the state), for the operation of which new rules had to be laboriously worked out, a process involving many setbacks and much in-fighting. The revolution imbued social institutions with the geometric principles of the Cartesian tradition, and set about turning France into an ethnically homogeneous whole in which, after a long period of vacillation, all citizens were placed at a formally equal distance from the legal person of the state, with its unprecedented prestige and power.

Within the new institutional framework citizens became engaged in a prolonged struggle on behalf of particular interpretations and realisations of the great principles of revolution: liberty, equality and fraternity. It was soon discovered that liberty and equality cannot always be squared with each other and that if fraternity has to bridge the gap between them, it must result in their mutual limitation. In short, the linkage of the three revolutionary slogans was bound to produce contradictions in their common implementation.

Despite this difficulty, several positive measures may be listed as already generally accepted in the first stages of the revolution: the abolition of judicial torture; religious tolerance; the enfranchisement of those subjected to seigneurial duties (and in some areas even serfdom); guaranteed property rights; and finally equality in law and taxation.

Within this general framework of changes there were two particular issues which were of paramount importance and which divided the revolutionaries and made the post-revolutionary consolidation particularly difficult. The first issue was how far the shift from privilege by birth to privilege by wealth should go; whether wealth should provide advantages only by its sheer social weight, or whether it should also bring privileges into the political sphere, in the form of a suffrage limited by a property census.[1]

The second bone of contention concerned the economic system, and in particular the question of whether the economy had to be left to the spontaneous regulation of supply and demand (free market), as the physiocrats wanted, or whether there should be some government control, especially of prices and supplies of staple consumer goods. Partisans of the second view often referred to Rousseau's principle that the enjoyment of property should be subordinate to the interests of society as a whole.

The class issue

Modern historiography on the French revolution has brought about a thorough, painstaking revision of what are seen as preconceived ideas or hasty general-isations.[2] The principal criticism concerns the thesis that the main underlying issue of the revolution was the class struggle between the bourgeoisie and the aristocracy. According to de Tocqueville's classical formulation, the crux of the matter really lay here:

> The French nobility had stubbornly held aloof from the other classes and had succeeded in getting themselves exempted from most of their duties to the community, fondly imagining they could keep their lofty status while evading its obligations. At first it seemed they had succeeded, but soon a curious internal malady attacked them, whose effect was, so to speak, to make them gradually crumple up, though no external pressure of any kind was brought to bear. The more their immunities increased, the poorer they became. On the other hand, the middle class (of being merged into which they were so much afraid) grew steadily richer and more enlightened without their aid and, in fact, at their expense. Thus the nobles, who had refused to regard the bourgeois as allies or even fellow citizens, were forced to envisage them as their rivals, before long as their enemies, and finally as their masters.[3]

This statement bears out both the Marxian and the Weberian elaboration of the issue. It reveals both the class contradiction and the disproportion between wealth, power and status as the main driving forces in the conflict.

The class interpretation (bourgeoisie versus aristocracy) has been subjected to serious criticism on grounds that can be summarised as follows: the bourgeoisie and the nobles were part of a propertied, land-owning élite and in many respects their interests coincided. This point has been put forward most forcefully by Cobban.[4] If there were tensions within the propertied classes, they affected only some of their particular sections, such as venal office-holders and the impoverished petty nobility which, as Lucas observed, was most hostile to the government of 1787–8.[5] Nor was the nobility unwilling to meet the bourgeoisie on their own terrain of economic enterprise.

Before the revolution, the most acute tension was between the royal administration and the privileged estates whose interests were protected by the regional juridical corporation known as *parlements*. The main bone of contention was the incidence and level of taxation. Attempts of the ministers of the Crown to increase the tax return by spreading its burden more evenly met with fierce opposition from the *parlements*, who used the traditional right to remonstrate against royal edicts; eventually, in order to stop the fiscal reform more effectively, they demanded the convening of the Estates General. Thus, as Theda Skocpol pointed out, they unwittingly opened the door to something more unpleasant, namely the revolution.[6]

Even Soboul, who otherwise adheres to the traditional Marxist dichotomy of class struggle between nobility and bourgeoisie, admits that within the latter class there were several groups, such as *roturiers*, *officiers* and even *la grande bourgeoisie financière*, which were all integrated, though to different degrees, into the traditional economic and social structure. In Soboul's view, only the commercial and industrial bourgeoisie, which suffocated within the ancient economic framework, consciously opposed the system.[7]

In Doyle's words, the pre-revolutionary bourgeoisie had no class consciousness, the ultimate aspiration of most of them being to become nobles.

> The bourgeois was not content to be what he was; a passenger on the social escalator, he was constantly shedding the traces of his low ancestry, all the time attempting to behave more and more like those he hoped he or his descendants might ultimately join.[8]

On the strength of these arguments, it seems that the bourgeois had to be shaken out of their 'quasi-feudal' mentality by the doctrinarians of revolution, by those less numerous but more influential ideologist-politicians recruited from and supported by what, in Cobban's terms, was the true revolutionary bourgeoisie, namely 'primarily the declining class of officers and the lawyers and other professional men'.[9] Their successes in the first years of revolution were striking. In the supreme representative bodies (whatever their official name of the day), it was the lawyers and various office-holders, mainly from outside Paris, who constituted the overwhelming majority.

But is this a sufficient reason to discard the epithet 'bourgeois' when attempting to characterise the French revolution? Does this argument invalidate the finding that, at the end of the day, power and prestige became more related to wealth than to birth? Furthermore, does the contradiction between aristocracy and bourgeoisie, or, to put it more succinctly, between aristocracy and timocracy, exhaust all the class contradictions that the French Revolution revealed?

There was yet another, perhaps even more grave, class contradiction in the French revolution, namely that between the bourgeoisie and the urban *menu peuple* (socio-economically lesser people), which on the political plane issued in a conflict between timocracy and democracy. Confrontations resulting from this contradiction opened up the second front of, or rather within, the revolution. Whereas in the Czech and English revolutions the extreme left made only a transient appearance, in the French Revolution it represented an undercurrent which on several occasions made an impact on the main course of events.

Blurred by the poverty line cutting across the divide between the small craftspeople and hired workforce, fenced off by the *loi le Chapelier*, the class-based struggle of the extreme left crept furtively onto the stage of revolution. Its harbinger was *la Grande Peur* in the countryside and peasant unrest. It appeared in the heart of events on the Champ de Mars on 17 July 1791, gathered momentum during the subsequent years of the high tide of revolution, became muted in the period of the Directory,[10] but broke out intermittently and at long intervals during the restoration monarchy. In June 1848 it issued in a short but tough civil war and in 1871 this type of conflict assumed still wider dimensions.

In this struggle the main issues were those two key controversies that divided the revolutionary forces most bitterly: the extent of property rights and the extent of suffrage. The first issue involved a struggle between those who stood for a completely free market and free enterprise and those who wanted their limitation by government intervention and the right of the workforce, whether employed or self-employed, to associate. This controversy remained an issue throughout the whole process of revolution; as it came to an end, the rights of property, free enterprise and a free market became safeguarded; the bourgeoisie was victorious.

The extent of suffrage during the whole process of revolution varied according to the type of the regime. Under the monarchy (including that from 1791–3) the issue was resolved according to the timocratic principle: vote and eligibility depended on a certain amount of tax paid, the amount being much higher for those eligible. Hence the French label 'la monarchie censitaire'. Under the republic, suffrage for legislative assembly was granted to all adult males (only insanity, criminal record, etc., were reasons for exclusion). Under the empire, this principle was preserved, but with the decline of the power of the legislative assembly it lost its practical meaning. The century from the end of the revolution (in our reckoning) to the time of writing has made universal suffrage the main avenue for attack on unlimited rights of property. In all these struggles for the heritage of the revolution there is a contradiction which invites both a Marxian and an Aristotelian interpretation.

A word has yet to be said about the contradiction between the productive forces and the mode of production, which is the other, more basic, form of the Marxian contradiction. Here the quest for facts and figures is much more difficult than in the case of the class contradictions. The crux of the matter is whether the *ancien régime* acted as a brake on the development of the productive forces, i.e. on the application of a new technology and new, more efficient methods of economic organisation. The scattered evidence points to the conclusion that the *ancien régime* was an irresolute supporter of economic progress rather than its opponent. There was a conscious drive for economic improvements which found its outlet in what G.V. Taylor has called 'the court capitalism',[11] but the complicated and inequitable structure of taxes, customs and seigneurial duties hampered their implementation. The abolition of these obstacles produced a new legal framework for faster economic development: accumulated funds were no longer squandered on buying offices, although landed property long remained the most cherished object of private investment. In contrast to contemporary England, private investment in industry and commerce developed at a much slower pace. The capitalist mode of production, if anything can be described in these terms, was, even more than the self-conscious bourgeoisie, a child of the later stages of the revolutionary process.

The attack on the Church and Christianity

The French revolution not only brought about a shift in worldly values; it also attacked the Christian beliefs that provided the transcendental orientation of the West European civilisation of that epoch. Understandably, the religious aspect of the French revolution was far less pronounced than in the case of the English and above all the Czech revolutions. The gradual transformation of the Latin Christian civilisation into a secular, utilitarian and individualistic civilisation of modernity[12] made considerable progress during the four centuries that separated the intellectual prelude of the Czech from that of the French revolution. Nevertheless, towards the close of the eighteenth century, God, in the traditional garb of the established Christian Churches, was far from dead, and the revolutionaries had to take up a stance towards Him.

As in fourteenth-century Bohemia, so too in eighteenth-century France the religious needs of the population were catered for almost exclusively by the Catholic Church. In contrast to pre-Hussite Bohemia, however, the Catholic Church in pre-revolutionary France did not enjoy exclusive command over people's minds. Its victory over Calvinist heresy and the Jansenists' softening of orthodoxy had sapped too much of its spiritual energy to leave it strong enough to withstand the onslaught of the Enlightenment. The revolution encountered the Church in a position that had been weakened and even undermined, especially in those circles such as the upper nobility that were supposed to be its faithful supporters.

In that respect there was a similarity to the position of the Anglican Church on the eve of the Puritan revolution. Yet whereas in the English revolution the alternative to the established orthodoxy was yet another, more determined, brand of Christian belief and practice, in the French case all the avenues for such an alternative were apparently exhausted. Not only the Roman Catholic Church as an institution but Christianity as a world-view in general was challenged.

The anti-Christian movement culminated in November 1793 in the declaration of the cult of the Supreme Being manifested in festivals and temples of Reason, in non-Christian names given to children and, most conspicuously, in the secular calendar, and, last but not least, in the cult of *saints, patriotes et martyrs de la liberté*.[13] Yet the anti-Christians themselves were not united: the straightforward atheists were opposed by deists who eventually won the upper hand under Jacobin rule.

The confrontation of the state with the Church in matters of wealth and power, however, was much more serious than the confrontation of deistic or atheistic thought with Christian tenets. As in the Czech revolution, the confiscation of Church property was an important element of the revolutionary struggle; the acknowledgement, in principle, of these confiscations by those concerned substantially contributed in due course to the restoration compromise. Furthermore, the attempt to detach the clergy from their head abroad (the pope) and to subordinate them to the authority of the lay state resulted in a kind of schism, a split into constitutional and refractory priests. This split embittered ecclesiastical life long after the anti-clerical policy of the government had been lifted.

The frontal assault on Christianity did not last long. After the failure of experiments with theophilanthropy and the decadary cult, the Directory lost interest in an official state religion. It disestablished the constitutional Church and, while the lay state confirmed its religious neutrality, the refractory priests were allowed to hold private worship provided they had taken the *petit serment* of loyalty to the Republic.

During his consulate and his first years as emperor, Napoleon continued with a policy of compromise. But his autocratic bent – reviving more strongly than ever the aspirations of French kings to be in command of a Gallican Church – led him to a renewed confrontation with Rome, which after a period of papal concessions (marked by the concordat of 1802) culminated in the pope being made the emperor's prisoner in 1809. Fortunately for the pope, Napoleon's defeat in the Russian campaign put an end to what looked almost like an echo of the great struggle for investiture six or seven centuries earlier. As then, so again now, the papacy survived its imperial counterpart. The half-military, half-monastic lay education of boys introduced by Napoleon was short-lived. With the restoration, education was again taken over by the clergy.

The Second Republic did not last long enough to implement its programme of lay education. The Second Empire, being in need of clerical support and wanting to detach the French clergy from their loyalty to the pope, was ready to make them concessions, and entrusted to them all primary and also much secondary education. The clerical monopoly of education was broken only in 1882, when compulsory primary education was introduced by law (Jules Ferry) and a network of secular state schools began to be built all over the country.[14] Yet the secular, pluralistic civilisation, whose birth was so vigorously helped by the French revolution, had not established its own monopoly; the Churches were allowed to run their own education system. The issue was recently revived, on the occasion of the centenary of the Jules Ferry reform, by the socialist government under President Mitterrand, but seems to have been resolved in favour of continuing pluralism in the spiritual sphere.

Multiple dysfunction and the main fronts in the revolution

In our quest for individual elements of the multiple dysfunction preceding and/or accentuating the French revolution, we may be helped by the quintuple structure mapped onto the revolution by Lefebvre.[15] The first four revolts or, as he put it, 'revolutions', are extrapolated from Mathiez's account: first, in 1787, the aristocratic revolution against the Court; second, in 1789, the revolution of the Third Estate against the prerogatives of the first two Estates; third, in August

1792, the democratic and republican revolution against the compromise tendencies within the National Assembly; and fourth, in June 1793, the social democratic revolution supported by the plebeian masses against the lack of concern for their needs.

To this scheme based on Mathiez, Lefebvre added a fifth revolution, that of the peasants, which occurred independently of the main causes and political events of the overall revolutionary process. The beginnings of the peasants' revolution can be dated to March 1789 and its final eruptions traced up to 1793. In Lefebvre's view this revolution was also autonomous in its results. Without it the Constituent Assembly would not have gone as far as it did in the famous night session of 4 August, when it solemnly abolished the remnants of feudalism: seigneurial dues and privileges, venality of judicial offices and other inequities. However, many exemptions from that law, as well as the imposition of redemption payments, reduced the practical impact of that abolition. Only on 17 July 1793, after continued peasant unrest and riots in the countryside, was a new law passed cancelling most of these limitations.

Within our morphological framework, the five 'revolutions' are particular, ramifying features of the compression, explosion and oscillation phases of the French revolution. In terms of our etiological considerations they reflect contradictions, most of which have already been discussed by de Tocqueville. Although since de Tocqueville's day the knowledge of the causes and the course of the French revolution has considerably increased, some of his observations require only slight qualification.

What we have described as the Tocquevillian contradiction is only one point in his analysis. In its economic aspects it has been modified by Labrousse.[16] According to his findings there was, during the forty years between 1730 and 1770, a period of sustained economic growth which, however, came to an abrupt end with the beginning of the 1770s. A period of bad harvests led to a protracted economic depression lasting – with minor interruptions – until the outbreak of revolution. Expectations, however, continued to rise, not only because people had become accustomed to the upward trend but also because, as a result of criticism, people were becoming increasingly aware of structural injustices in the social system.[17] The tension was aggravated by the fact that the government decided to follow the advice of the physiocrats and embarked on a policy of *laissez-faire* at the very moment when the boom gave way to a protracted depression; thus the decontrol of the supply of grain and bread resulted in an unprecedented increase in the price of these staple commodities.[18]

The salience of individual fronts in the revolution fluctuated according to the many coups and reverses, in which the different level of determination sometimes played a decisive role. Historians have pointed out the king's indecision or even weakness at several critical moments. Whether Louis XVI behaved like a Paretian fox may be disputed, but he was certainly not a prototypical lion. (To test the Paretian mutation among the sovereign rulers we would be obliged to go back as far as the accession of Louis XV to the throne.) On the other hand, the hardening of attitudes among the revolutionaries, culminating in their sending each other to the guillotine, may be viewed as an example of the opposite behaviour mutation.

Finally, the armed struggle brought the Khaldunian contradiction into the open. On the whole, with several qualifications, the fighting spirit of the revolutionary armies proved superior to the traditional recruits. As in the Hussite revolution, however, this contrast operated more against the foreign enemies than against the domestic ones. The counter-revolutionary peasants of the Vendée and Britanny showed a fighting spirit and determination which can by no means be considered as inferior to that of the revolutionaries. On the contrary, the Vendéean armies proved to be more consistent in their enthusiasm.

Yet it seems that the *esprit de corps* in the French revolutionary army was more rapidly affected by disturbing influences than was the case in the Czech and English revolutionary armies. The *levée en masse*, which in practice meant conscription of those who could not buy themselves off, brought to the army people without any ideological or martial motivation. Although there was much spontaneous enthusiasm, so that the army indeed became a great school of patriotism,[19] there were also frequent desertions. As the army had to live off the country it made little difference whether its soldiers came to suppress the counter-revolutionaries, or to liberate the would-be revolutionaries in neighbouring countries. It seems that it was mainly the tremendous military successes that helped to overcome the difficulties arising out of these circumstances. Exporting revolution by force of arms, however, proved a failure.[20]

In terms of political differentiation, France's revolutionary century was much more variegated than that of any other revolution in our study. This, however, was a matter of nuances rather than of basic political positions which remained, with only slight modifications, fairly stable throughout the whole revolutionary process. Ranging from the right to the left, and divided into three periods demarcated by the main turning points, the main political positions can be approximately assessed as shown in Table 3.1.

The supporters of the restored monarchy were divided with respect to their loyalty to one or other of the two branches of the Bourbon house. Supporters of the imperial regime were a kind of hybrid within the fivefold spectrum. The position of Napoleon I can be located somewhere between the revolutionary centre and the revolutionary right; that of Napoleon III was rather between the revolutionary centre and the revolutionary left. Girondists and Jacobins were people of basically the same socio-economic and socio-cultural complexion. Only the occasional, tactical cooperation with the *sans-culottes* gave the Jacobins a slight populist flavour. A similar nuance of orientation can be observed with respect to the Bonapartists and republicans in phase 3. Unlike the other political groupings the extreme left was not strong enough to make its internal dissensions visible.

Within this time span the morphology of the French revolution can be visualised as shown in Figure 7.3 (page 197) and in the adjoining chronological table.

Table 3.1 Spectrum of political differentiation in the French revolution

	Phase 1 (1789–99)	Phase 2 (1800–48)	Phase 3 (1848–71)
For *ancien régime*	Aristocratic opposition, Royalists	–	–
		Legitimists	–
Revolutionary right	*Feuillants*		
Revolutionary centre	Girondists	Orleanists, Bonapartists	Liberals, Bonapartists
Revolutionary left	Jacobins		Republicans
Extreme left	Enraged, Babuvists		Democrat-socialists

From onset to oscillation

The onset of the French bourgeois revolution can be dated to the middle of the eighteenth century, when the growing irreligious bent among intellectuals manifested itself in the work on the French Encyclopaedia. The period of nearly thirty years from 1751 to 1780 was a phase of mental ferment. Towards its close, in 1778, Voltaire and Rousseau died, each of whom had substantially contributed to the shift in values. Eight years earlier a prolonged period of sustained economic growth had come to an end. In 1776 Turgot, pushed by his physiocratic supporters, attempted a moderate reform of the inequitable tax system but, confronted with aristocratic opposition, had to resign. In 1778 France started its military intervention in favour of the British–American colonies in their struggle for independence. The war was financed mainly by growing debts, the accumulated amount of which reached disastrous proportions by 1786. This precipitated the confrontation: in 1787 Calonne's attempt to resolve the financial crisis by fiscal reform was foiled by the combined forces of aristocratic opposition and inter-ministerial rivalry. There thus began what Mathiez described as the aristocratic revolt, and what in our model has been conceived as a phase of compression.

The institutionalisation of the revolutionary forces took place in a similar way to that of the English revolution. The king, being in dire financial need, had to deal with what were then considered to be the representatives of the country, i.e. the Estates General. Unlike the English Parliament, however, the Estates General were a rather obsolete institution, and were therefore more susceptible to innovation. Deputies for the Third Estate were elected by delegates of local communities, where all male taxpayers over 25 could vote. Also at their meetings, lists of local grievances (*cahiers de doléances*) were drawn up. The claim of the elected representatives of the Third Estate to represent the nation at large was the crux of what may be metaphorically called a constitutional revolution: it was to have grave social consequences. The constitutional revolution, however, had to be helped by a real explosion of revolutionary forces. In asking the Constituent Assembly to dissolve and in forcing Necker, whom people considered as a guarantor of a low-price policy, to resign, Louis XVI himself pulled the trigger. The result was the uprising in Paris and the conquest of the Bastille, the main prison of the city. Nothing could better symbolise the outbreak of revolution.

Once the king had capitulated on the constitutional issue, albeit with mental reservations, dual power or sovereignty was legally established. Unlike in England, however, it did not lead to a full-scale civil war; the political struggle took instead the form of a chess game, with only the occasional display of force in which the king tended always to be the loser. A more consistent Paretian fox than his Stuart counterpart, Louis XVI survived for barely four years after the explosion, whereas Charles I managed to fight and manoeuvre for nine years after the confrontation had begun. Thus in France the symbolic destruction of the *ancien régime* – the execution of the king – entered into the rising tide of oscillation, while in England it coincided with a later phase of interception.

Of the three revolutions discussed so far, the oscillation in the French revolution had the fastest pulsation, but with that hectic rhythm it was short-lived, lasting barely four years. Although for some observers the revolution ended with the Thermidor of 1794, and for others with the Brumaire of 1799, in terms of our model the struggle for the shape of post-revolutionary France experienced only its first decade. During that period not only the extreme left but also the main left (the Jacobins) were eliminated for a long time from the political contest.

The plebeian masses who were not represented by the main political parties of the 1790s appeared on the stage of revolution right from the beginning. The peasantry rioted before the conquest of the Bastille and the first clash between the revolutionary forces of order on the one hand and the radicals on the other occurred on 17 July 1791. In N. Hampson's words:

> The 'massacre' of the Champ de Mars marked the end of the period when it was possible to think of the Revolution in Paris as a united movement against the aristocracy. Bailly, at his trial in 1793, described the agitators of July 1791 as 'the people, above all, those who wanted liberty for all, who were determined that the prestige of the two defeated orders should not be annexed by one section known as the bourgeoisie'. It is significant that this sharp class distinction, which impressed contemporary observers, should have arisen over an issue that had no immediate relevance to social or economic policy. A new line had been drawn in blood between those who were prepared to make concessions to the *ancien régime*, to restore order and end the Revolution and those who were not, and who now classed the conservative revolutionaries among the enemies of the nation – and the forces of order had shot and sabred more men in one day than the Parisian crowds had lynched in the first two years of the Revolution. In Paris, although not to the same extent in the provinces, the defence of a largely bourgeois revolution was already passing into the hands of *sans-culottes*, while the majority of the bourgeois leaders were now prepared to offer to the king the concessions they had refused in 1789, lest they should be pushed towards political democracy and the social levelling that they expected it to bring. The Champ de Mars affair both revealed and accelerated this division.[21]

From then on, for several successive years, the late spring or summer in Paris became a season of gradual shifts of the seat of power from the right to the left. Those nightmares of the Comte de Clairmont-Tonnère, the '*oscillations populaires*', became reality.[22] French historiography describes the dramatic turning points in the revolution simply as '*les journées*'.

On 10 August 1792 a Paris uprising speeded up the deposition of the king and new elections were ordered on the basis of universal male suffrage. The declaration of the Republic followed on 22 September. Two days earlier, at Valmy, the tide of the war against foreign intervention turned in France's favour.

In late spring (31 May–2 June) of 1793 the government of the Girondists – the revolutionary centre – was overthrown by a Paris uprising, and the Jacobins – the revolutionary left – took over. In contrast to other revolutions the rule of the revolutionary left was short-lived – barely fourteen months. That short period, however, was conspicuous by virtue of its unprecedented dynamic. During that time the innovative impulses seem to have known no limits: not only a new state but also a new religion was to be installed. Terror became the main weapon of the government, which purported to embody the general will as conceived by Rousseau. The plebeian masses enforced some concessions, deviations from the economic principle of *laissez-faire*, but their political representatives were either thrown into prison (e.g. J. Roux, who eventually died there), or guillotined (e.g. Hébert). Thus, as in the Hussite and Puritan revolutions, forces of the extreme left were suppressed by their next of kin in the revolutionary spectrum.

From oscillation to reversal

Calvinist Puritans were not alone in denying the plebeian masses the right to revolt. The philosophy of the physiocrats led to similar conclusions. As Cobban has put it, 'the revolution was to be more ruthless than the *ancien régime* in its refusal to admit that the populace had any legitimate grievances, or that any government action was needed to remedy them'.[23] In vain the *sans-culottes* and their political spokesmen referred to Rousseau's claim that the enjoyment of property rights was subordinate to the interests of society. All factions, from the constitutional monarchists on the right to the Jacobins on the left, were against government intervention in economic matters, and were appalled by the prospect of a possible redistribution of landed property to the benefit of small peasants.[24]

Towards the end of July 1794 the Jacobin rule was overthrown; the disappointed *sans-culottes* did not come to the aid of Robespierre and Saint-Just. Subsequently an attempt was made to intercept the seat of power at the position of the revolutionary centre, which from the beginning of the revolution had been represented mainly by the Girondist faction. A new constitution of 1795 re-emphasised the timocratic principle; the suffrage for a bicameral Legislative Assembly was limited by a property census. Although elected by the legislative chambers, the five-member supreme executive, the Directory, assumed sweeping powers which enabled it to interfere with the election results.

In spite of all these authoritarian measures, the political oscillation was not brought under control. In the late spring of 1795 there was a leftist uprising, followed in October by an uprising organised by the Royalists. In May 1796 the extreme left tried for the second time, but their plot, the Conspiracy of the Equals, led by Babeuf, was uncovered and suppressed. A year later the monarchists were successful in the national election but the Directory, afraid of their political take-over, undertook a kind of Pride's Purge against them (the *coup d'état* of 18 Fructidor, Year V). The spring elections of 1798 brought electoral success for the left, the Jacobins, and again the Directory's response was a purge of about a hundred of their deputies from the National Assembly (the *coup d'état* of 22 Floréal, Year VI). In the 1799 elections the left was again successful; the Jacobins won a majority, and eventually forced some personal changes in the Directory and attempted to set up a tougher revolutionary regime. The centre became alarmed and looked for a general who might help them to change the constitution.

All these oscillations at the top of the power pyramid could not be without effect on the mood in the country. The government was not in a position to safeguard order and the security of its subjects. It seems that in Year VIII the situation was at its worst: in Ponteil's words, this was a year of disorder, robbery, demoralisation and crime. The army sent to fight the brigands itself often indulged in pillage. The law was largely held in disrespect and the instability of the conditions of life, both material and otherwise, caused much suffering.[25]

Then came the return from Egypt of Napoleon, and his emergence as the most suitable candidate for enforcing a tightening of the republican regime. The result was the famous *coup d'état* of 18 Brumaire, Year VIII. The seat of power was intercepted at what to begin with appeared to be the position of the centre but was gradually shifted to a personal rule somewhere between the centre and the right of the revolutionary spectrum.

The phenomenon of personal rule is by no means peculiar to the French revolution. The closer we get to the mass society of modernity, the more successful and long-lasting it becomes as an element of revolutionary processes. In the Hussite revolution it appeared in the rather muted form of the ascendancy of the military commander-in-chief, Prokop the Shaven; in the English revolution it assumed the form of the Lord Protector; in France it surpassed both in splendour by creating an emperor. But even his imperial purple was, in terms of real power, but a thin veil when compared with the power enjoyed by Stalin in the Russian revolution.

Napoleon's regime was a hybrid stricken by paradoxes. Its very success was the main cause of its own undoing. Born of a republic which was unable to solve the contradictions within its own power base, Napoleon's regime preserved its trappings for a while, until the advantage of established law and order and national prestige on an unprecedented scale made the vestiges of a republic dispensable. Meanwhile, to the notables of wealth, whose privileges continued to be respected, were added notables of merit (*les collèges électoraux, les sénatoreries* and, above all, *la légion d'honneur*), and eventually a new, imperial aristocracy. On the other hand, the aristocrats of the *ancien régime*, provided they wanted to fit in, were invited to return. Thus the republican principle was amply abrogated, while at the same time the opening of new channels of social mobility made the social stratification of French society less rigid. Timocracy, meritocracy and a twofold hereditary aristocracy constituted an interlocked pluralism of élites which, in the context of France's ambition to become a highly developed great power, opened the door to yet another type of élite – the technocratic one.

All these new élites, however, had to accept their place within the elaborate hierarchical structure of power. Their activities were encouraged, provided that their aims coincided with Napoleon's wishes. None of the different bodies – the Senate, the Legislative Assembly, the Tribunate and the State Council – was representative of the nation; their members were appointed or at least had to be approved by the autocrat. Their function was purely consultative; they were supposed to provide the ruler with an expert opinion and to work out projects approved or decided on by him. Only when military fortune seemed to have abandoned Napoleon for good did these people dare to behave independently.[26]

Napoleon's economic policy was also a kind of hybrid. Although adhering to the principle of *laissez-faire*, which put employers in a stronger position than employees, in times of economic crisis Napoleon did not hesitate to embark on a sort of Keynesian policy of public works. Being a thorough pragmatist, Napoleon did not fall victim to any ideology, except that of his own glorification. In pursuing the latter aim, he ceased to be a pragmatist. Pushing expansion to the extreme, he overstretched the resources of his own nation and also the power of his own genius.

Although, under Napoleon, France lost its bid for the domination of Europe, its main revolutionary achievement – a modern nation-state, well-equipped with bureaucratic, military and educational facilities – received its most effective elaboration.

From reversal to the first consolidation

The restoration in France was not the outcome of internal policies as in England or Bohemia, but primarily a result of defeat in a foreign war.

The restoration compromise, the beginning of which was interrupted by Napoleon's short-lived return to power, lasted with some minor fluctuations throughout the whole of the reign of Louis XVIII. Even Charles X's rule started with the observance of this compromise but the tendency to embark on a full-fledged restoration (restoration pressure) soon became apparent. The Charles's Four Ordinances of 1830 precipitated the crisis.

In terms of our model, the so-called July revolution can be considered the first consolidation overthrow in the French revolutionary process. During the subsequent eighteen years, the seat of power was located approximately at the position of the revolutionary centre. The parallel with the Glorious Revolution of 1688 in England and with George of Poděbrady's conquest of Prague in 1448 is obvious. But as will be seen later, Louis-Philippe's regime did not bring about a final consolidation. Given the amplitude of the French revolution, an English-type or Czech-type consolidation was not enough.

The restoration compromise met a considerable number of bourgeois demands. Wealth continued to play a more important role than birth in social stratification. As de Sauvigny put it, 'the three-hundred-franc voters and the thousand-franc candidates formed a new privileged class in the nation'.[27] This, in combination with a wider access to higher education, provided a broader channel of upward social mobility than there had been under the *ancien régime*. On the other hand, the restoration regime adopted without modification the laws by means of which the revolutionary regime safeguarded the economic principle of *laissez-faire* and the unequal position of employers and employees before the law.

The consolidation overthrow of 1830 was a further step in the strengthening of the timocratic *vis-à-vis* the aristocratic power base. Louis-Philippe's rule was a bourgeois monarchy *par excellence*, with a slightly enlarged basis of power. Male suffrage was extended to a lower census level, from 300 down to 200 francs for an elector; from 1,000 down to 500 francs for the candidates. But what was of greater importance was that France embarked on a process of industrialisation. Railway construction provided the main impetus, and the investment multiplier produced the well-known Keynesian effect, but eventually the expansionist intentions outstripped the available financial resources.

In Girard's account,[28] the sequence of events was as follows. From 1842 state aid to companies accelerated the building of the railway network, which in its turn spurred on speculation which surpassed the potential of the capital market. In 1845 a financial crisis broke out. On top of that, in 1846 large-scale inundations, a bad harvest and an increase in food prices had a severe impact on the population in large areas of France. Some areas, however, were not affected at all and the subsequent year, 1847, brought a good harvest and a drop in prices. Only industry seems to have suffered a period of stagnation, which as far as the working class was concerned affected wages rather than the cost of living. Although the distress was not general, the prestige of the regime received a severe blow. As it operated on a basis of compromise between the different factions of right and centre, it was susceptible to breakdown when some factions became dissatisfied. At the beginning of 1848, people who expected more from the regime than it had delivered, turned to the issues which had been put aside by the compromise but which had not been forgotten. Demands were voiced for a more representative government. The revolution acquired a new lease of life.

The second turn of the revolution

The collapse of the Orleanist regime in February 1848 once again threw open the issues which had apparently been dormant during the preceding twenty-three years. The Second Republic decided to extend its power base by reintroducing universal suffrage. The replacement of a timocratic by a democratic principle seemed to result from a new coalition, or rather compromise, between the bourgeoisie and the lower classes in town and countryside. This, however, proved to be a non-starter, especially as far as the urban proletariat was concerned.

The year 1848 was one of several paradoxes. In February a violent overthrow of the monarchy took place, which, however, cost little blood. A more serious event was the subsequent civil war in Paris in June, in which those who wanted to carry the revolution further were defeated. A repetition of the Champs de Mars confrontation of 1791 occurred on a much larger scale. Thus the Second Republic, which in February was installed with the help of the working people of Paris, suppressed these very people four months later.

Surprisingly but understandably, universal male suffrage, which increased the number of those entitled to vote from about a quarter of a million to more than nine million, strengthened the position of the conservatives. Even in Paris the candidates of the left, such as Ledru Rollin and Louis Blanc, fared rather badly, despite their notoriety.[29] Furthermore, the Second Republic provided a framework for rallying the different factions of the right and centre into a workable alliance. As Thiers put it, 'la république est le régime qui nous divise le moins'.[30]

Yet although not only Thiers but also others, including de Tocqueville, believed that a republic without republicans might prove viable, in the event it did not. The Second Republic got into difficulties similar to those of the first one. The basis of popular support became too narrow. The masses, especially those in the countryside, which constituted the decisive majority of the electorate, preferred a strong hand at the helm; they wanted somebody appealing enough to arouse popular enthusiasm and above all to assure the stability of their holdings, economic conditions and social status. For this purpose, the combination of some sort of populism with a quasi-dynastic prestige proved to be the most effective. Thus it came about that in December 1848, after all the avenues for parliamentary compromise had been exhausted, Louis-Napoleon was elected president of the Republic by a three-quarters majority. By a *coup d'état* in December 1851, he changed the presidency into a virtual dictatorship and in December 1852 he assumed the title of emperor. In both instances the deed was approved by a plebiscite.

The parallel with Napoleon I is obvious, but the differences are significant. Napoleon III learned from the mistakes of his illustrious uncle, and tried to bolster his personal rule with some conspicuously democratic features. He understood that, as de Sauvigny put it, 'the more dictatorial a régime is, the more it needs the support of the uneducated masses'.[31] The universal manhood suffrage which he had to make a permanent feature of French policy, proved to be an ingenious device for transforming the political mood of the silent majority into a limited and occasional political activity. Moreover, in contrast to the First Empire, the pre-1830 restoration regime and the Second Republic, which all became more rigid with the passage of time, the Second Empire moved towards a more liberal type of government.[32] Furthermore, the election activity provided, as Campbell said, 'an apprenticeship for the Republicans who in 1848 had failed to sell their programme on any vast scale'.[33]

In his economic policy, too, Napoleon III was more imaginative than his predecessor. As Blanchard and Girard put it, Louis-Napoleon forged a partnership with the Saint-Simonians rather than with *laissez-faire* people. This resulted in a policy focused on the construction of a national railroad network and on the development of a banking system capable of providing a modern economy with sufficient capital.[34] When in 1856 the boom, which had largely been propelled by speculation, came to an end, and private initiative slackened, the government stepped in. In 1860 it started a diversified programme of public works, such as urban renewal, construction of roads and canals, land reclamation and reafforestation financed largely by deficit spending. Yet the political liberalisation which was in progress at the same time encouraged rather orthodox fiscal policies and more respect for autonomous market forces.

On the whole, it can be assumed that the Second Empire was a period of considerable economic growth in which, however, different groups of the population participated very unevenly. Although the living standards of the working class increased as well, the growth of the real income and wealth of the middle and especially upper classes was incomparably higher. The yawning socio-economic gap between the classes contradicted the principle of political equality embodied in universal suffrage. A sense of relative deprivation of an aspirational type was bound to add fuel to the time-honoured tensions. These tensions, however, did not bring the regime down. What did was – as in the case of Napoleon I – the hubris of imperial prestige, the overestimation of national military capacity, which led to defeat in a foreign war. Then the Republic got its third opportunity.

In order for a republican parliamentary regime to be established in France, the great revolutionary process had to undergo a twofold cycle. The basic stages of the revolutionary process had to be repeated: explosion (1789 and 1848), tightening (two imperial regimes, each falling in a foreign war), restoration (1814 and 1815) and consolidation overthrow (1830 and 1870). The Republic, which twice failed to establish itself and collapsed under its own internal tensions (1799 and 1852), however, got a third turn in 1870, when it managed to consolidate itself for a long time. A corollary of this threefold rally was a threefold rout of those who did not want a republic as a political framework for free market forces, but a republic as a political framework for the promotion of social welfare.

The dramatic confrontations of the Parisian plebeians with their upper-class opposites in 1793, 1848 and 1871 revealed a contradiction which can be described in both Marxian and Aristotelian terms. Beyond any doubt, these confrontations resulted from different class interests, but the fact that they became increasingly acute was a result of changing value orientations. The hierarchical structure of society considered natural by the *ancien régime* and also by the First Empire only gradually lost support in people's minds. The electoral equality brought by the revolutionary left and eventually established by the Second Empire called into question the acceptance of hierarchical structures in the socio-economic sphere. Once the principle of electoral equality won the day, the limited scope for satisfying those who expected from democracy not only equal rights but also equal opportunities, became apparent.

The dramatic opening up of this issue by the Paris Commune heralded a new phase in French, and also to a large extent European, history. At the time of writing the main elements of this phase are still with us. The French revolution, understood as a long-term process lasting about a century, re-established the rule of the propertied classes, but in a less determined and safeguarded form than that pertaining under the *ancien régime*. Neither birth nor wealth remained legal conditions of political status. But two important measures which helped the non-propertied classes to increase their chances beyond mere equality before the law, i.e. universal primary education and the abolition of laws prohibiting workers' associations, were introduced only at the dawn of a new, post-revolution era of history; in 1882 and 1884 respectively. At the same time, the idea of lay education as the most important corollary of a lay state won the day. The main elements of the transformation of European civilisation were completed. France happened to be the country in which this transformation occurred in a most dramatic and manifest way, but its impact resounded all over Europe, and its last echo was the so-called February revolution of 1917 in Russia.

Notes

1. Although with respect to the political circumstances of the time the right to vote was not necessarily meaningful (the first elections after the introduction of universal suffrage brought barely a 10 per cent turn-out and in later instances the highly-centralised executive power had ample opportunity for manipulation), its long-term implications must not be underestimated.
2. For a concise overview of that debate, see the first chapter in W. Doyle, *Origins of the French Revolution* (Oxford University Press, London, 1980) appositely entitled 'A consensus and its collapse: Writings on revolutionary origins since 1939' (pp. 7–40).
3. A. de Tocqueville, *The Ancien Régime and the French Revolution* (Fontana Library, Manchester, 1969), pp. 157–8.
4. A. Cobban, *The Social Interpretation of the French Revolution* (Cambridge University Press, London, 1968).
5. C. Lucas, 'Nobles, bourgeois and the origin of the French Revolution', in D. Johnson (ed.), *French Society and the Revolution* (Cambridge University Press, London, 1976), p. 95.
6. T. Skocpol, *States and Social Revolutions* (Cambridge University Press, London, 1979), p. 62.
7. A. Soboul, *Comprendre la révolution* (Maspero, Paris, 1981), pp. 30–1.
8. W. Doyle, *Origins*, pp. 130–1.
9. A. Cobban, *Aspects of the French Revolution* (Norton, New York, 1970) pp. 110–11.
10. In Lefebvre's view, this was due to the coincidence of good harvests and a period of deflation during which the workers were in a position to defend their wages (G. Lefebvre, *The Directory*, Routledge & Kegan Paul, London, 1965, p. 153).

11. G.V. Taylor, 'The Paris Bourse on the eve of the Revolution, 1781–1789', *American Historical Review*, vol. LXVII, 1962, pp. 976–7.
12. This description is only a substitute for an appropriate name for that civilisation. For what is suggested as a more apposite label, see my article 'Civilisation and religion', *Religion*, vol. 12 (1982), pp. 29–47.
13. Cf. a telling account in A. Soboul, *Paysans, sans-culottes et Jacobins* (Claureuil, Paris, 1966), pp. 183–202.
14. For an analysis of this breakthrough, see for instance A. Prost, *Histoire de l'enseignement en France 1800–1967* (A. Colin, Paris, 1968).
15. G. Lefebvre, 'Die französische Revolution und die Bauern', in W. Grab and H. Koplenig (eds), *Die Debatte um die französische Revolution* (Nymphenburger Verlag, Munich, 1975).
16. C.E. Labrousse, *Esquisse du mouvement des prix et des revenus en France au XVIIIe siècle* (2 vols, Paris, 1933); *La Crise de l'économie franaise á la fin de l'Ancien Régime et au début de la Révolution* (PUF, Paris, 1944); quoted from Doyle, *Origins*, p. 31.
17. One of the least illuminated corners of the vast complex of socio-economic issues prior to the French revolution is the popular image of enclosures. In comparison with England they were much less widespread and consequently less important. On the other hand, the question of whom they were intended to benefit is still more difficult to answer. Opinions, each supported by partial evidence, range from the view that enclosures favoured the rich peasants, to the diametrically opposite view that they were required rather by the poor ones. The former was widely shared by most scholars in the field, the latter has been put forward by Cobban, *The Social Interpretation*, pp. 112–17.
18. According to Labrousse, spending on bread constituted, before the revolution, about 50 per cent of a worker's family budget, and as a result of a much faster growth of prices than wages it rose, by 1793, to 88 per cent of total expenses (quoted from Doyle, *Origins*, p. 161).
19. The following verses of a song composed by a rank-and-file soldier of the Charente batallion can serve as an example of the spirited atmosphere in the revolutionary army:

> La liberté n'est donc que dans la loi;
> La loi, de tous la volonté suprême,
> C'est mon ouvrage, elle est faite par moi,
> Soumis aux lois, j'obéis à moi-même.

(Quoted from Soboul, *Paysans*, p. 218.)
20. For a critical account of the military aspects of the French revolution, see especially J.P. Bertrand, 'Voies nouvelles pour l'histoire militaire de la Révolution', in A. Mathiez and G. Lefebvre (eds), *Colloque* (Bibliothèque Nationale, Paris, 1978).
21. N. Hampson, *A Social History of the French Revolution* (Routledge, London, 1963), pp. 106–7.
22. *Ibid.*, p. 87.
23. Cobban, *The Social Interpretation*, p. 144.
24. As Alan Forrest has, however, shown, the first years of revolution were not so harsh in this respect. There were a lot of job-creating schemes organised by local authorities and supported by the Comité de Mendicité in Paris. But most of these *ateliers* had not survived Year III, 'for yet again the Revolution had failed to live up to its original promise' (A. Forrest, *The French Revolution and the Poor*, Blackwell, Oxford, 1981, pp. 99–113).

25. F. Ponteil, *Napoléon Ier et l'organisation autoritaire de la France* (A. Colin, Paris, 1956), pp. 7–22.
26. *Ibid.* and I. Collins, *Napoleon and his Parliaments, 1800–1815* (Arnold, London, 1979).
27. G. de Bertier de Sauvigny, *The Bourbon Restoration* (University of Pennsylvania Press, Philadelphia, 1966), p. 245.
28. L. Girard, *La IIe république, 1848–1851* (Colman Levy, Paris, 1968), pp. 30–1.
29. L. Girard, *ibid.*, pp. 114–16.
30. *Ibid.*, p. 228.
31. De Sauvigny, p. 443.
32. S.L. Campbell, *The Second Empire Revisited* (Rutgers University Press, NJ, 1969), p. 26.
33. *Ibid.*, p. 22.
34. *Ibid.*, pp. 158, 190ff.

4

□

Russia (1825–   )

General remarks

The great Russian revolution of October 1917, those 'ten days that shook the world', was one of the decisive formative events in a prolonged revolutionary process, whose origins have to be sought much further back in the past than is commonly assumed to be the case.

The whole revolutionary process which, in the October days, acquired such a conspicuous leftward drift did not by that token become a proletarian revolution in the Marxist sense. It definitely had proletarian undertones, not dissimilar to those of the French revolution, but revolutionary hagiography made these undertones into a halo. From subordinate participation in 1905 through the self-conscious breakthrough in October 1917 until the autumn of 1918, and perhaps to an extent up to the abortive Kronstadt uprising in 1921, the industrial proletariat could be considered not only as the main recruiting ground for the revolutionary armies but also as that social group whose representatives had some influence on the course of events. Thereafter the political leadership fell exclusively to politicians – ideologists, in short ideocrats, whose social origins were in the middle rather than the working class. How far the subsequent rule was favourable to the proletariat is a matter of factual analysis; if anything, it had fostered upward social mobility of individual workers rather than their position as a class.[1] The large-scale recruitment of industrial workers to the party and state 'apparats' which took place during the 1920s and 1930s, and the improved opportunities for workers' descendants to acquire higher education, did not appreciably diminish the traditional gap between the élite and the labouring classes, a gap as conspicuous in terms of power as in terms of living standards and social status. Eventually, people came to the helm whose main qualification for a commanding position was a dedicated commitment to a highly centralised leadership claiming a monopoly of the interpretation of one particular doctrine.

As this ideocracy was comparatively limited in numbers and as the running of state and a modern economy (which itself became state-owned) required not only a bureaucracy of a more-or-less traditional type but also an acquaintance with particular techniques (skills), the ideocrats needed to include in their apparat different groups of specialists, e.g. technical (technocrats) and military (machiocrats). Keeping them ideologically conformist required yet another specialised profession, the state security police – the phylacocracy. All these different '-cracies' form the bulk of what the official Soviet terminology called the 'working intelligentsia', but what a Trotskyist defector, James Burnham, preferred to label the 'managerial class'.[2] Malia coined for all of them an apposite complex term: *bureaucratie universelle idéocratique*.[3] Since their living standards emulated those of the bourgeoisie in the Western world, they may be described as a 'salaried bourgeoisie'.

With any of those labels much of the charm of the Soviet revolution disappears. A political scientist would look in vain for any vestiges of Soviet democracy, a sociologist would hardly find Soviet society destratified in a way suggested by the example of the Paris Commune. An economist looking at the type of economic organisation, production regulator and morphology of growth, would see in the Soviet system an alternative rather than a successive stage to the capitalist mode of production.

From where, then, did the Russian revolution derive its epoch-making image, if neither its political nor its socio-economic achievements justified its programmed intentions? In my opinion the crux of the matter lies in that macro-sociological dimension that can best be described in terms of the development and transformation of civilisation. Under the banner of Marxism, the Soviet ideocracy seemed to have resolved a long-standing crucial problem of Russia: its adaptation to the technological development of the Western world without the loss of its identity as a separate civilisation. The 200-year-long struggle between the Westernisers and the traditionalists was resolved by a third means. The reception of a Western ideology, radically opposed to the societal system of its own birthplace, an ideology revised and adapted to the needs of a thoroughgoing societal reconstruction and to the peculiarities of an alien tradition, not only was to save Russia's face but also to provide an example for other nations in a similar position.

This message of the Russian revolution, however, did not have a lasting effect. The October revolution switched the whole process in a direction that its supporters had not anticipated. The contrast between the image spread by propaganda on the one hand, and the realities of everyday life on the other was staggering; after seventy years of continuous drama, in which the suffering of millions overshadowed the splendour of imperial glory, the process of revolution was to be redirected to the path trodden before the Great October. Understandably, given the conditions of a tougher autocracy bequeathed to Russia by Stalin, a new, third phase of Russian revolution could start only after the calls from below met a response from an autocrat who grasped the whole tragedy of the Bolshevik derailment.

At the beginning it seemed that the gist of the change would be more simple: the spiritless despotism of the Soviet establishment would be replaced by enlightened absolutism, which would breathe new life into the fossilised structure of Soviet society. The exogenous nature of the revolution, however, required a different solution from that which was suitable for the situation 200 years earlier. Towards the close of the twentieth century, the third phase of the Russian revolution had to deploy the full gamut of liberal and democratic policies. At the same time, so it seems, the process had to shed its revolutionary trappings and embark on a long-overdue, thoroughgoing adaptation to the world that could not be caught up with, let alone overtaken, by the system and methods created in the earlier phases of revolution.

Historical roots

Bearing in mind the long-term dimension, it may be worthwhile to look into the origins of Russia's identity not only as a nation but also as a civilisation. As is well known, Russia received its Christianity not from Rome, as most European nations did, but from Byzantium. Like the Byzantine Empire, Russia became, albeit for a shorter period of history, subject to the domination of Ural-Altaic peoples. This severed its direct links with other parts of Europe. Like the Orthodox Christian communities in southeastern Europe, Russia's spiritual outlook and its rhythm of development differed from the general European pattern.

The Roman Catholic doctrine of the Two Swords did not find a corresponding echo in the Russian political establishment, which provided no scope for a viable polarity between the secular and ecclesiastical powers. Also the autonomy of estates – above all of the aristocracy and to some extent of the burghers – which in the West provided an element of pluralism within the secular power structure, lasted for only a short while, and in a relatively attenuated form, in Russia. Its political regime shared rather the pattern widespread in most parts of the non-European world – a mixture of, or oscillation between, the feudal and the despotic type of polity; her socio-economic system produced in the warlords' ownership of the land and in the bondage of the peasants a kind of stratification which by its rigidity prevented any substantial circulation of the élite.

In its cultural history Russia experienced neither a renaissance nor a reformation. In spite of the attempts of some historians to compare Ivan the Terrible with Renaissance princes, and in spite of the assertions, propounded especially by Soviet historians, that neither the Reformation nor the Counter-Reformation left Russia untouched,[4] the cultural development of Russia until the beginning of the seventeenth century was conspicuous by the absence of any substantial innovation.

From the thirteenth century onwards, Russia was exposed to two types of foreign pressure: the Mongol-Tartar from the East and the European from the West. Whereas the first pressure was fully eliminated within three centuries and Russia itself embarked on an imperial *Drang nach Osten* (eastward drive), the West constituted a constant, albeit intermittent, danger or at least irritation. Starting with the Teutonic Knights in the Baltic area, the pressure intensified in the seventeenth century when Russia was confronted with the expansion of the aristocratic confederacy of Poland and Lithuania and their counter-reformation Catholicism. The main danger lay in the growing feeling among knowledgeable people that Western Christianity had something that appeared to be superior to Russian Orthodoxy. Patriarch Nikon (in office 1652–66) probably had this in mind when he attempted to make Russian Orthodoxy more competitive with Catholicism while reinvigorating its Greek ingredients. But any innovation in Russia was difficult to achieve; even such a comparatively moderate reform as that undertaken by Nikon could not be achieved without alienating a substantial part of the Russian population which clung to a meticulous preservation of the traditional ritual.

Meanwhile, however, Western Christianity embarked on a process of thoroughgoing civilisational reconstruction, which put the West still further ahead of Russia. Under these circumstances, Peter the Great opted for the newly emerging spirit of the West, with which he had become acquainted during his sojourn in the Netherlands and Great Britain, and embarked on outright Europeanisation. The Aristotelian contradiction between two paradigms, each of which embraced not just a social philosophy but a whole world-view, could not be more apparent. The task was enormous because Western civilisation was to be transplanted to Russia not in its traditional but in its new secular utilitarian version, which at that time was starting to assume its characteristic features.

There was, however, a striking contradiction within the Petrian mode of Westernisation – a contradiction which outlived him: the enslaved masses of the peasantry had to provide the labour force and cannon fodder for all new ventures, without in any way partaking of the benefits of the great transformation which was put in motion at the upper levels of the body social.

Western civilisation increased its sphere of influence not only through the sheer weight of its technical and organisational superiority, but also by virtue of its new ideas, which in the wake of the French revolution became an issue of primary importance. In Russia they affected only the literate élite, who were drawn more often than not from the ranks of the aristocracy. Not all seem to have realised the nation-wide impact of these corrosive ideas. Catherine II flirted with them as if they were merely an intellectual game. But they started to produce an unwanted effect: the defection of intellectuals from the traditional values – both from those of the East and from those of the West. In 1801 a pupil of one of the Western *philosophes*, Alexander I, ascended the throne, leading to expectations of an era of reform.

But before anything tangible could happen, the expansionist (imperialistic) stage of the French revolution confronted Russia with the additional challenge of a direct assault. As a result the anti-reformist forces were strengthened and the proponent of a constitution, Count Speransky – in a way the Russian counterpart of the French Turgot – had to leave for exile in Siberia (1812). The expectations that had been aroused produced among the reformist intelligentsia the typical effect of an aspirational deprivation (cf. p. 34). Within the context of Russian society, their cream was to be found among the young nobility, largely officers in the Guards regiment who organised themselves in the Union of Salvation or, under a later name, the Society of True and Faithful Sons of the Fatherland. Many of them did not see any way out of the impasse other than armed insurrection. Yet their ranks and programmes were divided in a way somewhat reminiscent of the French revolution. All were for the abolition of serfdom but their concepts of civil liberty differed. The northern wing led by Muraviev resembled the Girondists: they stood for a constitutional monarchy, a federal organisation of the state and a suffrage limited by property census. On the other hand, the southern wing led by Pestel advocated, in a Jacobin fashion, a strongly centralised and authoritarian government and an egalitarian and disciplined society endowed with universal suffrage; their plans for 'democratic centralism' and their policing methods foreshadowed not only Bolshevik practice but also the policy implemented by Stalin.[5] The contradictions that were later to mark the Russian revolution thus appeared on a minor scale already a hundred years before it took place in full vigour.

Although easily suppressed, the irresolute insurrection of the Decembrists (so called because of the date of the attempted insurrection in 1825) became a landmark in Russian history. Despite being limited to a small section of the upper strata, its aim was not merely a palace *coup d'état* on the occasion of a new emperor ascending the throne, but a premature overture to a social revolution.

Hitherto, revolutionary uprisings (or, as we prefer to call them, revolts or rebellions) in Russia had been carried out by illiterate masses led by semi-literate leaders, such as Ryazin or Pugachev, mainly on the geographical fringe of the Russian Empire. In 1825, however, it was the intelligentsia in the capital that took the lead and also bore the brunt of the repression. From then on, the intelligentsia, irrespective of whether it was recruited from the aristocracy or from the bourgeoisie, became a permanent focus of dissent.

Yet, as is well known, an intelligentsia on its own is not in a position to make a revolution. Thus the main problem was whether it would find an ally strong and brave enough to become an adequate recruiting ground for the revolutionary struggle. At the beginning it seemed to be obvious that this revolutionary ally would be the peasantry, hard-pressed by serfdom and poverty. As the most oppressed and exploited social stratum they were supposed to have the greatest interest in social change. Yet their immobility and inherent conservatism prevented them from taking part in any significant social action except sporadic local revolts.

The long-overdue abolition of serfdom in 1861 resulted from the government's need for greater economic efficiency rather than from pressure by the peasants themselves. It was precipitated by Russia's defeat in the Crimean War, which revealed, even to those who least wanted to see it, Russia's overall backwardness. However, what the peasants got by the decree, i.e. personal freedom without acquisition of adequate land, did not make their destiny any better.

Before the emancipation, peasants held only a small part of the estate's land for their own work and use. Communities of peasants (individual *obshchinas*) were collectively responsible for the fulfilment of all obligations (work and payments) to their landlords, who at the same time exercised a wide range of the state's jurisdiction over their subjects. After the emancipation, the nobles in the less fertile regions ceded some extra lands to their former serfs in return for hefty redemption payments. As the latter were advanced to the nobles by the state, the allotment-holders were to remain tied to the land for a further forty-nine years. Elsewhere the nobles preferred to reduce the size of the peasants' holdings, thus forcing them to rent or work their landlords' soil. In either case there was no incentive to improve the technology of agriculture.

The populist movement that aimed to channel the peasants' discontent into purposeful action failed to make headway. Neither the leadership offered by the intelligentsia nor their attempts to identify with the peasant masses could spur the latter to resolute action. The most disappointing events for the enthusiasts were in 1874 when they launched a grand campaign of 'going to the people'. They found no positive response, and sometimes even encountered hostility.

The whole story of the Russian peasantry indicates the tenacity of the semi-religious belief in the tsar's good intentions, which supposedly only the bad will of his entourage and landlords prevented from being properly implemented in the country. Whatever they might have said in the peasants' favour, townspeople were likewise not trusted.

The need for industrialisation

What Peter the Great himself realised was that Russia needed industry, which in its turn needed people who could finance its rise and look after its operation. Peter and his disciples undertook to 'manufacture the manufacturers'.[6] However, it proved easier to create a bureaucracy than an entrepreneurial class by imperial command. The state manufacture was conceived as a transitory educative stage, intended for transfer to private hands later. Privileges such as tax exemptions and the right to exploit servile peasant labour were bestowed on those private manufacturers who wanted to carry on. However, in the absence of some equivalent to the Protestant ethic, the government had to keep its watchful eye on pseudo-manufacturers who tended to use their privileges for other than industrial purposes. Thus, because of its many regulations, and whatever its intentions, Peter's policy was closer to the practice of mercantilism than to the policies that had brought wealth to England and Holland – Peter's examples.[7] Although the effects of Peter's policy were limited, it nevertheless provided an impetus and left a legacy to future generations.

Not until about 1830 did new forms of industrial organisation and technology start to appear on a larger scale. This gave official Soviet historiography an opportunity to locate the beginning of the industrial revolution in Russia in that decade. However, industry was to remain for a long time a host of scattered islands in the peasant sea of Russia.[8]

The lack of a sustained entrepreneurial spirit seems to have been one of the main obstacles to matching the capitalist achievement of Western Europe. Russia's nascent industry had to rely more on government guidance than on the spontaneity of individuals. Only after the defeat in the Crimean War (1854–6) did the government shift to a policy of non-intervention,[9] or rather of limited intervention by financial measures only.

The large-scale construction of railroads, together with industrialisation, needed large-scale imports, which in their turn required foreign loans. For that purpose a free foreign trade and a freely convertible currency were deemed to be necessary preconditions. After several unsuccessful attempts, Russia eventually began under Witte's ministry to create these conditions. Large imports and the heavy interest on loans were financed by increased taxation, and above all by the growing demands on the peasants, who had to produce an ever-increasing commercial crop, even at the cost of a lower living standard. This became especially acute at a time of falling world prices in the late 1880s. In 1891 even a famine broke out, which forced the government to adopt some protective or expansionist measures such as import duties and high government investment in railroads and heavy industry. Up to the end of the century Russia managed to maintain a trade surplus and a high rate of industrial growth, but at the cost of a progressive impoverishment of the peasantry which constituted about three-quarters of the total population.

Stalin did not initiate something completely new when he embarked on his industrialisation drive at the cost of the peasants; he only made it more ruthless, more costly and also more conspicuous. The economic policies pursued by Peter, Witte and Stalin were based on the same assumption, namely that the primary accumulation of capital and the building up of the empire's military strength had to be achieved by an increased exploitation of the peasantry. Whether as serfs (under Peter), or exposed to the rigours of the market (under Witte), or in the bondage of socialist *kolkhozes* (under Stalin), the Russian peasant had to go through the ordeal of sacrifice for the benefit of the upper classes and imperial grandeur.

But before the last and harshest chapter of their exploitation took place, the peasants experienced three brief spells during which there seemed to be some hope of their becoming equals with the other subjects of the empire. The first was the period of Stolypin's ministry (1906–12), when peasants were encouraged to leave their traditional communes and improve their position through free enterprise, a policy that opened a channel of upward mobility for those strong enough to take the chance. The second was after the Bolsheviks took over and sanctioned the earlier spontaneous revolutionary appropriation of the baronial lands by the peasants (November 1917). The third came with the New Economic Policy from 1921, when the peasants were allowed to use that land according to their own devices. But none of these policies was allowed to last long enough to bring sizeable benefits even to those who were able to play the game.

Multiple dysfunction or total disintegration?

While the peasantry bore the brunt of imperial policy, the intelligentsia indulged in the struggle for social change, the precise contents of which, however, differed according to the ideological orientation of the individual factions. This book is not the place to retell the story which has been described and analysed many times before. For the purpose of this study we need only to see whether the etiological considerations discussed in the cases of the Czech, English and French revolutions apply also to the Russian case, and whether there were perhaps some other elements of the multiple dysfunction that gave rise to the revolution and/or were instrumental in the shaping of its outcome.

In what we have called the onset of the revolutionary process, the main motivation, the main driving force behind the quest for change, was the realisation of Russia's backwardness *vis-à-vis* Western Europe (the external factor). This realisation was particularly reinforced by the tremendous gap between the Europeanised and non-Europeanised elements within Russia itself (the internal factor).

People in possession of wealth and education were dissatisfied with their exclusion from any political decision-making – a Weberian type of contrast between inferior political status and higher economic position and prestige. The emancipated peasant masses wanted more land at their disposal. Their economic position did not match their newly acquired status of free peasants – another type of Weberian disproportion. Finally, the rudimentary industrial proletariat resented their harsh working conditions and low living standards, a sort of deprivation which – as it seems to have been a constant factor – can hardly be qualified by a further epithet. Thus the main contradictions which we have identified as the salient components of a multiple dysfunction also appeared in pre-revolutionary Russia.

The economic depression of 1899 served to highlight these contradictions. The collapse of the boom accentuated by the stopping of foreign loans produced the psychological effect that can be described as aspirational deprivation.

As Laue has indicated, Russia's economic progress, whether it was achieved as a result of a policy of *laissez-faire*, or of a planned and centrally managed economy, was obstructed by a hostile social and political framework. The

Russian *kupechestvo* was sluggish and inflexible; the peasantry, legally separated from the rest of Russian society, was not accustomed to individual private enterprise.[10] There did not exist a capitalist class strong enough to struggle for emancipation from the traditional economic or political framework. What provided the impetus for change was the idea, held by the Westernised intelligentsia and shared by both the power élite and the counter-élite, that Russia had to be steered onto the road of progress and brought up to the level of the most highly developed nations of the world.

Seen in Marxian terms, it was the contradiction between the productive potential as revealed by the development of the West, and the real productivity resulting from the conditions in the East. In Aristotelian terms, it was the contrast between, on the one hand, the traditional values of an autocratic society where the whole population, although structured in a highly differentiated hierarchy with ascribed status, existed in a position of servitude *vis-à-vis* the autocrat, and, on the other hand, the liberal, achievement-orientated society of the West, where competition took place both in the economic and in the political sphere.

Up to this point there was no consensus within the camp of the modernisers concerning the means or even the aims of the envisaged change. The opposition of the traditionalists who sought salvation in the time-honoured Orthodox Christian virtues gave the quest for the means of modernisation a particular twist.

The tsar wanted to be faithful to his oath of allegiance to the autocratic tradition, but he lacked the effective means to strengthen Russia sufficiently to prevent her from collapsing under the impact of the First World War. The contrast between the power of coercion over people and the power to direct the country's resources – both human and material – towards a planned aim revealed beyond any doubt the inadequacy of the *ancien régime*.

Here we come across a specific contrast which we have not yet touched upon in the section on etiology of revolution (pages 31–8). This contradiction has been amply discussed by the analysts. Isaac Deutscher described it as the 'contrast between the status and importance of Tsarist Russia as a great power and the archaic weakness of her social structure, between the splendours of her empire and the wretchedness of her institutions'.[11] We shall meet this contradiction again when discussing the other two exogenous revolutions, the Chinese and Turkish ones.

Not only the political regime, however, but also that part of the society that was sufficiently Westernised and thus qualified for the task of closing the technological gap, proved inadequate to this undertaking.

Malia, who did not investigate the civilisational dimension but focused on a structural analysis, discovered that a specific feature of the Russian situation was the underdevelopment of its civil society. In Malia's understanding, civil society is constituted by those social cells capable of organising themselves independently of the state and of looking after their own needs – either on the strength of certain common riches or capacities, whether professional, intellectual, etc., or because they are uniquely able to provide a particular service for the society as a whole.[12]

Thus it was owing to the weakness of the civil society that, after three years of what Malia considers the first democratic and total war in history, not only the state power collapsed but also the whole civil society disintegrated. Another year of chaos, in which peasants and workers were allowed to take over the land and factories respectively, and thus to wipe out the landlords and capitalists as social classes, led to a complete abolition of civil society in Russia. Although this happened independently of the will of the Bolsheviks, it very much helped their cause.

On that account the year 1918 can be seen as the key year of the Russian revolution. In that year the party which, until then, had shown quite a few conspiratorial features went through a mutation into a truly Leninist party, which in the course of subsequent years took over the role of the civil society in Russia. In Malia's view the years 1919 to 1920 witnessed a unique historical substitution, namely the substitution of a party state operating by means of a universal ideocratic bureaucracy, for a diseased civil society. It was the ideology that gave this universal bureaucracy its cohesion, its *raison d'être*, its messianism and its extraordinary strength.[13]

In our terms, the Aristotelian contradiction entered the scene in an accentuated form. The construction of a new integrative force on the debris of all the traditional pillars of integration was a task that – were one to look for parallels – one could only compare to the situation of victorious conquerors building their own civilisation on top of the one they have destroyed.

The above-mentioned mutation in the integrative forces of the society was not observed by outsiders alone, nor was it restricted to the propertied classes. On the evidence collected by Horský,[14] Lenin – the main actor in the revolution – had a similar insight, but from the other end of the stratification spectrum, when he said: '[the] industrial proletariat ... in our country, owing to the war and to the desperate poverty and ruin, has become declassed, i.e. dislodged from its class groove, and has ceased to exist as a proletariat'.[15]

This statement has to be understood against the background of the fact that by the end of 1920 (the end of the civil war) industrial production had dropped to below 15 per cent of its pre-war level and money had lost all value. In the steel and coal industries, which are as a rule the strongholds of the industrial proletariat, production fell below 3 per cent. Most workers had to abandon their factories and look for work in the countryside. Those who stayed were either unemployed or lived by selling the meagre output or factory tools on the black market. Wages paid to the workers covered barely a fifth of their living expenses.

Horský's comments bring Lenin's observation into a logical context with Malia's argument: 'thus the political stage was temporarily abandoned by that societal agent who in the imagination of the classics [i.e. of Marxism] was to become the main actor and guarantor of the revolutionary transformation of the bourgeois society'.[16] Horský also mentions Bucharin who, referring in 1925 to the Russia of 1921, saw in it an image of a dying human society.

As early as 1921, however, the Russian proletariat started occasionally to re-emerge as an articulate social grouping. Whether this occurred in the form of workers' opposition within the party, or as an attempt at military self-assertion, such as the Kronstadt uprising of March 1921, it was, in any case, too late. In the meantime the party state had already built the basic framework of its societal power and provided it with adequate means of coercion. It was no longer a question of a dictatorship of the proletariat through the institution of elected Soviets; a dictatorship was established over the whole society using the Soviets, appointed by the party, as an instrument of mobilisation rather than consultation. The atomised masses faced their rulers without the protection of adequate intermediary institutions.[17]

In this context we have to make a clear-cut distinction between the necessities resulting from the temporary situation and necessities resulting from the general conditions of the society in question.

The necessity resulting from the temporary situation would have similar effects in any country irrespective of its socio-cultural background. Once production sinks to such a level that there is almost nothing to distribute, the society has first to solve its production problems. This means taking measures to increase production, which in turn implies disciplining the workers. The greater the falling off in discipline, the sterner the measures that might be required.[18] In this context yet another point has to be stressed: namely, that if anybody is capable of getting such measures accepted, it is a workers' party. Being nearest to the workers, and having won a good deal of their trust, it is in a position to convince or, if necessary, to coerce them to follow a line which under normal circumstances they would be hardly likely to follow.[19]

Lenin knew what had to be done in such circumstances. Yet the question may be asked whether he did only what was necessary to pull the country out of its economic collapse, or whether he went much further. In order to promote production, was it necessary to establish a one-party dictatorship? It is difficult to speculate but one thing is clear, namely that the two contingencies coincided: the need to get out of the mess and the need to do it in the way most appropriate to the working attitudes and political culture of the people concerned. These latter – as students of Russian history know all too well – provided little scope for democratic or pluralistic ways of resolving problems.

Finally, what about the Paretian and Khaldunian contrasts in the Russian revolution? Unlike the cases of the other revolutions discussed in this book, in Russia these contrasts do not seem to have been particularly conspicuous. Although the Empress Alexandra would have liked to see Nicholas II use more force against his opponents, his behaviour in the crisis cannot be compared to the vacillation of the monarch trapped in other revolutions. However, if there was any lack of resoluteness on the part of the tsar it was far surpassed by the hesitations of the liberal opposition.

As there was a war, the behaviour of the army was the most decisive factor in the critical days, and there was little scope for others to manoeuvre. The liberals, not being in command of armed forces, could hardly be reproached for not behaving more resolutely.[20] Their hand was forced by spontaneous riots in the capital, sparked off by the administrative incompetence of the local authorities who could not provide regular supplies for the working population. Eventually the generals completed the February revolution by compelling the tsar to abdicate. The autocracy obviously lost its national appeal because it was not able to perform its patriotic duty, i.e. conduct the war successfully. The contrast between imperial aspirations and imperial achievement entered a critical stage.

Thus there does not seem to have been much scope for the Paretian contrast in the Russian revolution unless we regard the emigration of some two million people from the upper classes as a fox-like reaction to the revolution. On the other hand, after the Bolsheviks took power, the officer corps regained its martial spirit in the civil war; all the White Army commanders, such as Denikin, Kolchak, Yudenich and Wrangel, were able to mobilise between them forces that were only slightly inferior in numbers to those actually brought to the battlefields by the Bolsheviks, whose conscript armies suffered from a considerable rate of desertion. It seems that it was not so much a superior fighting spirit as the strategic advantage (holding the heart of the country with its better railway network and thus shorter lines of internal communication) that operated in the Bolsheviks' favour.[21] On the other hand, the counter-revolutionaries were often weakened by their political incompetence and internal dissent. Introducing a tough military dictatorship in the territories held by their armies, they estranged and eventually clashed with the democratic and socialist opponents of the Bolsheviks in the towns, and, hesitating to acknowledge the peasants' claims to their newly acquired land, they deprived themselves of support in the villages. Thus it was the Bolsheviks' superiority in Aristotelian terms, i.e. the more attractive concept of social justice for which they stood in those days, that won for them the support of some wavering segments of the civil population. Furthermore, the help provided by the Western powers for the White armies allowed the Bolsheviks to appeal to patriotic sentiments.

The relative weakness, or rather inefficiency, of the armies on both sides in the civil war can best be illustrated by the amazing intervention of the Czechoslovak Legion comprising some 40,000 men. Recruited from Austro-Hungarian prisoners of war of Czech and Slovak ethnic nationality in order to fight on Russia's side for the national independence of their homeland, they had to stop this fight when, in March 1918, the Bolsheviks concluded the peace treaty with Germany and her allies in Brest Litovsk. The Legion was supposed to be transported over the Pacific Ocean to the battlefields of France. *En route*, however, misunderstandings with local Bolshevik authorities multiplied and the attempt to disarm the Legion and to redirect its movements provoked a confrontation, as a result of which the Czechoslovak Legion took control of the transport centres in the Middle Volga and the Ural regions, and of the whole Trans-Siberian railway. This move, which the Bolshevik army was not in a position to prevent, allowed Admiral Kolchak to establish his power base in West Siberia, but he could hold it only as long as the Czechoslovak Legion acting on behalf of the Allied Command were willing to provide him with their support. As the Czechoslovaks preferred not to be involved in internal Russian matters and as the Kolchaks' dictatorial reign and terrorist methods appalled them, the gradual withdrawal of their Legion from Siberia also meant the end of Kolchak.[22]

Western paradigm and Russian reality

From the beginning of the nineteenth century until about the end of the first quarter of the twentieth century those actively involved in political developments in Russia thought and acted under the impact of the French revolution. Its experience provided both the liberals and the socialists with paradigms applicable to their own aims and means. But the counter-revolutionaries also took some lessons from it, though, as Malia has rightly observed, not as successfully as, for instance, the governments of Prussia between 1848 and 1914.

For the liberals the French revolution provided a ready-made model, a constitutional regime with legislative assemblies providing for a pluralist system of representation and allowing a free interaction of market forces. This model also provided guidelines for warding off socialists' bids for power.

For the socialists the model was contained in Marxian theory. Based on the experience of the whole revolutionary century in France, this theory taught how the defeated forces of what at the beginning of the French revolution were the urban 'plebeian masses' and at the end the urban 'working class', could win and transform a bourgeois society into a socialist one.

Both models provided a straightforward lesson and both were up to a point mutually compatible. According to the first model the Constitutional Democrats and their allies had to follow the course of the French revolution, possibly in a more straightforward way. According to the second, the socialists had first of all to help the liberals carry out their bourgeois revolution; then in due course, when the development of the productive forces had outgrown the capitalist mode of production, they had to attempt to make their own revolution. Were the development of capitalism in Russia to proceed fast enough, the socialist revolution in Russia might coincide with the socialist revolution in the whole of Europe, or at least in its most important countries, above all Germany. This would be the best guarantee of the successful achievement of the socialist revolution on an international scale.

Neither model, however, turned out to be applicable in the Russian case. The liberals failed in 1905 and again in 1917. The democratic socialists' participation on the second occasion was of little help. In October of the same year a political party of a new type claiming to be the vanguard of the urban working class won power in the capital cities and the heart of Russia.

The collapse of the state power and the disintegration of the civil society mentioned above enabled the Bolsheviks to build up their own establishment. Under the given circumstances this took them far from the ideals of socialist democracy. Both the revolutionary situation in which several groupings were competing for power, and the disintegrated societal structure where there were hardly any coherent, let alone organised, groups, led them to what may be seen as the shift from the left to the right of the whole revolutionary spectrum.

The need to hold on to power against other revolutionary groupings led, as in most revolutions, to a revolutionary dictatorship. The need to reintegrate a societal structure in which all the pillars of civil society had been destroyed, required even more strength and mobilising power than any revolutionary dictatorship could have produced. Whether we call the ensuing system state socialism or state capitalism does not matter. At any rate it did not correspond to what the promoters of the two models, liberal and socialist, expected from the revolution.

Karl Kautsky and Rosa Luxemburg realised in the very first stages of Soviet power that it was deviating from the socialist path. For Trotsky the light dawned only when he himself lost power. To many Western Marxists the Stalinist deviation or, as some called it, 'revisionism', became apparent only when, years after the Second World War, the Soviet regime stifled the attempts of its satellite nations to follow a more pronounced socialist course.

Irrespective of when the facts entered the consciousness of the observers, one key question arises from that development: why did Russia deviate so much from the programmed path? On the strength of what has been said so far, the answer is obvious: because the programmes, whether liberal or socialist, did not suit conditions in Russia. They were derived from the French experience and applicable only within the general framework of Western European civilisation. Russia was not yet sufficiently Westernised to allow such a Western-type transformation. Those who had thought that the transplantation of Western civilisation onto Russian soil was well advanced, turned out to have been the victims of a great illusion.[23] The period of over 200 years which had elapsed since Peter the Great began a selective Europeanisation of Russia and affected only a small part of the population. It produced an upper layer which found little spiritual or social contact with the peasant and lower-class urban masses, together constituting about 90 per cent of Russia's total population.

Any revolution, if it were to be successful, had to gain a base that went beyond the 10 per cent or so of Russians who thought in terms of Western political concepts and who were interested in Western institutions. The revolutionaries had to mobilise the non-Europeanised masses; they had to adopt methods suited to the habits and understanding of the people concerned, i.e. they had to respect the native rather than the foreign tradition.

Like the enlightened Romanovs, the Bolshevik leaders learned from West European technicians and philosophers, but unlike the Romanovs they chose to be guided by that West European philosophy which on the one hand was in fierce opposition to the whole societal system of the West,[24] and on the other was best suited to the Russian tradition. The Marxian–Hegelian compound could be used to rationalise something more formidable than the limited absolutism of Western Europe, which as a matter of principle did not exceed the political sphere. The Marxian–Hegelian philosophy fitted the needs of a complete, almost transcendental absolutism endowing the government with the totality of ideological, political and economic power. Furthermore, the policy derived from that philosophy canvassed the support of the industrial proletariat which, in contrast to what happened in Western Europe, in Russia did not enter the stage of history later than the bourgeoisie. Consequently, both these social classes were on approximately the same footing as far as their political experience was concerned.

Under Lenin, the legacy of Peter the Great was brought closer to the roots of the Russian tradition and was enriched by a programme of emancipation for the workers, who had to bear the brunt of industrialisation; in Stalin, creator of the new ruling class, the ghosts of Ivan the Terrible, Pugachev and Rasputin found their combined reincarnation, and Potemkin's window-dressing was brought to a new height of perfection. Bucharin, Zinoviev, Kamenev, Trotsky and other Old Guard Bolsheviks had to go because they did not want to give up their great illusion; not being able to rid themselves of the imagery of the French revolution, they wanted to achieve at least some part of the programme of the socialist revolution – a programme which, however, had been conceived in quite another world, a world where personal freedom and co-determination in social matters had acquired some real meaning. Stalin, with his Orthodox Christian, Georgian background, with his superficial, or rather vulgarised, knowledge of Marxism already revised by Lenin, and with his complete lack of scruples, was in a better position than anybody else to lay the foundations of the post-revolutionary establishment and to staff it with a new, privileged, political class of executives serving a Great Power idea. Thus Holy Russia became the Sacred Fatherland of socialism, which in the Great Patriotic War welded together its time-honoured nationalism and the messianic spirit of past and future expansion.[25]

The leadership's belief that they were in possession of a scientific truth and a superior doctrine ('the teaching of all teachings, the art of all arts') provided them with a subjective justification for taking command of the whole population without consulting them about the wisdom of their policies. As Ulam has pointed out, this contempt for their subjects' own views[26] found its theoretical justification in Lenin's brochure, *What is to be Done?*, published in 1902.[27] According to Lenin, the history of every country shows that the working class on its own is able to develop only trade-union consciousness. The workers' spontaneous striving for professional and economic gains had to be combated, and the working class had to be imbued with a revolutionary spirit which could only be brought to it from outside, by enlightened intellectuals.

Stalin merely carried on what his predecessor had begun: he pushed the shift across the revolutionary spectrum initiated by Lenin to the utmost limits of autocracy. In so doing, he brought the state philosophy (Marxism–Leninism) down to the intellectual and moral level of those from whom the universal ideocratic bureaucracy was to be recruited: newcomers from the towns and countryside whose primary interest was their individual promotion through the newly opened bureaucratic channels of social mobility. As S. Fitzpatrick put it:

> The new cadres were from the people but no longer of it, for they had been upwardly mobile. They were beneficiaries of the Revolution, but by the same token disposed to be loyal to the régime and most unlikely to be revolutionary. To be sure, only a skilled dialectician could relate Stalin's élite-building to the Revolution's socialist objectives.[28]

The Stalinian shift towards despotism took place in two stages: the first in 1927–9 when all opposition to Stalin within the party was eliminated; the second in 1936–8 when, as a result of great purges and fabricated trials, four-fifths of the party cadres and three-quarters of the party membership were exchanged for newcomers. The personal structure of the Bolshevik party was thus completely changed. Within twenty years of October 1917 the revolutionary vanguard of the working class was transformed into a party of docile servants, obedient to the will of one man who was in absolute command of all the means of production, education and compulsion.

With the help of such a party the time-honoured dream of the great Russian tsars could be realised: the whole country was mobilised – whether by stick or by carrot – to unprecedented achievements, and Russia constructed an economic base capable of sustaining the military might of a great international power. The contrast between the status of a great power and the archaic weakness of the social structure was abolished. The splendour of the new empire was matched by the elaborateness and toughness of its institutions.[29]

But much of the time-honoured discrepancy remained; it was merely reduced or shifted to another area. It survived in its most conspicuous form as a disproportion between, on the one hand, the highly developed technology used for military and space exploration purposes, and on the other, the rather backward technology and organisation serving the purposes of mass consumption.

The revolutionary spectrum and the course of revolution

In trying to analyse the individual streams and forces in the Soviet revolution in similar terms to those used for the other five revolutions, we encounter a particular complication, namely the difficulty of mapping them onto the continuum of the right/left spectrum. Given the fact that the revolution was initiated in the name of a Western ideology, it would seem legitimate to use Western ideas of what is left and what is right to identify and differentiate the revolutionaries. This evaluation is identical with what may be called the view *ex ante* of the revolution. However, in looking at these differences from the vantage point of the Russian tradition and long-term developments which may be identified with the *ex post* view, we get quite a different picture, especially if we equate the leftward move with increasing intensity of change. The two alternative evaluations can be juxtaposed in the way shown in Table 4.1.

Table 4.1 Spectrum of political differentiation in the Russian revolution

	In Western concepts The view *ex ante*	Viewed in the Russian tradition The view *ex post*
Counter-revolutionaries	'Seventeenth October' 'Black Hundred' and the White Armies	'Seventeenth October' 'Black Hundred' and the White Armies
Revolutionary extreme right	Constitutional Democrats	Stalin
Revolutionary right	Mensheviks	Bolsheviks: Lenin Trotsky Bucharin
Revolutionary centre	Socialist Revolutionaries	Socialist Revolutionaries
Revolutionary left	Bolsheviks: Bucharin Lenin Stalin Trotsky	Constitutional Democrats Mensheviks
Extreme left	Anarchists	Anarchists

Whereas the first column in Table 4.1 reproduces the conventional view, the second column rearranges the individual groupings according to the degree of deviation from the *status quo* – a *status quo* understood in terms of the traditional values and inherent trends of Russian history. Only the centre and both extreme wings of the spectrum are identical in the two configurations. This is due to the fact that, by definition, the *status quo* has to be located at one end of the spectrum. Anarchism also, by definition, does not fit into any organised scheme unless we are ready to view it as an ever-present tendency in Russia, a tendency that surfaces whenever an interregnum provides a suitable occasion.

The Socialist Revolutionaries are also, in a sense, a peculiarly Russian group; in contrast to the Bolsheviks, however, they were driven further to the left, more towards the anarchist pole. In this sense the so-called left Socialist Revolutionaries, who for a while cooperated with the Bolsheviks, should rather, in our view, be seen as their right wing. On the other hand, their mainstream representatives participated in the short-lived, post-February coalition government.

The Constitutional Democrats and the Mensheviks emerged as the most complete Westernisers. The former leaned towards the West in its contemporary form, the latter wanted to share its socialist future. In a sense, the Mensheviks were perhaps less alien to the spirit of Russia than the Constitutional Democrats.

On the eve of the revolution and during its early stages the Bolsheviks represented the most highly disciplined group. As soon as they assumed exclusive power, the natural tendency towards differentiation inherent in any social grouping could operate only within the framework of their party. Irrespective of temporary fluctuations and also personal changes of mind, the so-called Trotskyist group can be seen as the most internationally minded and most Westernised of all the Bolshevik groups. Stalin, despite his original caution, moved eventually to the other pole. However individual nuances of agricultural policy may be classified in Western terms (Trotsky-left, Bucharin-right, and the centrist Stalin eventually adopting Trotsky's leftish stance) within the Russian context, the collectivisation seems to have been more in line with the Russian tradition than Stolypin's policy of social differentiation in the countryside.

Bearing in mind this twofold evaluation, we can better understand the meaning of the shifts across the board of the revolutionary spectrum in the graphical presentation of the course of the Russian revolution (Figure 7.4, page 201).

The year 1905 can be seen as a rehearsal for what came in full force in 1917. In 1905 the attempted revolution failed to produce the desired effects. However, the tsarist regime, being militarily engaged in the Far East, was bound to make some temporary concessions to the liberals. When, however, the armies returned and the government succeeded in re-establishing discipline, a harsh repression of the radical elements permitted a gradual restoration of autocracy.

The lesson that can be drawn with hindsight is that there was no hope of change while the military power of the regime was still intact. Thus a successful revolution could only be precipitated by a shattering war. The catalyst occurred after less than three years of the First World War, in which the resources of Russia were not only overstretched, but the individual contradictions listed earlier entered a very acute stage.

With the combination of a tightened autocracy, material shortages, lost battles and growing suffering, the situation gradually became explosive. The triggers were pulled, as it were, anonymously, by the objective conditions of the impasse and the subjective will to overcome it. Each political group proceeded in its own way.

In this context one particular feature of the Russian revolution has to be mentioned, namely the specific type of institutionalisation which, in contrast to the case of the three revolutions analysed earlier, materialised on the far-left wing of the revolutionary spectrum. Given the conditions in autocratic Russia, where the upper classes were left without any institutional bases of their own, the urban working class, whose historical emergence – as we have already mentioned – did not lag behind that of the bourgeoisie, was able to organise its own representative assemblies – the Soviets – as the institutional basis of its own power aspirations. In October 1905 such Soviets emerged in St Petersburg, Moscow and some other industrial and communication centres, but they did not survive the government backlash in the following year.

After the February revolution in 1917, however, the Soviets had a better chance. In a chaotic situation, the democratic parties managed to constitute a provisional, coalition government, headed at first by a constitutional democrat and later by a socialist revolutionary (Kerensky). Although this shift was in tune with the general mood in the country,[30] the provisional government's endeavour to fulfil its international commitments and to continue the war cost it a good deal of popular support. On the other hand, the Soviets, who were standing for peace, propagated a popular cause; and more importantly, most of them fell under the control of a strong-willed Bolshevik leadership.

The sequence of the revolutionary events is well known. Suffice it here to say that the February explosion occurred as a spontaneous action of all the dissatisfied groups; it was the result of the contradictions listed earlier. The victorious revolutionary regime, however, was not in a position to consolidate its authority. In Western terms, the oscillation took the form of a leftward drift – from February to October 1917 and further until the autumn of 1918. Then, however, came Lenin's rightward shift and the consequent suppression of all other left-wing parties.

The civil war that followed produced some oscillation of the seat of power which, in the outlying provinces, continued until the close of 1920, when the last counter-revolutionary campaign was defeated. Then, throughout most of Russia, the seat of power can be considered as intercepted at the position of the party dictatorship, which at that time was already well to the right of the revolutionary centre understood in Western terms. The abortive Kronstadt uprising in March 1921 and the later gradual suppression of the workers' opposition within the Bolshevik party were the dramatic manifestations of that shift.

In 1922, when Stalin became the general secretary of the Bolshevik party, a further decisive step in the shift initiated by Lenin was accomplished. A further tightening of the military regime and perversion of the revolutionary ideals occurred towards the end of the 1920s, when political discussion within the party was eliminated and the decision was taken to destroy the economic independence of the peasantry at a huge cost.

At this point a twenty-five-year period of autocracy, unprecedented in Russian history, set in. The extended continuity of Stalin's autocracy and of his political style did not, however, exclude alterations of policy, which, in view of their social impact, were analogous to the shifts of the seat of power among individual revolutionary groups observed in other revolutions. From 1927/8 to 1953, the seat of power was firmly in Stalin's hands, but his policy changed in one or two important aspects at almost regular intervals.

Stalin started with a 'great leap forward': the collectivisation of agriculture, the extraction of an extraordinarily high 'surplus product' from the peasantry and the rapid construction of heavy industry at the cost of neglecting other needs. This was the content of the first Five Year Plan (1928–32). On the international level, he maintained a policy of hostility towards all political movements other than communist parties obedient to Moscow.

The second Five Year Plan (1933–7) brought some concessions to the consumers and collective farmers and, somewhat later, relaxation of the hostility towards socialist parties abroad. This was the period of the popular fronts – a response to the advance of 'rightist' parties throughout Europe and Japan. Internally most of the Bolshevik Old Guard were liquidated; the Bolshevik party completely changed its complexion.

From 1938 it was mainly international developments that influenced Soviet policy. There was a welcome opportunity to break what was seen as the encirclement of the USSR by capitalist powers and moreover to profit from an inter-capitalist war.

Seeing the main danger in the capitalist West, in particular in the United States, Stalin decided to give some support to Hitler in order to help him to deal heavier blows to the West. The belligerents were expected to weaken each other to such an extent that the USSR, while remaining neutral, could dictate the conditions of peace, or even better, export its revolution to the countries exhausted by the war. But it was Hitler's decision to foil this calculation. Contrary to Stalin's expectation, he launched a concentrated attack on the Soviet Union which thus became involved in the war on the side of the West.

Despite the tremendous input of resources into the military and industrial build-up, Russia, in the first one and a half years of its war with Nazi Germany, suffered a more shattering blow than it had received in the First World War. Hitler's blunders, however, saved Stalin. The excessive strain placed on the German forces waging a war on all sides of the Reich, the German failure to exploit the centrifugal tendencies within the Soviet Union, the exemplary endurance and heroism of Russians largely motivated by nationalistic appeals, and, last but not least, the Allied economic and military help to Soviet Russia – these were the main causes of the turning of the tide. At the turn of the year 1942/3 the Soviet retreat was halted and soon changed into an advance which, in the event, was to last until 1948, well after the end of the war. In that year the Western boundary of what was to become not only the Soviet sphere of interest but also a socio-economically and politically homogenised 'Soviet bloc' was demarcated. Thus, eventually, what was to be gained by supporting Hitler was won, though for a much higher cost, by helping to defeat him.

Stalin enjoyed his personal rule over the enlarged empire for another five years. This period was characterised by the reversal of the previous cultural relaxation, which had been imposed by the war conditions and the alliance with Western powers. Towards the end of the period, a new purge seemed to be imminent. The trial of some prominent doctors accused of having caused the deaths of one or two politicians and of planning to cause the deaths of a number of generals was an ominous sign of things to come.

Stalin's death, however, was a turning point. The relaxation of the dictatorial grip started almost immediately. The exposure of the 'doctors' plot' as a criminal fabrication, and the large-scale amnesty for inmates of the concentration camps, brought unexpected relief and satisfaction throughout the country. Khrushchev's twofold exposure of Stalin's crimes, at the 20th Party Congress in 1956 and at the 22nd Congress in 1961, can be seen as the main act of de-Stalinisation. In terms of our model, this represented a shift from Stalin's position to Lenin's. However, Khrushchev's failure to embark on the transition from socialism to communism as he had foolishly promised, and his ill-coordinated reorganisation measures which worsened rather than improved the economic situation, provided a welcome opportunity for those who did not want to see any major deviation from Stalin's practices.

The internal evolution of the Soviet Union since Khrushchev's fall in 1964 can be described as a continuous but more-or-less hidden struggle between the two basic tendencies within the Bolshevik tradition, Stalinist and Leninist; the former standing for a personal, the latter for a rather collective, dictatorship. To judge by Medvedev's account, after the pendulum had shifted so much towards Lenin's position in 1961, there followed a slow but continuous move towards more Stalinist policies. Medvedev claims that Stalin's full rehabilitation was prepared to coincide with the occasion of his ninetieth birthday in 1969 but was abandoned on the insistence mainly of the Polish and Hungarian Communist parties.[31]

Wherever the truth may lie, the essentials of the matter seem certain. The pattern of the revolutionary process in Russia after Stalin's death can be characterised as a quest for a balance between the respective legacies of Lenin and Stalin. In that sense we may suggest that there was a tendency to consolidate the political system somewhere around the centre of the dictatorship spectrum. Yet the obvious failure to achieve the main objectives of the revolution, to build up a new society which would be socially more just and technically and economically more efficient than the previous societies had been, provoked the need to change the course of development again. The revolutionary process entered the phase when the best way out of the impasse was to be the return to the starting period.

Specific features in the Russian revolution: terror and export of revolution

Two specific features in the Russian revolution deserve a brief comment: (a) the recurrent and extensive use of terror; and (b) the emergence of the Soviet-type (satellite) regimes in quite a few other countries. The results of Bolshevik social engineering as they appeared by the end of the Second World War were exported elsewhere, either by military conquest or by winning over the leaders of domestic revolutions to adopt the Soviet interpretation and application of Marxism–Leninism.

In general, terror, as an orchestrated persecution of particular groups of the population deemed dangerous to the ruling faction of the day, is a feature of the tightening phase in a revolutionary process. Its aim is to eliminate the most dreaded foes and to scare the rest. The frequency and intensity of terror varies considerably from country to country. Terror, practised in the Jacobin stage of the French revolution, is a classic example of the phenomenon. In Russia the terror developed into a stratagem which was used repeatedly. Although the threat of oppression and harsh treatment of individuals was never absent, one can identify five particular waves of terror or of intensified repression of whole groups of the population after the Bolsheviks seized power. The first wave was initiated by Lenin in the spring and summer of 1918. Although this wave of the 'red' terror was declared by Lenin to be finished by August 1918, its overspill lasted until the 10th Congress of the party in 1921, when the New Economic Policy was inaugurated. Its counterpart was the 'white' terror unleashed by the counter-revolutionary armies on territories temporarily conquered by them.

The second wave of terror or mass repression was initiated by Stalin in the autumn of 1928. Its main target was the peasantry, first, as a kind of rehearsal, in the Ural and Siberian areas, then from 1929 to 1932 in the country as a whole. Particularly affected was the Ukraine. As a by-product of that terror, all sorts of private enterprises, however small-scale they might be, were also eliminated.

The third wave (1936–8) of terror and persecution, the second of those orchestrated by Stalin, was directed against his opponents in the party and against all people of standing who might have been in some way dangerous to Stalin's undertakings. In principle, therefore, it was directed against the party cadres and the intelligentsia in general.

The fourth wave of mass punitive repression affected all people belonging to nationalities suspected of collaboration with the Germans during the Second World War – the Balkars, the Chechens, the Ingush, the Kalmyks, the Karachays, the Meshkets, the Wolga Germans and the Crimean Tatars; and additionally, after the war, the Greeks in the Black Sea areas.[32]

The fifth wave of terror, or rather summary retribution, was aimed at Russian prisoners in the Second World War. On the assumption that, because Russia was engaged in a life-and-death struggle against Nazi Germany, all USSR soldiers were expected to prefer death to captivity, those who allowed themselves to become German prisoners and after the war returned to the USSR were sent to concentration camps as a punishment for their unpatriotic behaviour, and, perhaps more importantly, as a precaution against possible infiltration by foreign agents.

On the evidence of the fabricated 'doctors' plot', a sixth wave of terror, this time against people suspected of 'divided loyalties', was in preparation in 1953. This, however, did not materialise owing to Stalin's death and the subsequent wave of liberalisation.

This persistence of terror in the Russian revolution is usually blamed on Stalin's personal cruelty. He definitely was the main villain, but the fact that so many people went along with what he did, and that, despite later revelations about the terror and the persecution of innocent people, Stalin's memory is still honoured in some parts of Russia, indicates that the propensity to use terror against one's enemies was not a feature alien to Russian political culture. Apparently, the traditional tendency to accept cruelty from the autocrat as his legitimate prerogative was combined with,[33] and strengthened by, the claim that the Bolshevik regime was acting in furtherance of a historical necessity, as revealed by an allegedly scientific doctrine of societal development – a necessity which, given the difficult internal and external conditions in which Russia found herself, did not allow for too many scruples.

The emergence of satellite regimes outside the USSR itself is a salient feature of the international implications of the Bolshevik revolution. A comparison with the French revolution may be useful. The ideas of the French revolution, too, were found susceptible for export; there was a series of attempts to found republics on the French model in the neighbouring countries. Something similar happened during the course of the Bolshevik revolution, but in a considerably different way. The original attempt to instigate revolutions in neighbouring countries, especially Germany, failed. Despite several repetitions between 1919 and 1923, the multiple dysfunction there was not of sufficient magnitude to produce a revolutionary situation. Unlike the young French Republic, the young Soviet Union was not in a position to help foreign revolutions. Rather, it had to make territorial concessions to its neighbours or temporarily allow some non-Russian territories to emancipate themselves from Soviet rule.[34] Therefore the Soviet satellite revolutions had to be postponed until the international situation was more favourable. This happened with Hitler's 'help' in the wake of the Second World War.

Then, all countries that the Soviet armies had entered during the course of the war, irrespective of whether they were conquerors or liberators, were forced to transform their political and socio-economic systems according to the Soviet example. Combined pressure, on the one hand from the local communists who everywhere had to be accepted into the government and gained the key posts in the armed forces and police, and on the other hand from the menace of interference by Soviet armies or their actual intervention, did the job within three years of the end of the war. Thus Bulgaria, Czechoslovakia, East Germany, Hungary, Poland and Romania became, in all important matters, dependent on the USSR. Only Yugoslavia and Albania, where the Soviet military presence was marginal and where the local communists' take-over was due mainly to their success in a civil war, managed to preserve their independence and build their political and socio-economic systems in a different way: Yugoslavia tended towards more relaxation and genuine federalisation; Albania stuck firmly to an all-embracing tight control on all walks of life.

Another suitable destination for the export of the Bolshevik revolution seemed to be the underdeveloped countries of Asia, Africa and partly also Latin America, where tensions arose from conditions similar to those in pre-revolutionary Russia, namely from the challenge of Western civilisation. An attempt at the expansion of the satellite sphere into South Korea (1950–1), however, was thwarted, as was the attempt in 1962 to make Cuba a Soviet base for nuclear weapons. Cuba, however, developed into a genuine Soviet satellite in the Western hemisphere, having been largely dependent politically and economically on the USSR and its allies.

The halt called to this expansion was a temporary one. As soon as the leftist regimes in several African and Middle Eastern countries, after performing a Lenin-type right-wing shift, reorientated their foreign policy towards the USSR, the Soviet Union used this opportunity to restart its expansion, this time by diplomatic means and military aid rather than by direct military intervention. Though not always successful and sometimes suffering setbacks, the most conspicuous being in Egypt and Somalia, the USSR was able to gain and, until its own collapse, sustain footholds on both sides of the Gulf of Aden and in what was once French Indochina.

This type of indirect expansion, in which Cuba also played a helpful military role, characterised the period from the end of the 1960s until 1979, when again a direct military expansion, this time into Afghanistan, took place. For the military intervention in Afghanistan a suitable scenario was provided by the Iranian revolution. In this development there seems to be a certain parallel with the configuration of the 1930s and 1940s. In 1939 the anti-Western regime in Germany eliminated Poland from the political map of Europe, isolated the Baltic states, and exposed them, along with the eastern Polish territories, to Soviet occupation. The power vacuum created in Central Europe by Hitler's defeat opened that area to a further Soviet advance. The Iranian anti-Western Ayatollahdom has created a similar situation with respect to Afghanistan.

Unlike the revolutionary or Napoleonic expansion of France, however, the Soviet Stalinist and post-Stalinist expansion was carried on in an extremely cautious way. The USSR was careful not to engage itself directly and simultaneously on several fronts as had, for instance, both Napoleon and Hitler. Both common sense and a knowledge of history provided a sufficient warning. The Chosen People had to preserve their bastion intact while performing their missionary task and waging their holy wars, as far as possible, by proxy.

Why the new turn of events?

As has been stressed earlier, there is no single cause that can provide a satisfactory explanation for the course of historical events. The quest for an understanding of the unexpected turn of events in the course of the Russian revolution is a case in point to consider multiple causation.

Throughout the USSR there was a growing feeling of disappointment with the achievements of the regime. The promise of catching up and overtaking the capitalist world not only did not materialise, but the gap in living standards and quality of life between capitalist and socialist 'modes of production' began to widen unfavourably for the USSR. As the catching up and overtaking was a key element of the Soviet doctrine, indeed the main point in its mundane eschatology, the doctrine itself was bound to suffer a credibility setback.[35]

This was all the more embarrassing as there was no further excuse for a continued tightening of the belt. The construction of socialism in one country, a construction based on large-scale industrialisation and undertaken with the utmost brutality, was completed. The immediate human cost, estimated at 15–20 million dead, appeared to many as a futile sacrifice. With a still higher human cost, the devastating German attack on the USSR in the Second World War turned, with the assistance of the Western Allies, into a Soviet victory. The gain from the newly acquired territories and satellite countries, however, was soon offset by extended support for further revolutionary movements and socialist regimes throughout the world.

The situation perceived by growing numbers of people can be described as a twofold relative deprivation: with respect to aspiration at home, and, despite strenuous effort to conceal the facts, in comparison with life abroad. Nevertheless, there was still continuous pride in the achievements of the USSR as a superpower, a position that emerged from the Second World War. But this pride was eventually eroded in an extremely difficult campaign which, after seven years of bitter fighting, resulted in complete failure. The comparison between the Soviet withdrawal from Afghanistan and the American withdrawal from Vietnam became commonplace in international political commentaries. The fact that the enemy had also lost face earlier was of little consolation.

Meanwhile, people began to be aware of yet another cost of socialist industrialisation: its disastrous ecological impact. The fact that the statistics about various aspects of human life ceased to be published could not conceal the continuous decline in the birth rate and life expectancy, the worsening of health conditions and the growing rates of infant mortality and abortion.

The loss of credibility in the official doctrine produced an ideological void which could not be filled by anything that would provide a common link for the multi-ethnic Soviet Union as a whole. The only available alternatives were ethnic and/or religious loyalties. Nationalism, strengthened by particular religious allegiances, became the strongest factor, especially Great Russian nationalism from which the Soviet regime drew abundantly. On the one hand, the federal structure of the USSR, ingeniously devised by Stalin, acknowledged a certain degree of cultural, and in particular linguistic, self-determination for each ethnic group. On the other hand, however, the highly centralised Communist Party, the *de jure* and *de facto* leading force in the whole federation, prevented any centrifugal tendencies from developing into a serious menace. The right of Union republics to secede, declared by the Constitution, was made dependent on so many conditions that its practical use was quite illusory. With the widening of the credibility gap, the ideological grip over the non-Russian territories was gradually substituted by the 'old boy network', where vested interests survived by striking informal deals with the influential sections of the domestic population, such as the cotton growers in Uzbekistan.

The official self-criticism in the USSR now slowly emerging described this situation as a 'stagnation'. In many respects it was really a decline which could not remain concealed from those who dared to push the critique into the open. The international situation allowed them to go further still.

Here we come to a point which has rarely been discussed by scholars in the field. Observers who followed the demographic trends in various parts of the world could not fail to realise that both the superpowers, the USSR and the United States, were beginning to represent a dwindling share of the world population. In one particular area, i.e. the Middle East, where both superpowers had a stake, the demographic upsurge was given a strong and menacing impetus by the resurgence of militant Islam.

The rival superpowers, followed by their respective allies, did not hesitate to supply sophisticated weaponry to those countries whose policies appeared to them, directly or indirectly, favourable to their respective interests. While in their direct contacts the superpowers were engaged in the cold war, in the Middle East and elsewhere they waged their little hot wars by proxy. Gradually, however, a new awareness began to surface, namely that eventually these proxies might become even more dangerous than the main foe. They had an uncomfortable propensity for switching sides whenever it seemed to them that the other superpower might be more helpful. How difficult the containment of pugnacious peoples might become, even in the face of technical superiority, was amply demonstrated by the failure of the two superpowers in Vietnam and Afghanistan.

In contrast to the volatile situation around the periphery, the core, dominated by the rivalling power blocs, presented a stable framework for a power game, short of using arms. Paradoxically, but also quite rationally, the tremendous striking power of the superpowers and their capability for mutual annihilation was the main deterrent, restraining the cold war from slipping into a hot one.

The balance of fear between the two blocs, however, was not correspondingly echoed by the smaller states possessing nuclear weapons. The drive for self-preservation pushed both superpowers to rid themselves of the lethal menace, while at the same time securing the non-proliferation of nuclear weaponry. Although the mutual mistrust was enormous, nevertheless the need to halt the deadly nuclear arms race led to cautious but persistent negotiations. Despite many bluffs and setbacks, the underlying trend was clear: to stop the race and to contain the danger from other quarters.

In such a situation, those in the USSR who were conscious of the need for a substantial restructuring of the political and economic system could move ahead. Although many risks were still to be faced, the danger of a real hot war between the two blocs could rightly be considered as non-existent. Thus Gorbachev could start his great venture – the timing was right. However, the task was beyond Gorbachev's (and perhaps anybody else's) capability. It eventually slipped out of his hands.

Gorbachev's programme of openness (*glasnost*) and reconstruction (*perestroika*) presented a conscious response to internal challenges. As a result, the Russian revolution entered its third phase; it had started as a revolution from above, as it did in the time of Peter the Great. But gradually, with the growing openness, spontaneous ideas and programmes began to surface. As at the beginning of a revolution from below, after the opening breakthrough had been made, opinions began to differentiate. At stake were the extent and speed of economic reform aiming at the transition to a market economy, and the filling of the quasi-democratic institutions with real democratic content. This implied a new constitutional status for individual member republics, autonomous republics and regions of the Russian federation.

But once the door for spontaneous development had been opened, there was no way for a coordinated, let alone a systematic, tackling of the key issues. More successful abroad than at home, Gorbachev failed to steer the multifaceted reform through the various bodies and their shades of opinion. Although international tension became diffused and the standing of the USSR in world politics temporarily increased, at home the latent tensions came into the open. Eventually, in August 1991, a *coup* was mounted by conservative elements in the Communist Party, and Gorbachev was kept isolated in his holiday resort at Crimea. The time for manoeuvring was over. The situation required a person of action, who would not shrink from taking the lead at the barricades. In such a capacity, Yeltsin, who had been elected president of the Russian Federal Republic in June 1991, stepped in. Gorbachev returned to Moscow, his position shattered, and the dissolution of the USSR was hastened.

As could be expected, it was the ethnic differentiation, based on language and partly also on religion, that appeared the most divisive of all the possible splits. The right of the Union's constituent (member) republics to secede, a right embodied in the Soviet Constitution merely as window-dressing, began to be taken seriously. All the fifteen republics constituting the Union declared their sovereignty and only nine of them joined – though with different degrees of involvement – the newly created Commonwealth of Independent States (Alma Ata Declaration of December 1991). But this was not the end of the fissiparous process. A considerable number of smaller ethnic groups which, under the Soviet Constitution, were endowed with a lesser status of autonomy than that of a republic, joined the drive for more independence.[36]

Two years earlier, the Soviet leadership, with Gorbachev still in full command, had allowed the nominally sovereign states and member countries of the Warsaw Pact to emancipate themselves from Soviet tutelage. In this respect the Soviet leadership showed more readiness and less resistance than the British and the French, who had disbanded their colonial empires thirty to forty years earlier.

It seemed that once the myths of the Great Proletarian Revolution and the Socialist Fatherland had lost their emotional and, to some extent, their doctrinal appeal, the old-fashioned colonial mentality, which meanwhile had become widely discredited, could not be revived as a legitimate substitute for the lost ideological bond.

It is difficult to imagine any other pragmatic reason for non-interference in the emancipation process than the obvious inability to hold the whole complex together by force. Although the military hardware and striking capacity were fully available, the necessary fighting spirit could no longer be aroused after the experience of Afghanistan. Economic interests were certainly at stake, but the state of the Soviet economy was so dismal that its total reconstruction, possibly with Western help, appeared a better prospect than the already diminishing advantages of maintaining the dominant position in the Council for Mutual Economic Assistance, the economic counterpart of the Warsaw Pact.

The collapse of the empire: the Russian revolution comes full circle

The emancipation of the so-called satellite states from the domination of the USSR has often been described as a series of revolutions. In terms of the typology suggested in this book, however, these events certainly cannot be considered revolutions in the proper sense of the word. The overthrow of the *anciens régimes* occurred in a surprisingly non-violent way. Action was taken both from below and from above. With the exception of Romania, there was no real fighting, only mass demonstration, strikes and clashes with the police. There were no barricades, and neither the army nor the workers' militia interfered. Technically, it was a negotiated transfer of power; its consequences, however, are far-reaching. The metaphor of revolution can justifiably be applied to the resulting social change.

The opposition had shown its willingness to negotiate in order to achieve more civil liberties, in particular freedom of speech and freedom of the press, for many years. The call for a dialogue with the authorities was repeatedly voiced by various dissident groups. But the will on the communist side to enter into such a dialogue and negotiate only emerged as a result of changes in the USSR. In Poland, attempts at a negotiated settlement had taken place as early as 1981. Here the opposition had managed to become institutionalised in the independent trade union, known as Solidarity, which had a large membership. Soviet pressure on the Polish government, however, prevented these efforts from coming to fruition.[37]

In the late 1980s the Soviet grip over the satellite communist regimes began to relax; regimes accustomed to following the Soviet lead found themselves without any secure guidance. Communist leaders who did not want to emulate the Soviet example of 'openness' (*glasnost*) and 'reconstruction' (*perestroika*) found themselves in an unexpected dilemma. They began to realise that in their own country they could no longer rely on Soviet help against the opposition. Perhaps they were even encouraged to yield. The situation was not quite clear in this respect. Contradictory signals were emitted to the satellites because in the USSR various groups were still engaged in a power struggle. Some communist leaders, such as those in East Germany and Czechoslovakia, wanted to believe that Gorbachev's leadership was a temporary phenomenon, and that they would be able to survive his era of reform by merely paying lip-service to its principles. Nevertheless, their resolve to defend their monopoly of power by force was shattered; consequently they preferred to appease the domestic opposition. As the opposition lacked any means of armed struggle, it was possible to embark on negotiation with the intention of diffusing the tension and surviving, possibly with a compromise arrangement.

Eventually, the old ruling class yielded more than it had intended. The *ancien régime* had to go, but its 'cadres' were able to retain most of their positions, particularly in the economy, culture and even in state administration. Only collaboration with the secret police became an obstacle to assuming high office. In contrast, when the communists had taken power in the late 1940s, their 'imported revolution' did not offer the defeated ruling class any escape route from their ruin. The emancipation from communist rule, which was simultaneously national liberation from foreign domination, was easier; it was carried out under the assumption that the old regime would not use force and the new regime would refrain from retribution. Even in Romania, where force was used, it was only perpetrated by part of the *ancien régime*. Communist converts to democracy stepped in on the other side of the barricade, thus securing for themselves a better prospect of survival than was the case elsewhere.

Having stressed the absence of revolutionary violence in the demise of the communist regimes in 1989–90, we must not forget that the comparatively quiet transfer of power was preceded by two serious revolutionary attempts, within a decade of the communist take-over, aimed at shaking off communist domination: the first in 1953 in East Germany, and the other in 1956 in Hungary. In Berlin and other East German cities it was mainly a workers' uprising, and thus it can be qualified as an attempt at a social revolution. In Hungary the revolt had a broader base; it was a full-fledged national revolution in which the anti-Soviet (i.e. national) communists, headed by Imre Nagy, played a key role. Both these revolutions were brutally suppressed by Soviet military intervention. In Hungary, the cost in lives (both from fighting and executions) has been estimated at 4,500; around 20,000 were arrested, and many more were deported to the Soviet Union. About 200,000 (2 per cent of the total population) left the country to go into exile.[38]

A less radical communist opposition to Soviet domination was latent in Poland. It surfaced for the first time in 1956; but its leader, Gomulka, preferred not to upset the dominant position of the USSR. Twelve years later, in 1968, the reform communists, with Dubček at the helm, took over the positions of leadership in Czechoslovakia, but their attempts to introduce substantial economic and political reforms were frustrated by Soviet military intervention (this being formally, the intervention of all the Warsaw Pact countries except Romania). About 140,000 people (1 per cent of Czechoslovakia's population) went into exile in 1968–9, as had happened after the communist take-over in 1948.[39] From then on no further attempts at secession (horizontal revolution) were undertaken. Only the Polish workers, enjoying the spiritual support of the Catholic Church (most Poles are practising Catholics) kept the spirit of defiance alive.

All this had to be briefly mentioned in order to show that the negotiated transfers of power in 1989–90 were the culmination of earlier and more dramatic – albeit frustrated – attempts at emancipation.

Through negotiation, power was bound to be transferred gradually. Understandably, the communists tried to retain as much power as possible for themselves. For that purpose they had to change sides. There were two alternative tactics available: either to play the dedicated democrats or to become fervent nationalists. For the crypto-communists there was no problem of adaptation.

Conversion to democracy, whether feigned or sincere (often passively accepted as a 'historical necessity'), not only provided a good opportunity for a further career but also enabled the transformation of the traditional, all power-seeking, Communist Party into a more-or-less acquiescing segment of the pluralistic political and economic structure. The market economy, with its new prospects for advancement, provided many suitable substitutes for the loss of powerful positions.

With the exception of the main communist faction in the Czech republic, the communists adopted another name. This, however, made little impact on their electoral appeal. Yet their reorientation and, on the other hand, the failure of new governments to steer the socio-economic transformation without too much hardship, give them a chance of resuming some influence on further development.

Where local conditions were propitious, embracing nationalism offered the communists more opportunity for self-assertion. As nationalists they could even attempt to cling to power. Before 1989, national communism or, rather, communist nationalism had been a well-tried method of keeping tight control. The Romanian and Bulgarian communist leaderships, in particular, played this card with vigour and ruthlessness; ethnic minorities were the main victims.

The shift from communism to nationalism was a comparatively easy undertaking. Marx and Lenin might have gone, but the commanding heights in society and the economy must be preserved! Autocephalic orthodox churches, traditionally identified with the national cause, provided welcome spiritual support to post-communist nationalism. Occasionally, other churches or religious bodies also offered similar help.

The most virulent kind of nationalism emerged, however, from a comparatively mild kind of communism in Yugoslavia. Under Tito's leadership the communists there had assumed power, not with the help of the Soviet armies but as a result of their victory in a civil war which ran parallel with the struggle against the German and Italian occupation during the Second World War. Defying Soviet domination, the Yugoslav communists managed to develop their own, more market-orientated and also more open brand of socialism; this also permitted a more meaningful federation than was the case with the federal arrangement in the USSR. But the collapse of communism all over Europe and, above all, the disappearance of the menace represented by the imperial aspirations of the USSR, stripped Yugoslavia of its main unifying link. As had been amply demonstrated during the Second World War, the common Serbo-Croat language alone, without any ideological back-up, was no effective substitute for the traditional allegiance to a particular religion and connected culture. Divisions along religious and ethnic lines, combined with a tribal mentality and resentment of cohabitation in mixed settlements, constitute a latent danger of bitter conflict. Once these conflicts break out, frequently leading to atrocities, they may become a repeated phenomenon. Yugoslavia and the Lebanon are the best examples of this retrograde development.

In the Soviet Union itself the conversion of communists into nationalists had begun to spread long before the demise of the communist regime. For those Russians who were proud of the imperial grandeur of the USSR, there was little difference between the two creeds. Among the non-Russians, nationalism arose mainly from discontent with the dominant position of Russians and of the Russian language in the federation. But in the ethnically mixed territories, where members of several non-Russian nations lived together, nationalism was stimulated more by the mutual rivalry of these smaller nations. The collapse of dictatorship and the disintegration of the USSR brought all these rivalries and enmities into the open. Nationalism has become most virulent in those areas where language, religion and a tribal mentality constituted an insoluble union, such as that in the Caucasus area. Where religious bonds united several nations, such as in Central Asia, the situation became more complicated. Linguistic, 'lay' nationalism clashed with communalism based on religious allegiance. Turkey, with her remarkable record of Westernisation, is the paradigm for the lay nationalists, whereas Iran, with her outright rejection of the Euro-American civilisation, is attractive to those who favour religious revival. Thus the need to cope with the Western challenge meets in Central Asia, and also among other Muslim peoples in the former USSR, with two alternative responses; both are different from the response offered by communist Russia. For the Muslims in the USSR it is no longer Lenin but either Kemal Atatürk or Ayatollah Khomeini who poses as the model of a revolutionary hero worth following.

For the Russians and the other two Slavic nations, the Ukrainians and the Belorussians, there are no new choices. The dilemma that has haunted Russia since Peter the Great has resurfaced with a new vigour. The alternatives to complete Westernisation are various brands of hybridisation.

At the time of writing these lines (January 1994) the forces aiming at a hybrid political and socio-economic structure were gathering momentum. The division of power which emerged in Russia after the break-up of the Soviet Union prevented any consistent economic policy. Measures undertaken by the radical reformists in the government were counteracted by the inflationary policy of the National Bank. The resulting chaos led to widespread disillusionment with what was supposed to be a socio-economic transformation. At the same time the autonomous republics and regions, inhabited by non-Russian nationalities, began to arrogate to themselves more independence.

In spring 1993, two different drafts for the badly needed new Russian constitution were prepared: one by the president and the other by the Supreme Soviet (the bicameral legislative body elected from a much broader 'Congress of People's Deputies' elected by direct popular vote). The Supreme Soviet declined to respect Yeltsin's victory in the national referendum of 25 April 1993. In September Yeltsin dissolved the whole Parliament and called a new election, together with a referendum on his version of the constitution for 12 December. The Supreme Soviet refused to obey and elected the acting vice-president to the post of President of the Russian Federation instead of Yeltsin. The escalating confrontation, in which the Parliament building was put under siege and the supporters of the Parliament's leaders fired the first shots, was resolved by the Army which gave its support to Yeltsin. The Parliament building was stormed and the opposition leaders were arrested.

However the vote of December 1993 did not get rid of the dual power situation. Although Yeltsin, by a slight margin, won his constitution, the elections for the bicameral parliament under that constitution brought the reformers a crushing defeat. Radical xenophobic nationalists emerged as the strongest party. Their alliance with other antireformist parties and groupings indicated that Russia's Westernisation is not going to be an easy matter.

As in the other countries of the former Soviet Union, Russia has to work out a viable functional division of power and tackle the problems of a fundamental socio-economic transformation. The extent of the autonomy of Russia's various regions has to be clearly defined, and the issue of the political status of areas disputed between individual states has to be resolved. In many places, effective measures have to be taken against the rampant rate of organised crime. Finally, and this is the most delicate issue, Russia's leadership must decide to what extent it should be concerned with the development in other former Soviet republics, in particular those where ethnic, ideological and personal rivalries constitute a serious menace to peace in a wider area. Examples, at the time of writing, include Transcaucasia and parts of Central Asia.

Will the semi-Westernised Russia, with 25 million ethnic Russians living in other former Soviet republics where they may be exposed to various kinds of discrimination, be poised to resume the role of 'Pax Sovietica' but carry it out more subtly and skilfully than her predecessor managed to do? Or will other forces, in particular those that have emerged from the exogenous revolutions in Asia, enter the field?

Notes

1. This point has been appositely summarised in S. Fitzpatrick, *The Russian Revolution* (Oxford University Press, London, 1982) esp. pp. 96–7, 133–4 and 159–60.
2. J. Burnham, *The Managerial Revolution* (Pelican, London, 1945).
3. M. Malia, *Comprendre la Révolution russe* (Seuil, Paris, 1980), pp. 128, 214 and *passim*.
4. Cf. references made by P. Dukes, *A History of Russia* (Macmillan, London, 1974), p. 42.
5. As Ulam rightly observed, there was even an Orwellian touch to Pestel's projects, as when he suggested naming the secret police 'The Department of High Order and Benevolence' (A.B. Ulam, *Russia's Failed Revolution*, Weidenfeld & Nicolson, London, 1981, p. 36). For a detailed account of the Decembrist movement and its significance see A. G. Mazour, *The First Russian Revolution 1825* (Stanford University Press, CA, 1963).
6. S. Blanc, 'The economic policy of Peter the Great' in W.L Blackwell (ed.), *Russian Economic Development from Peter the Great to Stalin* (New Viewpoints, New York, 1974), p. 38.
7. *Ibid.*, p. 48.
8. Significantly, the rising capitalist class in Russia was largely recruited from religious minorities, such as Old Believers, Skoptsy and Jews, who were discriminated against because of their non-conformism. Among the Old Believers there was a good deal of communal collectivism (the sect's leadership was virtually in command of an accumulated fund to which individuals were often forced to bequeath their property), but the process of secularisation, starting from about the mid-nineteenth century, undermined their collectivistic, quasi-monastic ethic. Thus, within the span of one or two generations, a materialistic, property-conscious individualism was substituted for a highly developed self-denying propensity to work and save. For more detail see W.L. Blackwell, 'The Old Believers and the rise of private industrial enterprise in early 19th century Moscow', in Blackwell, pp. 139–58.
9. T.H. von Laue, 'The state and the economy', in *ibid.*, p. 202.
10. *Ibid.*, pp. 209–10.
11. I. Deutscher, *The Unfinished Revolution: Russia 1917–1967* (Oxford University Press, London, 1967), p. 14.
12. Malia, p. 213 and *passim*.
13. *Ibid.*, pp. 139 and 214 and *passim*.
14. V. Horský, 'Dějinný kontext Říjnové revoluce' (Historical context of the October Revolution), *Sociologický časopis* (Prague, 1968), pp. 1–17 and 125–45.
15. Lenin's *Collected Works*, vol. 33 (Foreign Languages Publishing House, Moscow, 1966), p. 65.
16. Horský, p. 129.
17. This point is stressed, with reference to the writings of R. Aron, H. Arendt and W. Kornhauser, by R. Pethybridge, *The Social Prelude to Stalinism* (Macmillan, London, 1974), pp. 241–2.
18. This was the situation in which the trade unions were assigned the role of promoting the 'iron but just proletarian discipline' (resolution passed by the All-Russian Congress of Trade Unions on 2 April 1918; published in I.M. Volkov *et al.* eds, *Sbornik dokumentov i materialov po istorii SSSR sovetskogo perioda*, Moscow University Press, 1966, p. 76).
19. This discovery was made by many who experienced the socialist transformation of their country after the Second World War. Only the next of kin can convince or suppress their more radical cousins. France's de Gaulle was the best person to give up Algeria and Israel's Begin was the best person to give up the Sinai peninsula.

20. The lack of understanding between the liberals and the army is witnessed by P.N. Milyukov, *Vospominaniya*, Izd-vo Chekhova, New York, 1955, vol. II, pt 8.
21. Malia, pp. 142–4.
22. V.M. Fic, *The Bolsheviks and the Czechoslovak Legion: The origin of their armed conflict, March–May 1918* (Abhinav, New Delhi, 1978), and also P. Fleming, *The Fate of Admiral Kolchak* (Hart-Davis, London, 1963).
23. Paradoxically, the victims of that kind of optimism numbered not only Karl Kautsky, whose expectations of 1902 concerning 'Russia's help in clearing the air in the West' were soon to be utterly diappointed (cf. his later writings), but also an experienced expert on Russia, the philosopher statesman and first president of the Czechoslovak Republic, T.G. Masaryk, who at the beginning of the 1920s still gave the hypothesis of Russia's Westernised development more than the benefit of the doubt. For a discussion of the roots and the consequences of this illusion see J. Krejčí, 'Masaryk and revolution', in M. Čapek and K. Hrubý (eds), *T.G. Masaryk in Perspective* (SVU Press, Ann Arbor, 1981), pp. 173–89.
24. As A.J. Toynbee (*A Study of History*, vol. III, Oxford University Press, London, 1934, pp. 200–2) perceptively observed, Marxism is a kind of Western heresy which precisely because of this flavour, is more readily acceptable to foreign civilisations menaced by the overpowering strength of the West.
25. Isaac Deutscher summarised the essence of this historical development as follows:

> the transition from Leninism to Stalinism consisted in the abandonment of a revolutionary internationalist tradition in favour of the sacred egoism of Soviet Russia; and in the suppression of Bolshevism's pristine attachment to proletarian democracy in favour of an autocratic system of government. The isolation of the Russian revolution resulted in its mental self-isolation and in its spiritual and political adaptation to the primordial Russian tradition. Stalinism represented the amalgamation of Western European Marxism with Russian barbarism. (I. Deutscher, *Russia after Stalin*, Jonathan Cape, London, 1969), p. 34.

26. A.B. Ulam, *The Unfinished Revolution* (Random House, New York, 1960), pp. 270–1.
27. V.I. Lenin, *What is to be Done?* (International Publications, New York, 1969), pp. 31–41.
28. Fitzpatrick, *Russian Revolution*, p. 160.
29. How much tougher the police apparatus became under the Bolsheviks as compared with under the tsars is described in R. Hingley, *The Russian Secret Police; Muscovite, Imperial Russian and Soviet political security operations 1565–1970* (Hutchinson, London, 1970).
30. The elections to the ill-fated Constituent Assembly which took place in November 1917 – though incomplete in nation-wide coverage (44.4 million out of about 160 million of the total population) – showed the approximate support for individual political groupings. The Socialist Revolutionaries polled over 40 per cent, the Bolsheviks 24 per cent, the Mensheviks barely 3 per cent, the Constitutional Democrats barely 5 per cent and other groups, in Soviet sources classified as Russian or non-Russian petit bourgeois and bourgeois nationalist and others (such as the Cossacks), polled the remaining 28 per cent of votes. (L.M. Spirin, *Klassy i partii v grazhdanskoi voine v Rossii*, Izd. Mysl', Moscow, 1968, pp. 59 and 416–19.)
31. R.A. Medvedev, *On Stalin and Stalinism* (Oxford University Press, London, 1979) pp. 178–82.
32. For detail see for instance R. Conquest, *The Nation Killers: The Soviet deportation of nationalities* (Macmillan, London, 1970).

33. In this context, we may refer to the influential teaching of Joseph of Volokolamsk (1439–1518), a clergyman whose views were largely adopted by the Orthodox Church in Russia, and who maintained that the tsar was equal in power to God, from whom he had received the authority to resolve all secular and ecclesiastical matters in his country. (D. Tschiżewskij, *Das heilige Russland: russische Geistesgeschichte*, vol. I, Rowohlt, Hamburg, 1959, pp. 70ff.)

34. The most conspicuous case was that of the Transcaucasian republics whose independence was liquidated by the combination of Bolshevik plots and Soviet military intervention. Georgia survived, under its widely supported Menshevik government, until February 1921. The Baltic republics were a little more fortunate; they were incorporated into the USSR only on the eve of the Second World War.

35. As the detailed studies of Western Kremlinologists (many of Russian origin) revealed, the standard of living remained below the pre-First World War level for a long time. Until the early 1950s the average standard of living only twice exceeded that of 1913: at the end of the 1920s (at the height of the New Economic Policy which allowed the peasants free disposition of their property after the demise of War Communism) and at the end of the 1930s (towards the end of the second Five Year Plan in the final stages of the great purge of the Bolshevik cadres). Only in the mid-1950s, after Stalin's death and a decade after the Second World War, did the increase in living standards become more enduring. At that time millions of prisoners were released from the concentration and labour camps. Despite a significant improvement, the gap in living standards between the USSR and the West was becoming still wider. In comparison with the West, smaller income differentials were outweighed by a much greater contrast as far as the personal freedom of individual citizens was concerned. Almost everybody was under some sort of administrative constraint although the degree varied considerably.

36. The development is analysed in A. Pravda (ed.), *The End of the Outer Empire, Soviet–East European Relations in Transition, 1985–90* (The Royal Institute of International Affairs, Sage Publications, London, 1992). For a brief descriptive account of the sequence of events see C. Tilly, *European Revolutions, 1492–1992* (Blackwell, Oxford, 1993), pp. 228–32. For a wider context see G. Swain and N. Swain, *Eastern Europe since 1945* (Macmillan, London, 1993).

37. For a comprehensive account see. L. Goodwyn, *Breaking the Barrier: The rise of Solidarity in Poland* (Oxford University Press, Oxford, 1991).

38. The story of the Hungarian uprising is told in M. Molnár, *Budapest 1956: A history of the Hungarian revolution* (Allen & Unwin, London, 1971).

39. J. Krejčí, *Czechoslovakia at the Crossroads of European History* (I.B. Tauris, London, 1990, p. 191).

5

□

Turkey (1876–   )

The nature of the revolution

Seen in the context of this study, the Turkish revolution is a parallel case to the Russian and Chinese revolutions. All of them happened during the same period and all of them were particular responses to one and the same much wider challenge: the challenge of the dynamic West European, and later Euro-American, civilisation, encroaching on the outside world.

Significantly, the actors in the Turkish revolution saw it most clearly in that light, i.e. in terms of a conflict between the less efficient domestic and the more efficient foreign civilisation. The fateful consequences of this gap or, rather, lag had already been realised long before the revolution, and had led to a series of reforms or attempts at reform which were aimed at introducing West European technology, skills and organisation into the military and administrative apparatus of the Ottoman Empire.

In Turkey, in contrast to Russia, the process of Westernisation collided with the impregnable barrier of religion and law which considered the whole of European culture as unworthy of interest. Whereas Peter the Great and his followers could bypass religious opposition, in the world of Islam the fortress of religion and religiously grounded law had eventually to be stormed by a frontal attack. Thus, in contrast to Russia, the period of Europeanisation, which in Turkey preceded the revolution, did not create a stratum large enough to breed the illusion (either at home or abroad) that the civilisational barrier between the challengers and the challenged had already been lifted.

Unlike China, Turkey did not possess that sort of exclusive, clearly demarcated socio-cultural heritage which, sustained by several millenia and supported by an extraordinarily vast population, gave China a particularly strong self-contained identity and made it an almost impregnable and culturally self-sufficient world. In contrast to China, Ottoman Turkey did not possess a civilisation of its own. The Turkic nations embraced the already well-developed Islamic civilisation, and the Ottoman Turks, having carved out their domain in an area abounding in countless vestiges of other civilisations, had to create a particular pluralistic framework which enabled them to preserve both their newly acquired Islamic identity in its orthodox Sunnite version and their domination over the different subject peoples, who only partly shared their civilisation.

Furthermore, unlike the Russians and Chinese, who were well aware of what they were and how they differed from the rest of the world, the Turks did not pay too much attention to their Turkishness. They were called Turks by foreigners rather than by themselves. The inhabitants of what is nowadays Turkey saw themselves primarily as Muslims; only the primitive peasants of Anatolia were, condescendingly, described as Turks. It was religion, not ethnicity, which gave them a sense of dignified belonging. Only in second place did they see themselves as subjects of the Ottoman sultans, an awareness which, however, was blurred by the fact that the Ottoman sultan happened also to be the caliph, i.e. the titular head of the whole Sunnite Muslim community both within and without the Ottoman Empire.

The idea that the Turkish-speaking Muslims of the Ottoman Empire might be primarily Turks and be proud of it came to them only through the revolution. The revolution awakened in them a national consciousness and made of what remained of the dissolved multi-ethnic and multi-religious empire a nation-state. As a result of the revolution, the institutional and symbolic vestiges of the supranational Islamic civilisation, including its Arabic script, were discarded, and the Turks were provided with a secular nation-state with West European type institutions and Latin script, without being deprived of their Islamic creed. Furthermore, the Turkish language was purified of the most intrusive Arabic and Persian influences. Because this was the nub of the changes brought about by the Turkish revolution and because nationalism played an almost exclusive role in it – unlike in the other revolutions strongly coloured by nationalistic motifs, such as the Czech, the French and the Chinese ones – we may appositely apply to the Turkish revolution the differentiating epithet 'national'.

The creation of a self-conscious Turkish nation and nation-state was, however, not the only aim. It was understood as a constituent part of a thorough Europeanisation or Westernisation which, as has already been said, had to elevate the population of Turkey to the cultural and technological level of the West European nations; the developmental gap between Western Europe and the lands of the Ottoman Empire was to be abolished.

As in Russia and China there were, of course, different proposals with respect to the degree of change to be brought about. In Turkey, too, there were attempts at a compromise solution. But, after more than one hundred years, the decision in favour of complete Europeanisation won the upper hand. Contrary to the case of Russia and China, a specific way out of the impasse which might have drawn more upon domestic resources remained within the realm of theoretical considerations. In the view of those who led the revolution to final victory, the

Turks had no choice other than a wholesale reception of the West European way of life. As one of the most radical Westernisers, Abdullah Cevdet, put it, 'There is no second civilisation; civilisation means European civilisation, and it must be imported with both its roses and its thorns'.[1] Also for Kemal Atatürk, the founder of modern Turkey, there was no other civilisation to choose. In view of its pluralistic structuring, especially with respect to its geographical division into sovereign nation-states, the Western, or Euro-American, civilisation could best serve both needs: undisputed national identity and civilisational dynamism. Last, but not least, it did not require a religious conversion.

In a sense, the Turkish revolution simply completed by a bold, general sweep what previous generations had attempted to achieve only partially and by piecemeal reforms. The most far-reaching changes could be achieved only after the compromise-prone semi-*ancien régime* had been destroyed and the revolutionary dictatorship could impose its will upon a nation carved out of a differently shaped societal compound.

It remains to be seen whether such an imposed civilisational transplant can be properly assimilated by the Turkish people.

The ethno-religious slant of the social structure

As is well known, the Ottoman Empire was a multi-racial, multi-lingual and multi-religious society. It was upheld by a system of unequal partnership in which religious allegiance played the most important role. The whole population was divided among religious communities to which people owed their primary loyalty. The Muslim community, the *ümmet* (better known under the Arabic equivalent *umma*) was at the top of the social pyramid. However, it did not constitute an institutional association. All its communal functions were provided by the Ottoman establishment, the *din-u-devlet*, a polity that made no distinction between state and religion. All other religious communities constituted their own, to a large extent autonomous, communal associations, the *millets*. Each *millet* had its own jurisdiction over its members, and usually, but not necessarily, used its own language or languages and generally also its own writing.[2]

As a rule only the Muslims – whether born as such or converted – were called to serve the state in either the civil or the armed services. The others were exempt from this duty, but had to pay an extra poll tax. Conversions from Islam to any other religion were forbidden, while conversions to Islam were in practice encouraged but in fact happened mainly in the case of the *devşirme*, those drafted to the imperial services from among the adolescent males of the Christian population. The reason for this practice was that, in contrast to the general principle of closed communities (whether religious or professional) to which everybody was assigned, 'the military and administrative orders of the central government should possess no roots in the society and should bear allegiance only to their ruler'.[3]

In comparison with pre-Enlightenment Europe, Ottoman society was tolerant and in some senses even more pluralistic, although this tolerant pluralism operated on an unequal basis and with some discrimination.

Although, with the exception of Jews, the ethno-religious groups were socially diversified (they cultivated land and engaged in crafts and small trade), there was a considerable difference between Greeks and Armenians on the one hand, and Turks and other nationalities such as the Balkan Slavs, Albanians, Kurds, etc., on the other. The Greek and Armenian diaspora outside their compactly settled regions were predominantly engaged in craft and commerce. As a result of this the division of labour acquired in many cities a strong ethno-religious bias. Furthermore, a good deal of foreign trade was left to the foreigners – West European merchants; thus the main contacts with the expanding European economy were in the hands of foreigners and/or ethno-religious minorities – Greeks, Armenians and Jews.

As a result of this situation, there was little scope within the Turkish-speaking community for the emergence of their own bourgeoisie via the usual channels of development, i.e. by means of large-scale trade and manufacturing. The Muslim, Turkish-speaking bourgeoisie developed in the first instance from the government service, by and large *pari passu* with its Europeanisation throughout the nineteenth century. Teachers, army officers, doctors and technicians (especially in the field of telecommunications), i.e. mainly the salaried strata, were its backbone. The entrepreneurial bourgeoisie entered the stage only later, roughly with the beginning of the twentieth century.[4] Until then, it was only the urban artisanat and local merchants who constituted a sort of lower middle class in Turkish society. With a very limited level of industrialisation before the revolution, the industrial proletariat cropped up only in a few urban centres; since it was numerically weak and of diverse ethnic stock its role in the revolution, carried out under nationalistic banners, could not be a significant one.

The equality of Ottoman subjects irrespective of religion, proclaimed in 1839 by the Noble Rescript of the Rose Chamber (*Hatt-i-Serif* of *Gülhane*), but implemented only later, rather gradually and with qualifications, implied that all Ottoman subjects became citizens on equal terms. This meant that the Christians and Jews were to lose their communal autonomy but were to become eligible for civil and eventually also military service. They were supposed to acquire an undifferentiated Ottoman national consciousness.[5] The same process of substituting national for religious loyalties awoke among the subject ethnic groups the sense of their own national identity. The Greeks, the Serbs, the Bulgarians and eventually the Albanians succeeded in building – by a piecemeal process of insurrection and conquest (wars of independence) – their own nation-states in what had been the European part of the Ottoman Empire, so-called Rumelia.

In Anatolia the main ethnic Christian minorities were the Armenians, in the northeastern corner, and the Greeks, scattered all over the coastal areas and especially in the cities. These minorities got into an extremely difficult position.

On the one hand, the abolition of the *millets* formally made them equal citizens of the empire; on the other hand, the principle of nationalism, which gradually affected all the ethnic groups within the empire, opened up to them the perspective of a national independence. This was not so feasible for the Greeks, who lived in diaspora, as for the Armenians, who in part inhabited compact territories. Here too, however, the demarcation would have been difficult because the clusters of Armenian, Turkish and Kurdish villages were dispersed throughout the whole area, and in the cities too there were separate Turkish and Armenian quarters. The Ottoman principle of the *millets* was well suited to this situation. On the basis of personal allegiance it enabled all members of the ethno-religious community to enjoy communal partnership and protection. Once the system of the *millets* was abolished, however, the Armenians and Greeks had either to merge their national identity with the Ottoman one or to try to obtain, and be incorporated into, their own nation-states.

In the Greek case this dilemma was eventually resolved, after the Greek defeat in the 1919–22 war, by a large-scale exchange of population between Greece and Turkey which, in spite of immense hardship and even deaths (the most notorious being the massacre of the Greek civilian population after the fall of Smyrna in 1922), nevertheless provided a viable basis for the two nations to coexist in the long term as reasonably peaceful neighbours. Unfortunately the case of the Armenians was completely resolved by the most atrocious means of a carefully organised and executed genocide.[6]

As most of the Armenian and Greek property left behind was appropriated by the Muslim population, either by Turkish immigrants from the European areas of the former empire (whose numbers, however, were incomparably inferior to those killed or expelled), or (more often) by Turkish or Kurdish neighbours, it may be inferred that a by-no-means negligible redistribution of wealth took place which may have counteracted somewhat the possible emergence of socio-economic tensions in the areas concerned.

Etiological considerations

If we try to find out which of the main contradictions listed as elements of the multiple dysfunction in the introductory chapter of this book appeared as causes, precipitants or factors of the further development of the Turkish revolution, we arrive at a picture somewhat different from the other instances analysed in this study.

Basically, in the Turkish case the main contradiction was the same as in the case of Russia, namely, to borrow Isaac Deutscher's terms, the contrast between the status and importance of a great power and the archaic weakness of its social structure and institutions. Within this general parallel, however, there was one significant difference. In Russia the status and importance of a great power was largely achieved by means of the Petrine and post-Petrine Westernisation which, however insufficient, nevertheless created a new, efficient army and also, to some extent, a functioning administration. In Turkey, the status of great power had been achieved by other means and in a much earlier epoch; its status was the result of Ottoman creativity within the context of the late Islamic civilisation from the thirteenth to the sixteenth century. The problem was that from then to the close of the seventeenth century the situation changed so much that the Ottoman Empire remained, in most aspects of societal life, far behind Western Europe.

Furthermore, in contrast to Russia, the Turkish position was not complicated by contradictions resulting from a partial Europeanisation. There was neither a significant Turkish entrepreneurial bourgeoisie, nor a rudimentary working class, nor indeed a wide currency for the imagery of the French revolution, or rather revolutions, which would make these two classes the supposed main actors in the revolution. The military superiority of the West was seen as the result of its technical and organisational superiority. For some it appeared sufficient to learn or to borrow particular skills and implant them into the context of the Ottoman state and Islamic civilisation. But the more perspicacious observers soon realised that an implant of 'productive forces' was not possible without a commensurate change in the 'mode of production', and that in the long run neither of these two would be possible without adapting the totality of people's values and priorities to such a comprehensive change. In the view of Kemal Atatürk and his associates, the change necessary to make Turkey equal in strength with its European foes and neighbours required a reorientation from a fideistic, closed world-view towards an open, inquisitive and pragmatic outlook. Thus, the leaders in the Turkish revolution possessed, perhaps without noticing it, both Marxian and Aristotelian insights on this issue.

The other aspect of the Marxian contradiction, namely the class contradiction, was in the Turkish revolution conspicuous by its insignificance. The power of what may be described as the feudal classes (*derebeys*) had already been destroyed much earlier in the teens of the nineteenth century, by the Sultan Mahmud II. The rather capitalist landlords and the rich peasants seem not to have been strongly involved on either side of the political divide, in any case not strongly enough to allow the conclusion that they identified themselves with or supported a particular political grouping. Thus it is difficult to construct a picture in which either the entrepreneurial bourgeoisie as a class, or the industrial proletariat, or even the peasantry, could be considered as social agents in the revolution. Although between the Young Turk and the Kemalist periods a certain shift from the upper to the middle strata can be observed within the body of the reformers/revolutionaries, hardly any far-reaching structural conclusions can be drawn from this shift. In the Turkish revolution the masses played a more docile role than they did in any other revolution discussed in this study. The urban proletariat was almost non-existent, the peasantry was extremely acquiescent and suffered its role as cannon fodder even more submissively than the Russian peasantry, trained for centuries in the self-denying, kenotic spirit of Orthodox Christianity. Only after the collapse of the Ottoman Empire in 1918 did the example of the Russian revolution give rise to some political activity among the disgruntled peasants. In some villages even peasant Soviets were active for a short time.[7] More impact was made by the Green Army (a movement combining socialist, Islamic and nationalist slogans), but this was soon integrated into the Kemalist mould.

We have to bear in mind that by the turn of the nineteenth century, i.e. on the eve of revolution, the social stratification of the Turkish village was not favourable to the development of conscious, ideologically sustained, social dissent. The large estates were only partly owned by absentee merchant landlords. The villages were dominated by the rich peasants, the *ağas*, whose property had largely developed from tax farming, abolished and replaced by freehold ownership under the land law of 1858. As these *ağas* lived in their domains and took direct care of their holdings, they developed a personal relationship with the small peasants who in several respects were dependent on them: in renting land from them (and then working there as share croppers), or in being hired by them as labourers, and, last but not least, in borrowing from them at a high rate of interest (which might have been paid in kind by additional services). The close, face-to-face relationship between the rich and the poor peasants discouraged open hostilities. Furthermore, the rich ones, being the only communication link between the villages and the outside world, were in a position to prevent the penetration of foreign influences into the countryside.[8] Although, as B. Lewis points out, Turkish folk literature in the nineteenth century and fiction in the twentieth century reveal a bitter struggle between the impoverished, unhappy peasants and the landlords who exploited them, the only peasant champion was the bandit – a Robin Hood type of response to the oppression.[9]

The heaviest burden for the small peasant was the tithe (*osur*) measured as a proportion of the gross production of the land, paid most often in kind, and collected by the tax farmer or landlord. It was abolished only in the second wave of reforms after the Kemalist victory in 1925. The other salient point of the Kemalist revolution that affected the peasantry, land reform, was decreed twenty years later in 1945, but its implementation has so far had little effect on the distribution of land in the country.[10]

Looking into the other contradictions scrutinised in our study, we see that both the Weberian and the Tocquevillian contradictions appeared in a slightly distorted form. The first reform moves were carried out by people at the top of the traditional power hierarchy. As their primary aim was the modernisation of the armed forces, the introduction of Western-type education for young officers was a priority. Thus a new social group of young, well-educated people emerged; their service in the armed forces brought them to a realisation of the yawning gap between what they were supposed to do and what they could actually do within the limiting constraints of the Ottoman system. The contrast was therefore not so much between wealth and social status, as between the image of potential achievement on the one hand, and the constricting political and social conditions which prevented this potential from being realised on the other. This contrast could, of course, also involve some economic grievances, but by themselves these might have led to action other than that for which the Young Turks eventually opted: conspiracy and, in 1908, military uprising against the sultan's government. Their action may be understood as a result of an intense aspirational deprivation resulting from the thirty years of Abdülhamid's despotic rule – a rule bolstered by the use of European technology and organisational methods.

As far as the Paretian contradiction is concerned, we can see its vestiges in the contrast between the behaviour of the Sultan Abdülhamid, and of the young Turkish leaders, especially their ruthless triumvirate (Enver, Cemal and Talât); and above all in the contrast between the Ottoman traditionalists and the Kemalists.

And what about the Khaldunian contrast? We would look in vain for it in the period before 1920. If there was anything of the kind it operated in favour of ethnic groups that emancipated themselves from the Ottoman rule, i.e. the advantage of a stronger motivation to fight was on the side of the Turks' enemies. Only in 1920, when Anatolia was endangered and the 'new model army' was created by Kemal and his associates, did the bygone martial spirit begin to reappear on the Turkish side, eventually proving a match for the invading forces. Only then can we talk of the superior fighting spirit of the Turkish army, but we must not overestimate the numbers of those who were imbued by that spirit. It seems that they were officers rather than the rank-and-file peasant conscripts whose fatigue – after ten years of incessant warfare – could hardly be overcome by any exhortations.[11] That amnesty extended to the bands of brigands who took part in what was understood as a war of national liberation illustrates the point.[12]

Finally, a brief comment on the precipitants and triggers. The precipitants of the 1908 explosion can be seen in circumstances which B. Lewis has described as follows:

> In the Far East, an Oriental but constitutional Japan had a few years previously defeated a European but autocratic Russia – and both Russia and Persia had accepted this demonstration of the superiority of democratic institutions, and had introduced, the one by precaution, the other by revolution, constitutional and parliamentary *régimes*. In Europe, the meeting of the English and Russian sovereigns at Reval on 9–10 June 1908 portended the obsequies of the Sick Man of Europe, and suggested an urgent need for the constitutional nostrum. And in the Empire, a wave of mutinies or rather strikes spread from Anatolia to Rumelia as Abdülhamid's unpaid, underfed and ragged soldiery rose in desperation to demand the satisfaction of a few basic, minimum human needs.[13]

And what triggered the explosion was the discovery of the officers' conspiracy, which forced them to strike earlier than originally intended.[14]

In the case of the 1920 explosion, it is difficult to disentangle the precipitants and triggers from the main causation, let alone to distinguish between them. The foreign, mainly British, occupation of the capital and the Straits, the harsh conditions of the Treaty of Sèvres, involving the loss of what before 1915 had been the Armenian homeland, the sultan's readiness to fulfil these conditions, and the attack by French, Italian and above all Greek armed forces on Anatolia – all these were simultaneous events which at one and the same time caused, precipitated and triggered the national War of Independence within what were deemed to be the just ethnic borders.

The morphology of adaptation

Since in Turkey the main issue was one of the civilisational transformation, and as the revolutionary process culminated in measures aiming at outright Westernisation, it might seem sensible to conceive of the revolutionary spectrum in Western terms. However, a political differentiation of the European type, with its familiar right-left labels, became applicable only after the main revolutionary struggle was over and the revolutionary process entered its later phase of consolidation. What was happening before can hardly be squeezed into a scheme based on the terminology of the French revolution.

Instead of looking for a generally applicable political spectrum, we must look, rather, for a sequence of positions which characterise the individual stages of development. We shall identify these positions later in the book. For the moment, however, let us distinguish two main periods: first, a period of adaptation, when Europeanisation, more or less partial, was envisaged as a device for saving the Ottoman Empire and preserving it in its historical borders; second, a period of transformation when Europeanisation, this time a thorough one, was understood as a means of providing the Turks, within their ethnic borders, with their own modern, independent, secular nation-state. Both periods were marked by hectic phases of revolutionary explosion and oscillation: the adaptation period towards its end (1908–13), and the transformation period at its beginning (1918–23).

The first reform attempts started with the impact of the French revolution. They were initiated by the Sultan Selim III in 1792 but ended in 1807 with what may be described as a pre-emptive counter-revolution by the united front of the *ulema* (jurists/theologians) and the *janissaries* (standing army), as a result of which Selim III was deposed and many of his reformers killed.

For the second period of reform the ground was prepared by a fourfold clearing operation undertaken by the Sultan Mahmud II (1808–38). First, in 1812, Mahmud II began to suppress the *derebeys* (lords of the valleys), whom Lewis describes as 'a kind of feudal vassal-princes ruling over autonomous, hereditary principalities',[15] and whose rule extended over vast stretches of southwestern, central and northeastern Anatolia. In 1826 there followed the destruction of the Ottoman master institution, the *janissaries*, which had, from the thirteenth to the sixteenth century, proved to be one of the most efficient military establishments in world history, but had then gradually degenerated into an inefficient, privileged and exploitative incubus. Finally, the military fiefs (*timars*) were abolished and government control was extended to cover the pious foundations (*evkâf*) which had constituted the main source of the independent economic power of the *ulema*.

Thus the way was open for the second reform period, the *Tanzimat* (reorganisation) under the Sultan Abdülmecid, to begin. Initiated in 1839 by the Noble Rescript of the Rose Chamber, the reforms were fairly far-reaching, albeit, in the view of critical observers, rather superficial. These reforms introduced into Ottoman society the concept of a secular state which was in straight contradiction to the Islamic tradition. Thus, almost imperceptibly, religious criteria started to be separated from the practice of government. Unfortunately, as Mardin put it, 'the *Tanzimat* statesmen contributed nothing to replace the *Şeriat* as a measuring rod of good and evil in politics'.[16] Nevertheless the *Tanzimat* period provided some important segments of what may, with some qualification, be described as the intelligentsia, such as doctors, technicians, teachers and army officers, with a specialised Western-type education. The young army officers, in particular, were favoured with a quite comprehensive and demanding education which in time equipped them to be the natural leaders of the revolution.

But the continuation of the reforms was brought to a halt by the accession in 1861 of a new sultan, Abdülaziz, during whose reign the reformers and the sultan parted company. This may be considered as the beginning of what we described in our model as the onset phase of the revolutionary process.

Developments were complicated by a twofold failure of the *Tanzimat* to live up to expectations. It promoted neither national independence nor economic progress. On the one hand, the Western powers found the reforms inadequate and increased their economic pressure, as well as pressing for greater protection of non-Muslim religious groups. On the other hand, the disruptive effect of the reforms and increasing European interference in the internal affairs of the Ottoman Empire produced growing anti-Western and anti-Christian feelings.

In order to overcome the deadlock, a new generation of reformers, the so-called Young Ottomans, looked for a solution in the introduction of a constitutional regime, under which the ruler and the government would be brought under the control of representatives of the people.[17] Another innovation was that these representatives were to be drawn from the whole population, irrespective of religious and ethnic affiliation.

In 1875 the mood was exacerbated when the protracted financial crisis of the empire culminated in bankruptcy (the parallel bankruptcy of semi-independent Egypt led to the acquisition of the majority shares of the Suez Canal by the United Kingdom).

In 1876, after some confusion in the capital, when counter-reform riots took place and two sultans were deposed, the reformers and the sultan (Abdülhamid) came together for a short while, and their agreement resulted in the first Ottoman constitution. This, however, was not based on the idea of the sovereignty of the people but on the idea of the sovereignty of God, the sultan being his vice-regent, and the constitution only a part of the *Şeriat*. Thus the function of the elected national assembly was only consultative and the sultan was entitled to prorogue it at will and at any time. This eventually happened in February 1878, after the constitution failed to impress the European powers and Russia started hostilities by helping Romania to proclaim its independence from Ottoman sovereignty.

From 1878 until 1908 the sultan ruled as an autocrat, supporting only that kind of Westernisation which, in his opinion, seemed likely to strengthen the empire and his own position.[18] Yet such a selective Westernisation was no longer acceptable to that part of the new élite which had already acquired a more Europeanised world-view and whose main programmatic catch-words became 'union' (i.e. of all ethnic and religious groups in one Ottoman nation) and 'progress' (i.e. social transformation through educational and economic measures). In terms of our morphological model the period 1878–1908 can be considered a period of compression.

The explosion came in July 1908 when the Young Turks, organised in the Committee of Union and Progress, staged a successful military uprising (sometimes called the 'Constitutional revolution') and forced the sultan to reactivate the constitution of 1876, to order elections, to appoint a government in accordance with the Committee's demands and, eventually, to resign. The new sultan, Mehmed Resad, became a stooge of the Committee. After a suppressed counter-*coup* by the conservatives in 1909 (another attempt at counter-revolution) the Committee of Union and Progress took all the government posts. Yet Italy's successful attack on Tripolitania in 1911 undermined the Committee's prestige, which had already been damaged by a series of international setbacks at the time of the revolution.[19]

A new party, the Liberal Union, also criticised the dictatorial and terroristic methods of the Committee. In July 1912, a military group ('Saviour Officers') forced the appointment of a more liberal government, the so-called 'great cabinet', but the concerted attack of the Balkan states on Turkey in October 1912 made its position extremely difficult. In view of all these events the first five years of the Young Turks' rule may be considered as a phase of oscillation.

According to Berkes's analysis, there were three schools of thought during that time: the Islamists, the Westernists and the Turkists. The Islamists of that period admitted that the Muslims were far behind the West, as regards both material and non-material civilisation, but this in their view was due to the fact that Islamic law (the *Şeriat*) was not applied thoroughly to all details of life. Furthermore, in the past, Muslims had contributed more to science than had the Europe of that time: there was no reason that they should not do so again in the future. The Westernists, on the other hand, ascribed Turkey's plight to the mental barrier created by Islam. They were mainly concerned to appropriate the Western mode of thinking: for them the technical and organisational achievements of Western civilisation were manifestations of Western ideas and values. Finally, the Turkists, whose main theorist was Ziya Gökalp, located the essence of Western civilisation not so much in rationalism or humanism, but in a nationalism in which religion also played a part. Thus Western civilisation was for them an acceptable framework for Turkish national self-assertion. This understanding allowed them to Westernise and at the same time to fight against Western imperialism. It also enabled them to substitute a clearly circumscribed concept of the Turkish nation (defined by the possession of its own literary language) for the artificial concept of a multi-ethnic, multi-lingual Ottoman nation.[20]

In January 1913 tension within the Young Turks' camp was accentuated by the defeats in the Balkan War. The Committee exploited rumours that the government wanted to make further concessions to Bulgaria, and assumed dictatorial power by a military *coup*. It held on to power for the subsequent five years, during which time (from October 1914 to October 1918) Ottoman Turkey took part in what was to become its most disastrous war (the First World War). In terms of our model this second five-year period of the Young Turks' rule can be described as a period of tightening. It also saw the most conspicuous acts of terror directed against the main enemies of united and progressive Ottomanism within what was considered the Turkish heartland.

In 1918, as a result of the defeat in the First World War and the capitulation and flight of the Young Turk leaders, the seat of power returned to the sultan, but considerable limitations were imposed on his exercise of power by the presence of the foreign occupation forces and by the crippling effects of the Peace Treaty of Sèvres. The reversal resulted in a shadowy and also short-lived restoration of what, in view of the reforms already implemented, can best be described as the semi-*ancien régime*. Nevertheless, the new sultan, Vahideddin, did his best to abolish at least the most recent reforms. Recognising the unbeatable strength of the Allied powers, he hoped to exploit his position as caliph, in which capacity he aimed to be head of all the Sunni Muslims of the British and French empires. Since Great Britain ruled over more Muslims than anyone else, Muslim unity under the British wing seemed to some Islamists the best way out of the impasse resulting from the lost war.[21]

The morphology of transformation

Understandably in such a situation, the Turkist current in Ottoman society assumed the role of saviour. Its Associations for the Defence of Rights, and Mustafa Kemal's 'Liberation Army', ignited what can be described in terms of our model as the second explosion. A short but intense civil war, combined with a war against foreign powers attempting to extend their colonial empires (France, Italy) or to enlarge their own state (Greece) into Anatolia, set in. During this, the second period of oscillation, the Westernists joined the Turkists, and the Islamists were defeated.

In 1920 the political spectrum was temporarily complicated by the appearance of a communist element. The so-called Easterners came upon the scene, urging the Turks to follow the Bolshevik example. From among the disgruntled peasants, partisan units, the so-called Green Army, were recruited, and in the National Assembly the 'Populist' group advocated socialist policies. But the progress of the pro-Soviet Communist Party was checked by the official Turkish Communist Party created and dominated by Atatürk, and eventually foiled finally by the defeat of the partisan units whose Circassian commander fled to the advancing Greeks.[22]

The expansion of the national war of liberation into pan-Turkic ventures as some radical nationalists proposed was likewise successfully prevented by Atatürk and his People's Party.

In 1922/3 the seat of power was intercepted at the Kemalist position and the break with the past was symbolised with the proclamation of a republic and with the new, more favourable, Peace Treaty of Lausanne. At that time also, the dualism of the old and new institutions initiated during the *Tanzimat* period came to an end. During the subsequent five years the most far-reaching reforms, aiming at Turkey's complete Europeanisation, were proclaimed. Suffice it to mention the following: the abolition of the caliphate and of religious jurisdiction in public and family matters; the banning of religious orders and Islamic headgear; and the adoption of the European calendar, the Swiss Civil Code, the Latin script and international numbers.

With respect to the completeness of civilisational transformation in the West European sense, Kemal's People's Party was without doubt the most radical grouping. There was none to the left of it from this point of view. However, with respect to the type of polity and methods of governing, the Kemalists occupied more of a middle position between the Committee of Union and Progress and the liberals of the preceding phase of the revolution; although in matters of government they were nearer to the Committee, in their stress on political education and the involvement of the masses they did their best to pave the way for further liberalisation and the development of a pluralistic framework.

The end of the Second World War heralded the consolidation period in the process of the civilisational transformation of Turkey. The main issue became how to make a polity and society, differentiated according to the West European pattern, a going concern. In terms of the principles of revolution the nub of the matter has been the interpretation of, and emphasis on, individual items of Atatürk's six-point programme: republicanism, nationalism, secularism, statism, populism and revolutionism (or, as some translate the Turkish *inkilâpçilik*, reformism).[23]

The decisive step occurred only after the Second World War when President Inönü allowed the opposition to compete in genuinely free elections. From then on the political spectrum started to develop in a more West European way. The Republican People's Party considered itself to be the true heir of Kemalism. The Democrat Party moved to the left in its attitude to pluralism, but rightwards in other respects, such as in socio-economic and religious matters;[24] eventually, however, it started to rule in an authoritarian manner, as its predecessor in government, the Republican People's Party, had done.

In May 1960, fearing that Atatürk's path might be abandoned, the military took over the government by a *coup d'état*, staged political trials and held power until the autumn of 1961. In sympathetic circles this move was seen as furthering the revolution or 'hailed as a reforging of an Ottoman alliance between the men of the sword and the men of the pen'.[25] The final result was a new constitution (approved by referendum in 1961) which differed from Atatürk's constitution of 1924 in that it diffused the supreme power among a larger number of bodies, allowed for greater personal freedom and proclaimed the principles of the welfare state, thus giving the 'populism' that had been a major item of Atatürk's programme a more concrete and binding interpretation.

In 1965 the Justice Party (successor to the disbanded Democrat Party) won elections in yet another shift towards liberalism. Soon after, under its new leader Ecevit, the Republican People's Party changed its complexion; hitherto the defender of Atatürk's legacy, it became the advocate of social reform on a more ambitious scale. Yet, as Kemal Karpat observed, the Constitution of 1961, which gave this endeavour its *placet*, neither took fully into account the country's economic weakness, nor provided the executive with the necessary power to enforce these reforms. As another manifestation of this ideological shift, Ecevit began to substitute the term 'people of Turkey' for the term 'Turkish nation', thus pointing to a non-ethnic facet of integration.[26] On the other hand, the tension arising from the increased and often culturally disruptive social mobility (especially the migration from the country into shanty towns) made accommodation with the secularised socio-political framework questionable for some people. The revival of Islamic values seemed to them to offer an alternative solution.

Within six years of its overwhelming victory, the Justice Party, led by Demirel, was to find itself in a difficult situation. Economic growth and the spread of education raised people's expectations far beyond the limits of what could possibly be fulfilled. The growing or increasingly visible income differentials also became disturbing. Things of this kind would produce no particular problems in a traditional Islamic society. However, in a society whose literate strata were educated in the spirit of equality and of human rights, shortcomings in this area aroused misgivings which, reinforced by other types of disproportion, upset the general consensus. Although the discontent was voiced mainly in some urban areas, the sense of relative aspirational deprivation began to present a serious problem in Europeanised Turkey. Strikes, labour and student unrest again alarmed the generals. This time, however, they did not stage a *coup*, but satisfied themselves with participation in, or rather supervision of, the civil government; the so-called guided democracy, buttressed by martial law, lasted from March 1971 until October 1973. Meanwhile some liberal provisions of the constitution were cancelled and government control tightened.

Yet problems arising from inadequate and unbalanced economic growth, and from the as yet unsettled relationship between the secular state and the religious demands of its population, required a more decisive kind of action than coalition and compromise normally allowed. Only when in July 1974, under the premiership of Ecevit, the Turkish army invaded and occupied northern Cyprus, did a wave of nationalism bring the hostile parties closer together for a time.

In the late 1970s both the extreme left and the extreme right opposition resorted to violence, which by the end of 1979 had assumed staggering proportions. In 1980, therefore, the military seized power again. As in the previous instances this was intended as a temporary measure, to re-establish law and order. A new constitution was drawn up approximately according to the pattern of the French Fifth Republic.[27] The pluralistic framework was supposed to be preserved but within narrower limits, i.e. excluding the extreme right and left. In so far as the extremes were represented by political parties whose programmes were based on religious and class allegiance respectively, this limitation was quite in line with Atatürk's principles.

Earlier, I described the years after 1950 as a period of consolidation. In that period the seat of power became for the first time an object of electoral contest, but this process has periodically been interrupted by military 'rectifications'. While the first of these (1960–1) pushed the pendulum to the left and the second (1970–3) took it more to the right, the third (1980–1) steered a middle course.

In that sense the repeated military interventions may be seen in terms of our model as a sort of consolidation overthrow. Although they are not directed against pressures to restore the *ancien régime* (the classical restoration), as was the case with the consolidation overthrows in the three West European revolutions, they follow a similar aim, namely the consolidation of the revolutionary heritage near the central position of its political spectrum. This, in the given circumstances of a largely successful Westernisation, is somewhere between the presidential (rather authoritarian) and the parliamentary (more liberal) type of republic.

Thus in the Turkish case, too, we can identify all the main phases of our morphological model of revolution, though with some significant modifications. These can be clearly seen from Figure 7.5, (page 204), which covers the period from the first reform attempts until 1993.

During this time span the five main political and ideological positions can be described in terms of the type of regime that they managed, or at least tried, to establish: *ancien régime*, reorganised empire, constitutional empire, presidential republic and parliamentary republic. The reorganised empire was the aim of the sultans Selim III (1789–1807), Mahmud II (1808–39) and Abdülmecid

(1839–61); the constitutional empire was on the programme of the Young Ottomans, and later, from around 1900, of the Young Turks; but their strongest grouping, the Committee of Union and Progress, after gaining exclusive power in 1913 made the constitution a dead letter. The presidential republic (1923 onwards) was the work of Kemal Atatürk and his Republican People's Party, and was continued by President Inönü until 1950. The parliamentary republic opened the door to a wider political diversification, which in conditions of unbalanced economic growth and intensified social mobility (both vertical and geographical) could not but result in an accentuated polarisation.

The period of the presidential republic coincided with the most intensive phase of Europeanisation. However, its political complexion paralleled the authoritarian regimes of the West, a type which in Western Europe was due to disappear within thirty years or so after the Second World War. If Turkey wanted to Westernise fully, it had to consolidate its revolution on the basis of a more pluralistic type of political regime.

The consolidation phase started with the opening up of the possibility of political contest via parliamentary elections; the seat of power then began to move between positions which gradually became comparable with those encountered in Western Europe. Yet these moves were accompanied by violence, incompatible with the usual running of a parliamentary democracy. This, and the occasional outbursts of Islamic opposition to the secularised state and society, made the army leadership, which considered itself the legitimate guardian of Atatürk's legacy, apprehensive. The army's periodic interference indicated that the consolidation phase of the revolutionary process was not yet over.

From the third military 'rectification' (1980–1) until the time of writing (winter 1993), the consolidation process has, on the whole, been upheld. The need to join the European Union as a full member – there are good economic and political reasons for such an affiliation – is a further motivation for Turkey to adapt its political regime and its socio-economic system to the European pattern. The threat to further consolidation is threefold: (a) political, class-based radicalism; (b) religious radicalism; and (c) the government's refusal to grant ethnic minority rights to the Kurds, of whom there are approximately 12 million (i.e. over 20 per cent of Turkey's total population).

The radicalism of the left-wing groups had been a perennial phenomenon since the early days of revolution. The radicalism of the Orthodox Muslims, however, which had been rather muted under the Kemalist dictatorship, had been gradually evoked as a resonance of the upsurge of Islamic fundamentalism throughout the Middle East. Both these types of opposition to the Turkish republican establishment drew their main support from that part of the population which had not been in a position to enjoy any benefit from the sustained economic growth (from 1980 to 1990 the per capita annual growth of GDP was over 3 per cent). The surplus of the peasant population (in 1990 this was 45 per cent of the total labour force) could not easily be absorbed into other industries.

The collapse of the Soviet Empire gave Turkey an opportunity to expand its influence to the neighbouring nations in Central Asia. The political and ideological orientation of these Muslim nations is now torn between the two contrasting paradigms of the Islamic response to the Western challenge: the paradigm of adaptation and cohabitation represented by Turkey, on the one hand, and the paradigm of rejection and confrontation represented by the Islamic Republic of Iran, on the other.

Thus the demise of one post-revolutionary establishment and its ideology has cleared the way for the expansion of two other schools of thought born of revolution. Having embraced the secular philosophy of Marxism, the Soviet Union aimed at striking a middle road between rejection and adaptation of the Western (Euro-American) paradigm of civilisation. The Turkish and Iranian establishments are not inclined to such a compromise. It remains to be seen whether they will follow their chosen contradictory paths in respecting each other's endeavour as acceptable alternatives, or whether they will eventually become engaged in confrontation.

In conclusion, a word has to be said on the future prospects for maintaining and safeguarding the achievements of the Turkish revolution. As has been said earlier, it would be premature to pass final judgement on the long-term effects of Turkey's Europeanisation. A great deal depends on two circumstances: first, whether those who believe in Islam will be willing to practise it in its purely religious form divorced from the political attributes with which it has been integrated in the past; and second, whether Turkey will be able to develop an institutional framework which will enable it to regulate conflicts of a political, socio-economic and ethnic nature. As B. Toprak put it:

> the religious dimension in Turkish politics is closely related to two different kinds of problems. One real – the cultural gap between the Westernised *élite* and the more traditional masses; and the other perceived – the lack of serious *élite* commitment to socio-economic change in the countryside.[28]

The accumulation of unresolved problems may revitalise the opposition against the secularising and Westernising development of Turkish society and thus upset the delicate balance between what Ziya Gökalp conceived as the Turks' tripartite membership in their nation, Islamic faith and Western civilisation.

Notes

1. Quoted from B. Lewis, *The Emergence of Modern Turkey* (Oxford University Press, London, 1961), p. 231. In a broader context, the same passage is quoted in N. Berkes, *The Development of Secularism in Turkey* (McGill University Press, Montreal, 1964), pp. 357–8.
2. As language was less important that religion the Greek and Slavonic Orthodox Christians were lumped together into one *millet*; the Turkish-speaking Christians

belonged to the respective Christian *millets*, Orthodox or Armenian, and Greek-speaking Muslims to the Islamic *ümmet*.

3. Berkes, p. 12.
4. Cf. N. Neyzi, 'The middle classes in Turkey', in K. H. Karpat (ed.), *Social Change and Politics in Turkey* (E.J. Brill, Leiden, 1973), p. 124.
5. Measures aiming at the creation of one unified Ottoman nation culminated in the law of August 1909 prohibiting the formation of political associations based on or bearing the name of ethnic or national groups, and in the closing of all minority clubs and associations in Rumelia. Steps were also taken for the first time to conscript non-Muslims into the armed forces (Lewis, pp. 213–14).
6. The main massacres and deportations during which the deportees were killed or starved to death took place in 1915, before the Russian occupation of Armenia. Further mass killings of Armenians occurred later, especially in 1920, in the wake of the French campaigns in Cilicia, and also during the Turkish campaign against that part of Armenia which had been ceded to Russia in 1878 and which during the time of that campaign (1918–20) enjoyed a short-lived independence. Direct responsibility for the main holocaust of 1915, claiming about one million victims, rests with the Committee of Union and Progress and in particular with Enver Paşa, who is generally held to be the main instigator of the whole campaign. These Young Turks thus foreshadowed by twenty years the other, more refined and extensive, genocide, namely the Nazi extermination of millions of Jews. The third large-scale extermination of people within what may be called the wider European orbit took place on class, instead of racial, grounds under the Stalinist phase of the Bolshevik rule in Russia.
7. E.H. Carr, *The Bolshevik Revolution 1917–1923* (Penguin, Harmondsworth, 1966), vol. 3, pp. 299–301.
8. This point is especially stressed by D. Ergil, *Social History of the Turkish National Struggle 1919–22* (Sind Sagar Academy, Lahore, n.d.), p. 145. Unfortunately, much pertinent information in this study is impaired by very bad editing and also some inaccuracies and sweeping assumptions.
9. Lewis, p. 444.
10. On the agrarian problems and land reform see for instance F. Ahmad, *The Turkish Experiment in Democracy 1950–1975* (Royal Institute of International Affairs, London, 1977), pp. 132–7 and 276–8.
11. In Berkes's words, 'the real peasant unrest was shown in the peasants' attempts to avert the burdens of another war' (p. 441).
12. This, however, did not turn all the brigands into reliable allies of the revolution. Often, when they had helped to deliver some territories from foreign occupation and then, looking for compensation for their efforts, turned on the liberated peasantry, they became a nuisance and had to be combated as enemies of the revolution. The communists' attempts to gain these bands for their own cause met with a poor response. In 1921 most of them were incorporated into the Nationalist Army as regulars. Some, however, went over to the Greek side, thus showing a complete lack of loyalty to their ethnic fellows. (For more detail, see D. Ergil, pp. 196–8.)
13. Lewis, pp. 202–3.
14. F. Ahmad, *The Young Turks* (Clarendon Press, Oxford, 1969), p. 2.
15. Lewis, p. 441.
16. S. Mardin, *The Genesis of Young Ottoman Thought* (Princeton University Press, NJ, 1962), pp. 117–18.
17. There was much scholastic reasoning, for instance that the constitutional government represented a case of consensus (*icma*) of the community, which according to tradition was one of the four legitimate ways of interpreting and applying the *Şeriat*. The

justification for the constitutional government was sought in those verses of the Koran that recommended some sort of consultation, especially Sura III, verse 159 and Sura LXV, verse 6. When read in their context, however, these verses had no relevance to the issues for which they were meant to serve as an argument. This way of arguing sprang from the time-honoured practice of abstracting verses or sentences from the Koran and applying them to problem-solving in terms of their lexicographical meaning (Berkes, pp. 217, 232 and ff.).

18. Oddly enough, one of the by-products of Europeanisation – and by no means a short-lived one – was a strengthening of despotism.

> There had been tyrants before in the House of Osman but the abrogation of the traditional restraints on the one hand, and the introduction of a new, Westernised apparatus of surveillance and repression on the other, had given to the Imperial absolutism of the Sultan a scope and an impact unknown in earlier times. (B. Lewis, p. 118).

This applies, however, not only to the rule of the sultans, but also to the Young Turks' Committee of Union and Progress and also, in a way, to the Kemalist dictatorship, which operated through the trappings of a parliamentary republic in which Atatürk's People's Party was not the only contestant.

19. In 1908 Austria formally annexed the already occupied Bosnia and Herzegovina, Bulgaria declared its full independence, and Crete announced its union with Greece.
20. Berkes, pp. 348–64.
21. *Ibid.*, pp. 432–4.
22. For a detailed account of this development see G.S. Harris, *The Origins of Communism in Turkey* (Stanford University Press, CA, 1967), pp. 69 and ff.
23. C.H. Dodd, *Democracy and Development in Turkey* (The Eothen Press, University of Hull, 1979), p. 87.
24. This relaxation of policy on religion appeared dangerous. Although on the one hand it met to some extent the religious needs of the population, on the other it enlarged the scope for political activity of those who, like the followers of Said Nursi, opposed the secular state on principle. Cf. E. Mortimer, *Faith and Power: The politics of Islam* (Faber & Faber, London, 1982), pp. 151–2.
25. Dodd, p. 59.
26. K.H. Karpat, 'Turkish democracy at impasse: Ideology, party politics and the third military intervention', *International Journal of Turkish Studies*, vol. 2, no. 1, 1981, pp. 29 and 35.
27. Unfortunately, the constitutional referendum was conducted in such a heavy-handed way that it is difficult to evaluate the real extent of the support for the new constitution and the new president, General Evren. Nevertheless, in view of the military regime's achievements in the field of public security and the economy, this support was no doubt substantial.
28. B. Toprak, *Islam and Political Development in Turkey* (E.J. Brill, Leiden, 1981), p. 122.

6

□

China (1895–   )

Germination and a prelude to revolution

Like Turkey and Russia, China was pushed towards revolution by a foreign challenge – by the impact of an alien civilisation. In the Chinese case, however, the gap between the foreign and the domestic civilisation was much wider than in the other two countries. On top of that, China was eventually confronted not only by one, but by two civilisations. No wonder that, faced with such a formidable challenge, it needed more time and effort to work out its own adequate response.

By the mid-nineteenth century Chinese society was in an extremely difficult situation. After 3,000 years during which one particular world-view either dominated or substantially influenced Chinese officialdom, all the possible aspects and nuances of this world-view had had the opportunity to be tried and eventually found wanting. There was nothing left of those elements of the Chinese tradition that might have been used as a basis for civilisational reconstruction. The mere transfer of the Heavenly Mandate to another dynasty ceased to provide the scope for redress and improvement.

Nor could the barbarians of the Northern Steppes imbue China with a new lease of life any more. It was the barbarians of the Southern Seas who, after having failed to establish themselves in China as missionaries during the first wave of the European overseas expansion, reappeared in the first half of the nineteenth century as merchants, diplomats and soldiers; in displaying an unprecedented superiority in arms, technology and social organisation, they forcefully opened a few doors to the Chinese subcontinent, through which the corrosive influence of the West started to pour into the ossifying fabric of Chinese society.

The first attempts to cope with the Western challenge took two different forms: the official one (from above), which grew only reluctantly out of the gradual accumulation of conflicts with the outside world; and the unofficial one (from below), which, however, matured only in the south of China. There it culminated in what is commonly known as the uprising or revolution of the Taipings.

The official reaction to the foreign challenge was slow and muted; the unofficial one was stormy, vigorous and permeated with elements of fantasy. Inspired by foreign sources and starting with a host of innovative moves which transcended the traditional concept of the withdrawal of the Heavenly Mandate, it eventually issued in yet another dynastic change adorned by a few extravagant paraphernalia.

The Taipings aimed for change of a kind that promised genuine revolution, and the situation in fact displayed some typical features of a standard revolutionary process.[1] A few alienated intellectuals – 'marginal men' – led by a repeatedly unsuccessful candidate for a Confucian degree, Hong Xiuquan, founded a group called the Society of the Worshippers of God which became a focus of socio-cultural innovation, a mixture of Confucian élitism and paternalism (for the new self-appointed élite) and Taoist-type egalitarianism (for the rank and file), on which was superimposed a sort of distorted Christianity. Hong Xiuquan presented himself as a younger brother of Jesus Christ and the Heavenly King of the Taiping Empire. Two of his lieutenants, also styled kings, had trances in which they spoke as God the Father and Jesus Christ respectively.

The perennial grievances of the poor peasantry, aggravated from the mid-nineteenth century by population pressures and the decline in public order; the long-standing resentment felt by the non-Chinese ethnic minorities in the area towards the intruders from the North (and within the latter, the antagonism between the descendants of two successive waves of Chinese immigrants); the anti-dynastic feelings among the nationally minded Chinese; and, eventually, the unsatisfied chafing aspirations of particular groups of workers, such as miners and charcoal burners – all these factors produced a fertile ground for revolutionary agitation. The progressive decay of government administration, a gradual weakening of the integrative function of Confucian doctrine,[2] and the inability of the ruling élite (bureaucracy and landlords) to cope with the Western challenge, gave the malcontents the opportunity to take action.[3]

Nothing can better illustrate the state of administrative and spiritual disintegration in China than the rapid progress of the strange revolutionaries who within three years conquered a considerable area of southeast China and established there their 'Heavenly Kingdom of Great Harmony' (*Taiping Tianguo*).

Within another three years, however, not only the greatness, but also the misery, of their victory became apparent – the misery of a half-baked syncretism which could hardly overcome its internal contradictions, let alone gain the support of the traditionally educated strata. On the one hand, there was a strict discipline and levelling among the rank and file, applied not only to the allocation of food and other consumer goods (the land belonged to the 'sacred treasury' which was fully at the disposition of the rulers), but also to the sexes which, until the time of the final victory, had to live separately and under strict military rules; on the other hand, there were the princely position and the imperial status of the leaders, who indulged in luxurious and licentious lives and personal rivalry – which eventually undermined the morale of the Taiping movement and made it just as exploitative as the *ancien régime*, if not more so.[4]

There were, however, further circumstances which operated against the Taipings. As they put forward some very strange religious concepts which were not properly amalgamated with the Chinese tradition, they estranged the traditional scholars who, though looking askance at the Manchu dynasty, eventually found that this dynasty was more in line with the genuine Chinese tradition than the strange ideas of the Taipings. Moreover, the attractive idea of equality realised at the bottom of the Taiping community was frustrated by the contrasting behaviour of the leadership. There was no large-scale desertion of intellectuals from the *ancien régime*: the intellectual leadership was recruited from marginal strata, and the strange, foreign elements in the Taiping ideology were rather repugnant to the full-fledged literati. The only asset of the Taiping ideology was that it succeeded in uniting people of different socio-economic and ethnic backgrounds. Yet the experiment did not last long enough to show how the underlying contradictions and tensions might have been resolved.

Also the morphology of the Taiping revolution reveals some particular features that are dissimilar to the pattern of other revolutions. The uprising started on the periphery. There was no sudden explosion, but instead a creeping upheaval; there was no conquest of the capital but a carving out of a separate empire in the southern provinces. This gave a strong horizontal element to the revolution, which eventually provided the government with a good opportunity to strike back. Also, under these circumstances, the perversion of the revolutionary ideal was more dangerous for the revolutionary establishment than it would have been if the whole country had been conquered. On the other hand, the peasantry, who at the beginning of the revolution appeared to be its main beneficiaries, turned out, as in most other instances of peasant uprising, to be its main victims. The Taiping movement consummated itself before attaining its goal. It was an abortive revolution in the true sense of the word.

The Taiping revolution coincided with another large-scale rebellion, that of the Nian, whose leader assumed the title 'Lord of the Great Han Alliance' (Han meaning ethnic Chinese, as opposed to Manchus). The Nian, however, followed the more traditional pattern of insurrection, where the bid for a Heavenly Mandate could hardly be distinguished from organised banditry. In purely military terms, however, this movement was quite efficient.

There were also two repetitions of the Opium War and a series of major insurrections of the Muslim population in Yunnan, Xinjiang and Gansu. As a result, the Manchu dynasty was able to take the wind out of the insurgents' sails and to pose as the defender of true Chinese values against both foreigners and domestic dissidents. This gave the conservatives some credit and also the respite they needed to rally themselves and adapt to the changing conditions around China. Yet this rally was due more to a revival of traditional attitudes and even virtues (as far as administration and army discipline was concerned) in the provinces than to the endeavours of central government. This strengthened the tendency towards territorial disintegration initiated at the time of the rebellions. It may be assumed that the central government missed the last opportunity to mend its ways.

Reform or revolution?

It is astonishing that the Japanese example of successful modernisation had to wait so long before making an impact on the Chinese mind. Only after the Chinese had suffered a humiliating defeat (1894–5) at the hands of these fast and successful converts to Western know-how did some people in leading positions start to think seriously about reforms. In China, however, there was no scope for a Meiji-type restoration. A short-lived (Hundred Days) reform cabinet in 1898 was dismissed by the empress dowager despite the comparatively enlightened attitude of the regent, Prince Gong. After channelling popular feeling into xenophobic outbursts (the Boxer uprising of 1899–1900), the conservatives remained masters of the situation.

Yet another humiliation, the conquest and plunder of Peking by the punitive expedition of Western powers and the resultant further encroachments on Chinese sovereignty, finally persuaded the Manchu government to embark on extensive reforms. Even the ideational basis was to be changed. In September 1905, the traditional examinations based on neo-Confucian doctrine were abolished. The state was to be rebuilt following the model of the most efficient and prosperous Western states; this implied the gradual development of a parliamentary regime. In the first instance, regional consultative assemblies based on a very limited suffrage (the timocratic principle) were elected. They met for the first time in October 1909. Elections for a nation-wide Parliament were promised for 1913. Provincial assemblies, however, became centres of fierce opposition. It became increasingly clear that only another transfer of the Heavenly Mandate could bring China out of the impasse. Japan's victory over Russia, won largely on Chinese territory (1904–5), provided another illustration of the powerful results that a successful Westernisation can produce.

There were basically two types of people who were ready to assume the role of protagonists: the moderates, envisaging only technical innovations, and the radicals, aiming at thoroughgoing structural change, combined with a new ideological orientation. The plurality of schools of thought which had existed in classical times was rediscovered as a virtue, and a better knowledge of European and American philosophy and science started to spread among intellectuals in big cities. As was to be expected, students were the most ardent supporters of radicalism.

Unfortunately for the government, all this came too late. As Chesneaux *et al.* put it, 'since the aim of the reform was conservative, it could not win over the progressive forces, and since its effects were revolutionary, it estranged the vested interests'.[5] Considering all the circumstances, this was, as de Tocqueville discovered in the case of the French revolution, 'the most perilous moment, when a bad government sought to mend its ways'.[6]

A civilisational transformation in China was long overdue. All the proposals voiced by enlightened but isolated Confucian scholars to revitalise the Confucian tradition, to imbue it with a more pragmatic outlook, with forward- rather than backward-looking paradigms, failed. New inspiration could only come from abroad. Nevertheless, there was still a tendency to look for inspiration in the Confucian tradition, whose real meaning had to be rediscovered – despite all the evidence to the contrary – in constant innovations. Kang Youwei was the main representative of this somersault approach. China, however, needed more foreign elements for its civilisational reconstruction. This course was epitomised by the father of the revolution and of modern China, Sun Yat-sen.

A revolutionary change of concepts does not, however, by itself mean a corresponding change in reality. The withdrawal of the Mandate of Heaven, the *geming*, lost its transcendental undertone but in essence remained what it had been before – a civil war, a chaos (*luan*), resulting eventually in re-established order (*heping*).[7] Yet the question emerged: what kind of order? The disappearance of Heaven from the formula implied the attempt to introduce a new pattern and type of change.

Although traditional attitudes continued to persist and a tendency developed to graft only individual elements onto them, there was nevertheless an increasing sense of a spiritual vacuum which had to be filled by something new. Subsequent Chinese history can perhaps best be understood as a dramatic quest for a new ideational basis and organisational framework for societal integration.

The first round of revolution: the mandate of the people or yet another Mandate of Heaven?

The conventional date for the start of the Great Chinese Revolution (the date of the explosion) is 10 October 1911, which is the day of the insurrection of the garrison in the city of Wuchang. This precipitated the course of events during which the fate of the dynasty depended on one wavering general who followed his own personal policy. On 1 January 1912, Sun Yat-sen was inaugurated in Nanjing as president of the Chinese Republic. As during the Taiping rebellion, Nanjing again became the capital. This time, however, the new regime installed there aimed at taking the whole of China. Yet the situation was nowhere near ripe for this. Sun Yat-sen represented a numerically tiny segment of the Chinese population – those who believed that only by emulating the Westerners in their knowledge, technology and institutions could China regain its national identity and prestige. The republic was just the symbol of a complex acculturation.

No wonder that the first round of the revolution was marked by the struggle between modernisers, i.e. Westernisers, on the one hand, and traditionalists on the other, with of course a wide spectrum of half-shades in between. As the state power was already considerably weakened from the time of the Taiping rebellion, and the real power was in the hands of local dignitaries – military rather than civil – it was extremely difficult to reunite China by merely political means. The situation offered an opportunity for the adventurer, Yuan Shikai, who, being in the favourable post of commander-in-chief, and knowing how to play opposing forces off against each other, tried, for the last time in Chinese history, to regain the balance between rulers and ruled by installing a new dynasty. Yuan Shikai first negotiated with Sun Yat-sen his own election to the presidency of the Chinese Republic (1912). Then he attempted a carefully staged seizure of absolute power. In 1913, Parliament and the provincial assemblies were disbanded. Towards the end of 1914, Yuan assumed the title of protector of the faith, and the Confucian rites at the Temple of Heaven were reintroduced. On 21 November 1915, a 'National Congress of Representatives' voted 'unanimously' for the restoration of the imperial regime.

It is difficult to say whether the social climate in China favoured such a traditional solution. Judging from the outcome, we may answer the question in the negative. Yet we have to bear in mind that it was the local army commanders, who had meanwhile slipped from Yuan's control, who prevented him from pursuing his policy further. The military disintegration of China was apparently a more serious impediment to the restoration of the monarchy than the revolutionary movement. The would-be emperor was forced to give up the idea and to make concessions to his opponents. Yet Yuan's sudden though natural death (1916) brought the whole game to an abrupt end. China completely disintegrated. The first round of the Chinese revolution was over, and one of the worst periods of chaos (*luan*) in Chinese history set in: from 1916 to 1919 the forces of revolution seemed to be defeated.

As, before, a new impetus towards reconstruction came from abroad. China again suffered humiliation. Although in the First World War – at the request of the Western allies – it joined the Four Power alliance, in the peace negotiations its interests were completely pushed aside and Japan, not China, was to acquire former German possessions on the Chinese mainland.

These events led, in May 1919, to what Chesneaux describes as 'patriotic protest against the humiliating situation imposed on China, and the powers' encouragement of Japanese ambitions'.[8] In Chinese history it is known as the May 4th Movement, which consisted of an eruption of demonstrations against the foreigners and against the compliant government. They issued in a boycott of Japanese goods. Although not much was achieved in practical terms, the impact on the Chinese intellectual climate was enormous. As a Western observer put it, 'May 4th was the day Confucius died'. The Chinese intelligentsia became more receptive than ever to Western influences.

This mood, however, did not imply the will to become Westernised, to embrace a foreign culture in order to be identified with it, but the will to use it for the defence and preservation of a Chinese national identity. Initially, the non-dogmatic, pragmatic, Anglo-Saxon approach provided the necessary inspiration. Had not the time-honoured reformers such as Wang Anshi (1021–86) and critical interpreters such as Gu Yanwu (1613–82) intended to open up Confucian doctrine to just such pragmatism?

Yet the part of the foreign world that influenced China in that direction was not particularly well disposed towards Chinese political aspirations; although the achievements of Anglo-American culture invited emulation, a more intimate relationship was hampered not only by the substantial difference between the cultural traditions, but also by a distrust which gathered momentum after each mutual conflict.

For subsequent developments in China, however, the events in Russia assumed greater importance. The fact that post-revolutionary Russia ceased – for a short while – to be an imperialistic power and solemnly renounced its claim to ex-territorial rights in China, could not but have a positive impact on the mood in that country. Also the fact that Russia's change of policy was a corollary of her new state philosophy – Marxism – was significant. Both the new Russia and Marxism enjoyed an advantageous position in the contest of ideas and sympathies. Even when, later on, Soviet Russia bitterly disappointed Chinese expectations, Marxism remained the intellectual weapon of the new China. Reinterpreted and remoulded according to Chinese needs and ways of thinking, Marxism gave China what it needed – a new, neatly packaged world-view in which the concept of a golden age to come had been substituted for the golden age of the past in the Chinese tradition.

On top of that, there was yet another most important asset which China drew from Marxism: a concern for the broad masses, for their involvement in the effort to change not only society but people's views and attitudes. Within the Chinese situation and in contrast to the disastrous experience of Soviet Russia, this concern turned eventually to the peasant, who thus became not only the main cannon fodder, but also, up to a point, the beneficiary of the revolution. These advantages, however, had yet to prove their real value through the ordeal of civil war.

The second round of revolution: Euro-American or Euro-Asian paradigm?

The May 4th Movement of 1919, the renewal of the republic in the south in 1921 and the foundation of the Communist Party in the same year together heralded the second round of the Chinese revolution. In its early stages both the republic and the communists were almost negligible currents in the rough sea of a disintegrating society plagued by the ever-changing, mutually warring local alliances of warlords and gentry. No wonder that, if China was to move ahead, the heirs of Sun Yat-sen and the communists had to strike out on a common course. At that stage the united front advised by Moscow seemed to be a matter of common sense. China had first to get rid of the chaos in order to be able to find its way out of backwardness and stagnation.

Yet the contradictions between the two sources of inspiration which China found in the outside world were insurmountable, and the Chinese leaders realised this sooner than their Russian advisers were ready to admit. There can be no doubt that Stalin and his Politburo had no illusions about the incompatibility of the Western world's way of life and thought with those of their own. Yet their doctrine asserted that in particular circumstances (those of colonial and semi-colonial nations that had not yet undergone bourgeois revolution) there should be one common policy for the followers of both ways. How wrong this judgement was is obvious and need not be dealt with in this context.

The head of the Guomindang, the Moscow-trained Chiang Kai-shek, was the first to draw practical conclusions from the realisation of this incompatibility. Before the victorious campaign against the warlords was brought to an end, he decided to attack and destroy his competitors. Yet the advantage of the first strike was not matched by a corresponding policy of thoroughgoing civilisational reconstruction; this became the Achilles' heel of the Guomindang's policy in China.

The story of the struggle between Chiang Kai-shek's Guomindang and the communists is too well known to be repeated here; only the main features relevant to the long-term development and the morphological pattern of revolution will be recalled.

The years 1926–8 brought a culmination of the process of reunification and at the same time a breaching of the alliance between the Guomindang and the communists. The warlords were expelled from most of China (and in that sense chaos was significantly limited), but at the same time a new front of internal dissension between the Guomindang and the communists was opened up.

The contest between the two paths of civilisational transformation became the main issue in the second round of the revolution. The question that had to be answered by this contest was whether China would, in principle, follow the example of the West European countries and North America, or the example of the new social system emerging in Russia. In socio-economic terms, this dichotomy is known as the alternative between capitalism and state socialism. In political terms, the dichotomy is more difficult to describe. Looking at practice rather than at programmes, we may say that in China it was a dichotomy between two types of dictatorship.

Before they could tackle this issue properly, the communists had to shift the focus of their campaign in a twofold way: geographically and structurally. The geographical shift was from the southeast to the northwest (the Long March), and the structural one was from the urban proletariat to the peasantry as the popular and military basis. Both these shifts were a matter of revolutionary strategy: the latter, however – the reliance on the peasantry instead of the urban proletariat – assumed fundamental importance for the communist movement at large.[9]

It is debatable how much the communists have rewarded the peasants' commitment to their cause in the civil war. There can be little doubt that during the war they succeeded, especially in the north, in winning the allegiance of the peasants. The Guomindang was hampered in this respect by too great a reliance on the traditional gentry and the newly emerging merchant class. Also, the emergence of the third contestant on the Chinese mainland – Japan – played a significant role. Of the three contestants, the communists were the most concerned with the peasants' lot. Even in the south, where they had less influence and which they conquered later, communist discipline seems to have had the upper hand over the looser behaviour of the disintegrating Guomindang armies. Although no immediate structural change was introduced in the liberated areas, the reduction of rents and taxes was experienced as a considerable relief by the peasantry who had for several decades suffered from disorder, and in many places also from the ravages of war. Furthermore, in that period, the communists embarked on teaching the peasants not to be submissive: 'to speak their bitterness instead of eat it'.[10]

The Japanese intervention, starting in 1931, seemed for some time to push the basic Guomindang–communist dichotomy into the background. Indeed, it complicated the situation in China until the final Allied victory in the Second World War in 1945. Although the Japanese government's social philosophy was much nearer to that of Chiang Kai-shek's Guomindang than to that of the communists, their nationalistic and imperialistic fervour did not allow them to come to agreement with Chiang's China. As the quest for the modernisation of China implied a restoration of national sovereignty and prestige, the Japanese attempt to win China's cooperation by means of a malleable stooge (significantly, they found a former left-winger in the Guomindang, Wang Jingwei, to fill that role) could not but end in failure. In the end, Japanese intervention in China proved to be more beneficial to the communists than to anybody else.[11] As Barrington Moore put it:

> the Japanese campaigns, in inducing the Guomindang officials and landlords to move out of the countryside and in terrorizing the destituted peasants by mopping up and extermination tactics, performed two essential revolutionary tasks for the Communists, the elimination of the old *élites* and the forging of solidarity among the oppressed.[12]

Meanwhile, however, the anti-Japanese mood in the country forced Chiang to accept the truce with the communists. Nothing could better illustrate the social atmosphere (which gradually paved the way for the communist victory) than the so-called Xian incident in December 1936: Chiang Kai-shek, taken prisoner by revolting troops who wanted to fight the Japanese rather than the communists, was rescued by the intercession of a communist envoy (Zhou Enlai), when he (Chiang) agreed to cease hostilities against the communists and to concentrate on the war against Japan.

Although the Xian agreement was very much against the wishes of the Guomindang leadership, and therefore not consistently observed by them, the Japanese themselves did their best to keep it alive by launching a full-scale attack on China. When they were eventually forced to withdraw from the Chinese mainland, the power vacuum they left was filled by the communists rather than by the Guomindang.

Thus the last chapter of the second round in the Chinese revolution was fought under a considerably changed balance of forces which neither the technical nor the economic help given by America to nationalist China could redress. The Guomindang advance in the 1946–7 campaign against the communists proved to be a temporary success. Although commanding greater economic resources and more numerous armies, their fighting spirit crumbled in the face of the more ideologically conscious, more dedicated and more disciplined communist armies. The policy of struggle combined with moderate reforms paid dividends. The improvements in the peasants' economic lot, the considerable effort to make them literate, the concern with their human dignity and promises of a still better future to come were the invaluable assets that differentiated the communist from the Guomindang recruits. The prolonged period of 'war communism' moulded the cadres for the new tasks ahead – the socialist society to come.

In 1949, when the Guomindang was driven from the Chinese mainland, the whole country became, for the first time since the beginning of the revolution, united under one rule. In terms of our morphological pattern, the 'oscillating seat of power' was fully 'intercepted'.

The third round of revolution: reception or reconstruction?

In 1949, with the decisive communist victory, there were strong indications that the period of revolution proper was over, and that further developments would assume a course similar to that taken by Soviet Russia. In reality, however, the revolution took another turn; it was yet another twenty years before the basic contours of the resulting orientation could be perceived.

Although, on the surface, there seemed to be no substantial dissensions among the new communist leadership, more perspicacious observers realised that already in 1950, Mao, who was then the undisputed head of both state and party, was becoming increasingly distrustful of the new bureaucratic and technocratic élite.[13] One must not overlook the fact that his attitude was in part shaped by the experience of post-Lenin developments in Soviet Russia. In spite of that feeling, Soviet Russia under Stalin's autocratic rule was still, for a few years to come, to be considered as the exemplary and leading power in the communist camp.

Like Russia, China started first with agrarian reform, i.e. the redistribution of land (1950–3), and only then proceeded to socialise industry and commerce (1954–6). Unlike the Russian communists, however, the Chinese unleashed the main wave of terror in connection with the agrarian reform, and kept it within the formal framework of revolutionary justice. People's tribunals expanded their activity against corruption and illegal practices in the cities (1951–2). There were around 300 million peasants who benefited from the reform which expropriated the landlords without indemnity, and divided their lands among the 'poor and middle peasants'. Tenant farming, forced labour and other traditional, feudal-type services demanded of the peasants were abolished.[14]

Meanwhile, Stalin died, and his heirs fulfilled his promise to withdraw from Manchuria; the Soviet–Chinese companies, another assertion of Russia's superior status *vis-à-vis* China, were also abolished. In 1954 China adopted a constitution framed, in principle, according to the Soviet model. Surprisingly, on that occasion, the Chinese communists forgot the primary role of the peasantry in the revolution. As if they wanted to overtake Russia, they equated, in legislating for representation to the National Congress, the political value of one city voter with that of eight rural voters; the first Soviet constitution put that difference at one to five only. As, however, in both communist states the whole constitution had little practical meaning (it served mainly propaganda purposes), this difference can be dismissed as mere ideological window-dressing.

So far there was no visible scope for substantial dissension within the party. 'Contradictions among the people' seemed to remain limited to questions of implementation rather than principles. Neither did the intervention in the Korean War (1950–3) seem to have aroused any particular controversy. The challenge came rather from the Western half of the communist world. Khrushchev's unexpected criticism of Stalin, and restlessness among the Central European satellites which, in the case of Hungary, surpassed the limits of what Mao considered 'contradictions among the people', provided the first opportunities for visible dissent. Seen with hindsight, the main matters that became subject to Chinese criticism, such as the stress on economic incentives in the USSR and the concept of peaceful coexistence with the capitalist world, appear to have been pretexts. The Chinese communists themselves eventually embarked on the same path. It seems that differences in policy were of minor importance: what mattered was the mutual loss of confidence. Soviet leaders were late to realise that a big nation such as China, with its own time-honoured civilisation, cannot be reduced to the position of an obedient satellite of the Bulgarian type. Chinese communists could not forgive their Russian tutors their arrogance, meanness and hegemonic aspirations. The cleavage was deep-felt and deep-seated: no change in policy could mend it. That explains why, despite the vagaries of Chinese policy, the Sino-Soviet split became a constant in all further developments.

Meanwhile China became a great laboratory for social experimentation. Its leadership wanted to show the fastest possible pace of social change. Although in those days Mao was the undisputed leader, he was far from an autocrat: some decisions seem to have been taken collectively and there was wide scope for compromise among different views. Also the prolonged period of administrative disintegration before 1949 left some marks of regional differentiation even within the party apparat. To the outside observer, the policy appeared erratic, full of amazing, abrupt shifts and volte-faces. Marxism–Leninism did not appear to be a safe guide for every situation.

From 1956 there were three years of exuberance: the birth control campaign, the Hundred Flowers policy (an opening for criticism on the intellectual level which, however, soon had to be clamped down because criticism exceeded the expected, basically loyalist, framework), the rectification campaign and the purge of small auxiliary parties in 1957. In 1958 came the Taiwan Straits crisis (welcomed or even instigated by the Chinese in order to support their other moves), the mass mobilisation, the Great Leap Forward and the organisation of communes, which implied a tight collectivisation of agriculture. In that the Soviet experience was not only emulated, but surpassed: collectivisation was more extensive, with regard to both agricultural and associated artisan activities. Although Stalinist-type terror does not seem to have been applied, one must not underestimate the hardships to which the peasantry, together with other village inhabitants, were exposed. There was a great levelling at the subsistence level, perhaps saving people from starvation but destroying incentives to increase production, an essential condition for the further success of the revolution. In summer 1958, people's communes began to be established in the cities, but the project was interrupted at the end of the year. In April 1959, Mao relinquished the position of head of state to Liu Shaoqi.

In 1959, a period of sobering-up set in, with bad harvests, the Tibet uprising, the allowing of private plots in agricultural collectives and an attempt to unseat Mao from the saddle (Peng Dehuai's criticism of the Great Leap Forward at the Central Committee plenum at Lushan). The following year saw the open break with the Soviet Union and the Soviet withdrawal of all economic and technical aid.

After the failure of the Great Leap Forward the emphasis was on a slower pace of change and economic development. Professionalism and a pragmatic approach rather than indoctrination were encouraged. As indirect criticism of Mao's hazardous policy continued, a polarisation within the party leadership became apparent. Mao looked to the army for compensation for the ground lost within the party.

As the basic controversies were put in veiled rather than straightforward terms (historical analogies or abstract formulae became their principal vehicles), the issues often assumed a strange doctrinal garb, such as the question as to whether 'two combining into one' or 'one dividing into two' was the right way. This cryptic formula stood for a serious political issue: whether the contending factions had to achieve a compromise and unite, or whether the struggle had to be fought to the end with the prospect of possibly tearing the party asunder. In another context, this formula meant whether cooperation with Soviet Russia against American intervention in Vietnam or elsewhere had to be given priority, or whether the Chinese party's radical divergence from the 'revisionist' Soviet leadership ruled out such a policy.

Concerning the internal contradictions, the compromise formula apparently had more support in the party apparat. Its weakness, however, was that hardly anyone dared to assail Mao directly. Although Mao's opponents were in a position to ban his voice from the Peking (Beijing) press, the party was not enough of a monolithic institution to prevent him from finding a mouthpiece in Shanghai; he could also utter his views in the great sign posters. Furthermore, with the help of the army and young militants, he was able to re-establish his supremacy in the country and to assail the party from without. This was the aim of the Cultural Revolution, to shake up the party in order to prevent it from ossifying. Mao seemed to be convinced that without a constant mental ferment China could not undergo that anthropological change which was the key message of Marxian eschatology. In that sense he seems to have been more Weberian than Marxist: he better understood consciousness as an independent variable, or rather as a variable dependent on much more than the economic base.[15]

Thus, a second period of exuberance (1963–8) got under way. This time not the intellectuals but the young generation had to help to save the movement from stagnation and the leadership from complacency, or as Mao saw it, political degeneration. The Great Proletarian Cultural Revolution (1966–8) had to make the Chinese (a) collective-minded, not only with respect to the extended family but also and mainly with respect to society as a whole, (b) egalitarian, (c) frugal, (d) hard-working for the bright future, (e) politically active, and last but not least, (f) versatile, multi-dimensional and non-alienated beings:

> With hammer in hand they will be able to do factory work; with hoe, plough or barrow they will be able to do farming; with the gun they will be able to fight the enemy and with the pen they will be able to express themselves in writing.[16]

With regard to the ultimate aim Mao remained faithful to the young Marx's utopian vision. In that sense the Great Proletarian Cultural Revolution appeared to be the boldest mass attempt to imbue the Marxist–Leninist establishment with unyielding revolutionary spirit. Chinese communists had to be saved from Soviet 'embourgeoisement'.

The boldness of Mao's attempt can best be appreciated retrospectively, when we realise the enormity of the risks he took. The party apparat disintegrated, the civil service largely collapsed and petty wars between factions often using the same slogans seemed to bring China to the brink of a civil war similar to that which had torn the country apart for the greater part of the century. Mao's craftsmanship, however, appeared superior to any other factor on the Chinese scene. With the help of the People's Liberation Army, also in its turn largely purged, he eventually re-established 'proletarian discipline' over the aroused passions of the young. This fact may be interpreted as an implicit avowal of Mao's failure to guide a permanent revolution. He himself had to exorcise the spirits invoked by his own magic. Yet Mao might have seen it otherwise – as a discreetly manipulated conflict, with a certain calculated risk. But who else in the world could afford a step like that? Solomon sees in Mao's repeated attempts to upset the established order a conscious effort to institutionalise some forms of conflict as a method for resolving contradictions.[17] If this was the case, and there is no reason not to believe it, Mao's otherwise good understanding of human nature in general, and of the Chinese in particular, failed him in this specific respect. Solomon believes that the main difficulty was due to the Chinese tradition that inhibited criticism of authority. One can, however, hardly imagine that in any other nation, people, attackers and assaulted alike, would have behaved otherwise. There may be some residue of Confucian naivety in Mao's thought. As the Roman genius once discovered, there have to be fixed rules for allowing conflict situations to emerge without wrecking the system. And as common sense and also our findings indicate, people cannot live in permanent turmoil.

The pacification of the revolutionary guards took place in a way that, twenty-five years earlier, James Burnham had found typical of the managerial revolution which, in his view, was then in progress in the USSR and in Nazi Germany. First, the masses were incited to opposition and revolt; then, when they had fulfilled this task and helped the new rulers firmly into the saddle, they were ruthlessly pacified.[18] (In the USSR and Germany it happened in a way that the *ancien régime* might hardly have dared to emulate while in China, the atrocities of the pre-revolutionary regimes could scarcely have been surpassed. This difference is significant for the evaluation of the civilisational reconstruction sought in all three cases.)

It seems that psychological and economic reasons contributed equally to the eventual reversal of the third round of the revolutionary process in China. The chaos became counterproductive; as we can infer from the revolutions studied so far, there is an approximate five-year limit to the period of sustained ferment. Within this time span the extraordinary energy that powers this phase seems to have become exhausted. The decline in production, which was already meagre by world standards, together with the growth in population, made it imperative to stop the chaos. The Chinese Cultural Revolution consumed itself in three years.

We should not be surprised that the reversal happened under Mao's own auspices. Although the policy went through a U-turn, the boss remained at the top. Here is a similarity with Stalin's position in the USSR. Stalin, too, did not hesitate to adopt his purged enemies' policy, such as Trotsky's programme of collectivisation and primary accumulation of capital; similarly, Mao did not hesitate to return to the policy for which his main, ignominiously deposed rival, Liu Shaoqi, stood. In comparison with Stalin, however, Mao was more civilised; not all his rivals within the élite were sent to the other world, and many of them later re-emerged from their banishment. As usual on such occasions, it was mainly the commoners, the rank and file, who paid the toll of blood and oblivion.

The consolidation period: what sort of reconstruction?

The 9th National Congress of the Chinese Communist Party in April 1969 can be considered as the formal winding up of the Cultural Revolution, but also as a strengthening of Mao's position. The thought of Mao Zedong was reaffirmed as the theoretical guide to China's national development, as the expression of Marxism–Leninism in 'the era in which imperialism is heading for total collapse and socialism is advancing to world-wide victory',[19] and Lin Biao, Mao's main supporter in the Cultural Revolution, was designated as his successor to the party leadership.

From then on, official policy began to return to a moderate path. The consolidation phase of revolution set in. In order to increase productivity, 'rational rewards' were reintroduced (an element of de-levelling); peasants could safely enjoy their private plots. Also, the reconstruction of the party apparatus was again taken in hand.

On this occasion, however, a new 'dialectical contradiction among the people' emerged. According to the official reinterpretation of events, Lin Biao, as head of the army, which in the virtual absence of a coordinated party apparatus was the only centrally organised force in the country, did not show any eagerness to consolidate another party apparatus which in a Marxist–Leninist state would necessarily have played a leading role. He continued to infiltrate his men into key positions of power and to oppose Mao's decision to start negotiating with the United States. Unfortunately for Lin Biao, his bid for power was cut short by his death in an air crash in 1971.

In the area of domestic policy, Mao apparently wanted to have a new Communist Party which would retain a certain element of the Cultural Revolution, such as measures for effecting the abolition of two types of contradiction: between intellectual and manual work, and between town and countryside. The May 7th Cadre Schools were destined to give able-bodied intellectuals and white-collar workers a re-education among the manual workers or peasants, while sending young people for a certain period to work in the villages. A substantial element in the re-education of the whole nation was a vigorous campaign against the Confucian heritage.

These practices, however, did not long survive Mao's death in September 1976. The consolidation process whose signs were already visible in 1970 gathered momentum. At the beginning, under the auspices of Mao's short-term successor, Chairman Hua Guofeng, it seemed that a compromise between Mao's heritage and the more pragmatic approach of his opponents might be achieved. Yet apparently because Mao's policy still had some vigorous supporters – the most notable were branded as the Gang of Four – a compromise, which would leave Mao all the glory and the pragmatists all the decision-making, was not feasible. Albeit cautiously and with some wavering at the beginning, the process of de-Maoisation was set in motion. Not only were Mao's wife and three old colleagues put on trial and duly sentenced, but Mao's thought itself became superseded by references to direct sources of Marxist thought; or, more significantly, empirical tests replaced quotations from the classics as the main criterion of truth.

The new policy was most vigorously promoted by the former general secretary of the Communist Party, Deng Xiaoping. Once a supporter of Mao, then pushed into the background by the Cultural Revolution, from where he returned to the limelight even before Mao's death, Deng became the main representative of the present consolidation phase of the Chinese revolution. Although formally neither the party chairman nor prime minister, Deng, within five years of Mao's death, succeeded in becoming the undisputed leader; all the Maoist or semi-Maoist elements have been cleared from the Politburo and other leading posts in the army and civil service since then. The 12th Congress of the Chinese Communist Party of September 1982 endorsed Deng's reconstruction of the state and party apparatuses. But at the same time, Hu Yaobang (secretary general of the party since the 1982 congress, which abolished the post of chairman), described the main goal as the building of 'a socialist spiritual civilisation with communist ideology as its core'.[20]

The basic idea of the new policy, announced in 1978, was a combination of a one-party authoritarian rule with elements of a market economy. In contrast to the political and ideological reserve, an open-door policy was to be applied to the economy. The door, however, was not fully opened. Remarkable successes in agriculture were not matched by a corresponding development in other industries. This disproportion led to dissatisfaction; the partial liberalisation of the economy aroused a desire for ideological and political liberalisation as well. The communist leadership was divided: the tendency towards further liberalisation clashed with the tendency to tighten the screw again. The 'seat of power' oscillated between these two poles.

Meanwhile, the discrepancy between the performance of individual industries on the one hand and government financial claims on the other brought about a strong inflationary pressure resulting in unrest among the urban population. In 1988, ten years after the declaration of the open-door policy, the government returned to some regulation combined with austerity measures.

The general dissatisfaction with the economic policy spilled over to the political sphere. Foreign ideas were entering through the door opened for foreign goods. Criticism of corruption and nepotism (seen as a betrayal of the puritanical tradition of the communist revolution) combined with criticism of evident failures in a policy based on dogmatic premises.

In mid-1989 mass student demonstrations broke out in the capital. During May the Central Square of Eternal Peace (Tiananmen) was occupied by students and their sympathisers from other sectors of the population. The communist leadership hesitated. The party general secretary, Zhao Ziyang, saw support for his reformist policy in the student movement. The students advertised him as the only man capable of saving China, and called for the resignation of the prime minister, Li Peng, the advocate of drastic measures. The military commander in the capital was loath to interfere. Gorbachev's state visit to Beijing at that time reminded everyone that even China's one-time great example, the Soviet Union, had now embarked on the path of reform. The impasse was eventually resolved by the 84-year-old Deng Xiaoping.

Like his predecessor, Mao, Deng knew that political power comes from the barrel of the gun. Thus he travelled around, rallying the military commanders outside the capital in order to suppress the student movement and causing considerable loss of life. The action started on 4 June, five days after the students had erected a Statue of Liberty (shaped like the one in New York) in Tiananmen Square. The reformist faction in the Communist Party did not take the opportunity to make a breakthrough. The students had manifested their bitterness with a symbol from another ideological orientation. Unwittingly perhaps, they echoed the first steps of the Chinese revolution, the legacy of its father – Sun Yat-sen.

The anti-reformists, however, could not fully exploit their victory. The same Deng Xiaoping who saved their careers, soon returned to the middle course, as declared in 1978; namely, a tight political regime combined with a growing share of the private and cooperative sectors in the expanding market economy. Thus it came about that, from 1978 to 1990, the share of state-owned firms in industrial production declined from 78 per cent to slightly over 50 per cent. During the same period, the real GNP had grown by an average of almost 9 per cent per year. In several coastal provinces foreign trade and foreign investment had been encouraged. Even Taiwanese investors were now welcomed (despite the fact that the People's Republic of China and Taiwan did not recognise each other).

Furthermore, according to the agreement with Great Britain, China will recover sovereignty over Hong Kong from 1 July 1997. Hong Kong's existing social and economic system and its present lifestyle are supposed to remain unchanged for another fifty years. There is a paradox in this transfer. Of all the Asian countries, it was communist China that tolerated foreign domination on part of its soil long after all the other colonies had gone. Furthermore, there seems to be no rush for a systemic unification with the mainland. Why should this be so? Anyway, the adjacent area of the province Guangdong is being developed in a similar fashion to that of Hong Kong. Is this a pointer to the future development of China as a whole? Or should a pluralism of socio-economic systems in one country be accepted as possible alternatives to the pluralism of ideological and political orientations?

Theoretical and comparative considerations

Having outlined the course of the Chinese revolution in idiographic terms, we may now proceed to nomothetic considerations: we shall test whether, or to what extent, our six disproportions or contradictions and our morphological model are applicable.

In the case of China, as in those of Turkey and Russia, the basic Marxian contradiction can be observed with shifted geographical parameters. The contradiction was between the advanced productive forces abroad and the antiquated mode of production at home, or, to borrow Deutscher's terms, between the status of a great power and the archaic weakness of its institutions.

As far as the class contradiction is concerned, the qualification has to be made that in pre-revolutionary China, classes may be supposed to have existed merely as classes 'in themselves'. In order to acquire class consciousness the peasantry and the rudimentary urban proletariat had to be educated. Although peasant rebellions were endemic, class contradictions did not in themselves generate truly revolutionary action. They could develop in this direction only in so far as they assumed the Aristotelian dimension, i.e. in so far as people became convinced that their grievances justified them in taking revolutionary action.

Chairman Mao was well aware of where the nub of the issue lay. He knew that power grows from the barrel of a gun, but that the gun has to fall into the hands of, and above all be under the command of, those whose minds have, in Marxian terms, the 'right consciousness' or, as Mao put it, have been 'rectified'. Politics and economics may provide the means; a socio-cultural, anthropological change is the goal and the crux of the matter.

The Weberian contradiction has also to be perceived against the background of the above-mentioned circumstances. As long as China remained moulded by Confucian tradition, the potential contradiction between the literati and the gentry was overcome by close family and interest links between these two groups. Only when the new Western-educated intelligentsia started to emerge did the disproportion between their ambitions and the opportunities for their satisfaction start to emerge. One might also see in the development of this disproportion an instance of the Tocquevillian theorem. When the expectations that had been aroused during the hundred days of reform rule in 1898 came to nought, and the persecution of the reformists set in, the aspirational deprivation in the protagonists' milieu must have been both abrupt and intense.

It is difficult to conceive of a similar development with regard to the peasantry. Peasant rebellions resulted, as a rule, from short-term or regional disturbances – climatic or political – and it is difficult to find a general trend in these happenings or to relate them in a sensible way to the preconditions of the revolution.

It follows from what we have said so far that the main contradiction that came to the fore, and according to which the social forces became divided, was of the Aristotelian type: the contradiction between different understandings of justice, between the traditional Chinese world-view and the world-views underlying the foreign challenge.

The foreign challenge, however, was far from uniform. Unlike in the case of Turkey and Russia, China was confronted with two foreign social philosophies, each commanding the 'cybernetic heights' of different civilisations: the Euro-American with its basically Benthamite values, and the Euro-Asian with its Marxist–Leninist creed. So there was not only a wide gap between what the traditional China stood for and what the foreign challenge suggested; the competition between two foreign alternatives turned the Chinese situation into a three-cornered contest which made the whole revolutionary process more complex and more prolonged. During this contest the traditionalists suffered from the main disadvantages of the Paretian contradiction. The imperial court adopted the fox-like attitude, whereas the lions cropped up from among ambitious warlords and later, to greater effect, from among leaders of the Guomindang and the Communist Party; the two last represented alternative responses to the foreign challenges. In the final confrontation between the communists and the Guomindang it was the Khaldunian contradiction (the difference in fighting spirit) that played the most decisive role in the communist victory.

But the whole story did not end with the victory of one side in the contest. The victorious communists rejected the Soviet Russian paradigm and embarked on the construction of their own type of civilisation. Thus the three-cornered contest issued in a fourth alternative with more scope for the selective appropriation of suitable elements from the three others. In contrast to other revolutions discussed in this book, China got into a situation in which its civilisational transformation had to be worked out within the competitive framework of four paradigms.

Finally, what about nationalistic motives, which played such an important role in the Czech, French and, above all, Turkish revolutions? Yes, nationalism too had its prominent role in the Chinese revolution. As Kemal Atatürk made it one of his Six Points, so Sun Yat-sen made it one (actually the first) of his Three Principles. But nationalism was by no means a recent phenomenon in China, as some have imagined. Its much earlier mighty upsurge can be observed in the period of the anti-Mongol struggle in the fourteenth century AD, which eventually led to a resuscitation of the empire under a native, Ming dynasty. Only its broad popular basis can be attributed – as Chalmers Johnson suggests – to the twentieth-century revolution.[21] (The only difficulty may be in judging where to allocate the credit for its new and extended upsurge – whether to the insolent intruders, especially the Japanese, or to the communists, who were infinitely better than the Guomindang at capitalising on the foreign assault and humiliation.) However, as Lucien Bianco has pointed out, the Chinese peasants' nationalism must not be exaggerated.[22] First, peasant nationalism was a North rather than South Chinese phenomenon, and second, the peasant policy of the communists was by no means of merely secondary importance. Without a tangible improvement of the peasants' material lot in the communist-controlled areas, the peasantry would hardly have been won over to their side during the civil war. But having achieved that, and having outbid the nationalism of the Guomindang, the communists, in Bianco's terms, 'brought Chinese nationalism to fruition'.

The pattern of the Chinese revolution, in terms of stages of development and shifts of the seat of power between different positions in the spectrum, may be characterised as follows. The very beginning was marked by an unusual event: a conservative-inspired uprising. The Boxer movement was aimed at restoring traditional values against foreign encroachments; paradoxically, it produced an explosion coupled with compression. The imperial government was rather ambiguous and even hypocritical in its policy towards the Boxers. They were partly contained, partly exploited as a tool against the foreigners; when they eventually failed they were suppressed. Due to the character of their uprising, their suppression cannot be considered a compression of the reconstruction process. Indeed, it was followed by an attempt to speed up reforms with the aim of keeping the dynasty at the helm. The government, however, promised more than it could or was willing to do; the disappointed expectations may be considered as a case of relative, aspirational deprivation (T. Gurr), or the development characterised by the so-called J-curve (J.C. Davies). The reforms were too fast for the conservatives and too slow for the moderates. In this phase, there was no compression of the type characterising vertical revolutions.

The genuine explosion (1911) was, like the Taiping uprising, a peripheral matter, but unlike the Taiping uprising it had a nation-wide potential which was soon manifested by Sun's short-lived compromise with Yuan (representing the domestic tradition). Their split and Yuan's victory gave way to a compression which, however, issued in the disintegration of China as a unitary state. This in our terms may be considered as the first period of oscillation in which the power was divided among local warlords and cliques. In 1923 the revolutionary forces of right and left formed an alliance which, however, survived only until 1927. In 1928, when the warlords were largely defeated or pacified through negotiations, the seat of power was, in respect of the greater part of the country, intercepted at the position of the Guomindang (accepting the Euro-American orientation).

With the Japanese annexation of Manchuria in 1931, a new phase of oscillation, a three-cornered contest set in. From 1936 (the Xian agreement) to 1945 (the end of the Second World War) the antagonism between the Guomindang and the communists was superseded by the war against Japan and its extreme right puppet regime led by Wang, and was thus somewhat muted. In 1946, however, it turned into a full-scale confrontation.

In 1949 the communists succeeded in establishing their power over the whole Chinese mainland and thus in fully intercepting the seat of power (following the Soviet example). From 1954 to 1966 there was a period marked by frequent and abrupt changes of policy. These shifts were due to different political orientations which eventually led to the turmoil of the Great Proletarian Cultural Revolution. The period 1963–1969 may be seen as yet another period of oscillation. The end of 1969 may be considered a watershed; the forces of consolidation began, shyly, to appear on the stage. After Mao's death in 1976 they gathered momentum.

During the consolidation process there were two contrasting influences with which the Chinese communist leadership had to contend. On the one hand the Soviet model continued to dominate the ideological scene, and on the other the Euro-American paradigm began to provide some inspiration for dealing with practical matters. Gradually, the Chinese domestic genius began to mould these two paradigms, usually seen as incompatible, into a viable compound.

As we have said already, there is here, as in the Soviet revolution, no Waterloo – no reversal. (The imperial regime established by the Japanese in Manchuria was a peripheral matter; moreover, its political and socio-economic system cannot be considered as a restoration of the *ancien régime*.) There is no explicit restoration; but there is a tendency towards a less radical break with the past than that envisaged by Mao and his supporters. In contrast to the Soviet revolution and pure vertical revolutions, however, there is no spontaneous extreme left. When it eventually emerges at a comparatively late stage, it is a movement initiated and largely manipulated from above (by Mao himself). Although in many instances it got out of control, it was eventually curtailed by the army, in principle acting on Mao's behalf.

Each interception in the Chinese revolution seems to have been accompanied by a tightening up, but these did not assume Soviet proportions. Neither, yet, has the People's China had the opportunity for expansion that Soviet Russia had. In contrast to Russia, shifts in policy were more linked with personal changes or with shifts in the power position of leading personalities. As in Russia, however, the victorious leader did not hesitate to adopt his arch-enemy's policies.

The civilisational dimension of the Chinese revolution

The decision to make a fundamental shift in foreign policy was the most sensational event in the Chinese revolution. Communist China's temporary rapprochement with the United States and the corresponding estrangement from the USSR marked one of the salient turning points in the history of communism. For this shift there is no adequate explanation in the Marxist doctrinal armoury. Describing the other side as revisionists or traitors is a partisan value judgement. A rational explanation, however, is quite simple if we accept that, above all class interests and doctrinal arguments, there are some ethno-geographical constants which provide particular societies with some basic, almost immutable, interests.

China was the only communist power that could afford to shape its policy without any regard to Soviet wishes. Once the Chinese communists realised that the United States presented a lesser danger for Chinese independence than the USSR, they drew practical conclusions from that fact, irrespective of the philosophical roots of their state ideology. What mattered was national communism serving national interests – in China, in particular, helping the country in its civilisational reconstruction. For this purpose, Marxism appeared to many Chinese intellectuals to be most useful.

Dialectical materialism could be seen as a new interpretation of Tao – the way of the Universe – which was at the basis of all the Chinese philosophies of the past. Also the dialectical rhythm of thesis and antithesis has, in the alternating rhythm of Yin and Yang, a time-honoured precedent in Chinese thought. Furthermore, there is a striking parallel between Marxism and Confucianism and their respective roles in society. No civilisation in the world, apart from the Chinese, was moulded by a predominantly secular philosophy such as Confucianism. Its transcendental features, as the Jesuit missionaries once rightly realised, were either weak, or of general nature, and could be easily assimilated.[23]

Like Marxism, Confucianism had its classics. Like Marxists, Confucians believed in the power of teaching, in the power of the word. For both, a correct doctrine was a precondition of correct consciousness. Like Marxists, Confucians prescribed how state and society should be organised. Understandably, after 2,000 years, Confucian strategies became obsolete. A doctrine or ideology could, however, as Solomon realised, de-personalise authority, by providing standards for scholarly criticism.[24] This may be dangerous for the Marxist establishment which would prefer – like the Catholic Church – to reserve the interpretation of the Holy Writ for the top hierarchy. It is difficult to imagine that Mao might have been sincerely willing to renounce this prerogative.

Despite these parallels, differences must not be overlooked. Confucianism was, in principle, backward-looking. Highlights of ancient history were its paradigms; legendary rulers of antiquity were the embodiment of wisdom and creativity. Marxism is, in principle, forward-looking. Its golden age is not in the past but in the future. However, in opening up the outlook into the future, Marxism fulfils the dreams of some Chinese thinkers, such as Kang Youwei, who wanted to reorientate Confucian thought towards an ideal age yet to come.

And what about the Mandate of Heaven? Confucians were supposed to know best about it, just as Marxists claim to know best about the laws of development – the laws of historical materialism. Thus, the Mandate of Heaven is replaced by the Mandate of a Correct Doctrine. Just as the Mandate of Heaven came to those who had the guts to acquire it by strength, so the Mandate of the Correct Doctrine comes to those who succeed in gaining command over the party apparatus. The principle of *geming* has scarcely changed.

Given these parallels, it is no wonder that Mao was so obsessed with the fight against Confucianism; the anti-Confucian campaign was one of the most determined undertakings of his latter days. The new philosophy of the state was not to be confused with the old one. This was particularly important with respect to Mao's interpretation of Marxism, which, in contrast to the Marxian vision, saw no end to the dialectics, but postulated an eternal (though progressively less acute) conflict of contradictions. The Confucian concept of harmony was especially repugnant to Mao's dialectical mind.

Filial piety, the main Confucian virtue, also came under attack from Mao. Here, however, he was ambiguous: he denied filial piety towards other father figures, but claimed it for himself. Indeed, the fact that he remained at the head of both state and party after the havoc caused by the Cultural Revolution was mainly due to that Confucian virtue. It is hardly imaginable that any communist establishment would want to throw this virtue into the dustbin of history. Redirected towards the right object, it is likely to be even more heavily promoted, especially as far as its societal aspect (filial piety towards the political leader or leaders) is concerned. Although the personality cult may occasionally be criticised, it will always be fostered, because personal charisma has so far proved socially more effective than its institutionalisation. With reference to China, Mao once explained to Edgar Snow that it was hard for people to overcome the habits of 3,000 years of emperor-worshipping tradition. Although he admitted that his cult became excessive during the Cultural Revolution, he accepted that there was always, and not only in China, a desire to be worshipped and a desire to worship.[25]

Here perhaps an element of Buddhist tradition, which, like Taoism, catered for the religious needs of the lower strata of the Chinese population, can be discovered. 'The cultic attention to Mao's own person' had, as Ninian Smart observed, 'some resemblance to the devotionalism of the Pure Land School and some other Mahayana sects'.[26] To overcome a time-honoured authority, Mao might have drawn for support on a more metaphysically orientated tradition than Confucianism. It remains to be seen whether, with Mao's death, this cultic need has gone for good as well.

Furthermore, Marxism provided an additional justification for the Taoist preference for equality. This particular aspect of the Chinese tradition, too, has been especially strongly emphasised in Mao's understanding of Marx. It remains to be seen how much of it, together with the eternal dialectics, survives in the post-Mao era.

Whatever happens, the basic prospect seems to be clear. There may be different policies; there may be conflicts between different groupings within the power élite or a counter-élite may even emerge; but it is unlikely that China would accept the lead of any other nation, even in the name of a shared ideology. Most probably China will go its own way, in building – with some elements borrowed from the outside world – its own post-Confucian civilisation.

Although China's newly acquired dynamism may not be as buoyant as that of the nineteenth-century West, it is unlikely that its leaders will succeed in taking a leaf from the book of time-honoured Taoist wisdom:

Therefore the sage rules
By emptying their hearts
And filling their bellies,
By weakening their ambitions
And toughening their sinews,
Always striving to make the people knowledgeless and desireless,
And seeing that those who have knowledge dare not interfere,
By thus acting through inaction,
All things are controlled.[27]

Notes

1. For a telling, abundantly documented, history of the Taiping uprising, see F. Michael, *The Taiping Rebellion: History and documents*, 3 vols (Washington University Press, 1966–72); short balanced accounts are available in G. Lewy, *Religion and Revolution* (Oxford University Press, New York, 1974), pp. 154–75, and in J. Chesneaux, M. Bastid and M. Bergère, *China from the Opium Wars to the 1911 Revolution* (Harvester, Brighton, 1976), pp. 89ff.
2. This can best be demonstrated by reference to the weakening and eventual abolition (in 1865) of the periodic briefing of the population on Confucian ethics. In my view, Barrington Moore, Jr (*Social Origins of Dictatorship and Democracy*, Penguin, Harmondsworth, 1969, p. 206) is right in seeing in this development one of the disintegrative features of Imperial China.
3. The Chinese power élite did not have, in sufficient numbers, the adaptive capacity to change their economic habits and assume an entrepreneurial role in industry, nor were they willing to give the government the chance to take over this role; there were not enough funds for investment because of the increasing corruption of the taxation system. For detail see Chung-li Chang, *The Chinese Gentry* (University of Washington Press, Seattle, 1967), pp. 43 and ff.
4. The populations of later 'liberated areas' were treated as a mere supply basis for the Taiping armies, and when the tide of military fortune turned against the Taipings a higher levy had to be taken from a shrinking base.
5. Chesneaux, Bastid and Bergère, p. 345.
6. The specificity of the Chinese situation may best be illustrated by the upheaval caused by central government's attempt in 1911 to buy all the railroad projects from the provincial group that had invested in them. As the investors were local gentry and mandarins, and as the provincial as opposed to the nation-wide consciousness was on the ascendant, it was easy to incite popular riots (in Sichuan a virtual uprising) against the already hated central govenment. (This episode coincided with the insurrection of the military garrison in Wuchang, which heralded the beginnning of the revolution.) It is questionable whether the railway issue can be understood as a 'trigger' for the outbreak of the revolution.
7. Chesneaux rightly says that the traditional Confucian term for 'discontinuance of the Mandate (*geming*) has been wrongly adopted by modern political movements to mean revolution. *Geming* aimed at restoring social order and reintegrating with cosmic order' (Chesneaux, Bastid and Bergère, p. 6). Yet there were a few exceptional cases, such as the uprising of Yellow Turbans toward the end of the second century AD when *geming* surpassed the scope of a revolt (whose main result was the change of personnel and improved performance) and assumed the dimensions of a revolution (the expected change of Heaven implied changes in the social system).

8. J. Chesneaux, F. Le Barbier and M. Bergère, *China from the 1911 revolution to liberation* (Harvester, Brighton, 1977), p. 68.
9. For a pertinent analysis of the Maoist strategy which brushed aside a basic article of Marxist–Leninist faith on the Communist Party as the vanguard and agent of the industrial proletariat, see, for example, B.I. Schwartz, *Chinese Communism and the Rise of Mao* (Harvard University Press, Cambridge, MA, 1964), pp. 188–200. For a more complex, and at the same time detailed, assessment of Mao's position and role in the great transformation of China see especially the accounts of eleven authors in D. Wilson (ed.), *Mao Tse-tung in the Scales of History* (Cambridge University Press, London, 1977).
10. R.H. Solomon, *Mao's Revolution and the Chinese Political Culture* (University of California Press, Berkeley, 1971), pp. 70, 195 and *passim*.
11. To be attacked by the enemy is not a bad thing but a good thing' was the gist of one of Mao's public statements in 1939. Quoted from *Selected Readings from the Works of Mao Tse-tung* (Foreign Languages Press, Peking, 1967), pp. 130–2.
12. Moore, *Social Origins*, p. 223.
13. Solomon, p. 250.
14. J. Chesneaux, *China: The People's Republic* (Harvester, Brighton, 1979), p. 44.
15. The phenomenon of the Cultural Revolution, its causation and course have been subject to a wide range of analyses by Western scholars. It would be out of proportion to review all the nuanced interpretations suggested by authors other than those already quoted. Suffice it only to say that in 1977 an American scholar (P.J. Hiniker, *Revolutionary Ideology and Chinese Reality: Dissonance under Mao*, Sage, London, 1977, pp. 297–302) listed seven rival explanations (including his own) of the Cultural Revolution. A thoughtful reading, however, reveals that these are not so much rival as partial explanations, fitting quite well into the comprehensive picture which, to my knowledge, has been most adequately presented by R. Solomon.
16. Mao's letter to Lin Biao on 7 May 1966, quoted from *The Economist* (25 November 1972), p. 52.
17. Solomon, p. 331.
18. J. Burnham, *The Managerial Revolution* (Pelican Books, London, 1945).
19. Solomon, p. 510.
20. Quoted from *The Economist* (11 September 1982), p. 14.
21. C.A. Johnson, *Peasant Nationalism and Communist Power: The emergence of revolutionary China 1937–45* (Stanford University Press, CA, 1962).
22. L Bianco, *Origins of the Chinese Revolution* (Stanford University Press, CA, 1971), pp. 153–66.
23. Confucianism was not supposed to cater for the religious needs of China's population. This task was fulfilled by Taoist priests and Buddhist monks; in spite of occasional rows, the two religions lived in symbiosis with the Confucian philosophy.
24. Solomon, p. 257.
25. E. Snow, *The Long Revolution* (Vintage, New York, 1971), pp. 169–70.
26. N. Smart, *Mao* (Collins, Glasgow, 1974), p. 92.
27. *Tao Te Ching*, translated by H.D. Dubs in his 'Taoism in China', in H.F. MacNair (ed.), *China* (California University Press, Berkeley, 1946).

7

□

Graphs and chronological tables

In the following pages the applications of our morphological model to the six test cases of 'great vertical revolutions' (Bohemia, England, France, Russia, Turkey and China) will be presented in the form of graphs. They should illustrate to what extent our model can reveal similarities (perhaps even regularities) in the great revolutionary processes of the vertical type. A brief comment on the morphological pattern of two other great vertical revolutions (in Iran and Mexico) will be added subsequently.

As has been said earlier, the visual presentation is given here in the form of two-dimensional graphs, the horizontal dimension being time, and the vertical the range of political concepts represented by particular groupings, parties or persons. These groupings can also be described as 'social vectors' in the sense explained in the section on morphology of revolution (pages 38–42), but for the sake of brevity we can label them simply 'positions'. The positions are ranged from the bottom to the top according to the extent of social change (understood in the broadest possible sense) to be achieved. (However irrationally conceived or blurred, some purpose is always present in a revolution.) Thus the defenders of the *status quo* are at the bottom, and the representatives of the most radical views and desire for change are at the top.

Anticipating possible criticism of the vertical scale that the author has used – for example, questioning the validity of equidistance between individual positions – it must be stressed that vertical scales are arbitrary in the following sense: it is only the direction of the movement (i.e. changes in power) and not the absolute magnitude of that change which our graphs attempt to present. Since the direction of change at any point along the horizontal axis would remain up or down respectively, no matter what transformation of the vertical scale we might reasonably have adopted, the appearance of the graph would not have been materially affected by such transformation.

As far as the three 'historical' or 'Western' revolutions (those in Bohemia, England and France) are concerned (in terms of our typology they are classified as endogenous), individual positions are described by conventional historical names. Furthermore, their location within the whole range of positions is, for the sake of comparison, marked from the bottom to the top in terms of a political spectrum moved from right to left.

All the three 'modern' or 'Eastern' revolutions (those in Russia, Turkey and China) happen to be exogenous revolutions in terms of our typology. This means that for the policy orientation of the groupings that contested power, foreign paradigms played key roles. As has been shown in the discussion of the political spectrum in these revolutions, the left-to-right ranking of individual positions does not make sense in their case. Individual positions are better described either by the type of political regime or by the names of the competing foreign paradigms.

Understandably, not all nuances within the political spectrum can be represented in the graphs. In particular, schism within, and mergers of, individual political or ideological groups have to be omitted. Thus various individual positions reflect only the main lines of political and ideological differentiation. The time span of active presence of the individual positions in the revolutionary process is indicated by a thickening of the horizontal line which locates it within the vertical dimension of the graph. Interruption of a thick line means that the group in question was suppressed or ceased to exist for other reasons. Often after such a break, the position may again start to play some significant role, possibly under a changed name.

The curve running horizontally through the graphs illustrates, though only approximately, changes in the power structure. To put it more succinctly, it indicates the shifts in the seat of power from one position to another. Different positions are, as a rule, represented by different persons. But wherever autocrats stayed longer at the helm (whether they represented the revolution or restoration), they often changed their policy to such an extent that, from the point of view of our analysis, this meant taking another position.

Frequently, however, the shifts in the seat of power did not affect the whole country. Especially in the earlier stages of the revolutionary process, individual areas are dominated by various competing groups. In such a case the graph illustrates only the movement in the greater part, or at the 'heart', of the country.

The turning points and other events that are significant for the course of revolution and for the assessment of its phases in terms of our morphological model are summarised in the chronological tables following individual graphs. Readers who are suspicious about my method of drawing the course of the shifting seat of power may use them for checking to what extent my judgement was based on empirical observations. As I have said previously in the introductory discussion on morphology, the graphs serve illustrative, not sociometric, purposes; they are not based on any quantitative measurement but on historians' accounts of individual revolutionary processes. Furthermore, the graphical presentation is intended only to assist comparison.

The graphs reveal more similarities in the case of revolutions described as endogenous. The morphological pattern of the Hussite revolution in Bohemia and that of the Puritan revolution in England especially resemble each other. The main difference is in the position and duration of the restoration. The pattern of the French revolution, however, is substantially different. As there was much more at stake, the revolutionary process took longer to reach the point at which issues other than those which had caused the revolution became paramount. The first flare-up and oscillation were short-lived, and the interception of the oscillating seat of power was achieved at a less radical position than in Bohemia and England. Imperial expansion gave the course of the revolution a particular twist which, after its collapse, resulted in a conspicuous strengthening of the forces promoting restoration. 'Revolutionary events' had to be repeated twice (in 1830 and 1848) in order to push through the main systemic changes. The two subsequent rounds of revolution not only caught up with what they failed to achieve in the earlier stages of revolution, but moved the pendulum further to the left and with more durable effect than was the case with the Hussite and Puritan revolutions.

The widely different patterns of revolution classified as exogenous (Russia, Turkey and China) are mainly due to the foreign nature of the challenge and to the resulting variations in response. In terms of our morphological model, this is reflected in the number of the competing paradigms. In the case of Turkey, there were only two such paradigms: the Ottoman (*ancien régime*) and the European (embraced by the new regime). In Russia there were three paradigms: the tsarist (*ancien régime*), the challenging European (followed by the leaders of the February revolution in 1917), and the Bolshevik/Soviet (resulting from the October Revolution in 1917). In China, four paradigms were involved in the contest: the traditional domestic, the Euro-American, the Soviet (Euro-Asian) and the new domestic one. What can be surmised at the time of writing is that the latter paradigm reflects inspiration from all the other three sources. There are further comments on these issues in the concluding section of the book.

Bohemia

See Figure 7.1.

Chronology to the morphological model of the Hussite revolution in Bohemia (the Czech revolution)

Onset and institutionalisation

1403	First controversies about Wyclif; riots
1409	The Decree of Kutná Hora; the university turns Hussite
1412	Struggle for indulgences
1414	The first administration of Holy Communion in both kinds

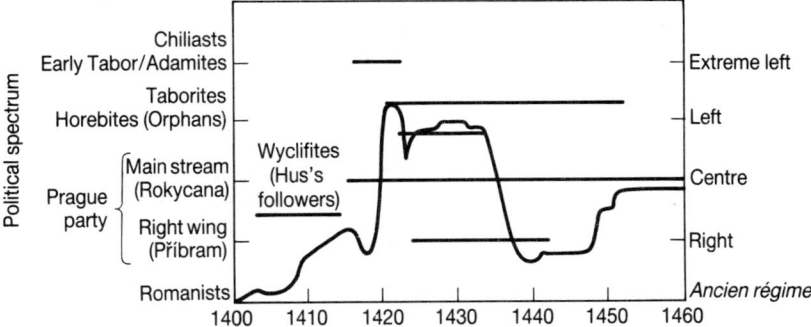

Note: The thick lines indicate the more-or-less institutionalised presence of the respective groupings.
The curve approximately indicates the shifts of the seat of power, or, in this particular case, the
geographical extent of the power of individual groupings.

Figure 7.1.   The pattern of the Czech revolution

1415	Martyrdom of Hus; a Utraquist covenant
1416	Prague University becomes authority on religious matters
1417	Emergence of the communities of radical reformers

Compression
1418–19	King's attempt at suppressing the Hussite movement

Explosion
1419	Defenestration; storms in Prague; gatherings on the mountains

Oscillation
1420	Chiliasm; founding of Tabor; the first crusade and the defeat of Sigismund; Four Articles of Prague
1421	Čáslav Diet; Želivský's rule in the New Town of Prague
1422	Žižka's break with the Tabor Hussites; the end of Želivský's rule

Interception
1424	Victory of Žižka and the Taborites over the Prague Hussites near Malešov; reconciliation with the Prague Hussites; Žižka's death; 'Orphans' and their agreement with the Taborites

Tightening
1426	Fixing of the Taborite doctrine; Prokop the Shaven commander-in-chief
1427	Rokycana's anti-Korybut *coup* in Prague

Expansion
1427	Beginning of military expeditions to foreign countries
1429	Beginning of negotiations with Sigismund
1431	Beginning of negotiations with the Basle Ecumenical Council
1433	A peace formula – the Compacts

Reversal

1434   Victory of the coalition of the Prague Hussites with the
              Romanists over the Taborites and Orphans (Battle of
              Lipany)

Restoration compromise

1436   Acceptance of the Compacts by the Bohemian and Moravian
              estates; the re-enthronement of Sigismund

Restoration pressure

1437   Efforts to restrict the Compacts; Rokycana's flight from Prague
1440   Regional truce agreements (*Landfrieden*); unification of eastern
              Bohemia under Hussite captains
1442   Reconciliation of Rokycana with Příbram; reunification of the
              Prague party
1444   Condemnation of the Taborite doctrine by the Prague Diet
1448   Attempt by a papal legate to carry off the original copy of the
              Compacts frustrated

Consolidation

1448   Conquest of Prague by George of Poděbrady
1450   Reconciliation of the Calixtin and Romanist nobility
1452   George becomes regent of the realm; surrender of Tabor
1457   Foundation of the Unity of Brethren
1458   George elected king of Bohemia

England

See Figure 7.2.

Chronology to the morphological model of the English revolution

Onset and institutionalisation
1628   Petition of Right

Compression
1629   Charles I dissolves Parliament; arrest of eleven opposition leaders
1632   Eliot's death

Explosions
1637–9   Insurrection of the Scots
1640   Restitution of Parliament; the Short and the Long Parliaments;
              dismissal and arrest of the king's counsellors, Strafford and
              Laud
1641   Grand Remonstrance
1642   Beginning of the war between the king and Parliament

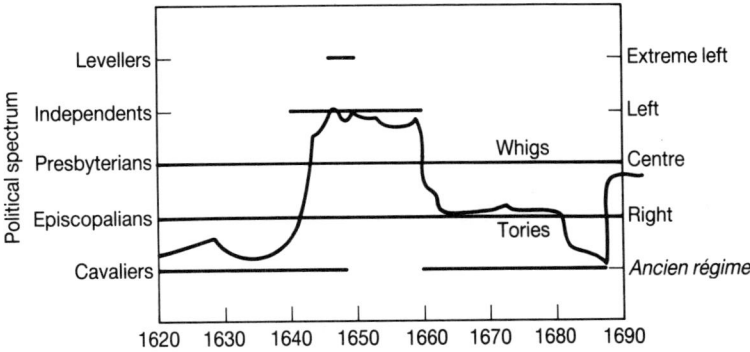

Note: The thick lines indicate the more-or-less institutionalised presence of the respective groupings. The curve approximately indicates the shifts of the seat of power.

Figure 7.2. The pattern of the English revolution

Oscillation

1642–5	'Cautious and conciliatory war'
1643	Solemn League and Covenant between the English Parliament and the Scots
1644–5	Parliamentary unity threatened; Self-denying Ordinance; New Model Army
1645	Cromwell's victory over the Royalists near Naseby
1646	City of London and Scottish Commissioner as pressure groups
1647	The king handed over to Parliament by the Scots; disagreement between Parliament and the army; Levellers' Agreement of the People presented to the Army Council in Putney; the king's escape and engagement with the Scots
1648	Renewal of the civil war; the king defeated; remonstrance of the army; Pride's Purge; the Rump Parliament

Interception and expansion

1649	Execution of Charles I; suppression of the Levellers; appearance of the Diggers; proclamation of the Commonwealth (republic); beginning of the expansion (to Ireland)
1651	Navigation Act
1651–2	End of the victorious campaign against Scotland and Ireland; beginning of the wars with the Netherlands

Tightening

1653	Dissolution of the Rump Parliament; 'nominated' Parliament ('of the Saints'); instrument of Government; Cromwell Lord Protector
1654	'Western Design' against Spanish Empire

| 1657 | Humble Petition and Advice; offer of the crown rejected by Cromwell but the right to nominate successor and members of a new Upper House accepted |
| 1658 | Cromwell's death |

Reversal

| 1659 | Resignation of Cromwell's son; Commonwealth revived |
| 1660 | Monck's march on London; Long Parliament restored |

Restoration compromise

1660	Declaration of Breda
1661–5	Clarendon Code; checking of the influence of Nonconformists
1667	Disturbances in London; expulsion of Chancellor Clarendon
1672	Declaration of Indulgence for the Protestant Nonconformists
1673	The same declaration revoked; Test Act
1679	Habeas Corpus Amendment Act
1679–81	Whigs strive to exclude James II from succession

Restoration pressure

1681	Charles II dissolves Parliament
1683	Suppression of the Whigs' and the Independents' conspiracy
1685	James II ascends to the throne; Monmouth's insurrection
1687	Catholics admitted to government offices by dispensation from the Test Act

Consolidation

| 1688 | Glorious Revolution |
| 1689 | Bill of Rights; Act of Toleration |

France

See Figure 7.3.

Chronology to the morphological model of the French revolution

Onset

1751–80	Work on and publication of Encyclopaedia
1770	End of a prolonged period of economic growth
1776	Turgot's attempt at a moderate reform frustrated
1778–83	Intervention in the American War of Independence
1786	Financial crisis revealed

Compression

| 1787–8 | Callone's reform attempts frustrated; rebellion of the privileged |
| 1788 | Disastrous harvest; convocation of Estates General |

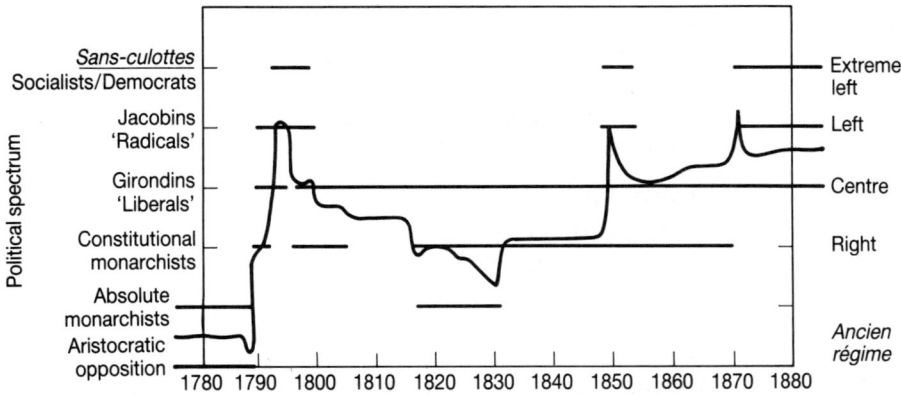

Note: The thick lines indicate the more-or-less institutionalised presence of the respective groupings. The curve approximately indicates the shifts in the seat of power, or in policy.

Figure 7.3. The pattern of the French revolution

Institutionalisation and explosion

1789   Peasants' unrest

The Third Estate declares itself National and then Constituent Assembly

Paris uprising (Bastille); peasants' pressure; abolition of 'feudalism'

Declaration of Rights; confiscation of Church's property

1790   Redemption of feudal rights decreed

The Church subject to the state's sovereignty

Oscillation

1791   Demonstration on the Champ de Mars

Abolition of corporations and guilds

1792   Uprising in Paris; Convent; proclamation of the Republic

Foreign intervention halted

Support of satellite revolutions; first annexations

1793   Execution of Louis XVI

Counter-revolutionary uprising in the provinces

Universal military service

Sans-culottes' uprising; fall of the Gironde government

Rule of the Jacobins; concessions to the *sans-culottes*

De-Christianisation attempts

Final abolition of feudal rights; terror

1794   Success of the *levée en masse*
              Suppression of the extreme left (Hébert) and of moderates
              (Danton)
              Fall of the Jacobin government; economic liberalism
              re-established

Subdued oscillation and expansion
1795   Conquest of the Netherlands
              Plebeian uprising in Paris suppressed; Directory
1796   War against the coalition; Pichegru defeated; Bonaparte
              victorious
              Babeuf's conspiracy suppressed
1797   Electoral success of constitutional monarchists; their expulsion
              from the National Assembly (*coup d'état* of Fructidor)
              Law on universal military service
1798   Electoral victory of the Jacobins; their expulsion from the
              National Assembly (*coup d'état* of Floréal)
1798–9   Bonaparte's Egyptian campaign
1799   The Third Directory (*coup d'état* of Prérial)

Interception, tightening and extended expansion
1799   The Consulate (*coup d'état* of Brumaire)
1801   The Concordat
1802   Standard secondary male education (*lycées*) established
1804   *Code civil des français* (from 1807 *Code Napoléon*) Napoleon
              confirmed as emperor by a plebiscite
1806   Continental system (blockade)
1808   Beginning of the campaign in the Iberian Peninsula
1810   Climax of the expansion; Napoleon's dynastic marriage
1812   Russian campaign and its collapse

Reversal
1813   Napoleon's defeat at Leipzig
1814   Foreign armies enter France; Napoleon's capitulation
              First restoration, Louis XVIII; compromise arrangement
              First Treaty of Paris; beginning of the Vienna Congress
1815   Napoleon's Hundred Days; Waterloo

Restoration compromise
1815   Second restoration; compromise revitalised
              Ultra-Royalist electoral victory
              Second Treaty of Paris; the Holy Alliance
1816   Leading republicans and Bonapartists banished;
              moderation of the regime
1817   Censitory (property owners') suffrage established
1818   Liberal opposition becomes vociferous

1820	Assassination of the Duc de Barry; trend towards the right
1822	Laws restricting the press
1824	Charles X

Restoration pressure

1825	Constitutional rights limited; compensation to returned *émigrés*
1827	Demonstrations and dissolution of National Guards
1830	Dissolution of the National Assembly; Four Ordinances

First consolidation overthrow

1830	'July Revolution'; Louis-Philippe
1831	Anti-clerical riots in Paris; weavers' uprising in Lyon
1832	Ultra-Royalist uprising in Vendée foiled
	Republican insurrection in Paris suppressed
1834	The second weavers' uprising in Lyon
1835	*Société des familles* (Blanqui)
1836	Louis-Napoleon's attempt at a *coup d'état* foiled
1846–7	Economic crisis

Second explosion and oscillation

1848	'February Revolution', the Second Republic; universal suffrage
	National workshops installed and then abolished
	Plebeian insurrection (June)
	Louis-Napoleon elected president (December)
1849	Temporary restriction of universal suffrage
1850	Increasing clerical influence in education

Second interception, tightening and attempts at expansion

1852	The Second Empire (Napoleon III)
1857	Government control of education; regime becomes less authoritarian
1860	Extension of the power of the National Assembly and the Senate; government-sponsored economic expansion
1862–7	Mexican adventure
1870	A new, more liberal, constitution approved by a plebiscite

Second consolidation

1870	Franco-Prussian War; Napoleon's defeat; the Third Republic
1871	France's capitulation; Paris Commune
1873	Failure of attempts at Royalist restoration
1876–7	MacMahon's flirtation with a monarchial restoration frustrated
1879	Republican majority in the Senate
1882	Compulsory primary education; lay state schools
1884	Trade unions legalised

Russia

See Figure 7.4.

Chronology to the morphological model of the Russian revolution

Foreshadowings
1818	First secret revolutionary association
1825	Decembrist attempt at a *coup d'état*
1830	Polish 'November' uprising; sailors' mutiny in the Black Sea Navy
1853–5	The Crimean War
1861	Abolition of serfdom

Onset
1862–3	Populist organisation of Land and Liberty
1863	Polish 'January' uprising
1868–9	Nechaev's and Tkachev's groups; programme of revolutionary activities
1874	Populists 'going to the people'
1878–81	Wave of terrorism and repression
1881	Assassination of Alexander II
1898	Social Democratic Party founded
1902	Socialist Revolutionary Party founded
1903	Rift in the Social Democratic Party; Bolsheviks versus Mensheviks
1904–5	Russo-Japanese War

First explosion
1905	Bloody Sunday; strikes and the first revolution
1906	Government concessions; Duma – consultative assembly on the basis of unequal elections; Stolypin's reform

Compression
1907	Successive limitations of concessions; government pressure on the Duma
1914–18	First World War

Second explosion and oscillation
1917	February revolution; first phase of oscillation; Kornilov's *putsch*; October revolution
1918	Short-lived coalition; expropriation of landed estates and factories; Peace of Brest Litovsk; transfer of capital to Moscow; the first terror
1918–20	Civil war and foreign intervention; secession of non-Russian territories
1919	Communist International founded

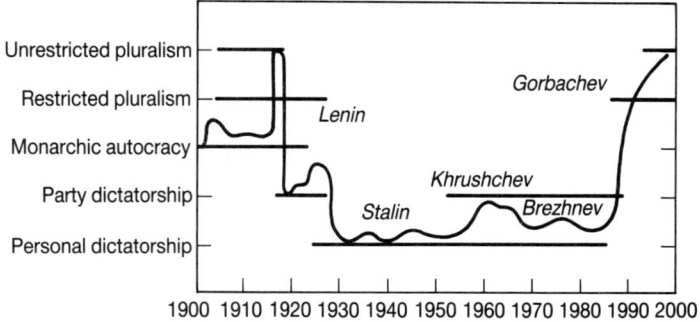

Note: The curve approximately indicates the shifts in the seat of power, or in policy

Figure 7.4.   The pattern of the Russian revolution

Interception

1920	Defeat of the counter-revolutionary armies; failure of the Bolsheviks to conquer Poland
1920–1	Sovietisation of Azerbaijan, Armenia and Georgia
1921	Kronstadt uprising; 10th Congress of the Communist Party; New Economic Policy; first purge
1922	Stalin general secretary; USSR constituted
1924	Lenin's death; first constitution of the USSR ratified

Tightening and perversion

1926–8	Stalin's opponents (Trotsky, Zinoviev, Kamenev, Bucharin, etc.) deprived of influence in the party
1928	First Five Year Plan launched
1929	Forced collectivisation of agriculture started; Trotsky banned; party in control of the trade unions
1929–32	Terror and famine in the countryside; destruction of individual peasantry; large-scale construction of heavy industry
1933–8	Second Five Year Plan; private plots allowed; consumer goods industry less discriminated against
1934	Assassination of Kirov
1936	Stalin's 'socialist' constitution
1936–8	Popular Front abroad; political trials at home; terror against the Old Bolshevik Guard and intelligentsia

First expansion

1939	Pressure on the Baltic states; agreement with Nazi Germany; fourth division of Poland
1939–40	War against Finland and annexation of its border territories
1940	Annexation of Bessarabia and Baltic states

Temporary, partial reversal
1941–2   German conquest of a great part of European USSR
1942–3   Battle of Stalingrad

Second expansion
1943–5   Soviet re-conquest of lost territories and conquest of the eastern part of central Europe; attempt to establish supremacy in Chinese Turkestan and northern Iran
1943–5   USSR acquires, on the basis of an agreement with its allies, a zone of influence in eastern and southeastern Europe
1943–8   Policy of cooperation with the 'national bourgeoisie' within the zone of influence
1947–8   Satellite 'revolutions'; Sovietisation of Poland, Czechoslovakia, East Germany, Hungary, Romania, Bulgaria and Albania; Yugoslavia rejects Soviet tutelage

Consolidation of the regime and of the empire
1953   Stalin's death; weakening of the state policy; East Berlin uprising
1953–6   Post-Stalinist thaw, most political prisoners released⁻
1953–64   Khrushchev first secretary of the Communist Party
1956   Polish semi-emancipation; Hungarian emancipation suppressed
1960–1   Sino-Soviet split; Albania allies with China
1962   Build-up of nuclear power base in Cuba foiled by the United States
1964   Brezhnev first secretary of the Communist Party
1965   Attempts to decentralise economy
1968   Emancipation of Czechoslovakia suppressed
1970   Attempts to get international guarantees for the *status quo* (consolidation of Soviet expansion) in Europe
1975   Acceptance of the post-1945 state borders in the Helsinki agreement; reluctance to honour provisions of the agreement aiming for a freer exchange of people and ideas between the two camps

Third expansion
1967 and 1973   Support for Arabs against Israel
1968–77   Temporary support for Somalia
1975   Intervention by proxy in Angola
1977   Support for the revolutions in Ethiopia and Mozambique
1979   Treaty with South Yemen (troops may be stationed)
1979–89   Military intervention in Afghanistan
1981–2   Emancipation of Polish trade unions suppressed

Reversal and restart
1982   Death of Brezhnev
1985   Gorbachev at the helm

1986	Beginning of *glasnost* (openness of information)
1987–8	Attempts at reconstruction; admission of pluralism; easing of international tensions; non-Russian nations strive for emancipation
1989	Fall of satellite regimes in Central and Southeastern Europe
1990	Political differentiation; Gorbachev tries to keep a middle course; failure of distribution system
1991	Democratic elections of the burgomasters and presidents of the Union republics; Yeltsin president of the Russian Federation; a military *coup* foiled; break-up of the USSR; Commonwealth of Independent States instead, but not all former Soviet republics join in
1992–3	Differentiation of political and economic developments in individual states; ethnic conflicts in the border areas; economic transformation most difficult; rivalry between the president and the Parliament in Russia; upsurge of nationalism

Turkey

See Figure 7.5.

Chronology to the morphological model of the Turkish revolution

A. ADAPTATION PERIOD

First phase of reforms

| 1792 | Selim III's new order |

Reversal

| 1807 | Selim III deposed |
| 1808 | Mahmud II |

Suppression of the traditional power bases

1812	Suppression of the *derebeys*
1826	Liquidation of the *janissaries*; government control of *evkâf*
1831	Abolition of the *timars*

Second phase of reforms

| 1839 | Abdülmecid's Rose Chamber Rescript; beginning of the *Tanzimat* |
| 1858 | Land law |

Reversal

| 1861 | Death of Abdülmecid; Abdülaziz's anti-reformist stance |

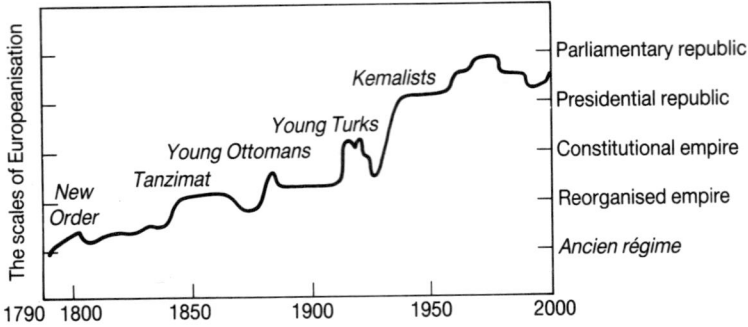

Note: The curve approximately indicates the shifts in the seat of power, or in policy.

Figure 7.5. The pattern of the Turkish revolution

Onset
1876   Abdülhamid accepts the constitution

Compression
1878   Abdülhamid starts ruling without constitution

Explosion
1908   Young Turks' revolution; constitution renewed

First oscillation
1909   Attempt at counter-revolution
1911–13   Loss of Tripolitania and most of Rumelia in wars
1912   Liberal government

First interception and tightening
1913   *Coup* and dictatorship of the Committee of Union and Progress
1914   Alliance with the German and Austro-Hungarian empires in First World War
1915   Massacres of the Armenians

Reversal
1918   Defeat, capitulation and restoration attempt

B. TRANSFORMATION PERIOD

Second explosion and oscillation
1919–22   Civil war and War of Independence

Second interception and tightening
1923   Republic and Treaty of Lausanne
1924   Republican constitution (executive supremacy)

1923–8	The main phase of reforms (Islam disestablished, civil code, Latin script, etc.)
1930–5	Further Europeanising reforms
1937	Kemalist social philosophy formulated – Six Arrows
1938	Atatürk's death
1939–45	Inönü's presidential regime

Consolidation

1945–50	Admission and founding of opposition parties
1950	Opening to the electoral contest
1950–60	Religious and economic liberalisation
1960–1	First military intervention
1961	Social-liberal constitution (division of power)
1965–70	A leftist upsurge
1971–3	Second military intervention; 'guided democracy'
1977–80	Political polarisation; mounting terrorism
1980–2	Third military intervention; ban on political parties
1982	Presidential constitution; law and order re-established
1983	New political parties admitted; Turgut Özal prime minister
1987	Ban on pre-1981 politicians lifted by popular referendum State of emergency in Kurdistan
1988	State of emergency in Istanbul revoked
1989	Özal (liberal) elected president
1990	Turkey becomes a paradigm for nationalists in ethnically related nations of former USSR
1993	Demirel (conservative) elected president Mrs Ciller prime minister

China

See Figure 7.6.

Chronology to the morphological model of the Chinese revolution

A. PRE-REVOLUTIONARY PERIOD

Foreign pressure

1839–42	First Opium War
1842	Treaty of Nanjing
1843	Society of the Worshippers of God founded (Hong Xiuqan)
1844–7	Doctrine of the Society of God conceived
1847	Edict of Tolerance for Christianity

First attempt at revolution

1850–1	Beginning of the Taiping uprising

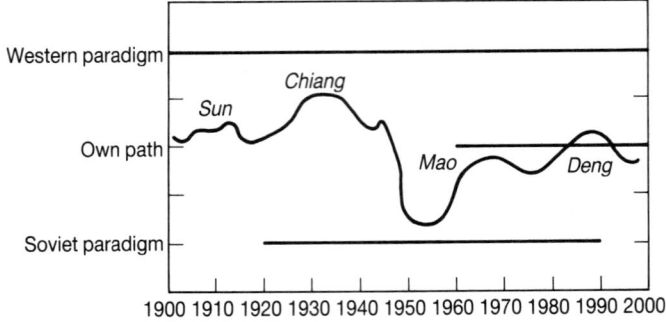

Note: The curve approximately indicates the shifts in the seat of power, or in policy

Figure 7.6. The pattern of the Chinese revolution

1852–3	Beginning of the Nian rebellion
1853	Conquest of Nanjing by the Taipings
1853	Muslim insurrection in Yunnan
1856	Rivalry among the Taiping leadership – internecine fighting, weakening of morale
1856–8	Second Opium War
1859–60	Third Opium War
1860	Beginning of Prince Gong's regency
1862	Muslim insurrection in Xinjiang and Gansu

Compression
1862–74	Rally of imperial power
1864	Re-conquest of Nanjing by imperial forces
1868	Liquidation of the last Taiping and Nian groups
1873–8	Suppression of Muslim uprisings
1884–5	Sino-French War
1894–5	Sino-Japanese War

Onset
1895	Collective memorandum of Guangdong and Hunan representatives Sun Yat-sen's abortive plot in Canton
1898	Reform cabinet lasting 103 days; its dismissal, and persecution of reformers
1899–1900	Boxer disturbances and military intervention by Great Powers
1905	Abolition of the Confucian examination system; revolutionary alliance 'The United League' founded – Sun Yat-sen chairman
1906	Abolition of slavery and of estate discrimination; preparation for a constituent assembly

1907	Sun Yat-sen's Three Points proclaimed
1909	Provincial assemblies elected (by limited electorate)
1910	Riots and petitions
1911	Nationalisation of railways opposed as a conservative measure

B. THE REVOLUTIONARY PROCESS

Explosion

| 1911 | Wuchang mutiny; Sun Yat-sen's revolution; Republic proclaimed in Nanjing |
| 1912 | Abdication of the Manchu dynasty; Guomindang founded; Yuan Shikai president |

Attempt at interception

1913	Tightening of Yuan's rule; abortive revolt in the south
1913–14	Guomindang, Parliament and provincial assemblies disbanded
1914	Sun Yat-sen in emigration
1915	Twenty-one Japanese demands
1915–16	Yuan Shikai's failed attempt to restore the monarchy

First oscillation and institutionalisation

1917	Virtual dissolution of China
1919	The 'May 4 Movement'
1921	Restoration of the Republic in the south; Communist Party founded
1923	At Soviet instigation, close cooperation between the Guomindang and the communists
1926	Expansion of the Republic from the south to the central provinces
1927	Beginning of Chiang Kai-shek's ascendancy in the Guomindang; Guomindang–communist split

Partial interception

1928	Guomindang's conquest of North China
1930–1	Three campaigns against the communists
1931	Japan occupies Manchuria
1932	Japanese intervention in Shanghai
1933–4	Guomindang's campaigns against the communists
1934–5	The 'Long March'
1935–6	Japanese pressure on North China
1936	Xian mutiny and agreement

Foreign intervention

1937	Japan starts full-scale war against China
1938	Japanese conquest of Shanghai and Nanjing
1939	Renewed tension between the Guomindang and the communists

1940	The New Democracy programme proclaimed by Mao Zedong; Wang Jingwei sets up a pro-Japanese government in Nanjing
1941–5	Pacific War
1942	Communist campaign for the rectification of conduct
1942	United Kingdom and United States abandon the unequal treaties

Second oscillation

1946–7	Guomindang offensive against the communists
1947	A turning point: the communist offensive
1948	Split in, and defection from, the Guomindang
1949–50	Complete defeat of the Guomindang forces on the mainland

Full interception – tightening up

1949	People's Republic of China proclaimed; Mao Zedong chairman of the party and head of state
1950–3	Involvement in the Korean War
1950–3	Agrarian reform; 'People's Tribunals'
1953	Soviet withdrawal from Manchuria; Soviet-Chinese companies abolished
1954	First constitution declared
1956–7	Birth control campaign; Hundred Flowers; rectification campaign; suppression of 'rightists'
1958	Taiwan Straits crisis; mass mobilisation; the Great Leap Forward; the communes
1959	Tibet uprising; Liu Shaoqi head of state
1960	Open breach with Soviet Russia
1961–2	Pragmatism prevails; professionalism encouraged

Third oscillation

1962–4	Polarisation within the leadership
1963	Army under Lin Biao increasingly engaged on Mao's side
1964	Party apparatus attempts to compromise while putting pressure on Mao
1965	Liu Shaoqi's firm hold on metropolitan area and outlying provinces; Mao finds support in Shanghai
1966–9	The 'Great Proletarian Cultural Revolution'
1967	Fall of Liu Shaoqi; minor civil wars; military insurrection in Wuhan
1968	Red Guards subjected to army proletarian discipline
1969	New party statutes – Lin Biao heir designate

Creeping interception

| 1969–70 | Return to economic incentives, private plots; reconstruction of the party apparatus started |

1971	Mao-Lin tension; Lin's air crash; UN membership for People's China
1972	Zhou Enlai virtually second to Mao; appeasement with United States; escalating tension between China and USSR
1972–3	Creeping rehabilitation of the victims of the Cultural Revolution
1974	Campaign against Confucius and Lin Biao
1976	Zhou Enlai's death; Hua Guofeng prime minister; second temporary eclipse of Deng Xiaoping; Mao's death; Hua Guofeng chairman; Mao's widow and three other radicals (Gang of Four) arrested
1977	Deng reinstated as a senior member of the Politburo; flood of wall-posters; campaign against the Gang of Four

Consolidation

1978	New constitution drafted; de-Maoisation sets in; beginning of economic 'open-door' policy
	Punitive expedition against Vietnam following the expulsion of ethnic Chinese from Vietnam and Vietnam's invasion of Kampuchea
1979	Policy of Four Modernisations; economic priorities shifted in favour of farming and urban consumption; Deng Xiaoping usurps some of the power nominally belonging to Hua
1980	Further opening to the West; attempts at keeping the balance between liberalisation and suppression of 'sedition'
1981	Deng in full command
1982	12th Congress of the Communist Party of China; new constitution declared
1984	Rapprochement with the United States; liberalisation in progress
1989	Students' freedom campaign and its bloody suppression in Tiananmen Square
1990–3	No political, but progressive, economic liberalisation

Part III

Two additional case studies

General note

According to the typology of revolution suggested in this book, the number of revolutions that could be classified as vertical from below, and which at the same time could be considered great, may be put at ten. If various vertical aspects of horizontal revolutions, or, in other words, if the transformative effects of secessionist wars (wars of liberation) are not taken into account, then the ten revolutions listed in Table I.1 (page 10) represent virtually all revolutions of that particular type in modern history – plus one revolution of the late Middle Ages. A similar assumption cannot be made with respect to the other types of revolution.

In the concluding part of this book, as in the introductory section, the focus will be on theoretical considerations. The search for a theory undertaken in the first edition of this book will be superseded by the suggestion of a theoretical framework. Consequently the author feels that the number of revolutions that serve as the empirical basis for theoretical conclusions should be increased by at least two other specimens: Iran and Mexico. This would then cover four-fifths of the given species. Both the Iranian and the Mexican revolutions of the twentieth century are, though to different degrees, responses to the European challenge.

In Iran the challenge was straightforward, the main issue of its revolution being comparable to that of Turkey and China. Unlike Turkey and China, however, the course of the Iranian revolution has not been a straight one. At first the response to the European challenge tended to follow the Ottoman line. Then, however, came the shift to a national monarchy inspired by the pre-Islamic tradition. Finally, the renaissance of the local version of Islam has turned the course of revolution to the outright rejection of the Western paradigm.

In Mexico, the exogenous parts of the drama (the painful process of adaptation) had been performed earlier. First, after the Spanish conquest in the sixteenth century, and second, in the secessionist war against the Spanish Crown (1810–21) and in its aftermath. The revolution that broke out in 1910 was already a domestic affair. The underlying issue can be described as groping for a viable coexistence of a twofold cultural heritage: that of the native Indios and that of the naturalised immigrants, the Creoles.

The two additional case studies (Iran and Mexico) will be discussed with the focus on general characteristics, such as the structure of causation and the contours of development, rather than on detail.

8

□

Iran (1906–)

General outline

As has been shown in the earlier case studies, exogenous revolutions were never a straightforward matter. The more alive the domestic traditions, and the more paradigms at stake, the more tortuous was the course of revolution, the more complex was the process of social transformation and the more marked this was by specific features.

The case of Iran further illustrates the point. Like other revolutions that broke out as a response to the challenge of the West, the Iranian revolution of the twentieth century had a long history. Furthermore, its course reveals a particular rhythm of a cyclical nature. After 170 years of strenuous and conflict-ridden effort, the quest for a compromise between the domestic and the foreign paradigms turned towards a revival of the past. Yet, in order to achieve that, the role of the leading clergy had to be adapted to the new circumstances. As the Twelver doctrine of Shiah, the dominant religion, was now under threat by no mere heresies but by the prospect of a wholly non-Islamic world-view, the official upholders of the true religion found themselves bound to intervene. They could no longer idly await the return of the Hidden Imam who, in his infallibility and might, would resolve the issues for them. In the absence of a trustworthy Muslim on the throne, the clerics were obliged to invent a new type of political regime which would keep Iranian society under the strict command of Islamic law.

In Iran (or Persia, as the country was then officially known), the first attempts at introducing a kind of new order started in 1797, five years later than in the Ottoman Empire. In Persia under the Qajars the impulse of the French revolution differed from that in the Ottoman domains on two counts. First, the issue was not only between the domestic (Islamic) and foreign (European) traditions, but also between the Islamic and pre-Islamic native traditions. Second, Iran's cultural identity was based not on ethnic (linguistic) but on religious grounds. *Ithna ashariya* (Shiah of the Twelve Imams) was the bond by which the political nation was constituted. Unlike Ottoman Turkey, Qajar Persia did not take part in the First World War and it was thus able to preserve its multi-ethnic state intact, whereas Turkey had to give up most of its non-Turkish territories.

The attempts at transformation, which took up most of the time between the Constitutionalist revolution of 1906–9 and the Islamic revolution of 1977–9, did not follow a clearly westernising course akin to the Kemalist transformation of Turkey. It was first the fame of the Safavids, then the still more glorious past of the Achaemenids, that diverted the shah from the straightforward path of Westernisation. Having estranged both the genius loci (the Shiite tradition) and the prevailing spirit of the times (the basic principles of Westernisation), the Pahlavi dynasty not only failed to achieve its objective but precipitated a violent backlash against any attempts at reconciliation between the domestic and foreign elements in Iranian culture.

In the late 1970s the 'modernising' process in Iran turned decisively anti-Western. If this is not merely a temporary aberration, and there is no compelling reason to believe that it is such, then the concept of modernisation, as Western social scientists understand it, deserves thorough re-evaluation.

Towards a constitutional monarchy: an incomplete revolution

The three successive Qajar shahs, who between them ruled for a whole century from 1797 to 1896, were less favourably impressed by the Western example than by the past splendours of the great Safavid shah, Abbas I (1588–1629), and were interested in taking over from the West only its military technique. However, the financing of a state-wide bureaucracy and of a viable standing army was rendered impossible by the vested interests of tribal chiefs, fief-holders and, to a considerable extent, the Shiite theologians. Only the sale of natural resources and commercial concessions to foreigners allowed the Qajars to keep their heads above water. Even the building up of an efficient military unit was entrusted to foreigners, the first example being the so-called Cossack brigade, founded in 1878.

Understandably, a weak and defenceless government easily became prey to the interests of the great powers, Russia and Great Britain, only their mutual distrust and jealousy making it possible for the Qajars to preserve a modicum of sovereignty.

Just as the subjects of the Ottoman rulers found a way out of their difficulties by learning from the encroaching Westerners, so did those of the Qajars. Inspiration came, however, not only from the West but also from reformist movements within Islam itself.

In the first half of the seventeenth century, the Iranian philosopher and mystic, Mulla Sadra, had already developed a theory of 'evolutionary modes of being' culminating in the Perfect Man, which was ingeniously fitted into Shiite theology.[1] But the concept of progress along Western lines provided more tangible results than the subtlety and speculation of a mystic could ever achieve. Nevertheless, the possibility of an alternative path towards progress, an alternative offering a domestic point of departure, had been indicated.

Movement in the direction of real reform gathered momentum during the rule of Muzaffar al Din Shah (1896–1906) whose inconsistent policies prompted the development of what may be described as a revolutionary situation. On the one hand he tightened the financial screw by steeply increasing taxes and lowering subsidies, while on the other hand significantly relaxing police control. Commercial, cultural and educational associations emerged, and the ideas of the French political philosophers and Russian Marxists achieved widespread currency. Disciples of the former organised themselves in a Masonic type of association, called the Society of Humanity, whereas the latter gave rise to two bodies – a social democratic party and the Revolutionary Committee. Dissent having thus become institutionalised, the rule of the Qajar shahs being akin less to that of true monarchs than to that of high kings of a tribal confederation, the political situation evinced all the governmental weakness that flows from duality of power in the capital. The fact that all strata of the population were adversely affected by the shah's fiscal policy (which by no means saved him from bankruptcy) gave the voice of the dissenters wide currency.

In 1905 several things happened which in terms of our morphological model may be described as precipitants. Abrahamian summarises them as follows:

> A bad harvest throughout the country; a sudden disruption in the northern trade caused by a cholera epidemic; by the Russo-Japanese War and by the subsequent revolution in Russia; and consequently a rapid increase in food prices. At the same time, the government, finding its customs revenues declining, its food costs rising, and its pleas for new foreign loans rejected, raised tariffs on native merchants and postponed loan repayments to local creditors.[2]

Three public protests, in which eventually even the *ulema* (theologians) were involved, not only met with no favourable response but even in one case (the third) called for the bloody suppression by the Cossacks. Large-scale demonstrations, followed by a general strike in which the *ulema* again took part, undermined government resolve. When eventually it was rumoured that even the Cossacks were preparing to defect, the shah gave in. After having appointed a liberal prime minister, he signed the proclamation convening a Constituent National Assembly. However, five days later, the shah died and his successor was averse to implementing his predecessor's promise. Furthermore, as in any other revolution, the revolutionaries were united only in their wish to topple the government; as far as further development was concerned, they were bitterly divided. Nevertheless, in August 1905 an electoral law was passed by the hurriedly convened Constituent Assembly and elections were held throughout the country. As the law was based on the status and censitary system (in Aristotle's terms, a highly geometrical equality) the upper strata, including the theologians, and the capital city, were strongly over-represented. Under these circumstances no clear-cut solution could be worked out.

The compromise was as follows: the Belgian constitution was chosen as the guideline, but with two substantial qualifications. Provincial councils were endowed with independent supervision of all reforms and the Twelver Shiah (*Ithna ashariya*) was declared the official religion. Heretical organisations and publications were to be banned. Furthermore, a 'supreme committee of *mujtahids* (high-ranking clerics) was to scrutinise all bills introduced into the parliament to ensure that no law contradicted Islamic law. The committee would sit until "the appearance of the Mahdi (May God Hasten His Glad Advent)" '.[3]

Thus the spirit of revolution, which might have responded positively to the foreign challenge, was killed before it could start to operate. It happened in a way that was to be repeated, with much more emphasis, seventy years later.

Nevertheless, the shah, although he had vowed to respect the constitution, looked for an opportunity to get rid of the embarrassing limitation of his powers. The opportunity for a counter-stroke (in terms of our morphological model, 'compression') was provided when the liberals began to press for a more representative electoral law and for a balanced budget. As this initiative coincided with a bad harvest and increasing food prices, the liberal policy became highly unpopular. Also the attempts at providing educational facilities for girls involved fierce opposition from the conservatives. For economic reasons the latter began to win the support of the lower classes. The tribal chiefs, facing loss of revenues from the budget, rallied behind the shah. The parliament (the *Majles*) continued to derive its main support from the middle classes – the traditional, the *bazaaris* and the modern intelligentsia.

In June 1908, the shah, who had received private financial aid to pay his Cossacks, decided to strike. Under a Russian colonel, the Cossack Brigade in Tehran easily defeated the volunteers who attempted to defend the *Majles* (National Assembly). However, in Tabriz and elsewhere in the country the shah's coup eventually failed. As the financial supplies to the royal treasury dried up, the shah took refuge in the Russian embassy.

The second National Assembly, elected on a much less socially skewed basis than the first one, convened in November 1909. But by this time it was no longer the Qajar restoration that menaced its existence; it was the bitter internal strife between the main parties, a strife accompanied from mid-1911 by tribal warfare in the provinces. In 1915 the central government held only the capital city. Luckily, however, Persia did not become involved, unlike most of her neighbours, in the First World War.

Nevertheless, there was constant threat from abroad. The Anglo-Russian agreement of 1907 and later the Anglo-Persian treaty of 1919 established in the country foreign zones of interest. Apart from the Russian-officered Cossacks there were now the British-officered South Persian Rifles and the Swedishofficered Gendarmerie. The Bolshevik revolution of 1917 in Russia seemed at first to have brought Persia relief from Russian pressure. But soon the Bolsheviks found new, ideological reasons for Russia's interference. There was no chance for any political party to 'intercept the oscillating seat of power'. Just as in France under the Directory, the situation became ripe for a Bonaparte.

The first empire and revolution from above

The way to a 'Bonapartist' solution was opened in February 1921 when a colonel in the Cossack division, Reza Khan, was promoted to the position of army commander and became a member of the cabinet. Within nine months he united all the armed forces under foreign officers under his own command. Furthermore, some skilful manoeuvring enabled Reza Khan to strike a deal with the Soviet government which had earlier supported the struggle of individual ethnic groups for independence from Persia. In October 1923, Reza Khan became prime minister. In December 1925, Reza Khan convened a Constitutional Assembly to depose the Qajar dynasty and to promote himself in their stead to the imperial throne. In April 1926 Reza Khan was crowned as the Shah-in Shah (king of kings) of Persia. For his dynasty he adopted the name of the Iranian language in the Middle Ages – the *pahlavi*.

Although there was considerable agitation in favour of a republic and Reza Khan might have been willing to follow the Turkish example, respect for the clergy favoured the monarchic solution.

Right from the beginning, the reforms in Persia were to be more respectful of the domestic tradition. In contrast to Kemal Atatürk's explicit programme of Westernisation (its six points encompassed republicanism, nationalism, secularism, statism, populism and reformism), Reza Shah proceeded more carefully. Instead of building a revolutionary establishment (with a political party providing the link with the activists in the population) like Kemal, Reza relied on the three traditional pillars of monarchic power: the standing army, the government bureaucracy and the court's patronage. A prolonged and bitter war for national liberation waged under Kemal's leadership provided the latter with higher prestige and a firmer mandate than was the case with Reza to undertake bold reforms. We have to bear in mind also the difference in cultural identities and traditions which made it easier for the Turks to embark on radical change. The substitution of the Latin alphabet for the Arabic script was easier with respect to the Turkish language, in which not so much had been written in earlier times, than in Persian with its abundant, sophisticated and ancient literature written in a particular type of the Arabic script.

Nevertheless, Persian society was likewise destined to undergo substantial changes. Education and the judiciary were to be withdrawn from the influence of the clergy and the political and social prerogatives of the upholders of Islam were to be significantly reduced. Women were to be admitted to work outside the home and were required to dress according to Western fashion. The state began to promote the development of industry and of the cities. Tribes were induced to abandon their traditional, often nomadic, way of life.

In 1934, as an act symbolic of closer coherence, Reza Shah changed the name of the country from Persia to Iran – a more comprehensive label. He also cancelled all capitulations (i.e. privileges) granted to foreigners under the Qajar regime. A year earlier a new, supposedly more equitable, Anglo-Iranian oil agreement was concluded.

The lack of political communication with the population, however, prevented the shah from taking credit for his reforms. The conservatives hated the innovations right from the beginning; the Westernised intelligentsia was dissatisfied with the excessive concentration of power at the top and with the despotic rule of the shah. Inflationary effects of high military expenditure and the court's extravagance were highly resented. Measures aiming at linguistic unification estranged the ethnic minorities and attempts at government control of religious education irritated even some of the more moderate of the clergy.

The accumulated tensions, however, were resolved by foreign intervention. Iran's 'Napoleon' did not need to lose a war in order to be despatched to exile. The Second World War created a situation in which the oil-rich Iran became a target for growing foreign interest and envy. Britain was concerned with maintaining a continuous supply of oil and with the safe route to India. Germany tried to exploit some affinities between its Nazi regime and Reza Shah's autocracy. When, however, the Germans attacked the Soviet Union and this country became, contrary to Stalin's earlier intentions, an ally of the United Kingdom, the common Anglo-Soviet intervention put an end to the risk of Reza Shah's possible cooperation with the Germans. Reza Shah the Great, as his sympathisers styled him, had to go, but the dynasty was to be preserved. The exiled shah's young son, Muhammad Reza Shah, ascended the throne and, under the circumstances of a renewed foreign presence, Iran once more had an opportunity for constitutional development.

Constitutional interlude and a fudged revolution

It took altogether twelve years before the new shah was able to follow up the policy of his father. During those twelve years the balance of power between the shah and the civil government provided some scope for attempts to build up a constitutional monarchy. Unfortunately, the constitutionalists were divided to such an extent that they could not pursue a coherent policy. Also the tribal chiefs often adversely intervened in the attempts at consolidation.

The main divisive issues were: land reform, ownership of the oil fields and the oil industry, and the political involvement of the clergy. Each of these issues often divided people into a variety of fronts, which prevented the emergence of coherent political groupings. Both the Westernisers and the Islamists were divided on these issues.

The tension between the shah and the government developed into an outright confrontation between May 1951 and August 1953. At that time the leader of an alliance of nationalist and reformist political parties, under the name of the National Front, Mohammad Mossadeq, took to extra-parliamentary means (the so-called 'street politics') in order to achieve his aims. His main concern was the nationalisation of the oil companies, the elimination of the executive power of the shah and, last but not least, the narrowing of the gap between the rich and the poor.

Understandably, although the nationalisation of the oil companies was extremely popular at home, it was not a good advertisement for Massadeq's diplomatic effort to obtain badly needed foreign credits. In July 1952, Mossadeq challenged the shah in using his own constitutional right to appoint the war minister. The shah refused to accept the appointment, whereupon Mossadeq resigned and appealed to the public. The popular response was enormous. Demonstrations and strikes paralysed economic life. Tehran city police disappeared from the streets. After a bloody confrontation with the demonstrators, the military commander, uncertain as to whether he could rely any longer on his troops, ordered them back to the barracks.

Exhilarant Mossadeq hastened to exploit his victory; he took over the ministry of war for himself, and began to purge the top brass in the armed forces. Martial law was used against his opponents and the shah was stripped of almost all executive power. Furthermore, Mossadeq decreed a land reform that established village councils and increased the peasants' share in the crop-sharing system in agriculture. The draft of a new tax bill shifted the burden of taxation from low to high income recipients. Thus Iran experienced the first serious steps towards a social revolution. The extent to which Islamic law was disregarded gave that revolution a conspicuously westernising twist. In both these respects, Mossadeq's National Front could rely on the support of the Tudeh (communist) Party.

The opposition to Mossadeq rallied not only the supporters of the Shah but also those of his enemies who, though liberal in principle, would have been adversely affected by the reforms, together with those (for example, the majority of the *ulema*) who opposed Mossadeq's measures for purely ideological reasons. Not only in the Senate, but also in the *Majles* (National Assembly – the Lower House), Mossadeq failed to muster a majority. In order to make the opposition ineffectual, all National Front deputies resigned, reducing the Assembly below its quorum, and thus, in effect, dissolving it. Mossadeq called for a national referendum.

Here, however, Mossadeq violated not only the constitution but also the principles of democracy of which he appeared to be a champion. Ballot boxes were divided into those for 'yes' votes and those for 'no' votes, and each was located in a different place. No wonder that 99.9 per cent of votes were cast for Mossadeq.

With such methods, Mossadeq alienated many of his former supporters. Not only many moderate clerics, but also groups representing liberal *bazaaris* left the National Front. More dangerously, the US administration, which since F.D. Roosevelt's presidency had looked quite favourably on the Iranian drive for independence, under General Eisenhower shifted to the support of British policy in Iran.

Under these circumstances, the disgruntled army officers could not only expect widespread approval for action against Mossadeq, but could also count on financial support from the United States. Their *coup d'état*, however, was not a straightforward matter. Its eventual success was due more to Mossadeq's blunders than to the prowess of the plotters. Mossadeq's intended arrest by the imperial guards was prevented by the pro-Mossadeq troops, who were allegedly tipped off by the Tudeh intelligence service. While the crowds, largely incited by the communist agitators, began to dominate the streets of Tehran and other cities, the shah preferred to escape to Baghdad. But Mossadeq, alarmed by the prospect of a communist take-over, accepted the promise of aid given to him by the American ambassador, provided that law and order were to be re-established, and directed the army to clear the streets of all demonstrators.

The armed forces did clear the streets, but they also cleared the prime minister's office of its incumbent. When, in a similar situation in 1918, the German social democratic interior minister, Noske, had asked the conservative homeguard to suppress the communist uprising in Berlin, he remained at his post when the task had been accomplished. Mossadeq, however, signed his political death warrant. The reinstated shah duly appreciated Mossadeq's helpful about-turn. While other enemies of the shah were executed or otherwise murdered (especially those of the Tudeh Party), Mossadeq and his associates received prison terms of three to five years. Those who had fudged the revolution did not deserve a harsher punishment.

The second empire and more revolution from above

The twenty-five years of the autocratic rule of Muhammad Reza Shah (1953–78) were often described as revolution from above. The shah himself called it the White Revolution. However, it was not wholly of his own making. To some extent it was imposed upon him by the criticism of his foreign mentors, whose goodwill was essential for his imperial ambitions. It seems that it was the Kennedy administration, in particular, that pushed him towards more radical reforms, initiated by his own, but disgraced, ministers.[4]

Unlike the six points or arrows declared by Kemal Atatürk, the six points put forward by the Iranian shah contained no declaration of principles but a description of concrete measures: land distribution, nationalisation of forests, privatisation of state factories, profit-sharing for individual workers, enfranchisement of women and promotion of literacy in the countryside.[5]

Although a nation-wide referendum in January 1965 endorsed the shah's programme by 99.9 per cent of the votes cast, in June of the same year, on the occasion of the mourning month of Muharram, a huge mass demonstration against the shah took place in the capital and other cities. As the most outspoken critic appeared to be the Ayatollah Khomeini, until then a little-known *mujtahid*, the imperial regime was denounced for corruption, rigging the elections, violating the constitution, censorship, suppression of opposition and of the freedom of the universities, neglecting the needs of merchants, workers and peasants, undermining beliefs, indiscriminate imitation of the West, granting privileges to foreigners, selling oil to Israel (the main enemy of Islam) and expounding bureaucratic centralisation.[6]

Thus as early as 1963, all the grievances that were to bring the shah to his ultimate fall sixteen years later had already been voiced, and the man who was to become the leader of the anti-shah revolution had already taken over the helm of that mass protest. It was like a rehearsal for the 1977–9 revolution. The parallel with the years 1905 and 1917 in Russia is striking. In both instances there was a highly developed revolutionary situation marked by coincidence of discontent for various reasons and uniting in opposition people who otherwise had little or even nothing in common. Already in 1963, Khomeini cleverly avoided in his speeches anything that might have divided the opposition, such as land reform and the extension of the voting right to women, although these two points were the most important ones for the bulk of the clerical opposition to the shah.[7]

The shah, however, learned nothing from this first encounter with Khomeini. He underestimated the superior socio-psychological wisdom of that cleric. The demonstrations were bloodily suppressed and Khomeini was banished to Turkey whence he moved to Najaf, the holy city of the Shiites in Iraq. From there, Khomeini could better launch his anti-shah propaganda. In the course of this, a new, mighty weapon of modern Western technology – audiotapes – was abundantly used with astonishing success. Just as in the Russian and Turkish revolutions a masterpiece of modern technology – the telegraph – became an efficient means of speedy mobilisation, in Iran sixty years later it was the recorded voice of God's messenger that was to be the main technological device for mobilising supporters.

But for more than a decade yet, the shah's position appeared unassailable to the outside world. All the great powers, the United States, the United Kingdom, the USSR and China, each for different reasons, adopted a friendly policy towards him. In many respects the White Revolution appeared to be successful. Literacy, student enrolment, industrialisation, urbanisation, women's emancipation (often more by push than pull) all made considerable progress. The soaring oil revenues made it possible also for the shah to build up formidable modern armed forces.

The cornerstone of the White Revolution, the modernisation of agriculture, however, was beset by two fatal flaws. First, it was to be carried through by a skilful manoeuvring against the vested interests of the class that otherwise provided the shah with his most loyal support. Second, and this turned out to be more fateful, the reform was to follow the shah's own understanding of modernity. Muhammad Reza Shah saw the future of Iran in a prosperous agriculture in large-scale agro-factories, unencumbered by the primitive nature of rural life and, what was particularly relevant for Iran, by a nomadic way of life.

In the first stage of land reform, peasants were to receive full possession of their lands. Reportedly, over one-seventh of the villages in Iran benefited from this first stage of the land distribution programme (compensation was to be paid in ten to fifteen years by instalments). Further on, in order to appease the landlords, the reforming process was toned down to a mere revision of tenancy rights. Eventually, when the disgruntled landlords could be more than adequately compensated by their participation in oil revenues (in 1972–3 the value added in oil production made up more than a half of GNP),[8] the redistribution of their land was resumed. But by this stage the land was no longer distributed among the peasants but assigned to production units, in which the peasants participated by taking negotiable property shares. Unlike the Mexican *ejidatarios*, the Iranian shareholders soon sold their shares and turned into wage-earning labourers while the estates were run by the state bureaucracy.

Not only rural life was destined for transformation. The traditional centres of crafts and commerce, the bazaars, were in their turn to make way for a new entrepreneurial class with factories and stores. The colourful community where people in all walks of economic, social and cultural life met in everyday intercourse, was now to be streamlined in accordance with the more specific demands of the division of labour. As in the Soviet Union, the development plans (first of seven, then of five years' duration) fostered mainly the heavy and armament industries. Military expenditure enjoyed a high priority; but in contrast with Russia, where the cost was to be extorted from the population, the militarisation of Iran was eased by high revenues from oil, in particular by the windfall profits after the steep price increase (more than twofold) of December 1973, which the shah pushed through at the Tehran conference of the Organisation of Petroleum Exporting Countries (OPEC).

However, what was to produce the most shattering innovation in Iranian society was the withdrawal of a growing section of social and family life from clerical jurisdiction and influence. As in Turkey, religion was to become a private matter for each citizen. However, Iranians were not as accustomed to the extra-shariate authority of their rulers as were the subjects of the Ottoman Empire, where secular law (*urf*) and imperial rescripts (*kanun name*) used to be well-established sources of jurisdiction. Furthermore, Shiites of the Iranian branch were less tolerant than the Sunnites and also less so than the Shiites elsewhere.

On top of all that, Muhammad Reza Shah added a particular irritant for the orthodox Shiites in further promoting elements of the pre-Islamic Iranian tradition. At a great celebration which took place in the ancient Persian capital Persepolis in 1971, the ancient Zoroastrian calendar was officially substituted for the Islamic one. Modern imperial glory was thus linked with a tradition going back 2,500 years into history.

In 1975, the shah realised that the government-sponsored, two-party system, introduced after the suppression of the riots in 1963, was of little use for mobilising political support, and decided to have only one political party, to be called 'Resurrection of Iran'. He did not understand that such a party, if it was to play such a mobilising role, would have to grow from below, from the grass roots, and be under the leadership of somebody who had emerged from the people, having proved his abilities in the daily struggle, often against heavy odds. A political party created by the decree of a despot has little chance of becoming a genuinely popular party. Thus, despite all efforts to make the party big and influential, the main pillars of the shah's power continued to be limited to his armed forces, complemented by the strong secret police best known by its acronym, SAVAK.

The fact that the one-party regime in Turkey had already been abandoned thirty years earlier and that Turkey had embarked on building a pluralistic parliamentary democracy was not deemed worthy of consideration. Friendly voices from abroad, recommending relaxation of despotism, remained unheeded. When they began to be taken seriously, it was already too late.

The Islamic counter-revolution: a genuine revolution from below

There is no paradox in the heading of this chapter. If, in using the term 'revolution', more stress is being laid on the extent and speed of social change, then Iran in the twentieth century experienced two such revolutions, each carried out in two bouts. The first came from below; its first bout occurred in 1906–9 (the 'constitutionalist revolution'), the second in 1951–3 (Mossadeq's National Front). The other revolution came from above. The first bout took place under Reza Shah the Great (1926–38) and the second bout under his son, Muhammad Reza Shah (1963–77). If more stress is laid on the way in which the revolution is carried out, on how many people are involved and on how shattering are the acts of revolution, then only the 'Islamic revolution', which broke out in 1978 and at the time of writing has not yet run its full course, deserves to be called a genuine revolution of the vertical type. A closer scrutiny will also show that it, too, contained some innovation, at least as far as the political regime is concerned, which, however, has to be assessed against the background of Islamic civilisation and its 1,300 years of development.

The Islamic revolution in Iran started as a revolution against the rule of an insensitive and inconsistently innovative regime. It was carried out by people of divergent, often contradictory, views, who for a short time became united with respect to what they wanted to be abolished, but not as to what they wanted to come afterwards. Jahangir Amuzegar dubbed this momentary multifaceted revolutionary front a 'rainbow coalition'.[9] It involved the widest possible spectrum of opinion, from radical Westernisers for whom the shah's White Revolution was a parody of what they wanted to take over from the

West, on the one hand, to the most radical Islamists, for whom any hint of Westernisation was an unacceptable anathema, on the other. The great variety of opinion in between these extremes made this wide spectrum still more incongruous. That this strange coalition did not fall apart before the despot and his regime were toppled was extraordinary in itself. Perhaps only the staggering contrast between the cultural backgrounds which distinguished the two sides in the conflict and moulded their leading personalities can explain the emergence of such a union of contradictions.

The same contrast between cultural backgrounds or ideological positions may also explain the fact that the revolution, won by a broad coalition of forces, was, with unprecedented speed, 'hijacked' by the grouping that stood at one extreme wing of the revolutionary spectrum. In terms of our morphological model the 'oscillating seat of power' was intercepted at a point beyond the conventional concepts of political right and left. As has been shown with respect to other exogenous revolutions, a three- (or more) cornered contest is out of the question in a two-dimensional model.

The specific nature of the Islamic revolution in Iran is reflected more in its morphological than in its etiological aspects. Our etiological comment in Part I of this book fits, although with important shifts of emphasis, the Iranian case too. Of all the basic contrasts that constitute a multiple dysfunction, the most significant was the Aristotelian contrast, i.e. the contrast between different concepts of justice.

At this point, a brief comment by way of comparison with other exogenous revolutions in twentieth-century Asia may be useful. As in the Chinese revolution, two modernising paradigms were available in Iran: the shah's pro-Western, but authoritarian model (cf. the Guomindang), and the communist (Tudeh Party) model, inspired by the Soviet example. A pluralistic, democratic alternative involving radical Westernisation was represented virtually only by intellectuals who appeared but rarely on the political scene. The communist paradigm, however, despite the dedication and fervour of its supporters, could not break through, and in the revolutionary situation the Tudeh Party looked for an alliance with others. In 1953 the communists supported the democrats, whereas in 1978 they made common cause with the Islamists who, contrary to expectation, became the main revolutionary force.

In China there was no parallel to that particularly Iranian phenomenon. Even in Turkey, another country where Islam has been the dominant religion, the Islamists did not become a strong 'vector' in the revolution. The Sunnite version of Islam and, as has been mentioned above, a well-established tradition of secular law running parallel to the sharia, did not provide the Islamists there with a strong motive for self-assertion. In Turkey, there was yet another specific grouping in the political spectrum: the nationalists, who were inspired by the Turkic ethnic tradition rather than by membership of the Islamic community, the *ümmet*. In Iran, the Turkic peoples (mainly the Azeris) were in the minority; the non-religious Azeris preferred to operate under the banner of the Tudeh, a theoretically international party. As has already been said, the unifying idea in Iran was religion, not language. Thus there was no scope for the Westernisers to unite with the nationalists against the Islamists as was the case in Turkey. In Iran there were the Shiite Islamists of the Twelve Imams who at the same time represented the strongest nationalist stream in the political spectrum. Whether under the shah, or later under Khomeini, granting specific rights to ethnic, let alone religious, minorities was unimaginable.

Within the Shiite version of political nationalism there were significant nuances. Quite a few were prone to look for a *modus vivendi* with Western ideas, provided that they could be somehow related to the Shiite tradition. Mehdi Bazargan, Ali Shariati and Albohassan Banisadr were particularly prominent in that respect. They all saw the contemporary state of the Islamic religion as inadequate to the situation, but believed there to be enough in the Shiite tradition capable of being revitalised to the point of resolving the contemporary problems. In short, 'modernisation' could be based on domestic foundations. Renaissance of the authentic Shiism of Ali was the main concern for Shariati, whereas Banisadr planned an Islamic republic and the economy of the future. Many revolutionary fighters (the *mujahedin*) dreamed of a theoretical synthesis between Islam and socialism. Like Shariati and Banisadr, they argued that the original Islam, as practised by the Prophet Muhammad, would eventually lead to a *tauhidi* society, a society of 'unity', where man is united with the product of his labour, with nature, and with all creation and ultimately with God. In a *tauhidi* society, 'all oppression and exploitation will crumble, and social solidarity based on Islamic principles will emerge'.[10]

Khomeini's views were more down to earth. For him, the key issues were the abolition of the monarchy and observance of the divine law. The Islamic state and society were to be supervised by the distinguished and just theologian-jurists.

Khomeini, however, refrained from making his vision of the Islamic republic the focus of his propaganda. From the time when the Shiites, being in a minority, became intermittently a target for repression, they developed a protective doctrine of dissimulation which allowed them to hide the true essence of their teaching from outsiders. Khomeini knew when to apply this doctrine. Only when the worst was over and the army, demoralised by the insecure and vacillating stand of the shah, followed Khomeini's call not to shoot at their Muslim co-religionist, did Khomeini fully reveal his plans.

But what were the other issues on which Khomeini could forge an alliance against the shah? Certainly, there was the discontent of all those who were left behind in the great economic forward march, whose expectations were not fulfilled, and who saw others being much more fortunate. The feeling of relative deprivation played an important role. Even the modernised middle class often felt a disturbing contrast between their economic advance on the one hand and the lack of opportunity for independent political self-assertion on the other. The development of the productive forces (technology) was well ahead of the mode of production (socio-economic and political).

The course of events precipitating and eventually triggering the revolution can be reviewed as follows. In November 1976, Jimmy Carter was elected president of the United States. Unlike his republican predecessors, he wanted the Iranian regime to observe human rights. Although his administration was not quite unanimous in its messages to the Iranian authorities, the shah realised that he could not rely any longer on unconditional American support. In the spring of 1977, the fifth economic plan (1973–8), based on an unrealistic assumption of a 26 per cent annual GDP increase, collapsed, causing bottlenecks, disruptions and inflation. Attempts to stave off collapse by government decrees and punitive measures had made the situation still worse. Release of some political prisoners and the easing of censorship enlarged the scope for the activity of the dissenters. The government's counter-propaganda was launched in the most unfortunate way. Although Khomeini was the right target, the published attack was so insulting and absurd that on the following day (8 January 1978) a huge demonstration in the holy city of Qom rallied people of various political shades to Khomeini's support. The security forces used arms and the revolutionary cause achieved its first martyrs.

In 1978 the shah tried to establish contact with the moderate mullahs, but in vain. Riots continued but the intervention of the armed forces was discouraged. Only when, on 8 September (known as Black Friday), the demonstrators shouted 'Death to the shah' and denounced the monarchy as 'nonsense' in an Islamic country, did the army open fire, causing many casualties. In response, strikes and work stoppages paralysed the country. At the request of the shah, Khomeini was expelled from his exile in Iraq and moved to Paris. As an old-fashioned cleric, located in the sophisticated French milieu, he was believed to be innocuous. On the contrary, however, in Paris Khomeini became known internationally and his prestige further increased. The shah, receiving no clear guidance from his American mentor, could not make up his mind as to whether to carry on with the concessions or to call in the army. But for any of these options it was already too late. Opposition, based on the mosques and organised in various political, partly militarised, groups was already sufficiently institutionalised to represent a second pivot in the power structure. Thus, on 16 January 1979, the shah left the country 'on a rest-and-rehabilitation vacation'. On 1 February 1979, Ayatollah Khomeini returned in glory to Tehran and on 5 February named the provisional government under Mehdi Bazargan, one-time political colleague of Mossadeq. On 10 February the military leadership declared the neutrality of the armed forces in political matters. The revolution proper was over. Further stages of the revolutionary process were to follow.

As soon as the *ancien régime* had been toppled, differences concerning what to do next came to the surface. Dilip Hiro described the unfolding political spectrum as follows:

Militant *ulema* loyal to Ayatollah Khomeini and their lay allies wanted an Islamic *régime* of an orthodox mould, led by clerics. Lay Islamic radicals, headed by Mehdi

Bazargan in the Liberation Movement, favoured a less rigid model than Khomeini loyalists. Liberal, secular forces, represented by the National Front of Karim Sanjabi, aspired to create social democracy in Iran. The leftist Islamic strand of the movement, dominated by the Mujahedin-e Khalq, wanted to create an egalitarian Islamic society through fusion of Islam and Marxism. Such Marxist–Leninist groups as the Fedai Khalq and the Tudeh visualised the current revolution as a step towards a socialist revolution to follow.[11]

In terms of our morphological model, the 'seat of power began to oscillate'. Nationalists of ethnic minorities were the first to challenge the government. The Kurds in the northwest, the Baluchs in the southeast and the Arabs in the southwest demanded autonomy. The Azeris were placated for some time by having their own Ayatollah – Shariatmandari – next to Khomeini in the leadership.

No less serious were the divisions along political lines throughout the country. The loosening of the grip of the shah's power allowed the Tudeh (communist) party to operate more freely. Two formerly guerilla organisations, one Marxist–Leninist and the other leftist Islamic, mobilised large crowds to support their struggle for a social revolution. They could not accept Khomeini's leadership without reservation. The Islamist *mujahedin* were prepared to give up their weapons, but only 'provided people's rights are guaranteed'. Yet Khomeini was intransigent. For him 'Democracy was another word for usurpation of God's authority to rule'.[12]

Within two years, the divergent views led to open warfare that cost more lives than the fight against the shah. The 'lions' of the revolution possessed more *assabiya* (*esprit de corps*) than the 'foxes' of the *ancien régime*. (Both the Paretian and the Khaldunian theorems could be applied to the Iranian situation at that time.) Violation of international law, such as the occupation of the American embassy and the taking hostage of its staff, was a by-product, an asset for the radicals, in the internecine war.

Within a year, a curious twist came to complicate the course of the Iranian revolution: foreign attack coming not from the enemies of Islam but from an Islamic neighbour – the Republic of Iraq. Blood was to be shed more within the *Dar al-Islam* than against the *Dar al-Harb* (the world outside Islam, the legitimate sphere of war). Ethnic and religious contrasts (Arabs against Persians, Sunnites against Shiites), contrasts exacerbated by the personal rivalry of self-righteous autocrats and irrelevant appeals to history, led to a ten-year war, costly in both human and material terms, which eventually led to stalemate.

Meanwhile, Khomeini was able, against the dissenting voice of a number of high-ranking clerics, to consolidate his uncontested position as the supreme interpreter of God's will and guardian of its implementation. Relying upon the grassroots support of his Islamic Republican Party and operating through the fifteen-member Islamic Revolutionary Council, he pushed through his concept of the supremacy and guardianship of the jurist-theologians (*villayet-e Faqih*).

This principle is based on the assumption that in the absence of an imam (the last, the Twelfth Imam, miraculously went into hiding 1,100 years ago), only a just Faqih is qualified to rule an Islamic state. Either he is recognised as such by the people (as was assumed to be the case with Khomeini), or a 'popularly elected' Assembly of experts chooses a single or a collective leadership.[13] The experts best qualified to do this are the highest-ranking clerics, known as *mujtahid*, of whom the ayatollahs (light of God) are the highest rank.[14]

The new constitution, approved in December 1979, by a 99.5 per cent vote in the referendum, is based on this principle. Iran has become an Islamic republic. The president and the *Majlis* (Islamic Consultative Assembly) are elected by popular vote. However, only acknowledged Islamic candidates and parties may compete. The Council of Guardians supervises the elections and the *Wali Faqih*, supported by his colleagues, takes care lest any legislative, executive or judiciary act should contradict the divine law as revealed in the Koran and sustained by the Shiite tradition.

Khomeini enjoyed his rule until his death in June 1989. Meanwhile the opposition was driven underground and officialdom became divided into a conservative (orthodox) and a reformed (pragmatic) faction. After Khomeini's death the Council of Experts elected President Khamenei as *Wali Faqih*. This, as well as the election of *Hojjatoleslam*[15] Hashemi Rafsanjani as president of the Republic in August 1989, and also the elections for the Council of Experts in 1990 and for the *Majlis* in 1992, shifted the balance in favour of the pragmatists. However, within the constitution and with a still large proportion of fanatical supporters of orthodoxy, the scope for a pragmatic policy remains limited.

As was the case with development in the Soviet Union, in Iran the doctrinal clamp-down and the vested interests of its guardians are also the main obstacles to allowing society any spontaneous development. Will there be an enlightened Faqih (as there was an enlightened general secretary in communist Russia), or is Iran to experience one more bout of revolution? Analogy with the other exogenous revolutions discussed in this volume points rather to the former alternative.

Notes

1. For more on this subject see Mangol Bayat-Philip, '*Tradition and change in Iranian socio-religious thought*', in *Modern Iran: The dialectics of continuity and change*, ed. M.E. Bonine and N.R. Keddie (SUNY, Albany, 1981), pp. 37 ff.
2. E. Abrahamian, *Iran Between Two Revolutions* (Princeton University Press, 1982), p. 81.
3. *Ibid.*, p. 90.
4. Cf. D. Hiro, *Iran under the Ayatollahs* (Routledge & Kegan Paul, London, 1985), pp. 43 ff.
5. For more detail and also points added later, see G. Lenczowski (ed.), *Iran under the Pahlavis* (Hoover Institution Press, Stanford, CA, 1978), p. 477.

6. Abrahamian, p. 425.
7. Both these idiosyncrasies were based on theological arguments. But only the subordinate position of women was explicitly demanded by the Koran. Also the way in which they were to dress was stated there. On the other hand, the argument against land reform was tortuously derived from a *hadith*. In Katouzian's translation the passage reads 'People have dominion over their persons and possessions' (H. Katouzian, *The Political Economy of Modern Iran*, Macmillan, London, 1981, p. 311 fn. 3).
8. Katouzian, p. 257.
9. J. Amuzegar, *The Dynamics of the Iranian Revolution* (SUNY, Albany, 1991), p. 14.
10. M. Kamrava, *Revolution in Iran: The roots of turmoil* (Routledge & Kegan Paul, London, 1990), p. 62.
11. Hiro, p. 103.
12. *Ibid.*, p. 106.
13. C. Bernard and Z. Khalilzad (eds), *'The Government of God': Iran's Islamic Republic* (Columbia University Press, New York, 1984), p. 121.
14. Kamrava, p. 79, quotes an estimate giving the total number of mullahs in Iran in 1978–9 as some 180,000. Of these only a few were styled Ayatollahs.
15. Clerical title of the category next to the ayatollahs.

9

□

Mexico (1910–   )

The long march to the revolution

The great Mexican revolution which broke out in 1910 cannot be properly understood without taking preceding developments into account; we need to go back to the time of the Spanish conquest in order to appreciate fully the complexity of issues which, after a long and turbulent course of events, culminated in a revolutionary situation.

Let us first consider the dramatis personae in the threefold structural perspective: ethnic (racial), social and religious. As far as the ethnic (racial) structure is concerned, the bulk of the population were aborigine Indians (the Indios). As a result of fighting, harsh treatment and epidemics, their numbers were substantially reduced (according to rough estimates, from twenty million in 1520 to slightly over four million in 1570) and the decline continued until the mid-seventeenth century to just over one million. From that point, the Indian population began to increase again.[1] Meanwhile, the immigrant Spaniards changed the racial structure of the population in two ways. On the one hand, they began to constitute a new indigenous segment of the population known as the Creoles. On the other hand, in contrast to the British, for instance, the Spanish conquerors did not refrain from mixed marriages. The result was a fast-growing, mixed type of population known as the mestizos. Mixing of mestizos with Indios or Creoles and the subsequent interbreeding of various types of racial mix created a wide-ranging shade of coloured population in Mexico. Some combinations were given particular names, but the whole lot became described as the *castas*.

The racial division was, and still is, only one element of the cultural divide. Language, religion and social status were, and to some extent still are, further divisive factors. The conquerors imposed on the natives both their language and their religion. For the Spanish, religion mattered more than language. All the natives were to be converted to Roman Catholicism. But the conversion has been far from complete. Although every part of society was penetrated, the proselytising did not sink deeply enough into the minds of the Indios. As a result, a kind of syncretic religion emerged in the countryside; domestic cults were carried on under the banner of Christian symbols and under the guise of Catholic rites, creating a colourful mixture of folklore.

Compared to the Indians and also to many of mixed race, the whites were, in the long run, less accommodating. The spirit of the French revolution, which through Spain had penetrated to Mexico, created a fateful breach within the white community. The anti-clerical liberals clashed with the devoted Catholics. In contrast to the French revolution, however, there was no attempt to promote a new religious cult or belief. It was not as a religion that the Catholic Church in Mexico was assailed, but as an organised power, a rival to the power of the state. As the vast wealth of the Church was at stake, the strife between the state and the ecclesiastical authorities became, on occasion, very bitter. But it was with respect to education in particular where the rift appeared irreconcilable. The severity of the confrontation between Church and state exceeded similar confrontations in European countries, both with respect to its duration and to the number of casualties.

No use of force was needed to spread the Spanish language. The Indians spoke various languages, none of which could develop into a kind of lingua franca. We must not forget that, because of their real or suspect cultic nature, the few literary documents produced in Indian languages (such as in Maya or Aztec) were largely destroyed by the over-zealous Catholic missionaries. Thus the Spanish language became a unifying factor that gradually filtered down from the upper strata to the lower echelons of society. There was no purposeful drive to denationalise the Indios, to deprive them forcibly of their mother tongue as, for instance, was practised by the English in Wales. Spaniards preferred to keep the Indios uneducated and illiterate. A well-meaning attempt by the Spanish government in the early days to provide the Indian aristocracy with a high level of European education was frustrated by the Spanish *in situ*, who feared competition by educated natives.

From the beginning, the Spanish immigrants assumed all power in the conquered country. As in Spain, the temporal (in Mexico mainly military) and spiritual (ecclesiastical) powers acted in close cooperation. The common aim was to keep the Indian population docile and ensure that they served their new masters. Royal directives from Madrid, occasionally embodied in well-intended decrees, were paid little attention and only in exceptional circumstances did Church representatives intercede on behalf of the subject population.

All the material needs of the conquerors were provided for by the natives. The new masters were allocated a number of village communes covering a certain area known as *encomienda*. The 'commended' villagers had to provide their lords (*encomenderos*) with a tribute in kind and various kinds of services. The village elders took responsibility for fulfilling these obligations. In addition, individuals were bound to render services for the 'public weal'. (A similar system had previously been practised by the Aztecs.)

As long as there were few masters and many potential servants, the burden of the commended Indians was supposed to be lighter than that of the peasants in Spain. But the growing immigration of the whites and above all the catastrophic decline in the Indian population increased this burden enormously, despite occasional protective measures undertaken by the royal authorities.

The drastic decline of the Indian population on the one hand, and the growing need for labour in the cities and in the plantations on the other, made labour a scarce commodity. The system of forced labour gradually gave way to free labour. The Indios, however, as well as the numerically growing *castas*, did not have much opportunity to benefit from this change. On the contrary, a new form of bondage – the 'debt peonage' – became widespread. The *hacendados* (plantation owners) made money advances to indigenes to attract them to live on the hacienda rather than in the villages. Gradually the use of this method was extended to other kinds of work as well. Thus, as Cumberland put it: 'The *encomienda* and the *repartimiento* died with the colonial period, but the debt peonage continued into the early twentieth century, exacerbating relations between labour and capital'.[2]

Tannenbaum quotes the following description of this system, the victims of which were known as *enganchaderos*:

> The people here live largely by supplying labor to the coffee plantations in the southern part of the State. They send out agents to the villages who advance some money to the Indians for which they make a cross on paper. These Indians are brought to town where they are collected in certain houses, each of which has an *aguardiente* shop. Here they are fed all of the drink they want. They use up what has been advanced to them and are allowed to have all of the drink they wish on credit. When they come to themselves they have used up not only the cash that was advanced to them, but their credit for the future. In debt, they start for the coffee plantations where they are allowed food on credit to be worked off. After many months and years of labor an Indian may succeed in working off his debt, but not always.[3]

Similar methods were used for other kinds of labour procurement. Rank-and-file soldiers, however, were recruited simply by using press-gangs to round up young males. Privates were also abundantly supplied by the prisons. Having said that, however, we must stress that the situation was far from uniform throughout the country. There were areas, especially in the less fertile and sparsely populated north, where Indians preserved a modicum of pride and freedom.

On the whole, it can be said, however, that there was no escape from what may be described as the 'relative deprivation of decremental type' among the lowest strata of Mexican society save in vagrancy, begging and banditry. The hard-pressed Indios had to wait for their opportunity of redress until another sector of population started to feel cheated of its just share in the common wealth. This came about when the indigenous white élite began to feel hostility against the *peninsulares*, i.e. those who came from the mother country to take all the high-ranking positions in Mexico.

Secession, chaos and the *porfiriato*

The libertarian message of the French revolution reached the Spanish colonies in the first decades of the nineteenth century. As a result the ruling élite there was split down the middle and the eventual outcome was secession from the Spanish Crown. In Mexico, however, this secession was not a straightforward process. When, in 1810, the well-meaning Catholic parish priests, such as Hidalgo and Morelos, started their war of liberation in the belief that the political independence of Mexico would alleviate the misery of the subject population, the frightened Creoles and the Church authorities rushed to help the royal armies to suppress the uprisings. But when the liberals, aided by a military intervention, assumed power in Madrid in the early 1820s and began to liberalise the colonial system and confiscate some Church property, the white population, in order to preserve their privileges, decided to sever their links with the mother country and proclaimed independence in 1821. The whole process, from 1810 to 1821, can be classified as a horizontal revolution.

However, the country was not ripe for independence. The noble declarations of politicians and constitutional lawyers were no match for the power that grew out of the barrel of the gun. From 1821 to 1867 the country was in constant turmoil. Revolutions in Calvert's and Tilly's understanding were almost everyday events. According to Cumberland's count, during the first fifty years of Mexico's independence over thirty different people served as president, heading more than fifty governments.[4] Federalists and centralists, republicans and monarchists, anti-clerical liberals and the Church supporters, swapped power as a result of bullets rather than ballots. It was also necessary to repel foreign encroachment and intervention by the strength of arms.

Meanwhile, the population continued to increase and the mestizo element became more assertive. Even pure Indians occasionally got to the top. Most conspicuous was the case of Benito Juarez, a liberal and staunch anti-clerical leader. After the overthrow of Maximilian the Habsburg, whose power rested on the support of the Church and above all on the French expeditionary army, Juarez, as Mexico's president, managed to inaugurate a short period of comparative calm. But his successor, who pushed the anti-Church policy to extremes, was overthrown in 1876 by Porfirio Diaz, who, though observing the trappings of elected presidency, then ruled as a dictator.

The thirty-five years of Diaz's dictatorship, often referred to as the *porfiriato*, were also sometimes described as a liberal revolution; a determined attempt was undertaken to transform Mexico into a fast-developing capitalist country.

Law and order were to be established, the tension between the state and the Church was to be eased, transport facilities to be built up, foreign expertise and investment to be encouraged, and, what concerned the Mexican people most, agriculture was to be opened up to large-scale commercial undertakings. There was an assumption that the common lands (*ejidos*) were not suitable for the development of agricultural production. From 1856 the legislature had encouraged villages to distribute their common lands among the heads of families. The latter were then in too weak a position to withstand the pressure from estate owners to buy up their plots. Another assumption was that there was much vacant land (*terrenos baldios*) to which there was no valid property title. According to a law of 1883, any organisation could obtain a contract from the government for surveying, i.e. for seeking out vacant land. The surveyors could take one-third of the land surveyed as payment and the rest was kept by the government for sale. Despite the provision in the law that some 'colonists' should be allowed to stay on the land, the opportunity for eviction and fraud was enormous. Small landholders and entire village communities were helpless against the surveyors' decision concerning the vacant lands. As a rule the courts did not recognise their holdings as lawful. A new land survey law of 1894 made the position of the smallholders still more difficult. At the same time commercialisation required more hired labour; this resulted in a further spread of debt bondage.

Under these circumstances the long-lasting rift within Mexican society deepened. On the one hand were those who enjoyed the fruits of the Porfirian boom, and on the other were the depossessed *peones*. Only the growing proportion of people of mixed race – by the end of the nineteenth century about 40 per cent of the total population – made the coincidence of social stratification with racial structure less frequent.

Despite the growing bitterness among the common folk, the decremental deprivation of the leaderless Indios resulted merely in riots and strikes. Only when other strata of the population began to teem with grievances did the situation start to be dangerous for the government.

The real revolution: war and reform

The *porfiriato* did not allow an adequate circulation of the élite. The Paretian contradiction between the old guard and the young generation longing for more wealth and power, gave rise to a sense of aspirational relative deprivation among the ambitious members of the Creole population. Thus a new discontent, this time within the élite, was added to that of the subject population. The blame fell on one and the same institution, Diaz's government. In 1904, a young *hacendado*, Francisco Madero, emerged as leader of the Creole opposition. From 1905 economic problems resulting from monetary and fiscal conditions led to a series of strikes and riots which were suppressed by force. Political opposition was harassed and in 1910 Madero was arrested. But the phase of 'compression' did not last long. The use of force triggered the explosion and in 1911 Diaz's government was overthrown.

According to our typology it looked more like a *coup d'état* which eventually resulted in a negotiated transfer of power than an explosion of genuine revolution. Nevertheless these events started a violent process of transformation, which can rightly be described as a great vertical revolution.

In Madero's revolution no reform programme was involved, merely the upholding of the constitution. Within two years, however, Madero was removed from power and murdered. A devastating civil war set in which was to last for fourteen years. Various pretenders for the presidency of a more-or-less liberal complexion, and various partisan armies, fought for power and, by implication, for social change. There was much purposeful action which was not, however, always properly articulated. Conspicuous regional differences underscored by the federal structure of the state were a contributing factor to the long-lasting chaos in the country.

As in the case of other great vertical revolutions, the political spectrum represented by military factions (revolutionary armies) can be described in terms of five positions. Conservative forces were represented mainly by those, such as Victoriano Huerta, who wanted to uphold the *ancien régime*, the *porfiriato*, but occasionally Catholic zealots also took to arms in order to defend the *fueros* (the privileges) of the Church which even Porfirio Diaz had not fully respected.

On the right wing of the revolution were the liberals, such as Madero, whose main merit was the lifting of censorship, allowing the '*glasnost*' which exposed the magnitude of the gulf between the people of Mexico. The revolutionary centre was taken by a range of liberals who, as the struggle went on, moved towards some acknowledgement of the necessity of social reform. The later presidents, Carranza, Obregón and Calles, may be named as the leading personalities in this group. Their subsequent presidential rule stretched over the decade 1917–28.

The revolutionary left had its outstanding leaders: first in Emiliano Zapata (killed in an ambush in 1919) and then, much later, in Lázaro Cárdenas. Zapata, an Indian peasant from the southern part of the country, himself a victim of the Porfirian drive to dispossess the peasants, had a clear aim: return or redistribution of the confiscated lands. His intellectual aide, Antonio Diaz Soto y Gama, drew up a consistent reform programme for the Zapatistas, also known as *agraristas*. Although its rationale was sympathetically viewed by many of the centre, its realisation had to wait until 1934, when Cárdenas took over the presidency. Then agrarian reform became a key factor in a much wider social reform, which covered, in particular, education, labour relations and ownership of national resources. Unlike in Russia, it was a reformist socialism that won the day in Mexico.

In this context it must be pointed out that the workers' movement only slowly began to play a significant role within the political spectrum of Mexico.

In contrast to other vertical revolutions, the extreme left in the Mexican revolution was not represented by radical programmatic thought as much as by the intractable personality of Pancho Villa. Commanding the largest army in the revolution, Villa certainly represented a strong social vector. However, as Frank Tannenbaum, a sympathetic student of the Mexican revolution, put it, 'it was not possible to work with Villa; he was going nowhere. Like a tornado, he was without purpose, without direction, a blind annihilating force'.[5] In January 1915, Villa's forces were destroyed by the army under Obregón, aided by the 'workers' battalions' and some groups of *agraristas*. Thus the extreme left was not eliminated by the left proper in the Mexican revolution as it was in other revolutions discussed in this volume, but by the centre; nevertheless, the left made a contribution.

Also, unlike in the other vertical revolutions, the radicals had to wait a long time before they came to power. The hectic (some call it the 'epic') phase of the revolution, which may also be described as a civil war and which, in terms of our morphological model, may be considered as the phase of oscillation, lasted for fourteen years. The loss of life was estimated at two million, i.e. over 13 per cent of the total population. The election of Plutarco Elias Calles in 1924 and the peaceful transfer of office can be considered as the key event that brought the warring phase of the revolution to an end. In terms of our model, the seat of power was 'intercepted' at the position of the centre.

The constitution, drafted mid-way through the warring phase of the revolution in 1917, could be regarded as a beacon for consolidation. But as soon as the fighting was over and the constitution had to be respected, its anti-clerical provisions aroused a renewed and vigorous protest from the Church hierarchy (earlier protests were launched at the time of drafting the constitution). The government reacted by exiling foreign priests, by closing Church schools and by exhorting the local administration to limit the number of clerics who could perform religious services. The Catholic zealots took to arms and for three years (1926–9) savage guerilla warfare ravaged several areas of the country. Eventually the ambassador for the United States mediated a compromise, but for a long time state–Church relations remained strained. Only at the time of writing does the atmosphere appear to have significantly improved.

As stated earlier, the oscillating seat of power was intercepted on the position of the revolutionary centre after fourteen years of war (1910–24). In the early 1930s the circumstances began to develop in favour of the revolutionary left. Apart from the sense of an unfinished job, it was the world-wide economic crisis, in particular, that gave a new impetus to the idea of social justice embodied in the Constitution of 1917. As a protective measure, many countries were turning to government intervention, regulated market and public spending. In 1933, when F.D. Roosevelt became president of the United States, this mighty neighbour of Mexico also embarked on such a policy. The danger of interference from this quarter now became less likely.

In Mexico the conflict between those who can be considered liberals (led by the former President Calles) and the socialists (led by General Cárdenas) was resolved at the ruling party's convention at Querétaro in 1933. On the basis of his wide-ranging social programme, Lázaro Cárdenas was chosen as the official party candidate for the presidency. Elected in 1934, Cárdenas had to remove to exile his rival, Calles, before he could embark on effectively realising his own party's programme conceived as a six-year plan. Social change which transformed the political revolution into a full-fledged revolution could now begin.

As more than three-quarters of the Mexican population lived in the countryside, the most revolutionary change was to take place there. During the civil war the drive to liquidate free villages and expropriate peasants in favour of the large estates had been stopped and legal ground for its reversal provided. The Constitution of 1917 gave the state legislatures the right to create free villages of resident plantation communities, and thus to recreate the *ejidos*. Unlike in communist revolutions, genuine cooperatives were upheld and, with some qualification, survived until the time of writing. In their original form they consisted of family plots with inalienable rights to landholding which reverted to the communal village for redistribution only if they were given up or if the *ejidos* member died without an heir.

During the warring phase of the revolution only about 5 per cent of the population working in agriculture received land under the provision of the constitution. From 1924 to 1934 this proportion increased to 21 per cent. During the six years of Cárdenas's presidency the number of the beneficiaries of the agrarian legislature doubled. Thus about 42 per cent of the agricultural population became *ejidatorios* with almost half of the total arable land in their possession.[6] Government-sponsored expertise and credit facilities were arranged to promote the viability of the *ejidos*. After Cárdenas, however, the redistribution process continued at a slower pace, but due to the higher increase of the agricultural population as a whole the proportion of *ejidatarios* declined.

To complete the picture of the improvements for people working in agriculture, we have to point out that the practice of debt peonage and the *tienda de raya* (the peon's obligation to buy goods in the hacienda's shop) had ceased during the early days of the revolution.

The rural population was not only to be socially upgraded but also culturally integrated with the urban sector. A nation-wide education programme became one of the pillars of the revolutionary transformation of Mexico. The most important innovation was the change of attitude towards the Indios. The Mexican government repudiated the idea that Indians were inferior beings and embarked on their education to such an extent that they could attain an equal status with the white population. If the Indians who stood at the lowest echelon of the social stratification had to be elevated, this applied even more to various *castas* between the Indios and the Creoles. Compulsory universal lay education, cultivating social cohesion beyond the *compandrago* (godfather) relationship, became the main instrument of nation-building.

Mass political mobilisation was another means of serving this purpose. In 1938, Cárdenas reorganised the National Revolutionary Party, from then on called the Party of the Mexican Revolution, on the basis of four sectors: workers, peasants, military and popular (residual). Despite huge differences in the numerical strength of these sectors, each received an equal voice on the party councils. This was of particular importance because occasional mutual tensions were to be resolved by negotiation rather than majorisation. (Political theory describes this system as consociation or pillarisation.) Furthermore, the 'capitalist' groups were required to form corporations under government supervision.[7]

The most daring revolutionary action taken by Cárdenas was the expropriation of oil companies which also occurred in 1938, the peak year of social change. The uproar among the affected owners, British and American, led to retaliatory measures such as the refusal to sell the chemicals necessary for the refining process, etc. Fortunately for Mexico, the outbreak of the Second World War, in which Mexico eventually became the ally of both the United Kingdom and the United States, eased the tension. Settlement with the United States was reached in 1941, and with the United Kingdom in 1947.[8]

After the habitual haggling in the ruling party council, General Avila Camacho was chosen as a candidate for the presidency and, as there was no challenge to the Party of Mexican Revolution, he was duly elected president in 1940. Although in principle he followed Cárdenas's path, Avila Camacho slowed down the rate of transformation in several respects. Redistribution of land was carried out at a slower pace, the government's attitude towards the Church became more conciliatory and more stress began to be laid on economic development, in particular on industrialisation. The ground was prepared for the consolidation phase of the revolution.

At this point two specific features of the Mexican revolution must be mentioned. The first was the capability to constrain personal leadership by the observance of rules for a regular change of leader. The president, elected by universal suffrage, but chosen in fact by the convention of the ruling party, could only serve one term, which formerly lasted for four years but was later increased to six. Second, there was a viable mix of socialist and corporatist elements with a modicum of democracy in the political structure. In a country that had suffered instability and turmoil for so long, the safeguarding of continuity, while allowing some opportunity for change, was a particular achievement.

Consolidation

The consolidating process in the wake of the Mexican revolution can best be illustrated by the role and power of the military within society. In 1940 the military sector in the Party of Mexican Revolution was abolished and military personnel were accorded representation as private persons in the popular sector.[9] In 1952, the first civilian candidate, Adolfo Ruiz Cortines, was elected president, followed in 1958 by another civilian, Adolfo Lopez Mateos. When social change was at its height, the proportion of the federal budget spent on the military sector substantially declined. Halfway through the civil war in 1917 it stood at 77 per cent; by the end of the war in 1924 it was down to 34 per cent, and declined to 21 per cent towards the end of Cárdenas's presidency. This downward trend continued until military expenditure stabilised at 7 per cent of the federal budget in 1956.[10] In 1990 defence expenditure accounted for less than 3 per cent of the federal budget.

Another remarkable feature of this consolidation was the sustained economic growth. From 1940 until the mid-1970s Mexico's gross domestic product in constant prices continued to increase by over 6 per cent per annum.[11] Meanwhile, improvements in health care, hygiene and, last but not least, living standards, more than halved the mortality rate, both general and infant, so that, with a constant birth rate, the natural increase rate of the population rose from barely 2 per cent in the late 1930s to 3.5 per cent in the late 1960s and throughout the 1970s. (In the mid-1920s the natural increase rate was 0.7 per cent; before the revolution this rate was only a fraction of that amount.)[12]

Under these circumstances it became increasingly difficult to uphold a rate of economic growth faster than the increase in population, in particular when the international economic climate began to require a more competitive approach to foreign trade. By the mid-1970s Mexico's population growth outstripped its economic growth.[13] During the 1980s the population growth slowed down significantly (the ten-year increase was 21 per cent), but the GDP growth rates remained low (merely 15 per cent).[14] Many people began to look for work abroad. Continuous emigration into the United States has become a mark of relative deprivation.

It was not only the economy that put to the test the wisdom of the social arrangements introduced by the revolution. The Partido Revolucionario Institucional (PRI), as the ruling party had been appropriately renamed in 1946, could no longer maintain that the extraordinarily high vote cast in its favour in various elections represented the genuine wish of the voters. Continuous complaints of manipulation, harassment of the opposition parties, and even of rigging the elections, made the electoral system questionable. The call for change was mounting.

More economic efficiency and more democracy became the main issues in the 1980s. In some ways these developments were similar to those in the Soviet Union which had embarked on an even more ambitious project of social transformation. But as can be seen from our narrative, the Mexican revolutionary establishment provided a much wider scope for adaptation than did the Soviet establishment. Just as social change had been effected by reform rather than by the use of force, the new needs were being tackled in a less dramatic way than in the Soviet Union.

In contrast to earlier elections, when 75–90 per cent of the votes for the official candidates was the norm, in the presidential elections of 1988 Carlos Salinas de Gortari won a 'mere' 50.74 per cent of the votes cast. His main rival, Cuahtemos Cárdenas Solarzano (son of Lázaro Cárdenas, the architect of the Mexican revolutionary establishment), gained 31.06 per cent of the vote. A right-wing candidate won 16.81 per cent.[15] This was beginning to look more plausible although serious complaints were voiced concerning election rigging. It also revealed divisions on serious ideological lines. At the time of writing, the young Cárdenas wants to keep the heritage of his father intact, while Salinas, struggling with the huge foreign debt, strives for competition, efficiency and comprehensive liberalisation. Similarly, in the elections for the Federal Chamber of Deputies in 1991 and also in the local elections, a new, though less conspicuous, variety of results could be witnessed. The move towards pluralism has been slow but steady.

Increased pluralism within the political structure was echoed in the state–Church relationship. The 1991 Amendment to the Constitution of 1917 permitted the recognition of Churches by individual states in the federation and allowed possession of property by the Churches, as well as the enfranchisement of the priests. The institutionalised revolution was slowly giving up its institutionalisation.

This tendency could not avoid the peasant sector, the low productivity of which was becoming a serious obstacle to economic growth. According to the law adopted by the Congress in February 1992, the programme of land distribution established in the Constitution of 1917 was to be discontinued and the *ejido* system relaxed. With the consent of the commune, the tenant farmers (*ejidatarios*) may become landowners, thus being able to mortgage, rent or sell their holdings. *Ejidos* may form joint ventures with private investors. A pilot project of a new farming method was launched in the northeastern state of Nuevo León.[16] Like the Chinese, so too were the Mexicans cautiously looking for a way out of the revolutionary establishment. But compared with the Chinese, the Mexicans had less dogma to overcome.

Comparison with the Russian and the Chinese revolutions made in the previous paragraphs points to one particular common feature of these three revolutions – namely the socialist nature of their revolutionary establishments. In all of them, socialism, though differently accentuated, represented the path along which the domestic tradition wanted to reassert itself against the corroding impact of Europeanisation.

The main difference between Mexico, on the one hand, and Russia and China, on the other, lies not only in the scope and intensity of socialist reglementation but also in its historical roots. The Mexican revolution, with its agrarian basis, re-established the domestic institution of autonomous village cooperatives with smallholder membership. Only railway, electricity, oil and much of commercial agriculture were nationalised. All other industries were left in the private sector. Trade unions remained an autonomous factor in society.

Socialism in Russia and China has followed a blueprint, and one of foreign provenance. It was brought to both countries as a by-product of the foreign challenge. In both Russia and China, socialism was conceived with the aim of penetrating into every area of society. It was imposed upon the agrarian and industrial sectors from above. Moreover, the agrarian sector which, as in Mexico, constituted the overwhelming majority of the population, was to bear the brunt of industrialisation.

These differences may also help to explain the different strategies for coping with the post-revolution problems in these three countries. Russia failed to make a viable blend of the foreign blueprint and the domestic tradition. China, confronted with two blueprints – the Euro-American and the Russian – tried hard to strike a balance between them. Mexico has no need to reconsider its racial and cultural blend, which is making progress slowly but surely and is moving ahead.[17]

As far as social change is concerned, Mexico's revolutionary process seems to be approaching the end in a similar way to other vertical revolutions which we have described as endogenous. The seat of power shifts to the centre of the original political spectrum. So far this process has been on the whole painless, as if all hell had been unleashed during the civil war when for fourteen years there was no stable government in the country. As stated earlier, the oscillating seat of power was first (in 1924) intercepted by the centre, and then (in 1934) by the left. This second interception was accompanied by a degree of tightening which, however, compared with other revolutions, was moderate. There was no organised government terror of the Jacobin or Bolshevik type. Spontaneous terror, however, occasionally cropped up; the most ferocious, though meaningless, was the terror exercised by both sides in the Cristero rebellion (1926–9), i.e. at the time when the power was still with the centre. The consolidation phase started comparatively smoothly.

On the first day of 1994, however, just as the North American Free Trade Agreement between the United States, Canada and Mexico was coming into force, an uprising broke out among the Indians of the southern state of Chiapas, calling themselves the Zapatist National Liberation Army, a timely reminder that President Salinas has to think more about the social cost of his economic liberalisation and the opening up of his country to a wider market. It is also a reminder that political liberalisation has not yet gone far enough to abolish the misuse of power concentrated in the Partido Revolucionario Institucional. The state Chiapas, in the underdeveloped south neglected by the federal government, has been particularly notorious for the tight oligarchic rule of the ruling party bosses and for the impossibility of redress for justified grievances. These mainly concerned flawed elections and exploitation often reminiscent of the *ancien régime* (cf. pp. 232–6).

At the time of writing it seems that after three weeks of heavy fighting, the federal authorities are poised for a negotiated resolution of the conflict. Foreign investment, badly needed, would not pour into a country beset by political unrest. Furthermore, the next presidential election is due in August 1994. As the days of an easy manipulation seem to be over, winning this election will be more difficult than ever before for the candidate of the ruling party. For many people democracy appears to be the best means for resolving the conflict between economic efficiency and social welfare.

By way of conclusion, it has to be pointed out that there is yet one particular feature which makes the Mexican revolution different from other revolutions discussed in this book. It is the sequence of two separate revolutions. In the first revolution, the Spanish settlers in Mexico, the Creoles, shook off the domination of their mother country. For them it was the war of liberation. In the second revolution, people of all races, Creoles, mestizos and Indios fought out an arrangement that abolished the most drastic inequalities and thus created conditions for their gradual, racial and cultural merger. The warring phase of that revolution may be described as a war of integration. To sum up, the horizontal revolution which broke out in 1810 created the Mexican state; the vertical revolution of a hundred years later, started to build up the Mexican nation.

Notes

1. For detail see C.C. Cumberland, *Mexico: The struggle for modernity* (Oxford University Press, New York, 1968), table on p. 367.
2. *Ibid.*, p. 83.
3. F. Tannenbaum, *Peace by Revolution: Mexico after 1910* (Columbia University Press, London, 1966), pp. 29–30.
4. Cumberland, *Mexico*, p. 141.
5. Tannenbaum, p. 60.
6. Data from J. Wilkie, *The Mexican Revolution: Federal expenditure and social change since 1910* (University of California Press, Berkeley, 1970), p. 194, and Cumberland, p. 369.
7. Wilkie, pp. 73–5.
8. Cumberland, pp. 312 ff.
9. Wilkie, p. 75.
10. E. Lieuwen, *Mexican Militarism: The political rise and fall of the revolutionary army 1910–1940* (University of New Mexico Press, Albuquerque, 1968), pp. 142 and 153.
11. C.W. Reynolds, *The Mexican Economy: Twentieth-century structure and growth* (Yale University Press, London, 1970), p. 22.
12. Cumberland, p. 366.
13. From 1970 to 1975 Mexico's GDP increased by 37 per cent; from 1975 to 1980 by merely 5 per cent. During the whole of the 1980s the population increased, at almost constant rate of growth, by 39 per cent.
14. Data from UN Statistical Yearbooks and the Statesman's Yearbooks.
15. *The Europa World Yearbook, 1991* vol. II (Europe Publications, London, 1992), p. 1883.
16. *The Economist*, 16 November 1991 and *Europa World Yearbook*, 1992.
17. According to the official data, Mexico's racial structure in per cent of the total population developed as follows:

	Amerindians	European origin	Mestizo	Total population (m)
1910	36	18	46	15.2
1980	29	16	55	66.8

(Quoted from the Statesman's Yearbooks.)

Part IV

Conclusions

THE SCOPE OF THE SUBJECT MATTER

As has been said in the Introduction note, simple, 'one-track' theories are not adequate for the explanation of complex phenomena. They may also not be quite appropriate for the categorisation of the subject matter.

These eight case studies, as well as my brief comments on revolutions in the 'bygone ages', illustrate how much individual revolutions are marked by specific features. But at the same time, comparison of these case studies reveals quite a few significant similarities. Their occurrence or absence is a helpful item for the typology of revolutions and also for the assessment of the limits within which a particular theoretical observation may be considered as valid.

Although our findings sometimes do allow a comment of a general nature, which more often than not is in tune with the observation of other authors, it would not be appropriate to generalise beyond the framework of our empirical evidence, or to put it more accurately, beyond the type of revolution that our case studies represent. This means that our theoretical suggestions claim validity only with respect to the great vertical revolutions, i.e. revolutions that fulfil the following conditions:

1. They broke out from below against the domestic (native) government.
2. After the overthrow of the *ancien régime*, they developed into a prolonged process of further revolutionary events, such as in-fighting, enforced adaptations, reversals, reforms, etc.
3. They resulted in significant changes of some key aspects of the culture and structure of the society, in particular of the prevailing ideology, political regime and economic control.

Before arriving at the final conclusions, a review of the main sections of our enquiry, namely the causes, the course and the outcome of the revolutions under

study, including the impact of individual revolutions on the outside world, may
be useful.

STRUCTURE OF CAUSATION

Most of the disproportions, contradictions or contrasts listed as elements of
multiple dysfunction in the section on etiology of revolution (pages 38–42) were
found in our eight revolutions, albeit in varying degrees of intensity. The
Aristotelian contrast of ideas, the gist of which is the contradictory understanding
of justice – a contrast which operates through what may be called mental ferment
– was clearly discernible in each case. Although the new concept of justice was
never a uniform one – there were always differences of interpretation –
and the outcome always differed to a greater or lesser extent from the intentions,
it was the necessary agent that triggered the transformation of interests into
some kind of revolutionary action. To borrow Daniel Marnet's terms, 'it
transformed men's minds; it made them lose the habit of respect for tradition
... it cleared the soil in which the seeds of new harvests could germinate'.[1]

The Marxian contradiction was less easy to identify. The class struggle was
not always at the forefront of events (its role was especially subdued in the
Czech and Turkish cases) and even where it was to play an important role, its
sides were not necessarily identical with the main divide between the revolutionary and counter-revolutionary forces. In the English and above all in the
French case the class struggle opened, so to speak, a second front of the
revolution. Nor in the Russian case could the identity of the class and political
alignments (i.e. communists with blue-collar workers) be preserved for more
than a short period. In the Chinese revolution the marriage between the
Communist Party and its supporting class (in this case, the peasants) lasted
much longer. As in China, so also in Mexico the main support for the vertical
revolution was among the peasants; they also derived significant benefits from
the outcome of the revolution. In Iran, the class struggle was superseded by
the confrontation of the clerics with the secularising tendencies of the monarchy.

Viewing the Marxian contradiction in terms of productive forces versus the
mode of production, we do not encounter such a difficulty. Oddly enough this
interpretation can best be applied in the case of Turkey and China. Their
political institutions and modes of production were the main obstacle to the
introduction of the more developed productive forces from abroad. The same,
to a lesser degree, can be said of Russia. On the other hand, as some more
recent research indicates, in the case of England and France the domestic mode
of production was not as hopelessly opposed to technological innovation as
was earlier thought to be the case. However, it may be argued that the
development of productive forces in those countries was accelerated by the
revolution. In the Czech case it does not seem that the revolution had any
particular effect on the development of the productive forces, unless we assume

that the Hussite revolution, via its side effects, prompted the re-establishment of serfdom, which in turn enabled large estates to be run on a more efficient commercial basis; this, however, was offset by the weakening of the urban economy. In Iran the development of productive forces was supported by the imperial regime (revolution from above), whereas the victorious revolution from below followed other priorities. In Mexico the revolutionaries were concerned with a just (equitable) mode of production rather than with economic growth. Only recently has the latter (promotion of productive forces) become a priority.

The contrast between the development of productive forces abroad and the archaic mode of production at home is virtually the economic counterpart, or rather aspect, of Deutscher's contradiction between the aspirations for great power status and the archaic social institutions. From whichever side they are viewed, the wish to catch up and, possibly, overtake appears to be the leitmotiv of three revolutions – the Russian, the Turkish and the Chinese.

Clearly this motivation need not be shared by the majority of the activists in the revolution. They may be driven primarily by a sense of some sort of relative deprivation. Such feelings, whether they are seen as deriving from frustrated expectations (Tocquevillian contrast) or from a disproportion between status and achievement (Weberian contrast), were doubtless a major ingredient of the inclination to rebel in all the cases that we have examined.

We have, furthermore, to bear in mind that relative deprivation was only partly an economic or political matter; the lack of maintenance values, i.e. the frustration caused by the staggering contrast between acknowledged moral principles and the actual practice of the authorities in charge of preserving those principles, contributed in one way or another to the motivation of revolutionary action in all our eight cases, most conspicuously perhaps in the Czech, English, Iranian and Chinese revolutions.

The last two contrasts mentioned in the introductory chapter, the Paretian and Khaldunian ones, are relevant to the course and outcome rather than to the causation of revolution. Nevertheless, if success (or lack of it) is the crucial factor in deciding whether a revolt becomes a revolution, we have to consider these two contrasts as equally important. On the whole it can be said that both the Paretian and the Khaldunian contrasts appeared, at least for a short while, in all eight instances under study, albeit with varying time spans and intensity. The fighting spirit was kept especially high during the period of foreign invasions, which lasted longest in the Czech and Chinese revolutions. In the case of the Russian revolution the full strength of the fighting spirit appeared rather belatedly, during what has officially been styled the Great Patriotic War (1941–5). In the Chinese and Turkish cases, the defensive patriotic wars, displaying a high degree of fighting spirit, coincided more closely with the main violent phases of the revolution. In the French revolution the fighting spirit seems to have been high, not only throughout the defensive but also during the offensive phase of the revolutionary process; here, however, it is difficult to separate the part played by patriotic fervour from that played by the superior military craftsmanship of Napoleon. In Iran the Khaldunian *assabiya* was at its highest point when the revolutionaries fought each other and when the victorious Khomeinian regime engaged in a war with Iraq.

The fact that the above-mentioned contrasts appeared at the same time or in close sequence does not in itself mean that the revolution was bound to break out; nor does the multiple dysfunction consisting of these disproportions, contradictions or contrasts encompass all the possible causes of revolution. Further circumstances must also be present if a revolutionary spirit is to issue in actual revolution.

In none of our eight revolutions were all the actors recruited from a single social class. The cooperation of different social groups at crucial moments of the revolution, such as explosion and consolidation, was a necessary precondition of its success. In the Czech case, for instance, the success of the Hussites was due to the cooperation of a part of the nobility, especially the gentry, the royal boroughs and the peasantry. The gentry provided the military expertise, while the royal boroughs produced the arms, and together with the peasantry furnished both enthusiastic recruits for the armies and, last but not least, the necessary economic backing. The English revolution was successful as long as a segment of the nobility, together with the yeomanry and the burghers, especially those of London, gave it support. As soon as the London Presbyterians and their religious brethren throughout the country shifted their support to the other side, the revolutionary regime became extremely shaky. In the French case the crucial breakthrough was made possible by the defection of some prominent nobles and clergymen to the Third Estate and by the dramatic support given to the latter by the plebeian masses of Paris. Subsequently the alliance between the bourgeoisie and peasantry played an essential role in preventing the revolution from taking a more radical course.

The cooperation of different social groups in the crucial phases of revolution seems to have been made possible by two circumstances: first, the fact that all the different sorts of deprivation experienced by individual social groups could be blamed on one general cause, one scapegoat – the existing political regime; and, second, the belief that the main grievances and deprivations could be put right by changing the leadership and institutions in accordance with the new ideology and its new understanding of justice.

In contrast to the convergent tendencies on the side of the reform (revolutionary) forces, there was in all eight cases a breach in the ranks of the *ancien régime*. This assumed the two familiar forms: (a) the defection of intellectuals; and (b) the emergence of a dual power or dual sovereignty (the second pivot). Defeat in a foreign war also played an important role in the weakening of the *ancien régime*.

The intellectuals' defection from the establishment has been amply discussed and analysed by the theorists of revolution; yet it seems that its full implications have not always been fully appreciated. To my knowledge there has been no successful revolution in which the revolutionary leadership has not been to a

substantial extent recruited from the cultural élite of the *ancien régime*. It would seem that if the mental ferment and the ideological amalgam discussed above are to be truly effective, they have to be initiated and expounded by those who understand the ideational basis of the establishment and are acquainted with the functioning of the *ancien régime*, so that they can attack it at its weakest point and at the same time develop ideas that appeal to the widely differentiated masses of the malcontent.

The importance of the dual power or dual sovereignty seems to have been more fully appreciated by scholars in the field. In our morphological model we have termed this phenomenon institutionalisation, thus laying stress on the fact that the opposition manages to find a base within the system from which it can legally organise its forces and propagate its ideas. This may happen well before the revolution breaks out, at a stage when the movement is still orientated towards peaceful reform, which it hopes to further with the support of a suitable institution within the system. In the Czech case it was the University of Prague and, in times of crisis, the secular estates that fulfilled this role; in the English case it was the House of Commons and the City Council of London; in the French case the *tiers état*. In the Chinese revolution it was the regional armed forces, traditionally more-or-less independent according to the varying strength of the central government; as a result of the Taiping uprising these armed forces acquired – by virtue of their much wider scale of operation and also of their ideological motivation – a particular importance and prestige. In the other two revolutions such institutions had to be newly created: the Soviets in the Russian revolution, and the Associations for the Defence of Rights in the Turkish revolution. Their armies and the People's Army in the second round of the Chinese revolution were also new creations. In these three non-Western revolutions, it was defeat or difficulties in a foreign war that made the splitting of the state's authority possible.

As long as the reform ideology could accommodate all the different interests there was scope for cooperation or at least parallel action, but as soon as the reformists became revolutionaries and overcame their main hurdle – as soon as the *ancien régime* ceased to represent a deadly menace to the forces of revolution – these forces fell apart. The revolutionaries became differentiated into factions with diverging interests and diverging interpretations of the revolutionary ideology.

THE COURSE OF REVOLUTIONS

The divisions among the revolutionaries, their shifting alliances and the outcome of their confrontations together determine the subsequent course of the revolution. These are the basic parameters of our morphological model illustrated in the graphs and itemised in the respective chronologies.

In the section on morphology of revolution (pages 31–43), I gave a description of the model and pointed to its two versions: one in which the revolutionary process is interrupted by a phase of restoration, and one in which there is no such explicit interruption. Having applied this model to the eight revolutions, we can now see clearly the distinction manifested by the presence or absence of a restoration.

In other respects the general development is similar. The revolutionaries soon become divided. Within a climate of enthusiasm and extensive mass participation in political or military action, the seat of power starts to move towards an increasingly radical position.[2]

Once the radicals have won enough power and want to take over responsibility for the government, they have to put a stop to this drift. If there is nevertheless a further move to the left, they have to eliminate the forces behind it, as happened with the Adamites in Bohemia, with the Levellers in England, with the Enraged and Babuvists in France, with the anarchists and workers' opposition in Russia, with the communists in Turkey, with the 'Gang of Four' (within an altered timetable) in China, with the *mujahedin* in Iran, and with the Villistas in Mexico.

Meanwhile, the victorious revolutionary faction discovers not only the charm of its exclusive rule but also its limits and liabilities. Its struggle with the other revolutionary factions means that it has to tighten its grip on all focuses of independent action or thought. To this end it has to extend the administrative and surveillance apparatus, and even to establish new means of compulsion.[3]

In so doing, the revolutionary faction in power abandons many of the noble principles preached before, or at the time of, the explosion of the revolution. Once the revolutionaries have to turn to the day-to-day business, they inevitably become more apprehensive concerning their power base. They might still believe that they are acting for the benefit of all, or almost all; they might still believe that at the end of the day everybody will recognise the beneficial effects of their doings; yet many of their subjects cannot fail to realise the gap between the lofty ideals and the not always inspiring reality, and will behave accordingly. The new rulers are thus inclined to use more effective means of compulsion – even terror for a time.

At this point the morphological pattern common to the six revolutions from which the model was abstracted comes to an end. Subsequent developments take one of two directions. Either the victorious revolutionary faction succeeds in strengthening its establishment to such an extent that the opposition to it remains ineffective; or the moderate revolutionaries and the counter-revolutionaries manage to strike up an alliance and overturn the revolutionary regime. The former was the case with the Russian, Turkish and Chinese revolutions; in the Czech, English and French ones it was the latter. The Iranian and Mexican revolutions, added later to the sample, belong (at least so far) to the former category.

The overthrow of the revolutionary regime, however, does not mean the end of the revolutionary process. As this overthrow had been brought about by the

coalition between the moderates in the revolutionary camp and the supporters of restoration, the latter had to observe the compromise that had made the coalition possible. But, as the course of the Czech, English and French revolutions indicates, the supporters of restoration ceased to observe the compromise and tried to enforce a full restoration of the *ancien régime*. This could not but lead to a realignment of forces. A new alliance was struck between moderates on both sides; with their mutual cooperation the consolidation could then materialise. This occurred, as shown on the graphs, at the position of what at the outbreak of revolution had been approximately the revolutionary centre.

If the revolutionary regime was not overthrown, its shape nevertheless did not remain substantially unchanged. Even in Russia and China, and above all in Turkey, the development towards a more central position between individual political and ideological tendencies took place. But in all these cases the changes were initiated within the revolutionary establishment itself; mounting pressure from below did not reach the point of an acute danger to the regime.

So far Turkey has moved furthest in that direction, China being the slowest. Russia, which at the beginning was overtaken by China, eventually made a dramatic upturn, the consequences of which remain to be seen. But the tendency everywhere points to a more balanced position between the political and ideological alternatives that emerged at the start of the revolution.

A similar tendency can also be observed in Mexico. Its revolutionary establishment is giving up its authoritarian grip and its *ejido* socialism experiences an opening towards a more efficient mode of production. With respect to Iran it is still too early to say whether the process at consolidation will take the way of yet another revolutionary event, or whether it will be brought about by the moderates within the revolutionary establishment. A sensible reinterpretation of Muhammad's message (many have already made an attempt in this direction) may give the Islamic republic a new, more viable turn.

One obvious reason for the aforementioned differences in the course of revolution may be seen in the different nature of the power structure and political culture in the countries concerned. It may be suggested that the pluralistic structure of power in Western Europe was so deeply rooted in the political structure of the society that it prevented those who had assumed supreme power from concentrating and extending its scope to such an extent that any reversal, any attempt at restoration of the *ancien régime*, was not feasible.

In contrast, Russia, Turkey, China and Iran, though allowing some elements of pluralism (mainly with respect to the religious bodies), did not provide these elements with enough opportunity to make their way to the top of the power pyramid. Only the painful realisation of the obvious setbacks, often brought to the surface by unrest in key sectors of the economy, induced the necessity of changing gear.

The Mexican revolution is a special case. Being a two-tier society, each tier belonging to a quite different culture, Mexico experienced a series of revolutions in each of which only a part of its staggering contrasts could be tackled.

The power structure and political culture, however, are only partial aspects of social and cultural differences, which in their totality differentiate the wholes, usually described as civilisations.[4]

At this point we come up against a particular differentiating feature in our sample of revolutions, which can be equally perceived in their causes, developments and outcomes. This feature is due to the contact of different civilisations, a contact in which one civilisation displays in some important walks of life superiority over the other, and thus creates a challenge which has to be answered in one way or another. The question affecting our investigation is whether such a contact with an alien civilisation can be identified as one of the major causes and features of revolution. If this is the case, then we describe the respective revolution as exogenous; if it is not the case, we describe it as endogenous (cf. the section on concept and types of revolution, pages 4–16).

On the basis of the evidence we have gathered, we can say that all three West European revolutions were endogenous. All of them were due, in civilisational terms, to internal causes. Whatever the influences from abroad that affected these three revolutions, they came from countries that belonged to the same civilisation as the country in which the revolution broke out and ran its full course. The three revolutions reflect specific crises in the development of the West European civilisation. They broke out in different areas, separated by long intervals. In the meantime, the Latin Christian civilisation, which the Czech revolution had attempted to reform, underwent a considerable transformation, for which its internal dynamics provided the main propelling force. In fact, all three revolutions, whether by removing obstacles or by accelerating the pace of development, proved to be important contributory factors in this process, the English revolution more so than the Czech, and the French, chronologically last of our three, most of all.

In contrast, the multiple dysfunction in the four non-Western revolutions was, if not wholly caused, then at least heavily aggravated, by contact with the contemporaneous Western (Euro-American) civilisation. In the case of tsarist Russia, the socio-economic and technological level of Westernisation was inadequate and its political form corresponded to what in the West was already out of date. Modern Europe, with its Anglo-American liberal and French revolutionary tradition, was an invitation to take a step forward. In Ottoman Turkey, proud of its glorious past as a mighty bulwark of Islamic civilisation, the revolution resulted from the sultan's failure to cope with the Western challenge, which after a duration of over two centuries had almost reduced the country to the state of a colony. In Pahlavi Iran the Islamic revolution resulted from the shah's failure to respond to the Western challenge in a sensible way. Even China, the most remote and populous of the four, and exposed to Western pressure for the shortest span of time, was not able to avoid the corroding influence of the West; eventually, it had to resolve its problems by revolution, in which the impact from abroad was even stronger than before.

The difference between the course of the endogenous revolutions on the one hand and the exogenous revolutions on the other is illustrated in the graphs (Chapter 7). In the case of endogenous revolutions the development, indicated by the curve of the seat of power, aims towards a kind of balance between the new and the old. The spectrum stretches from the *status quo ante* (extreme right) to the most daring innovations (extreme left). In the exogenous revolutions there are foreign paradigms which constitute the opposite pole to the *status quo*. Where there is only one foreign paradigm seriously considered by the revolutionaries, as in Turkey, then a two-dimensional graph adequately illustrates the development. Where there are, however, several paradigms at stake, as in Russia or in China, then the visual illustration is less straightforward but nonetheless, I hope, helpful.

The multiple choice of paradigms in the exogenous revolutions can be briefly reviewed as follows. While the Turkish nationalists envisaged in principle only one paradigm which was to be applied to their country, and this paradigm was found already developed in the Euro-American West, the Russian Bolsheviks and the Chinese communists opted for new paradigms of their own. While Turkey was to swap civilisations, Russia and China were to preserve their own civilisational identity. The difference between the last two countries was the number of paradigms involved in each case. In the Russian case there were three: (a) the semi-Europeanised *ancien régime*, (b) the fully Europeanised parliamentary state and civil society, and (c) the Soviet socialist establishment. In the Chinese case there were four alternatives: (a) the *ancien régime*, (b) the example of the Euro-American West (Guomindang), (c) the example of the USSR, and (d) the Chinese communist establishment. Taking the abortive attempts of the Taipings into consideration as well, and covering the 150 years which have elapsed between the First Opium War and the time of writing, we can count altogether five paradigms which emerged in the struggle for civilisational reconstruction in China.

In the process of the Iranian revolution (not included in the graphs) there are also four paradigms at stake: (a) the antiquated Qajar style, (b) the westernising constitutionalist style; (c) the westernising imperial (Pahlavi) style, and (d) the Islamic Republic.

The pattern of the vertical revolution in Mexico follows the two-dimensional spectrum of endogenous revolution. The vertical revolution in Mexico, however, was preceded by a development in which two particular events had transformative effects comparable with those of the great revolutions. These were first, the Spanish conquest in the sixteenth century; second, at the beginning of the nineteenth century, the secession from the Spanish crown (horizontal revolution). The vertical revolution of the twentieth century has only started to tackle the dysfunctional consequences of the Spanish conquest and the Creole domination. If the social and cultural integration of the Mexican peoples initiated by the vertical revolution eventually fails, the emergence of yet another dimension in the political spectrum cannot be ruled out.

THE OUTCOME OF REVOLUTIONS

A comparative evaluation of historical processes with respect to their outcome requires first a clarification of what is to be understood by this term. It means the amount of significant changes that occurred in some key aspects of human life in the society, such as power structure, economic control, jurisdiction, legal and social status of individual groups of population, scope of individual self-assertion, social mobility, etc. The amount and the patterns of alterations depend on the extent to which the prevailing views and value judgements concerning those social issues have changed too.

Here, again, I have to cross swords with all those who tend to eliminate the human mind from the course of social change in history, who underestimate the role of purposeful action. However subjective, volatile or blurred, it is always the human will that eventually decides whether to start to fight or to give up, whom to join and whom to abandon, whether to fit in or to play the odd one out, etc. In the hectic days of a revolution the number of people involved in politics may increase several times beyond the normal; people combine strength and thus, becoming 'social vectors', engage in a contest whose outcome may only remotely correspond with the views that had been held by the actors at the beginning of the confrontation.

Our comment raises two more questions: first, to what extent we can maintain that what happened really was caused by the revolution; whether perhaps even without that revolution, the development might have taken more or less the same direction. Recently, quite a few scholars have undertaken a thorough reassessment of what has been widely considered an established knowledge of individual revolutions.[5] However respectable their work may be, it leads us too far into the realms of speculation. In my opinion, it is safer to accept the assumption that, if the contrary is not obvious, the sequence of events implies also a causal link (*post hoc ergo propter hoc*) and that, if necessary, we may check this simplification by looking into a broader socio-historical context of the development.

The other question concerns the time dimension. Revolutions bring about various changes, great and small, of which only some are of longer duration, while others, such as changes precipitated under the temporary rule of the radicals, are merely ephemeral. Understandably, only changes of longer duration will be considered in this context. However, the time span of the duration, possibly with respect to particular issues, may be helpful for the comparative evaluation of the outcome of individual revolutions.

Bearing in mind what has been said about the outcome of revolutions in general, we may now briefly review the outcomes of the eight revolutions discussed in this volume.

The Hussite revolution in Bohemia and Moravia was carried out under the banner of a religious dispute. In this respect it established in the country an ecclesiastical dualism which, for almost two centuries, provided some (albeit

precarious) scope for the coexistence of various Christian denominations. During the Hussite revolution the political power and prestige of the royal boroughs *vis-à-vis* the other estates in the country significantly increased; the wealth and power of the ecclesiastical estate were substantially reduced. Within about eighty years from the consolidation that took place in the 1450s, the relative position of the estates began to return to the previous situation. The high aristocracy can be considered the main beneficiary. The advancement of the ethnic Czechs in the boroughs previously dominated by ethnic Germans, however, has remained unchanged in many of these places up to the time of writing.

The English revolution was dominated by two main confrontations: Parliament versus the Crown over political/economic power, and Nonconformist Protestants versus the episcopal establishment of the Anglican Church; in the last phase of the revolutionary process, all Protestants rose against the readmission of Roman Catholics to official public life. The outcome was as follows: on the political front Parliament won the upper hand; on the religious front the Anglican Church re-established its leading position, but other Protestant denominations were also acknowledged as legitimate religious bodies. As Parliament mainly represented the propertied classes, the increase of its power *vis-à-vis* the Crown enabled a speedier development of an unbridled market economy and connected social relationships. There was no radical backlash against these achievements. In line with general development in other parts of Europe, however, the population excluded from full citizenship either on social (economic) or religious grounds was slowly and gradually enfranchised.

The French revolution was fought mainly for political and socio-economic causes. Religious or, rather, ecclesiastical confrontation was merely a side issue. As far as the outcome is concerned, the French revolution brought about more substantial changes than any other endogenous revolution analysed in this book. It abolished seigneurial rights (remnants of feudalism), strengthened the legal position of private ownership and prepared the ground for egalitarian citizenship and representative democracy in an administratively centralised and linguistically unified lay state. These changes, however, could be completed only after several rounds of revolutionary events had cleared up the obstacles that the forces of an inegalitarian tradition piled up against such a broad spectrum of innovations. Throughout this process, the sense of French national identity was significantly enhanced.

The bicentenary of the conquest of the Bastille as the signal of the break-out of the revolution was celebrated in France in great style and, seemingly, with the widespread sympathies of the population. The dissenting voices did not seem to represent any serious danger to the official view of the French revolution as a glorious and, on the whole, beneficial act in French history. So far, save for a short period of the Vichy regime, the institutionalised legacy of the French revolution has not been questioned.

All the other revolutions in our sample are twentieth-century events and their long-term outcome still remains to be seen. Nevertheless, because many decades have already elapsed since their beginning, a prospective assessment of the outcome may be suggested.

The Mexican and the Turkish revolutions offer a comparatively safe ground for such an assessment. Although, in terms of our typology, the former was endogenous and the latter exogenous, nation-building was their common feature. The Turks were already an ethnic nation, but their national consciousness was submerged. They saw themselves primarily as Ottoman subjects and members of the largely arabicised Muslim religious community (*ümmet*) which, in the multi-religious empire, enjoyed the dominant position. In that situation 'Turk' was the term used for a peasant. The Westernisation (there was no other paradigm at stake) meant a psychological reorientation towards a Turkish national consciousness and lay state built according to the West European model. Promotion of the Turkish vernacular to a sophisticated literary language using Latin script was the change likely to last the longest. The transformation from a one-party dictatorship to a pluralistic democracy became the main issue of further political development; at the time of writing it seems to have made considerable progress.

In Mexico, which is a country where two quite different peoples and cultures (civilisations) live and mix together, the nation-building has been a very long process. As the main contrast between the two races (the Creoles and the Indios), and countless shades of mixing between them (the mestizos), was manifested mainly in the social status and the level of education, the nation-building first had to tackle this disparity. This was the main issue in the vertical Mexican revolution. The 'institutionalised revolution' – an authoritarian presidential regime supported by a broadly based political party – was well fitted for implementing social reforms, undertaken mainly for the benefit of the indigenous peasantry. After about forty years of quite successful development, however, the combination of unprecedented population growth and tougher competition in foreign trade and international money markets has created a situation where the need for a more efficient economy has become paramount. Calls for political pluralism also have become more frequent. The revolutionary establishment has responded to these challenges by economic and political liberalisation. The development is taking a similar direction to that in Turkey.

The Russian and Chinese revolutions are great not only because of the size of their countries but also because of the social change caused by these revolutions. In both these revolutions the victory in the struggle between various parties came to that political party which followed the most definite ideology and enforced its implementation most vigorously. With hindsight, it may be inferred that it was these two qualities – rigour and vigour – that spurred the largely successful drive for social change, but also that both these qualities became the main obstacles to the survival of these changes.

The Chinese revolutionary establishment realised earlier than the Russian that the ideological stance had to be modified by pragmatic considerations. Before this could happen, China was to go through the traumatic experience

of the Great Leap Forward and of the Great Proletarian Cultural Revolution. Its 'Helmsman' plunged it headlong into a turmoil from which it took many years to recover. The subsequent turn to pragmatism might be at least one salutary effect of this experience. Thus it happened that within twenty years from the communist victory over the Guomindang, the all-pervading socialism was relaxed, and, within a further fifteen years or so, reduced to the industrial and public service sectors. Also in its foreign policy, ideology gave way to pragmatic consideration. At the time of writing the communist leadership is looking for a balance between what may be described as a political dictatorship on the one hand, and a capitalist economy on the other. It remains to be seen whether the communist/capitalist compound will be more viable than were combinations of other types of dictatorship with the free market in the Far East.

The Russian communists pursued their transformatory zeal with more consistency than the Chinese (also, seemingly, by using terror). Against heavy odds, which were made still heavier by their paranoid leadership, they succeeded in transforming a predominantly peasant country into a highly industrialised, urbanised and literate society able to sustain a huge and sophisticated military apparatus. So equipped, the USSR could engage itself in helping to promote Soviet-type socialism all over the world. The cost of these achievements, however, was so excessive, in particular in human and ecological terms, that a thorough reconstruction of the whole system was deemed necessary. As those in charge failed to carry out the task (which would have amounted to a kind of revolution from above), the whole system collapsed and the USSR disintegrated.

What then remains as a more durable outcome of the Russian Bolshevik revolution? It is the level of modernisation and the geopolitical articulation of the country on ethnic lines. The former might have happened anyway, but under a milder regime in Russia it might have taken much more time and thus perhaps also have been less harmful. The latter – the recognition of the right of individual ethnic groups to an adequate, albeit by the conditions of the communist dictatorship limited, political status in what was declared a federation – was due to the Marxist ideology. When the Communist Party ceased to perform its centripetal role, the administrative framework of union republics, autonomous republics, autonomous regions, etc., provided a suitable ground for an easier emancipation of individual nationalities from what the Soviet national anthem had hailed as an 'insoluble union of the free republics'.

The Islamic phase of the revolutionary process in Iran is the most recent case discussed in this context. It would be premature to try to assess its outcome. Although the Islamic Republican Party does not aim at that kind of modernisation which had been envisaged by the communist parties in Russia and China, it shows the same rigour and vigour. With religion as the dominant issue and with the stress on practising religion, however, the Islamic revolution is more akin to the Hussite revolution in fifteenth-century Bohemia. Analogy offers the opportunity to imagine three alternatives. The moderates will succeed in dissociating the observance of the rigid ideology from real, everyday life (the

Chinese way); or they will attempt a reconstruction of both the theory and practice (the Russian way), whereby they might succeed or fail, or the moderates will strike an alliance with the supporters of a lay state and its constitutionalist tradition and defeat the radicals in a civil war (the Hussite way).

THE IMPACT OF REVOLUTIONS ABROAD

All three West European revolutions made some impact on the outside world; however, that of the French revolution was by far the most impressive.

The international repercussions of the Hussite revolution were intense but short-lived. It was not so much the domestic regime in the lands of the Bohemian Crown that was challenged, as the Roman Catholic Church – the main integrative institution of the West European civilisation of those days, whose doctrinal monopoly provided that civilisation with its authoritative ideational basis. In order to give their demands for reform more weight, the Hussites eventually started to undertake military raids into the neighbouring countries, thus extending their challenge abroad in an unmistakable fashion. However, once the challenge was contained by a compromise agreement in which the more moderate elements called the tune, the schism of Hussitism became localised to Bohemia and Moravia until another outbreak of reform, this time in a wider European context, revived in a more formidable way the challenge to the Roman Catholic integration of the European West.

In its religious content, the Hussite revolution foreshadowed the Protestant Reformation, which in turn was one of the main driving forces in the English revolution. There were also other aspects of the Hussite revolution which prefigured what was to follow in Europe. The strong and self-confident involvement of the Hussite burghers in what may be described as national politics was paralleled by the strong participation of the bourgeoisie in the English revolution and their dominant participation in the French revolution. Nationalism, which was another salient feature of the Hussite movement, re-emerged as one of the main forces in the French revolution, from where it spread all over Europe.

Taking these points into account, the Hussite revolution can be described as a proto-Protestant, proto-bourgeois and proto-national revolution. However, only its proto-Protestantism became a living legacy within a wider European context. John Hus was recognised with approval by Martin Luther and became a sort of John the Baptist of Lutheranism.

Compared with the Hussite revolution in Bohemia, the Puritan revolution in England was a rather parochial phenomenon. Its expansionist ventures beyond the British Isles were motivated by the commercial interests of the country rather than by the wish to carry the revolution abroad. Nevertheless the Puritan revolution also eventually acquired a wider appeal. This, however, happened through yet another revolution, that of the British colonies in North

America. There many of the ideas of the English revolution, such as the contractual character of the state, the principle of no taxation without representation, and the rights of the individual, religious tolerance, etc., became revitalised.

The American revolution gave additional impetus to ideas which at that time had also crystallised in France. The concept of what may be briefly described as the liberal establishment, both in the political and the economic sense, thus passed over from the Anglo-Saxon to the Romance world. The European monarchs who, in their fight against the estates' privileges, had managed to achieve some of their absolutist aspirations, and who by this achievement had inspired the Stuarts to follow a similar path, were eventually – like their less effective Stuart disciples – the losers.

One of the main international consequences of the French revolution was the establishment of constitutional, contractual regimes throughout much of Europe. The image of the French Republic with its social and nationalistic overtones was a source of inspiration, not only within the West European civilisation, which progressively shed its Latin Christian features and adopted a liberal, utilitarian and pluralistic world-view, but also beyond.

Of the two major legacies of the French revolution, republicanism and nationalism, it was the second that made the wider impact. French nationalism itself was a unifying and, in a way, levelling force. It set in train the progressive obliteration of regional differences and the absorption of ethnic minorities. In other parts of Europe, however, nationalism was a force that destroyed rather than fortified the existing state boundaries. Where an ethnic nation was divided among several states, nationalism wanted them to be absorbed into one nation state; where there was a multi-ethnic state, nationalism aimed to divide it so that each individual nationality might enjoy its own state. Thus the French revolution set in motion a process that transformed the political map of Europe. Gradually and more often than not, violently, the political borders were adapted to the ethnic borders. The process started with the unification of Italy and Germany, followed by the emancipation of subject nationalities in the Austro-Hungarian, Ottoman and Russian empires. Thus it happened that, while in 1820 more than half the population of Europe belonged to ethnic nations who either lacked a territorial political status of their own (state, federated or autonomous status) or were scattered among several dynastic states uninterested in their national aspirations, by 1920 the proportion of people belonging to such ethnic groups had declined to about 7 per cent of the total European population.[6]

The Ottoman reformers and revolutionaries prior to Atatürk believed that they could emulate the French example of nationalism as a unifying factor. If revolutionary France was able to reduce provincial particularities, including the languages of ethnic minorities, to minimal significance, why should the Europeanised Ottoman state not manage to do the same with its ethnic minorities? This reasoning, however, proved to be totally wrong on two counts: first, the minorities in Ottoman Turkey were distinguished not only by ethnic (i.e. basically linguistic) differences, but also to a large extent by their different religious and cultural traditions. Second, the proportion of ethnic minorities in the population of the Ottoman Empire was much higher than the proportion of ethnic minorities in France.[7] Atatürk, however, was wiser than his predecessors. He decided to cut his losses and build the Turkish national state more or less within the ethnic boundaries of the Turkish nation.[8]

The Russian Bolsheviks also proved to be wiser than the Young Turks. They formally consented to the self-determination of the non-Russian nationalities. However, to counter the wish for self-determination through the alternative of secession, the Bolsheviks transformed the Russian Empire into a federation, the Union of Soviet Socialist Republics, based on ethnic differences. Nevertheless, in order to reunite the borderland nationalities with 'Mother Russia', they eventually had to use force, under the assumption that it was the Communist Party, and not the other political parties of the respective nationalities, that represented the true interests of the people.

In revolutionary China the just treatment of the ethnic minorities, numerically less significant than in Russia, also became a particular issue; it was resolved by the granting of autonomous status to the minority regions. Unfortunately there is not enough evidence of how this has been received by the people concerned. What is well known are the difficulties that arose from the endeavour to integrate Tibet, with its totally different religious and social structure, into the People's Republic of China. The original Chinese attempt to convert the Tibetan Lamaist Buddhists to the Chinese brand of Marxism–Leninism seems to have failed; after considerable bloodshed the Chinese appear now to be ruthless with more caution.

Of the non-Western revolutions, the Russian one had the most widespread international impact. Being already partly Europeanised, and thus aiming for progress along European lines, revolutionary Russia was a promise and a paradigm for the emerging revolutionary forces throughout Western Europe. But being at the same time partly non-Western, and having built up an image of itself as the spearhead of the struggle for emancipation from the domination and encroachments of Western imperialism, it could not but provide an attractive example for the non-Western world as well.

Understandably, the Russian Bolshevik revolution inspired and fed similar tendencies in those European countries where there were signs of a multiple dysfunction and the *ancien régime* was shattered, and where in addition the imagery of the French revolution made much more sense than in Russia itself. In Germany and Hungary, which suffered defeat in the First World War, the communists attempted to emulate the Russian example. In Germany there took place between 1919 and 1923 a series of more or less local bids for power which, however, failed; Angress's term 'stillborn revolution' provides an apposite characterisation of those turbulent events.[9]

In Hungary the Bolshevik venture under Bela Kun was more impressive. Here the situation was somewhat reminiscent of what happened in Turkey. The

ethnic Hungarians, like the ethnic Turks, constituted a minority in their pre-war state. Their defeat in the First World War gave the subject nationalities the opportunity to secede and to found their own nation-states. The Hungarian communist attempt to regain some territories and incorporate them into what might have become a Soviet-type federation could not fail to arouse a sympathetic response among some Hungarian nationalists. Had he moved further in their direction Bela Kun might have played the role of a Hungarian Atatürk. But the attempted revolution's Bolshevik complexion, plus Hungary's landlocked geographical position *vis-à-vis* its numerically stronger neighbours, made this, too, an abortive venture.

The chances of any revolution following the path of the Russian revolution seemed to be greater outside Europe, where the inter-civilisational dimension provided a greater incentive for imitation; yet even there the revolutions went their own ways.

Between the Russian and the Turkish revolution there existed an ambiguous relationship. Although there was here little ground for cooperation, the fact that the Bolsheviks, in need of allies against the feared encirclement, declared their support for national movements of liberation from the colonial or semi-colonial domination of the capitalist powers, provided some ground for a temporary understanding with the Kemalist phase of the Turkish revolution. On the other hand, Atatürk showed a remarkable skill in integrating the sporadically emerging pro-Soviet groups and their military potential (the 'Green Army') into his own political framework and armed forces. The common interest of Russia and Turkey in not allowing the establishment of independent states in Transcaucasia also operated in favour of an understanding between the leaders of the two revolutions. As the Bolsheviks considered it to be their duty to help and direct the fraternal communist parties in other countries, however, a clash between the Turkish nationalists and the Russian Bolsheviks eventually became inevitable.

Much more intricate was the relationship between the Russian and the Chinese revolutions. In contrast to Turkey, in China the communists succeeded in establishing their own political organisation. In contrast to the Russian Bolshevik attempts to emancipate the Turkish communists from Atatürk's tutelage, in China the Soviets advocated and supported the alliance of the communists with the Guomindang, and even their submission to the Guomindang's leadership, against the better judgement of many Chinese communist leaders. The dramatic and paradoxical development of Sino-Soviet relationships is too well known to need repeating here. Suffice it to say only that the Chinese communists had embarked on their own independent policy well before the split with the Soviets became apparent. From January 1934, when the Bolshevik faction in the Chinese Communist Party excluded Mao Zedong from the actual leadership, leaving him only honorary president of the communist-held zones, until the summer of 1960, when the Soviet Union announced that it was withdrawing its technicians and ending its assistance to China, the discussion was kept under cover, as a purely internal family quarrel. Mao Zedong showed a remarkable capacity to conceal the real meaning of his acts, ignoring Soviet advice while outwardly preserving the decorum of acknowledging its wisdom. Although in fact he not only disagreed with, but also acted against, Stalin's wishes, he never publicly questioned Stalin's position as the top, senior leader of the world communist movement. This sort of 'filial piety' exercised by the Chinese communists even survived Stalin's death. In contrast to the Soviet Union and its satellites, in China there were no publicised attempts to dethrone Stalin from his pedestal – a reminder that even seemingly unequivocal symbols may be misleading.

The main impact of the Chinese revolution abroad was due to the romantic appeal of Mao Zedong's style rather than to the example of the revolutionary transformation of Chinese society. There were only a few countries (such as the Third World's Tanzania, or the already communist Albania which fell out with the USSR) that had direct official contact with, and received some real help from, the People's Republic of China. Otherwise there were mainly some revolutionary organisations engaged in terrorism, such as the Shining Path in Peru, and radical students admiring such activities all over the world, who considered themselves inspired by the teaching of Chairman Mao. Furthermore, some communist parties in the Third World, became divided into a pro-Soviet and a pro-Maoist branch.

The full impact abroad of the Iranian revolution has yet to be seen. Although carried out under the banner of a minority branch of Islam, the Twelvers Shiah, the Islamic revolution in Iran passed a message to the whole world of Islam. Export of that revolution became a practical proposition. The spiritual promoters of the Islamic revolution, in particular Ayatollah Khomeini, put their trust (so at least they declared) in the attractiveness of the fruits of the revolution, as demonstrated by the shining example of the Islamic republic.[10]

Yet, taking into account what has happened up to the time of writing, it was the revolution itself rather than its outcome that created a paradigm for emulation. The Islamic republic has failed to respond to the whole, complex challenge presented by the oppressive Pahlavi regime. Satisfied are only those who laid the main stress on strict observation of the Islamic law in its Shiite interpretation. Those who took part in the revolution with the aim of gaining more social justice and personal freedom felt frustrated.

Various kinds of social deprivation are precisely the issues that induce the poverty stricken masses in the Islamic countries to revolt against the more or less secular Westernised governments. Since the 1980s, Islamic fundamentalism has become the most likely source of inspiration to revolt in such circumstances. This, however, need not be the fundamentalism of Iranian Shiite type. There are several alternative autonomous foci for militant Islamic fundamentalism whether Shiite or Sunnite, the most notorious of which is that in the Sudan.

If there is any country where, in the near future, yet another Islamic revolution may take place, it is Algeria. The secular regime established after the war of liberation of 1954–62 (a horizontal revolution which shook off French domination) embarked on the creation of a socialist society. Its failure to sustain an economic growth commensurate with the high rate of population growth led to attempts at economic liberalisation which did nothing to improve the situation. Extremely high unemployment and the widening gap between rich and poor have discredited the Western models of political and economic organisation of society. To many (and as the cancelled second round of elections in 1992 indicated this might well be a majority) return to the basic principles of Islam appears to be the best way out of the impasse. At the beginning of 1994 the armed forces seem to provide the only effective support for the regime. All the other conditions of multiple dysfunction listed in this book as preconditions of a vertical revolution are present. Will the Algerian army do any better in saving the secular regime than did the army in Iran?

The Mexican vertical revolution made no particular impact on other countries. There was neither foreign intervention nor expansion abroad. Although the staggering racial and social contrast between the native and immigrant populations was a common feature of social life in many Latin American countries, the key issues that were at stake in the Mexican revolution were specific to that country. The socialistic elements in the Mexican revolution were widely acclaimed at the time of the post-revolutionary reforms but, since the 1950s, it was the Cuban rather than the Mexican revolution that provided inspiration to potential revolutionaries in south and central America. With the Cuban venture the message of revolution in Latin America acquired a Leninist, and partly also a Maoist, character. In other Latin American countries, much more than in Mexico, part of the Catholic clergy also became sympathetic to a revolution which promised to abolish the evils resulting from the profound cleavages in those racially mixed societies. However, in spite of many revolutions, revolts and civil wars throughout Latin America, none of them brought about social change comparable with the revolutions in Mexico and Cuba.

THEORETICAL OUTLINE

Although all kinds of revolution are touched upon in this book, the focus is on one type, namely the great vertical revolutions, i.e. revolutions from below which have transformative consequences in social life. My theoretical conclusions are based primarily on the eight case studies of this type of revolution. References to other vertical revolutions in the text, however, provide additional evidence to what is being said by way of conclusion.

A theoretical explanation of a complex phenomenon, which appears in the real world comparatively rarely and in many variations, is bound to be complex as well, if the theorist wants to avoid the pitfalls of a reductionist stance. Thus, such an explanation cannot evolve into one simple formula; it has to be conceived of as a summary of generalisations abstracted from an adequate number of case studies. Although the issue discussed in this volume is not why people rebel in general or why internal armed conflicts of any kind take place, the findings in this context may nevertheless be useful in such a broader sense as well.

As our case studies indicate, the manifest key issue in individual vertical revolutions varies considerably. The spectrum stretches from religious to socio-economic preoccupations. But the whole complex of issues that are at stake is always a mixture of elements ranging from the most abstract and noble to the most concrete and selfish preoccupations of people involved in revolution.

The orientation of the key issues depends on the two coordinates of social events – geographical space and historical time. To put it in more colourful, philosophical terms, the said orientation reflects the combination of the *genius loci* and the spirit of the time, the latter often blowing through a wider space than a local genius can comprehend.

In the mix, there always are at stake the issues of wealth and power (possession of one of them helps to acquire the other), security and self-realisation (often contrasting with each other), prestige and pleasure (the latter embracing a wide range of forms and circumstances) and, last but not least, the issue of satisfaction derived from the gains or advantages won by individual social groups involved in the confrontation, whether these groups are defined in terms of a tribe, nation, religious body, estate, class or political party. We may describe these coveted positions as social amenities. None of them can be considered more important than any other. There is no basis and no superstructure. Their comparative value for those involved in the process is a matter of each individual case.

A shift in distribution (allocation or appropriation) of these amenities between individual groups is the substance of the transformative effects of revolutions. These effects also correlate with the degree of atrocity of revolutionary events as well as with the length of the whole revolutionary process.

A struggle for, or at least attempts at, some redistribution (re-appropriation) of the aforementioned amenities is going on most of the time in most parts of the world. Such a struggle need not, however, necessarily ensue in what can be described as revolution. If there are some readily available institutions or procedures that can facilitate legal redistribution of social amenities, or if these redistributions are limited in their impact on those adversely affected, or if there are available adequately strong and disciplined armed forces, loyal to the government, then there is no scope for a revolt, let alone a revolution.

These case studies, as well as my references to other revolutions, have shown that great vertical revolutions do break out if the acute discontent affects various strata of population, which may be ready to revolt for different reasons, and, as has been said already, there are no legitimate (constitutional or customary) procedures available for tackling the causes of the discontent on the one hand, and no conditions for a timely suppression of the dissent by military means on the other. The plurality of social strata involved and the plurality of reasons for joining in can be described as a multiple causation which may be itemised as follows:

1. People of more than one social group resent the given distribution of social amenities; these people feel strongly that they have less of those amenities than they deserve. This sense of deficiency can be described as relative deprivation.
2. People may feel deprived (a) when they compare their situation with other people within their own country, (b) compare their situation with people in another country, (c) compare it with their own situation in the past, or (d) when their expectations, bolstered by some real advancement, are frustrated by a setback.
3. In order to become conducive to action the discontent needs a moral or an ideological justification. This may be derived either from traditional values which, however, may be subject to reinterpretation (in this case inspiration may come from an earlier stage in the domestic tradition), or from the values of an alien civilisation which, because of its manifest superiority in some key aspects of technology and/or culture, becomes a paradigm for inspiration or even imitation. Here is the root of our distinction between endogenous and exogenous revolutions.
4. A substantial contribution to the justification of redistribution of social amenities is made by intellectuals who defect from the government camp.
5. All the blame for the discontent, for various kinds of relative deprivation, is being put on the government of the day, which is being viewed as the main obstacle to the redistribution of social amenities.
6. Although there is no procedural framework for the required change in operation, some already established institutions assume the role of propounding such a change. This may be called the second pivot or the dual power.
7. If there are no such institutions, they are created from scratch, provided that the existing regime has been sufficiently weakened by foreign war (its armed forces having been defeated or engaged elsewhere) and/or by defections from the ranks of the élite.
8. The extent and the intensity of the resentment, its ideological justification and institutional support lead to the activation of an extraordinarily large number of people, who usually prefer to maintain a passive attitude towards politics.
9. *Vis-à-vis* the mounting tide of discontent, government policy becomes inconsistent. Shifting from repression to relaxation and back again, the government makes its own position still weaker.
10. The actual outbreak of revolution requires over and above these general conditions (which in their turn can be classified as either preconditions or accelerators) some triggering event such as the martyrdom of a revolutionary leader, the dismissal of a popular minister, the refusal by the government to fulfil its promises of reform, or attempts to suppress, or at least limit, the activity of the reformists.

Once a vertical revolution breaks out, it is likely that it will take a considerable time (several decades) before issues other than those that caused the revolution assume a greater importance. The whole period may be described as the revolutionary process.

The courses of the vertical revolutions under study reveal some significantly similar features. This is especially the case with the first stages of the revolutionary process, for which a common morphological model can be drawn. For a latter development two basic alternatives of the model are envisaged.

The first phase of the revolutionary process can be described as the onset. This is the phase during which the above-mentioned multiple causation unfolds. The second phase sets in if the government attempts to suppress, or at least to place limits on, the reform activities and their institutions (the phase of compression). The failure of these attempts is due to a broad coalition of forces, extending from the members of the élite who have defected on the one hand, to the politically activated, popular masses on the other. Once the *ancien régime* loses the decisive confrontation, the coalition of revolutionary forces falls apart and individual revolutionary factions begin to engage in in-fighting (explosion is followed by oscillation). The political differentiation can be conceptualised in terms of a fivefold political spectrum: supporters of the *ancien régime* on the one hand, and revolutionaries on the other, with the latter divided into right, centre, left and extreme left. In the first years of the revolutionary process the seat of power shifts to a more radical position, until one faction succeeds in establishing its exclusive power throughout the whole of the country or at least in its vital centre (interception of oscillating seat of power). The victorious faction is menaced not only by the forces of the *ancien régime* but also by the other revolutionary factions; consequently a tightening of the revolutionary rule (often in the form of a centralised dictatorship) and thus a perversion of the revolutionary ideal occurs. Foreign intervention or fear of it may lead to some sort of retaliatory or pre-emptive expansion.

The reaction to the tightening, perversion and expansion reveals a twofold pattern. Where there is a well-established pluralistic system which the revolutionary dictatorship cannot fully eliminate, there is the possibility of a realignment of forces and a compromise between the most moderate revolutionary faction (the revolutionary right) and the reform-minded supporters of the *ancien régime*. A formal restoration of substantial parts of the *ancien régime* presents an opportunity to those who aim at a full-fledged restoration. Attempts in this direction lead to a new realignment of forces. A coalition of the revolutionary centre with the revolutionary right strikes back and, by means of a kind of 'glorious revolution' or a series of such events, paves the way for a final consolidation.

Where there is no pluralistic system or tradition and therefore no prospect of a restoration compromise and its further consequences, the consolidation proceeds by changes of policy rather than by changes in the leadership. The revolutionary dictatorship tries to accommodate people with traditional, especially nationalistic, views, to secure privileges and stability for its new power base (the recruiting ground of the new élite) and occasionally also to improve its image abroad. The policy of the revolutionary establishments tends towards what corresponds to the central position within the political spectrum at the time when the first bout of revolution broke out. Thus, in this respect, there does not seem to be much difference between the two patterns of the course of vertical revolution.

The tendency for a revolution to result in some central position between the political forces that emerged at the onset of revolution may be explained by analogy with physical vectors. Also social forces may be identified by their magnitude and direction, the magnitude being defined in human as well as material terms, the direction in intent and energy input. The outcome is the resulting change described in idiographic terms.

There are also psychological reasons for the rhythm of the shifts in power structure or policy during the revolutionary process. There are certain time limits for the active involvement of people in tense situations. Individual phases identified in the course of our six revolutions from which the morphological model was abstracted reveal on average a five-year duration. In the two additional case studies, there is less regularity in this respect. But also, here, people's involvement in the struggle has shown certain, albeit more extended, limits. The excess of energy input on the side of the radicals over that of the moderates soon after the start of revolution on the one hand, and the reverse relationship in the later stages of the revolutionary process on the other, may also be due to the time span of sustainable tension.

It is important to point out that all the above-mentioned generalities concern only the procedural aspects of the phenomenon 'revolution'. It is the 'shell', or 'vehicle', and not the 'filling', or 'cargo', that is similar. Whereas the ways in which revolutions break out and take their full course reveal quite a few similarities, their socio-historical content, i.e. changes in social attitudes, relationships and institutions, are more variegated, and their individual elements are unique. Here is the idiographic approach which is more appropriate.

But if we take a wider look at the course of history, we may discover that a similar social change occurred in a country that had not experienced a revolution and avoided such a drastic confrontation. This is a field in which relative scopes for a nomothetic approach on the one hand, and an idiographic account on the other, are reversed. The content of social change taking place in a wider geographical area is a general phenomenon; the way it happens, whether via revolution or through any other means, is specific to each area. This specificity is more a matter for a historian, whereas the ongoing social change on a broader scale is more fitting for a systematic analysis by a social scientist.

Research on the borderline between history and social science abounds with pitfalls. The awareness of the multifaceted nature of social phenomena, the distinction between what is unique, what is repetitive and what may even be cyclical, with possible alterations according to the vantage point of the observation, is a helpful caveat against placing too much confidence in theoretical constructions. In my opinion, theorising in social science should never be detached from its empirical base. This, at least, I have tried not to do in this outline.

Notes

1. D. Marnet, 'The intellectual origins of the French Revolution', in W.F. Church (ed.), *The Influence of the Enlightenment on the French Revolution*, 2nd edn (D.C. Heath, Lexington, 1974), p. 112.
2. It may be surmised that those who want to win the first round of the revolution have to act according to the famous slogan of Lenin: 'no enemies to our left'.
3. In this context one cannot refrain from quoting de Jouvenel: 'the true historical function of Revolution is to renovate and strengthen Power. Let us stop greeting them as the reactions of the spirit of Liberty to the oppressor' (Bertrand de Jouvenel, *Power: The natural history of its growth*, Batchworth, London, 1952, p. 187).
4. For the concept of civilisation and its applicability in social science, see J. Krejčí, *Society in a Global Perspective*, pt II (SLON, Prague, 1993).
5. This is especially the case with the reassessment of the French revolution. The author most prominent in this field is François Furet. His books relevant to this point are included in the bibliography.
6. For more detail concerning this particular development, see J. Krejčí and V. Velimský, *Ethnic and Political Nations in Europe* (Croom Helm, London, 1981, pp. 61–73).
7. While in France – if the dichotomy between *langue d'oïl* and *langue d'oc* is not taken into account – the ethnic minorities embraced about 6 to 7 per cent of the population, in the Ottoman Empire the non-Turks constituted the majority of the population.
8. Only the Kurds, divided between Turkey (where in the 1965 census they were numbered as 7 per cent of the population), Iran and the newly constituted Iraq, remained a stateless nation.
9. W.T. Angress, *Stillborn Revolution: The communist bid for power in Germany 1921–23* (Princeton University Press, NJ, 1963). This book, however, does not cover the whole time span during which the Soviet example invited imitation.
10. For more detail see R.K. Ramazani, 'Iran's export of the revolution: politics, ends, and means'; and F. Rajaee, 'Iranian ideology and worldview: the cultural export of revolution', both in J.L. Esposito (ed.), *The Iranian Revolution, Its Global Impact* (Florida International University Press, Miami, 1990).

Bibliography

General

Amman, P., 'Revolution: A redefinition', *Political Science Quarterly*, vol. LXXVII, 1962, pp. 36–53

Angress, W.T., *Stillborn Revolution: The communist bid for power in Germany 1921–23*, Princeton University Press, NJ, 1963

Arendt, H., *On Revolution*, Faber & Faber, London, 1963

Aya, R., *Rethinking Revolutions and Collective Violence*, Het Spinhuis, Amsterdam, 1990

Barber, E.G., *The Bourgeoisie in Eighteenth-Century France*, Princeton University Press, NJ, 1955

Benoit-Smullyan, E., 'Status, status types and status interrelations', *American Sociological Review*, vol. IX, 1944, pp. 151–61

Beqiraj, M., *Peasantry in Revolution*, Cornell University Press, New York, 1966

Black, C.E. (ed.), *Comparative Modernisation*, Free Press, New York, 1976

Black, C.E. and T. Thornton (eds), *Communism and Revolution*, Princeton University Press, NJ, 1964

Blackey, R. (ed.), *Revolutions and Revolutionists,* Clio, Santa Barbara, 1982

Brinton, C., *The Anatomy of Revolution*, Jonathan Cape, London, 1953

Brooks, A., *The Theory of Social Revolutions*, Macmillan, New York, 1913

Brugger, B. and K. Hannan, *Modernisation and Revolution*, Croom Helm, London, 1983

Bühl, W.L., *Evolution und Revolution: Kritik der symmetrischen Soziologie*, W. Goldmann, München, 1970

Calvert, P., *A Study of Revolution*, Clarendon Press, Oxford, 1970

Calvert, P., *Politics, Power and Revolution*, Harvester, Brighton, 1982

Calvert, P., *Revolution and Counter-Revolution*, Open University Press, Milton Keynes, 1990

Cassinelli, C.W., *Total Revolution*, Clio, Santa Barbara, 1976

Church, C.H., *Revolution and Red Tape*, Clarendon Press, Oxford, 1981

Close, D. and C. Bridge, *Revolution: A Study of the Idea*, Croom Helm, London, 1985

Cohan, A.S., *Theories of Revolution*, Nelson, London, 1975

Dahrendorf, R., 'Über einige Probleme der soziologischen Theorie der Revolution', *Archives européens de sociologie*, vol. II, no. 1, 1961

Davies, J.C., 'Towards a theory of revolution', *American Sociological Review*, vol. XXVII, no. 1, 1962, pp. 5–19

Davies, J.C. (ed.), *When Men Revolt and Why*, Free Press, New York, 1971

De Fronzo, J., *Revolutions and Revolutionary Movements*, Westview Press, Oxford, 1991

Draper, H., *Karl Marx's Theory of Revolution*, 3 vols, Monthly Review Press, New York, 1977–86

Dunayevskaya, R., *Philosophy and Revolution*, Harvester, Brighton, 1982

Dunn, J., *Modern Revolutions: An introduction to the analysis of a political phenomenon*, 2nd edn, Cambridge University Press, Cambridge, 1989

Eckstein, H. (ed.), *Internal Wars,* Free Press, New York, 1964

Edwards, L.P., *The Natural History of Revolution*, reprint Russell & Russell, New York, 1965

Eisenstadt, S.N., *Revolution and the Transformation of Societies*, Free Press, New York, 1978

Eisenstadt, S.N., 'The breakdown of communist regimes', *Daedalus*, vol. 121, no. 2, 1992, pp. 21–42

Ellul, J., *Autopsy of Revolution*, Knopf, New York, 1971

Fabri, L., *Dictatorship and Revolution*, Cienfuegos Press, London, 1981

Forrest, W.G., *The Emergence of Greek Democracy*, World University Library, Weidenfeld & Nicolson, London, 1966

Friedland, W., Amy Barton, Bruce Dancis, Michael Rotkin and John Spiro, *Revolutionary Theory*, Allenheld & Osmun, Totowa, NJ, 1982

Friedrich, C.J., *Revolution*, Atherton, New York, 1966

Gernet, J., *A History of Chinese Civilization*, Cambridge University Press, London, 1982

Goldstone, J.A., *Revolution and Rebellion in the Early Modern World*, University of California Press, Berkeley, 1991

Goldstone, J.A. (ed.), *Revolutions: Theoretical, comparative and historical studies*, Harcourt Brace Jovanovich, San Diego, 1986

Goldstone, J.A., 'The comparative and historical study of revolutions', *Annual Review of Sociology*, vol. 8, 1982

Goldstone, J.A., 'Theories of revolution: The third generation', *World Politics*, vol. 23, no. 3, 1980

Greene, T.H., *Comparative Revolutionary Movements: The search for a theory and justice*, Prentice Hall, Englewood Cliffs, NJ, 1984

Griewank, K., *Der neuzeitliche Revolutionsbegriff: Entstehung und Entwicklung*, H. Böhlaus, Weimar, 1955

Grotanelli, C., 'Archaic forms of rebellion and their religious background' in B. Lincoln (ed.), *Religion, Rebellion and Revolution*, St Martin's Press, New York, 1985

Gurr, T.R., 'The revolution: Social change nexus', *Comparative Politics*, vol. 5, no. 3, 1973, pp. 359–92

Gurr, T.R., *Why Men Rebel*, Princeton University Press, NJ, 1971

Hagopian, M.N., *The Phenomenon of Revolution*, Harper & Row, New York, 1974

Hauner, M., 'The professionals and amateurs in national socialist foreign policy', in G. Hirschfeld and L. Kettenacker (eds), *The Führer State: Myth and Reality*, Klett, Cotta, Stuttgart, 1981

Hermassi, E., 'Toward a comparative study of revolution', *Comparative Studies in Society and History*, vol. 18, no. 2, 1976

Hitti, P.K., *History of the Arabs*, 10th edn, Macmillan, London, 1973

Hobsbawm, E., *The Age of Revolution, 1789–1848*, New American Library, New York, 1962

Hook, S., *Revolution, Reform and Social Justice: Studies in the theory and practice of Marxism*, Blackwell, London, 1976

Hopper, R.D., *Cybernation, Marginality and Revolution*, Oxford University Press, London, 1964

Hopper, R.D., 'The revolutionary process', *Social Forces*, vol. 28, no. 3, 1950, pp. 270 ff.

Horowitz, D., *Imperialism and Revolution*, Allen Lane, The Penguin Press, London, 1969

Huntington, S., *Political Order in Changing Societies*, Yale University Press, New Haven, 1968

Jessop, B., *Social Order, Reform and Revolution*, Herder & Herder, New York, 1972

Johnson, C., *Autopsy on People's War*, University of California Press, Berkeley, 1973

Johnson, C., *Revolution and Social System*, Hoover Institution Studies, Stanford University Press, CA, 1964

Johnson, C., *Revolutionary Change*, University of London Press, 1968

Jouvenel, B. de, *Power: The natural history of its growth*, Batchworth, London, 1952

Julien, C.A., *History of North Africa*, Routledge & Kegan Paul, London, 1970

Kann, R.A., *The Problems of Restoration*, University of California Press, Berkeley, 1968

Kelley, D.R., *The Beginning of Ideology*, Cambridge University Press, Cambridge, 1983

Khaldun, Ibn, *The Muqaddimah: An introduction to history*, vol. I, Routledge & Kegan Paul, London, 1958

Kimmel, M.S., *Revolution: A sociological interpretation*, Polity Press, Cambridge, 1990

Kissin, S.F., *Farewell to Revolution: Marxist philosophy and the modern world*, Weidenfeld & Nicolson, London, 1978

Klíma, O., *Mazdak: Geschichte einer sozialen Bewegung im Sassanidischen Persien*, ČSAV, Prague, 1957

Konrad, G. and I. Szelenyi, *The Intellectuals on the Road to Class Power*, Harvester, Brighton, 1979

Kramnick, I., 'Reflections on Revolution: Definition and explanation in recent scholarship', *History and Theory*, vol. XI, 1972

Krejčí, J., *Dějiny a revoluce (History and Revolution)*, Naše Vojsko, Prague, 1992

Krejčí, J., *Society in a Global Perspective*, SLON, Prague, 1993

Krejčí, J., 'Sociology or social science?', *History of European Ideas*, vol. 2, no. 2, 1981

Krejčí, J., *The Civilizations of Asia and the Middle East, Before the European Challenge*, Macmillan, London, 1990 (*Before the European Challenge, The Great Civilizations of Asia and the Middle East*, SUNY, New York, 1990)

Krejčí, J., *The Human Predicament: Its changing image*, Macmillan, London, 1993

Krejčí, J., *The Great Revolutions Compared: The search for a theory*, Harvester, Brighton, 1983

Krejčí, J. and V. Velimský, *Ethnic and Political Nations in Europe*, Croom Helm, London, 1981

Kuhn, T., *The Structure of Scientific Revolution*, Chicago University Press, 1970

Kumar, K. (ed.), *Revolution: The theory and practice of a European idea*, Weidenfeld & Nicolson, London, 1971

Lasswell, H. and D. Lerner (eds), *World Revolutionary Elites: Studies in coercive ideological movements*, MIT, Cambridge, Mass, 1965

Leiden, C. and K.M. Schmitt, *The Politics of Violence: Revolution in the modern world*, Prentice Hall, Englewood Cliffs, NJ, 1968

Lens, S., *The Promise and Pitfalls of Revolution*, United Church Press, Philadelphia, 1974

Lenski, G.E., 'Status crystallization: A non-vertical dimension of social status', *American Sociological Review*, vol. XIX, pp. 405–19, 1954

Lipset, S.M., *Revolution and Counterrevolution: Change and persistence in social structures*, Heinemann, London, 1969

Löwenthal, R., *Social Change and Cultural Crisis*, European Perspectives, Columbia University Press, Guildford, 1984

Luard, E., *War in International Society*, I.B. Tauris, London, 1986

Marcuse, H., *Reason and Revolution*, Routledge & Kegan Paul, London, 1969

Marnet, D., 'The intellectual origins of the French Revolution', in W.F. Church (ed.), *The Influence of the Enlightenment on the French Revolution*, 2nd edn, D.C. Heath, Lexington, 1974, p. 112

Marx, K., *Revolution and Counterrevolution*, Allen & Unwin, London, 1971

Marx, K., *Selected Writings in Sociology and Social Philosophy*, ed. T.B. Bottomore and M. Rubel, Penguin, Harmondsworth, 1961

Maspero, H., *China in Antiquity*, University of Massachusetts Press, Dawson, 1978

Maspero, H. and J. Escarra, *Les Institutions de la Chine*, Presses Universitaire de France, Paris, 1952

Meisel, J.H., *Counterrevolution: How revolutions die*, Atherton Press, New York, 1966

Mollat, M. and P. Wolff, *The Popular Revolutions of the Late Middle Ages*, Allen & Unwin, London, 1973

Monnerot, J., *Sociologie de la révolution*, Fayard, Paris, 1969

Moore, B., Jr, *Injustice: The social bases of obedience and revolt*, Macmillan, London, 1978

Moore, B., Jr, *Social Origins of Dictatorship and Democracy*, Penguin, Harmondsworth, 1966

Morison, S.E. (ed.), *American Revolution 1764–1788*, 2nd edn, Oxford University Press, London, 1970

Mortimer, E., *Faith and Power: The politics of Islam*, Faber & Faber, London, 1982

Neumann, S., 'The international civil war', *World Politics*, vol. I, 1978–9

Oglesby, R.R., *Internal War and the Search for Normative Order*, M. Nijhoff, The Hague, 1971

Olson, M., Jr, 'Rapid growth as a destabilising force', *Journal of Economic History*, vol. XXIII, 1963

O'Sullivan, N. (ed.), *Revolutionary Theory and Political Reality*, Harvester, Brighton, 1984

Paige, J., *Agrarian Revolution*, Free Press, New York, 1975

Palmer, R.R., *The Age of the Democratic Revolutions: A political history of Europe and America 1760–1800*, Princeton University Press, NJ, 1959

Palmer, R.R., *The Age of the Democratic Revolution: The struggle,* Princeton University Press, NJ, 1964

Pareto, V., *Manuale di economica politica*, Edizioni Bizzarri, Rome, 1965

Pareto, V., *The Mind and Society: A treatise on general sociology*, vol. II, Dover Books, New York, 1963

Pettee, G.S., *The Process of Revolution*, Harper & Row, New York, 1938

Pirenne, H., *Economic and Social History of Medieval Europe*, Kegan Paul, London, 1947

Polanyi, K., *The Great Transformation*, Beacon Press, Boston, 1957

Porter, R. and M. Teich (eds), *Revolution in History*, Cambridge University Press, 1986

Pye, W. and S. Verba (eds), *Political Culture and Political Development*, Princeton University Press, NJ, 1965

Rejal, M. and K. Phillips, *World Revolutionary Leaders*, F. Pinter, London, 1983

Revel, J.F., *How Democrats Perish*, Weidenfeld & Nicolson, London, 1985

Robertson, D., *Penguin Dictionary of Politics,* Penguin, London, 1985

Robertson, P., *Revolutions of 1848: A social history*, Harper & Row, New York, 1960

Romilly, J., *Problèmes de la démocratie grecque*, Hermann, Paris, 1975

Rosen, B.A. (ed.), *Iran since the Revolution*, Brooklyn College Studies on Society in Change, New York, 1985

Rudé, H., *Revolutionary Europe, 1783–1815*, World, Cleveland, 1964

Salert, B., *Revolutions and Revolutionaries,* Elsevier, New York, 1976

Savory, R., *Iran under the Safavids*, Cambridge University Press, London, 1980

Schmitt, B., *Repräsentation und Revolution*, C.H. Beck, München, 1970

Schoenbaum, D., *Hitler's Social Revolution: Class and status in Nazi Germany 1933–39*, Weidenfeld & Nicolson, London, 1967

Schrecker, P., 'Revolution as a problem in the philosophy of history', *Nomos*, vol. VIII, *Revolutions*, 1966

Schwartz, D.C., 'A theory of revolutionary behaviour', in J.C. Davies (ed.), *When Men Revolt and Why*, Free Press, New York, 1971

Scott, J.C., *The Moral Economy of the Peasant*, Yale University Press, New Haven, 1976

Seibt, F., *Revolution in Europa: Ursprung und Wege innerer Gewalt*, Süddeutscher Verlag, Munich, 1984

Seton-Watson, H., *The East European Revolution*, Hutchinson, London, 1985

Seton-Watson, H., *The Imperialist Revolutionaries*, Hutchinson, London, 1980

Shtromas, A., 'How the end of the Soviet system may come', in A. Shtromas and M. Kaplan (eds), *The Soviet Union and the Challenge of the Future*, vol. I, Paragon House, New York, 1988

Skocpol, T., *States and Social Revolutions: A comparative analysis of France, Russia and China*, Cambridge University Press, Cambridge, 1979

Skocpol, T. (ed.), *Vision and Method in Historical Sociology*, Cambridge University Press, New York, 1984

Skocpol, T. and M. Somers, 'The uses of comparative history in macrosocial inquiry', *Comparative Studies in Society and History*, vol. 22, no. 2, 1980

Skocpol, T. and E.K. Trimberger, 'Revolution in the world historical context of capitalism', *Berkeley Journal of Sociology*, vol. 22, 1977

Sorokin, P.A., *Social and Cultural Dynamics*, vol. III, *Fluctuation of Social Relationships, War and Revolution*, Allen & Unwin, London, 1937

Sorokin, P.A., *The Sociology of Revolution*, H. Fertig, New York, 1967

Stone, L., *The Causes of the English Revolution 1529–1642*, Routledge & Kegan Paul, London, 1972

Stone, L., 'Theories of revolution', *World Politics*, vol. XVIII, no. 2, 1966

Syme, R., *The Roman Revolution*, Oxford University Press, London, 1960

Tanter, R. and M. Midlarsky, 'A theory of revolution', *The Journal of Conflict Resolution*, vol. XI, no. 3, 1967

Taylor, A.J.P., *Revolutions and Revolutionaries*, Oxford University Press, London, 1981

Taylor, S., *Social Science and Revolutions*, Macmillan, London, 1984

Tholfsen, T.R., *Ideology and Revolution in Modern Europe*, Columbia University Press, New York, 1984

Tilly, C., *As Sociology Meets History*, Academic Press, New York, 1981

Tilly, C., 'Changing forms of revolution', Working paper no. 80, Center for Studies of Social Change, New School for Social Research, 1989

Tilly, C., *European Revolutions, 1492–1992*, Blackwell, Oxford, 1993

Tilly, C., *From Mobilization to Revolution*, Addison Wesley, London, 1978

Tilly, C., 'Routine conflicts and peasant rebellions in 17th century France', in R.P. Weller and S. Guggenheim (eds), *Power and Protest in the Countryside*, Duke University Press, Durham, 1982

Tilly, L. and C. Tilly, *Class Conflict and Collective Action*, Sage, London, 1981

Timasheff, N., *War and Revolution*, Sheed & Ward, New York, 1965

Trimberger, E.K., *Revolution from Above*, Transaction Books, NJ, 1978

Tucker, R.C., *The Marxian Revolutionary Idea*, Allen & Unwin, London, 1969

Urry, J., *Reference Groups and the Theory of Revolution*, Routledge & Kegan Paul, London, 1973

Venturis, F., *Roots of Revolution*, Grosset & Dunlap, New York, 1966

Waley, D., *The Italian City-Republics*, World University Library, Weidenfeld & Nicolson, London, 1969

Wallerstein, I., *The Capitalist World System*, vol. I, Cambridge University Press, New York, 1979

Wallerstein, I., *The Modern World System*, vol. I, Academic Press, New York, 1974
Wallerstein, I., *The Modern World System*, vol. II, Academic Press, New York, 1980
Wallerstein, I., *The Modern World System*, vol. III, Academic Press, San Diego, CA, 1989
Walton, J., *Reluctant Rebels: Comparative studies of revolutions and underdevelopment*, Colombia University Press, New York, 1984
Weber, M., *The Sociology of Religion*, Social Science Paperbacks in assoc. with Methuen, London, 1966
Weber, M., *The Theory of Social and Economic Organisation*, Free Press, New York, 1969
Willer, D. and G.K. Zollschan, 'Prolegomenon to a Theory of Revolution', in G.K. Zollschan and W. Hirsch (eds), *Explorations in Social Change*, Routledge & Kegan Paul, London, 1964
Woddis, J., *New Theories of Revolution*, Lawrence & Wishart, London, 1972
Wolin, S.S., 'The politics of the study of revolution', *Comparative Politics*, vol. 5, no. 3, 1973
Wood, G., 'The American Revolution', in L. Kaplan (ed.), *Revolutions: A comparative study*, Vintage Books, New York, 1973
Zaehner, R.C., *The Dawn and Twilight of Zoroastrianism*, Weidenfeld & Nicolson, London, 1961
Zagorin, P., *Rebels and Rulers*, 2 vols, (Cambridge University Press, Cambridge, 1982
Zollschan, G.K. and W. Hirsch (eds), *Social Change: Explorations, diagnoses and conjectures*, Schenkman, Cambridge, MA, 1976

Bohemia

Bartoš, F.M., *The Hussite Revolution 1424–1437*, Columbia University Press, New York, 1986
Betts, R.R., *Essays in Czech History*, Athlone Press, London, 1969
Brock, P., *The Political and Social Doctrines of the Unity of the Czech Brethren in the Fifteenth and Early Sixteenth Centuries*, Mouton, The Hague, 1957
Čornej, P., *Rozhledy, názory a postoje husitské inteligence v zrcadle dějepisectví 15. století*, Universita Karlova, Praha, 1986
Heymann, F.G., 'City rebellions in 15th-century Bohemia and their ideological and sociological background', *The Slavonic and East European Review* (London, June 1962), pp. 324–40
Heymann, F.G., *George of Bohemia: King of heretics*, Princeton University Press, NJ, 1965
Heymann, F.G., *John Žižka and the Hussite Revolution*, Princeton University Press, NJ, 1955
Heymann, F.G., 'The crusades against the Hussites' in K.M. Setto (ed.), *A History of the Crusades*, vol. III, *The Fourteenth and Fifteenth Centuries*, H.W. Hazard, Madison, WI, 1975
Heymann, F.G., 'The role of the towns in Bohemia of the later Middle Ages', *Journal of World History*, pt 5 (Paris, 1954)
Hlaváček, I., *Ze zpráv a kronik doby husitské*, Svoboda, Praha, 1981
Hrubý, K., 'Senior Communitas: Eine revolutionäre Institution der Prager Hussitischen Bürgerschaft in Bohemia', *Jahrbuch des Collegium Carolinum*, Band 13, R. Oldenburg Verlag, München-Wien, 1972
Jacob, E.F., 'The Bohemians at the Council of Basle 1433', in R. Seton-Watson (ed.), *Prague Essays*, Clarendon Press, Oxford, 1949
Kalivoda, R., *Husitská ideologie*, ČSAV, Praha, 1961
Kalivoda, R., *Revolution und Ideologie des Hussitismus*, Böhlau Verlag, Köln-Wien, 1976
Kaminský, H., *A History of the Hussite Revolution*, Berkeley and Los Angeles University Press, 1967

Kaminsky, H., 'Wyclifism as ideology of revolution', *Church History*, vol. 32, 1963, pp. 57–74

Kejř, B., *Husité*, Panorama, Praha, 1984

Klassen, J.M., 'The nobility and the making of the Hussite Revolution', *East European Quarterly*, Boulder, New York, 1978

Krejčí, J., *Czechoslovakia at the Crossroads of European History*, I.B. Tauris, London, 1990

Krejčí, J., 'The meaning of Hussitism', *Journal of Religious History*, vol. VIII, June 1974, pp. 3–20

Krofta, K., 'Bohemia in the 13th century' in *Cambridge Medieval History*, vol. VIII, Cambridge University Press, London, 1959, pp. 65–118

Krofta, K., *Dějiny selského stavu*, Laichter, Prague, 1949

Macek, J., *The Hussite Movement in Bohemia*, Lawrence & Wishart, London, 1965

Machovec, M., *Husovo učení a význam v tradici českého národa*, ČSAV, Praha, 1953

Míka, A., *Petr Chelčický*, Svobodné Slovo, Praha, 1963

Molnár, A. (ed.) *Husitské manifesty*, Odeon, Praha, 1986

Molnár, A., *Na rozhraní věků*, Vyšehrad, Praha, 1985

Odložilík, O., *The Hussite King: Bohemia in European affairs, 1440–1471*, Rutgers University Press, NJ, 1965

Pekař, J., *Postavy a problémy českých dějin*, Vyšehrad, Praha, 1990

Ransdorf, M., *Kapitoly z geneze husitské ideologie*, Univerzita Karlova, Praha, 1986

Seibt, F., 'Die Hussitenzeit als Kulturepoche', *Historische Zeitschrift*, Bd. 195, 1962, pp. 21–62

Seibt, F., *Hussitica: Zur Struktur einer Revolution*, Böhlau Verlag, Köln-Graz, 1965

Skalický, K., *Storia religiosa dei cechi e degli slovacchi*, La Casa di Matriona, Milano, 1987

Spinka, M., *John Hus: A biography*, Princeton University Press, NJ, 1968

Spinka, M., *John Hus and the Czech Reform*, Archon Books, Hamden, 1966

Spinka, M., *John Hus at the Council of Constance*, Columbia University Press, New York, 1965

Spinka, M., *John Hus' Concept of the Church*, Princeton University Press, NJ, 1966

Urbánek, R., *Lipany a konec polních vojsk*, Melantrich, Prague, 1934

Weltsch, R.E., *Archbishop John of Jenstein, 1348–1400*, Mouton, The Hague–Paris, 1968

Zeman, J.K. (ed.), *The Hussite Movement and the Reformation in Bohemia, Moravia and Slovakia 1350–1650*, Michigan Slavic Publications, University of Michigan Press, 1977

Ze zpráv a kronik doby husitské, Hlaváček, I. (ed.), Svoboda, Praha, 1981

England

Ashton, R., *The English Civil War: Conservatism and revolution 1603–1649*, Weidenfeld & Nicolson, London, 1978

Aylmer, G.E. (ed.), *The Interregnum: The quest for settlement 1646–60*, Macmillan, London, 1972

Beddard, R.A., 'The Restoration Church', in J.R. Jones (ed.), *The Restored Monarchy 1660–88*, Macmillan, London, 1979

Cook, C. and J. Wroughton, *English Historical Facts 1603–1688*, Macmillan, London, 1980

Cragg, G.R., *Puritanism in the Period of the Great Persecution, 1660–1688*, Cambridge University Press, London, 1957

Fletcher, A., *The Outbreak of the English Civil War*, E. Arnold, London, 1981

Hexter, J.H., *Reappraisals in History*, Longman, London, 1961

Hill, C., *Change and Continuity in Seventeenth-Century England*, Weidenfeld & Nicolson, London, 1975

Hill, C., *Intellectual Origins of the English Revolution*, Panther, London, 1972

Hill, C., *Puritanism and Revolution*, Secker & Warburg, London, 1965

Jones, C., M. Newitt and S. Roberts (eds), *Politics and People in Revolutionary England*, Blackwell, Oxford, 1986

Jones, J.R. (ed.), *The Restored Monarchy 1660–88*, Macmillan, London, 1979

Jones, J.R., 'Main trends in Restoration England', in J.R. Jones (ed.), *The Restored Monarchy 1660–88*, Macmillan, London, 1979

Kishlansky, M.A., *The Rise of the New Model Army*, Cambridge University Press, London, 1979

Manning, B., *The English People and the English Revolution*, Bookmarks, London, 1991

Miller, H., *The Early Tudor Peerage, 1485–1647*, MA thesis, 1950

Morrill, J.S., *Conservatives and Radicals in the English Civil War, 1630–1650* Longman, London, 1980

Morrill, J. (ed.), *The Impact of the English Civil War*, Collins & Brown, London, 1991

Ogg, D., *England in the Reigns of James II and William III*, Clarendon Press, Oxford, 1955

Pocock, J.G. (ed.), *Three British Revolutions: 1641, 1688, 1776*, Princeton University Press, NJ, 1980

Richardson, R.C., *The Debate on the English Revolution*, Methuen, London, 1977

Roots, I., *The Great Rebellion 1642–1660*, Batsford, London, 1966

Russell, C., *Parliaments and English Politics 1621–1629*, Clarendon Press, Oxford, 1979

Russell, C., *The Causes of the English Civil War*, Clarendon Press, Oxford, 1990

Russell, C., *The Fall of the British Monarchies 1637–1642*, Clarendon Press, Oxford, 1991

Russell, C. (ed.), *The Origins of the English Civil War*, Macmillan, London, 1973

Schenk, W., *The Concern for Social Justice in the Puritan Revolution*, Longman, London, 1948

Schoenfeld, M.P., *The Restored House of Lords*, Mouton, The Hague–Paris, 1967

Stone, L. (ed.), *Social Change and Revolution in England, 1540–1640*, Longman, London, 1977

Stone, L., *The Causes of the English Revolution, 1529–1642*, Routledge & Kegan Paul, London, 1972

Stone, L., 'The crisis of the aristocracy', in *Social Change and Revolution in England, 1540–1640*, Longman, London, 1977

Stone, L., 'The results of the English revolutions of the 17th century', in J.G.A. Pocock (ed.), *Three British Revolutions: 1641, 1688, 1776*, Princeton University Press, NJ, 1980

Tawney, R.H., *Religion and the Rise of Capitalism*, Penguin, Harmondsworth, 1938

Tawney, R.H., *The Agrarian Problem in the Sixteenth Century*, Longman, London, 1912

Thomas, K., 'The Levellers and the franchise', in G.E. Aylmer (ed.), *The Interregnum: The quest for settlement 1646–60*, Macmillan, London, 1972

Underdown, D., *Pride's Purge: Politics in the Puritan Revolution*, Clarendon Press, Oxford, 1971

Walzer, M., *The Revolution of the Saints: A study in the origins of radical politics*, Atheneum, New York, 1974

Western, J.R., *Monarchy and Revolution: The English State in the 1680s*, Blandford, London, 1972

Woodhouse, A.S.P. (ed.), *Puritanism and Liberty*, Dent, London, 1974

Woolrych, A.H., *Battles of the English Civil War*, Batsford, London, 1961

Woolrych, A.H., *Commonwealth to Protectorate*, Clarendon Press, Oxford, 1982

Woolrych, A.H., 'Last quests for a settlement 1657–1660', in G.E. Aylmer (ed.), *The Interregnum: The quest for settlement 1646–1660*, Macmillan, London, 1972

Yelling, J.A., *Common Field and Enclosure in England 1450–1850*, Macmillan, London, 1977

France

Amman, P. (ed.), *The Eighteenth Century Revolution – French or Western?: Problems of European civilisation*, Heath, Boston, 1963

Barber, E.G., *The Bourgeoisie in Eighteenth-Century France*, Princeton University Press, NJ, 1955

Bergeron, L., *France under Napoleon*, Princeton University Press, NJ, 1982

Bertrand, J.P., 'Voies nouvelles pour l'histoire militaire de la Révolution', in A. Mathiez and G. Lefebvre (eds), *Colloque*, Bibliothèque Nationale, Paris, 1978

Best, G. (ed.), *The Permanent Revolution: The French Revolution and its legacy, 1789–1989*, Chicago University Press, 1989

Campbell, S.L., *The Second Empire Revisited*, Rutgers University Press, NJ, 1969

Charle, C., *Histoire sociale de la France au XIXe siècle*, Seuil, Paris, 1991

Church, W.F. (ed.), *The Influence of the Enlightenment of the French Revolution*, 2nd edn, Heath, Lexington, 1974

Cobban, A., *Aspects of the French Revolution*, Norton, New York, 1970

Cobban, A., 'The French Revolution, orthodox and unorthodox: A review of reviews', *History*, vol. 52, 1967, pp. 149–59

Cobban, A., *The Social Interpretation of the French Revolution*, Cambridge University Press, London, 1968

Collins, I., *Napoleon and His Parliaments, 1800–1815*, Arnold, London, 1979

Doyle, W., *Origins of the French Revolution*, Oxford University Press, London, 1980

Doyle, W., *The Oxford History of the French Revolution*, Oxford University Press, London, 1989

Duguit, L., H. Monnier and R. Bonnard, *Les Constitutions et les principales lois politique de la France depuis 1789*, Auzias, Paris, 1952

Dupeux, G., *La Société française 1789–1970*, A. Colin, Paris, 1972

Forrest, A., *The French Revolution and the Poor*, Blackwell, Oxford, 1981

Furet, F., *Interpreting the French Revolution*, Cambridge University Press, London, 1981

Furet, F., *L'Héritage de la Révolution française*, Hachette, Paris, 1989

Furet, F., *Penser la Révolution française*, Gallimard, Paris, 1978

Furet, F. and M. Ozouf, *Dictionnaire critique de la Révolution française*, 4 vols, Flammarion, Paris, 1992

Gauthier, F., *Triomphe et mort du droit naturel en Révolution: 1789–1795–1802*, PUF, Paris, 1992

Girard, L., *La IIe république, 1848–1851*, Colman Levy, Paris, 1968

Godechot, J., *The Counter-Revolution: Doctrine and Action, 1789–1804*, Princeton University Press, NJ, 1981

Grab, W. and H. Koplenig (eds), *Die Debatte um die französische Revolution*, Nymphen-burger Verlag, Munich, 1975

Hampson, N., *A Social History of the French Revolution*, Routledge, London, 1963

Johnson, D. (ed.), *French Society and the Revolution*, Cambridge University Press, London, 1976

Jones, P., 'The peasantry of France on the eve of the French Revolution', *History of European Ideas*, vol. XII, 1990, pp. 335–50

Krejčí, J., 'Civilisation and religion', *Religion*, vol. 12, 1982, pp. 29–47

Labrousse, C.E., *Esquisse du mouvement des prix et des revenus en France au XVIIIe siècle*, 2 vols, Paris, 1933

Labrousse, C.E., *La Crise de l'économie française à la fin de l'ancien régime et au début de la Révolution*, PUF, Paris, 1944

Le Bon, G., *La Révolution française et la psychologie des révolutions*, Flammarion, Paris, 1912

Lefebvre, G., 'Die französische Revolution und die Bauern', in W. Grab and H. Koplenig (eds), *Die Debatte um die französische Revolution*, Nymphenburger Verlag, Munich, 1975

Lefebvre, G., *The Directory*, Routledge & Kegan Paul, London, 1965

Lucas, C., 'Nobles, bourgeois and the origin of the French Revolution', in D. Johnson (ed.), *French Society and the Revolution*, Cambridge University Press, London, 1976

Marx, K., *Der Achtzehnte Brumaire des Louis Bonaparte*, Hamburg, 1885

Marx, K., *Der Bürgerkrieg in Frankreich*, Berlin, 1891

Marx, K., *Klassenkämpfe in Frankreich*, Berlin, 1895

Mathiez, A. and G. Lefebvre (eds), *Colloque*, Bibliothèque Nationale, Paris, 1978

Meyer, J. and A. Corvisier, *La Révolution française*, 2 vols, Presses universitaire de France, Paris, 1991

Moulin, A., *Peasantry and Society in France since 1789*, Cambridge University Press, 1991

Ozouf, M., *L'Homme régénéré: essais sur la révolution française*, Gallimard, 1989

Palmer, R.R., *The World of the French Revolution*, Allen & Unwin, London, 1971

Ponteil, F., *Napoléon Ier et l'organisation autoritaire de la France*, A. Colin, Paris, 1956

Price, R. (ed.), *Revolution and Reaction: 1848 and the Second French Republic*, Croom Helm, London, 1975

Prost, A., *Histoire de l'enseignement en France 1800–1967*, A. Colin, Paris, 1968

Sauvigny, G. de Bertier de, *The Bourbon Restoration*, University of Pennsylvania Press, Philadelphia, 1966

Skocpol, T., *States and Social Revolutions*, Cambridge University Press, London, 1979

Soboul, A., *Comprendre la révolution*, Maspero, Paris, 1981

Soboul, A., *Paysans, sans-culottes et jacobins*, Claureuil, Paris, 1966

Sutherland, D., *France 1789–1815*, Oxford University Press, London, 1986

Taine, H., *L'ancien régime*, Complexe, Paris, 1991

Taylor, G.V., 'The Paris Bourse on the eve of the Revolution, 1781–1789', *American Historical Review*, vol. LXVII, 1962, pp. 976–87

Tocqueville, A. de, *The Ancien Regime and the French Revolution*, Fontana Library, Manchester, 1969

Vovelle, M. and A. de Baecque (eds), *Recherches sur la Révolution: un bilan des travaux scientifiques du bicentenaire*, L'institut d'histoire de la Révolution française, Paris, 1991

Russia

Abramovitch, R.R., *The Soviet Revolution 1917–1939*, Allen & Unwin, London, 1962

Anisimov, E.V., *The Reforms of Peter the Great: Progress through coercion in Russia*, M.E. Sharpe, New York, 1993

Bartlett, R. (ed.), *Land Commune and Peasant Community in Russia*, Macmillan, London, 1990

Billington, J.H., 'Six views of the Russian Revolution', *World Politics*, vol. XVIII, 1966, pp. 452–73

Blackwell, W.L. (ed.), *Russian Economic Development from Peter the Great to Stalin*, New Viewpoints, New York, 1974

Blackwell, W.L., 'The Old Believers and the rise of private industrial enterprise in early 19th century Moscow', in W.L. Blackwell (ed.), *Russian Economic Development from Peter the Great to Stalin*, New Viewpoints, New York, 1974

Blanc, S., 'The economic policy of Peter the Great', in W.L. Blackwell (ed.), *Russian Economic Development from Peter the Great to Stalin,* New Viewpoints, New York, 1974

Bremmer, I. and R. Taras (eds), *Nations and Politics in the Soviet Successor States*, Cambridge University Press, New York, 1993

Burnham, J., *The Managerial Revolution*, Pelican Books, London, 1945

Bushnell, J., *Mutiny amid Repression: Russian soldiers in the revolution of 1905–1906*, Indiana University Press, Bloomington, 1985

Carr, E.H., *The Bolshevik Revolution 1917–1923*, 3 vols, Macmillan, London, 1930–3

Conquest, R., *The Nation Killers: The Soviet deportation of nationalities*, Macmillan, London, 1970

Deutscher, I., *Russia after Stalin*, Jonathan Cape, London, 1969

Deutscher, I., *The Unfinished Revolution: Russia 1917–1967*, Oxford University Press, London, 1967

Dukes, P., *A History of Russia*, Macmillan, London, 1974

Dukes, P., *October and the World: Perspectives on the Russian Revolution*, Macmillan, London, 1979

Ferro, M., *October 1917: A social history of the Russian Revolution*, Routledge & Kegan Paul, London, 1980

Fic, V.M., *The Bolsheviks and the Czechoslovak Legion: The origin of their armed conflict, March–May 1918*, Abhinav, New Delhi, 1978

Fitzpatrick, S., *Cultural Revolution in Russia*, Indiana University Press, London, 1978

Fitzpatrick, S., *The Russian Revolution*, Oxford University Press, London, 1982

Fleming, P., *The Fate of Admiral Kolchak,* Hart-Davis, London, 1963

Gill, G.J., *Peasants and Government in the Russian Revolution*, Macmillan, London, 1979

Gleason, A., P. Kenez and R. Stites, *Bolshevik Culture*, Indiana University Press, Bloomington, 1986

Goodwyn, L., *Breaking the Barrier: The rise of Solidarity in Poland*, Oxford University Press, Oxford, 1991

Hingley, R., *The Russian Secret Police: Muscovite, Imperial Russian and Soviet political security operations 1565–1970*, Hutchinson, London, 1970

Horský, V., 'Dějinný kontext Říjnové revoluce', *Sociologický časopis*, Prague, 1968, pp. 1–17, 125–45

Hosking, G., *A History of the Soviet Union 1917–1991*, Fontana, London, 1992

Kort, M., *The Soviet Colossus: The rise and fall of the USSR*, Routledge, London, 1993

Krejčí, J., *Czechoslovakia at the Crossroads of European History*, I.B. Tauris, London, 1990

Krejčí, J., 'Elites and counter-elites in Soviet-type society', in A. Shtromas and M.A. Kaplan (eds), *The Soviet Union and the Challenge of the Future*, Paragon, New York, 1988

Krejčí, J., 'Masaryk and revolution', in M. Capek and K. Hrubý (eds), *T.G. Masaryk in Perspective*, SVU Press, Ann Arbor, 1981, pp. 173–89

Krejčí, J., 'The Russian Revolution as a response to challenge from without: An appraisal with hindsight', *The Journal of Communist Studies*, vol. 4, no. 2, London, 1988, pp. 125–41

Laue, T.H. von, 'The state and the economy', in W.L. Blackwell (ed.), *Russian Economic Development from Peter the Great to Stalin*, New Viewpoints, New York, 1974

Lenin, V.I., *Collected Works*, vol. 33, Foreign Languages Publishing House, Moscow, 1966

Lenin, V.I., *The Development of Capitalism in Russia*, Progress, Moscow, 1967

Lenin, V.I., *What is to be Done?*, International Publications, New York, 1969

Luckett, R., *The White Generals*, Longman, London, 1971

Malia, M., *Comprendre la Révolution russe*, Seuil, Paris, 1980

Mazour, A.G., *The First Russian Revolution 1825*, Stanford University Press, CA, 1963

McCauley, M., *The Russian Revolution and the Soviet State 1917–1921: Documents*, Macmillan, London, 1975

Medvedev, R.A., *On Stalin and Stalinism*, Oxford University Press, London, 1979

Milyukov, P., *Russia and its Crisis*, Collier Macmillan, London, 1962

Milyukov, P.N., *Vospominaniya*, Izd-vo Chechova, New York, 1955, vol. II, pt 8

Molnár, M., *Budapest 1956: A history of the Hungarian revolution*, Allen & Unwin, London, 1971

Nahylo, B. and V. Swoboda, *Soviet Disunion: A history of the nationalities problem in the USSR*, Free Press, New York, 1990

Pethybridge, R., *The Social Prelude to Stalinism*, Macmillan, London, 1974

Pipes, R., *The Russian Revolution*, Harvill, UK, 1990

Pravda, A. (ed.), *The End of the Outer Empire, Soviet–East European Relations in Transition, 1985–90*, The Royal Institute of International Affairs, Sage Publications, London, 1992

Rosenberg, W.G. and M.B. Young, *Transforming Russia and China*, Oxford University Press, London, 1982

Service, R., *The Bolshevik Party in Revolution 1917–1923*, Macmillan, London, 1979

Seton-Watson, H., *The Russian Empire 1801–1917*, Clarendon Press, Oxford, 1967

Shukman, H., *Lenin and the Russian Revolution*, Longman, London, 1977

Smith, S.A., *Red Petrograd: Revolution in the factories 1917–1918*, Cambridge University Press, London, 1983

Spirin, L.M., *Klassy i partii v grazhdanskoi voine v Rossii*, Izd. Mysl', Moscow, 1968

Swain, G. and N. Swain, *Eastern Europe since 1945*, Macmillan, London, 1993

Tilly, C., *European Revolutions, 1492–1992*, Blackwell, Oxford, 1993

Toynbee, A.J., *A Study of History*, 12 vols, Oxford University Press, London, 1934–64

Tschižewskij, D., *Das heilige Russland: russische Geistesgeschichte*, vol. I, Rowohlt, Hamburg, 1959

Ulam, A.B., *Russia's Failed Revolution*, Weidenfeld & Nicolson, London, 1981

Ulam, A.B., *The Unfinished Revolution*, Random House, New York, 1960

Volin, L., *A Century of Russian Agriculture*, Harvard University Press, Cambridge, Mass, 1970

Volkov, I.M., *et al.* (eds), *Sbornik dokumentov i materialov po istorii SSSR sovetskogo perioda*, Moscow University Press, 1966

Wayne, S.V. (ed.), *The Peasant in Nineteenth Century Russia*, Stanford University Press, CA, 1968

Westwood, J.N., *Endurance and Endeavour: Russian history 1812–1971*, Oxford University Press, London, 1981

Turkey

Ahmad, F., *The Turkish Experiment in Democracy 1950–1975*, Royal Institute of International Affairs, London, 1977

Ahmad, F., *The Young Turks*, Clarendon Press, Oxford, 1969

Allen, H.E., *The Turkish Transformation*, P. Greenwood, New York, 1968

Berkes, N., *The Development of Secularism in Turkey*, McGill University Press, Montreal, 1964

Carr, E.H., *The Bolshevik Revolution 1917–1923*, Penguin, Harmondsworth, 1966, pp. 299–301

Dodd, C.H., *Democracy and Development in Turkey*, The Eothen Press, University of Hull, 1979

Ergil, D., *Social History of the Turkish National Struggle 1919–22*, Sind Sagar Academy, Lahore, n.d.

Feroze, M.R., *Islam and Secularism in Post-Kemalist Turkey*, Islamic Research Institute, Islamabad, 1976

Hale, W., *The Political and Economic Development of Modern Turkey*, Croom Helm, London, 1981

Harris, G.S., *The Origins of Communism in Turkey*, Stanford University Press, CA, 1967

Karpat, K.H. (ed.), *Social Change and Politics in Turkey*, E.J. Brill, Leiden, 1973

Karpat, K.H., 'Turkish democracy at impasse: Ideology, party politics and the third military intervention', *International Journal of Turkish Studies*, vol. 2, no. 1, 1981, pp. 29–35

Kushner, D., *The Rise of Turkish Nationalism 1876–1977*, F. Cass, London, 1977

Landau, J., *Atatürk and the Modernization of Turkey*, Westview Press, New York, 1984

Lang, D.M., *The Armenians: A people in exile*, Allen & Unwin, London, 1981

Lewis, B., *The Emergence of Modern Turkey*, Oxford University Press, London, 1961

Mardin, S., *The Genesis of Young Ottoman Thought*, Princeton University Press, NJ, 1962

McCarthy, J., *Muslims and Minorities: The population of Ottoman Anatolia and the end of the empire*, New York University Press, 1983

Mortimer, E., *Faith and Power: The politics of Islam*, Faber & Faber, London, 1982

Neyzi, N., 'The middle classes in Turkey', in K.H. Karpat (ed.), *Social Change and Politics in Turkey*, E.J. Brill, Leiden, 1973

Ozbudun, E., *Social Change and Political Participation in Turkey*, Princeton University Press, NJ, 1976

Pamuk, G., *The Ottoman Empire and European Capitalism 1820–1913*, Cambridge University Press, London, 1987

Rustow, D.A., 'Turkey: The modernity of tradition', in W. Pye and S. Verba (eds), *Political Culture and Political Development*, Princeton University Press, NJ, 1965

Shaw, E.K. and S.J. Shaw, *History of the Ottoman Empire and Modern Turkey*, vol. 2, *Reform, Revolution and Republic 1808–1975*, Cambridge University Press, London, 1977

Shaw, S.J., *Between Old and New: The Ottoman Empire under Sultan Selim III, 1789–1807*, Harvard University Press, Cambridge, MA, 1971

Toprak, B., *Islam and Political Development in Turkey*, E.J. Brill, Leiden, 1981

Weiker, W.F., *Political Tutelage and Democracy in Turkey*, E.J. Brill, Leiden, 1973

Weiker, W.F., *The Turkish Revolution 1960–1961*, The Brookings Institute, Washington DC, 1963

China

Akamatsu, P., *Meiji 1868: Revolution and counter-revolution in Japan*, Allen & Unwin, London, 1972

Bianco, L., *Origins of the Chinese Revolution*, Stanford University Press, CA, 1971

Brady, J.P., *Justice and Politics in People's China*, University of Massachusetts Press, Boston, 1982

Brugger, B., *China: Liberation and transformation 1942–1962*, Croom Helm, London, 1981

Brugger, B., *China: Radicalism to revisionism 1962–1979*, Croom Helm, London, 1981

Brugger, B. (ed.), *China: The impact of the Cultural Revolution*, Croom Helm, London, 1978

Burnham, J., *The Managerial Revolution*, Pelican Books, London, 1945

Chesneaux, J., *China: The People's Republic*, Harvester, Brighton, 1979

Chesneaux, J., F. le Barbier and M. Bergère, *China from the 1911 revolution to liberation*, Harvester, Brighton, 1977

Chesneaux, J., M. Bastid and M. Bergère, *China from the Opium Wars to the 1911 Revolution*, Harvester, Brighton, 1976

Chung-li Chang, *The Chinese Gentry*, University of Washington Press, Seattle, 1967

Dietrich, C., *People's China*, Oxford University Press, New York, 1986

Dubbs, H.D., 'Taoism in China', in H.F. MacNair (ed.), *China*, California University Press, Berkeley, 1946

Ellison, H.J., *The Sino-Soviet Conflict: A global perspective*, Holdan Books, Oxford, 1982

Franke, W., *A Century of Chinese Revolution 1851–1949*, Blackwell, Oxford, 1981

Grasso, J., J. Corrin and M. Kort, *Modernization and Revolution in China*, M.E. Sharpe, New York, 1991

Gray, J., *Rebellions and Revolutions: China from the 1800s to the 1980s*, Oxford University Press, London, 1990

Harris, P., *Political China Observed: A Western perspective*, Croom Helm, London, 1981

Henkin, L., R. Edwards and A. Nathan, *Human Rights in Contemporary China*, Columbia University Press, New York, 1986

Hiniker, P.J., *Revolutionary Ideology and Chinese Reality: Dissonance under Mao*, Sage, London, 1977

Hsiung, J.C., *China's Bitter Victory: The war with Japan, 1937–1945*, M.E. Sharpe, New York, 1992

Hsü, I.C.Y., *The Rise of Modern China*, Oxford University Press, London, 1970

Huang, R., *China: A macro-history*, M.E. Sharpe, New York, 1988

Johnson, C.A., *Peasant Nationalism and Communist Power: The emergence of revolutionary China 1937–45*, Stanford University Press, CA, 1962

Kraus, R.C., *Class Conflict in Chinese Socialism*, University of Illinois Press, 1982

Levy, H.S., 'Yellow turban religion and rebellion at the end of Han', *Journal of the American Oriental Society*, vol. LXXVI, 1956, pp. 219–24

Lewy, G., *Religion and Revolution*, Oxford University Press, New York, 1974

MacNair, H.F. (ed.), *China*, California University Press, Berkeley, 1946

Mao Tse-tung, *Selected Readings from the Works of Mao Tse-tung*, Foreign Languages Press, Peking, 1967

Michael, F., *The Taiping Rebellion: History and documents*, 3 vols, Washington University Press, 1966–72

Moore, B., Jr, *Social Origins of Dictatorship and Democracy*, Penguin, Harmondsworth, 1969

Ngok, L. and L. Chi-keung (eds), *China: Development and challenge*, 4 vols, CAS, London, 1979–81

Rosenberg, W.G. and M.B. Young, *Transforming Russia and China*, Oxford University Press, London, 1982

Schram, S., *Mao Tse-tung*, Penguin, Harmondsworth, 1967

Schwartz, B.I., *Chinese Communism and the Rise of Mao*, Harvard University Press, Cambridge, MA, 1964

Schwartz, B.I., 'Modernization and the Maoist vision: Some reflections on Chinese communist goals', *China Quarterly*, no. 21, 1965, pp. 3–19

Smart, N., *Mao*, Collins, Glasgow, 1974

Snow, E., *The Long Revolution*, Vintage, New York, 1971

Solomon, R.H., *Mao's Revolution and the Chinese Political Culture*, University of California Press, Berkeley, 1971

Watson, D. (ed.), *Mao Tse-tung in the Scales of History*, Cambridge University Press, London, 1977

Iran

Abdulghan, J.M., *Iraq and Iran: The years of crisis*, Croom Helm, London, 1984

Abrahamian, E., *Iran Between Two Revolutions*, Princeton University Press, NJ, 1982

Akhavi, S., *Religion and Politics in Contemporary Iran*, SUNY, Albany, 1980

Algar, H., *The Roots of Islamic Revolution*, Open Press, London, 1983

Amuzegar, J., *The Dynamics of the Iranian Revolution*, SUNY, Albany, 1991

Arjomand, S.S., 'Iran's Islamic revolution in comparative perspective', *World Politics*, vol. XXXVIII, no. 3, April 1986

Arjomand, S.S., *The Turban for the Crown: The Islamic revolution in Iran*, Oxford University Press, New York, 1988

Bakhash, S., *The Reign of Ayatollahs: Iran and the Islamic revolution*, I.B. Tauris, London, 1985

Bashiriyeh, H., *The State and Revolution in Iran 1962–1982*, Croom Helm, London, 1984

Bayat-Philip, Mangol, 'Tradition and change in Iranian socio-religious thought', in M.E. Bonine and N.R. Keddie (eds), *Modern Iran: The dialectics of continuity and change*, SUNY, Albany, 1981

Bernard, C. and Z. Khalilzad (eds), *'The Government of God': Iran's Islamic Republic*, Columbia University Press, New York, 1984

Bonine, M.E. and N.R. Keddie (eds), *Modern Iran: The dialectics of continuity and change*, SUNY, Albany, 1981

Bosworth, E. and C. Hillenbrand, *Qajar Iran 1800–1925*, Edinburgh University Press, 1983

Browne, E.G., *The Persian Revolution of 1905–1909*, F. Cass, London, 1966

Enayat, H., *Modern Islamic Political Thought*, Macmillan, New York, 1982

Esposito, J.L. (ed.), *The Iranian Revolution: Its global impact*, Florida International University Press, Miami, 1990

Fischer, M.J., *Iran*, Harvard University Press, New Haven, 1980

Graham, R., *Iran: The illusion of power*, Croom Helm, London, 1979

Halliday, F., *Iran: Dictatorship and development*, 2nd edn, Penguin, Harmondsworth, 1979

Heikal, M., *The Return of the Ayatollah: The Iranian revolution from Mossadeq to Khomeini*, A. Deutsch, London, 1981

Hiro, D., *Iran under the Ayatollahs*, Routledge & Kegan Paul, London, 1985

Hussain, A. *Islamic Iran: Revolution and counter-revolution*, St Martin's Press, New York, 1985

Kamrava, M., *Revolution in Iran: The roots of turmoil*, Routledge & Kegan Paul, London, 1990

Katouzian, H., *The Political Economy of Modern Iran*, Macmillan, London, 1981

Kazemi, F., *Poverty and Revolution in Iran*, New York University Press, 1981

Keddie, N.R., *Roots of Revolution: An interpretative history of modern Iran*, Harvard University Press, New Haven, 1981

Lenczowski, G. (ed.), *Iran under the Pahlavis*, Hoover Institution Press, Stanford, CA, 1978

McEoin, D. and A. al-Shahi (eds), *Islam in the Modern World*, Croom Helm, London, 1982

Moghtader-Mojdehi, J.M., *Interpreting the Iranian Revolution*, Cambridge University Press, Cambridge, MA, 1986

Mottahedeh, R., *The Mantle of the Prophet: Religion and politics in Iran*, Penguin, Harmondsworth, 1987

Rajee, F., 'Iranian ideology and worldview: the cultural export of revolution', in J.L. Esposito (ed.), *The Iranian Revolution, Its Global Impact*, Florida International University Press, Miami, 1990

Ramazani, R.K., *Revolutionary Iran: Challenge and response in the Middle East*, Johns Hopkins University Press, Baltimore, 1986

Ramazani, R.K., 'Iran's export of the revolution: politics, ends and means', in J.L. Esposito (ed.), *The Iranian Revolution, Its Global Impact*, Florida International University Press, Miami, 1990

Sardar, Z., *The Future of Muslim Civilisation*, Croom Helm, London, 1980
Skocpol, T., 'Rentier state and Shi'a Islam in the Iranian revolution', *Theory and Society*, vol. XI, no. 3, 1982
Vatikiotis, P.J., *Islam and the Nation State*, Croom Helm, London, 1983
Zabih, S., *Iran since the Revolution*, Croom Helm, London, 1982

Mexico

Bazant, J., *A Concise History of Mexico*, Cambridge University Press, 1977
Bazant, J., *Alienation of the Church Wealth in Mexico: Social and economic aspects of the liberal revolution 1856–1875*, Cambridge University Press, 1971
Brading, D.A. (ed.), *Caudillo and Peasant in the Mexican Revolution*, Cambridge University Press, Cambridge, 1980
Cumberland, C.C., *Mexico: The struggle for modernity*, Oxford University Press, New York, 1968
Cumberland, C.C. (ed.), *The Meaning of the Mexican Revolution*, D.C. Heath, Boston, 1967
Eckstein, S., *The Poverty of Revolution: The state and the urban poor in Mexico*, Princeton University Press, NJ, 1977
Institute of Latin American Studies, *Mexico's Recent Economic Growth*, University of Texas Press, London, 1967
Knight, A., *The Mexican Revolution*, 2 vols, Cambridge University Press, 1986
Lieuwen, E., *Mexican Militarism: The political rise and fall of the revolutionary army*, University of New Mexico Press, Albuquerque, 1968
Meyer, J.A., *The Cristero Rebellion*, Cambridge University Press, 1976
Oudin, B., *Villa, Zapata et le Mexique en feu*, Gallimard, Paris, 1989
Philip, G. (ed.), *Politics in Mexico*, Croom Helm, London, 1985
Reynolds, C.W., *The Mexican Economy: Twentieth-century structure and growth*, Yale University Press, London, 1970
Ruiz, R.E., *Triumph and Tragedy: A history of the Mexican people*, Norton, New York, 1992
Tannenbaum, F., *Peace by Revolution: Mexico after 1910*, Columbia University Press, London, 1966
Vayssière, P., *Les révolutions d'Amérique Latine*, Seuil, Paris, 1991
Wilkie, J., *The Mexican Revolution: Federal expenditure and social change since 1910*, 2nd edn, University of California Press, Berkeley, 1970
Williamson, E., *The Penguin History of Latin America*, Penguin, London, 1992

Author index

As there are frequent comparisons in the text, the most often used concepts and names are referred to in the index only with respect to those pages where they are discussed in some detail.

Subject index

As there are frequent comparisons in the text, the most often used concepts and names are referred to in the index only with respect to those pages where they are discussed in some detail.